DEAR UTIA ———

HOPE YOU ENJOY YOUR
"CULINARY TOURING" AROUND
RUSSIA AS MUCH AS I DO ——
AND YOU DON'T NEED A VISA
OR PLANE TICKET!! love,
verochka

OCT 2016

CULINARIA
RUSSIA
A CELEBRATION OF FOOD AND TRADITION

CULINARIA
RUSSIA
A CELEBRATION OF FOOD AND TRADITION

Marion Trutter

Editor

Gregor M. Schmid

Photographer

h.f.ullmann

Abbreviations and quantities

1 oz	= 1 ounce = 28 g
1 lb	= 1 pound = 16 ounces
1 cup	= 8 ounces* (see below)
1 cup	= 8 fluid ounces = 250 milliliters (liquids) / 2 cups = 1 pint (liquids)
1 g	= 1 gram = $\frac{1}{1000}$ kilogram
1 kg	= 1 kilogram = 1000 grams = 2¼ lb
1 liter	= 1000 milliliters = approx 34 fluid ounces
125 ml	= approx 8 tablespoons = ½ cup
1 tbsp	= 1 level tablespoon = 15–20 g* (see below) = 15 ml (liquids)
1 tsp	= 1 level teaspoon = 3–5 g * (see below) = 5 ml (liquids)

With dry ingredients, the number of spoonfuls always refers to the processed raw materials, e.g.: 1 tbsp chopped onions; but 1 onion, peeled and chopped. The weight of dry ingredients varies significantly depending on the density factor, e.g. 1 cup flour weighs less than 1 cup butter.

Quantities given in the recipes: If not otherwise indicated, the recipes are calculated for four persons. Quantities in ingredients have been rounded up or down for convenience, where appropriate. Metric conversions may therefore not correspond exactly. It is important to use either American or metric measurements within a recipe.

It is advisable not to serve any dishes that contain raw egg to very young children, pregnant women, elderly people or anyone weakened by serious illness. If in any doubt consult your doctor. Be sure that all the eggs you use are fresh.

Names and descriptions in the original languages are transcribed here according to their pronunciation in English (for the Russian, according to the BGN/PCGN Romanization system). If spellings that deviate from this have become established, the latter have been used.

MIX
Paper
FSC FSC® C019646

© h.f.ullmann publishing GmbH
Original title: *Culinaria Russia – Russland, Ukraine, Georgien, Armenien, Aserbaidschan*
ISBN 978-3-8331-2183-8

Editor: Tanja Krombach
Editorial assistant: Maren Tribukait
Specialist editors: Prof. Dr. Nicolas Szafowal (Ukraine),
Prof. Dr. Jörg Stadelbauer (Georgia, Armenia), Dr. Wolfgang Thomann
(wine texts)
Editors: Christine Hamel (Russia, Georgia), Gertraud M. Trox (Ukraine,
Azerbaijan), Ortrun Egelkraut (Armenia)
Recipes editor: Barbara Wurzel
Designer: Sonja Loy
Design assistant: Sara Shahin
Picture editors: Silke Haas, Lilia Kouzmina-Tarassowa
Maps: Studio für Landkartentechnik, Norderstedt/Detlef Maiwald
Cover design: Roman Bold & Black based on an original layout
by Carol Stoffel
Front cover photos: Spoon: © Renee Comet Photography/Stockfood
Blini with caviar and lemon: © Christophe Madamour/Stockfood and
FoodPhotography/Stockfood
Back cover photo: © Gregor M. Schmid
Project coordinator: Isabel Weiler

© for this English edition: h.f.ullmann publishing GmbH

Special Edition

Translated by Nicola Coates, Katherine Taylor, and Rae Walter in
association with First Edition Translations Ltd, Cambridge, UK
Edited by Lin Thomas in association with First Edition Translations Ltd,
Cambridge UK
Typeset by The Write Idea in association with First Edition Translations
Ltd, Cambridge UK
Project management by Sheila Waller in association with First Edition
Translations Ltd, Cambridge UK

Overall responsibility for production: h.f.ullmann publishing GmbH,
Potsdam, Germany

Printed in China, 2015

ISBN 978-3-8480-0213-9

10 9 8 7 6 5 4 3 2 1
X IX VIII VII VI V IV III II I

Based on an idea by Ludwig Könemann

www.ullmann-publishing.com
newsletter@ullmann-publishing.com
facebook.com/ullmann.social

In this series:

Contents

Life, food and drink
between Europe and Asia

A culinary journey through Russia and the Ukraine, Georgia, Armenia, and Azerbaijan: in our mind's eye it conjures up images of caviar and Crimean champagne, piroshki and borscht, vodka, and sumptuous arrays of zakuski. Although these delicacies stem mainly from Russia and the Ukraine, they have created a worldwide reputation for the cuisine of this land that stretches from Europe into Asia. Less well known facts, however, are that Ukraine was the granary, the orchard, and the sugar bowl of the Soviet Union, that Georgia produces subtropical fruits and excellent wines, that the Azerbaijanis create exotic dishes from meat, fruit and spices, and that Armenia has kept its traditional cuisine alive for thousands of years.

In this book, we would like to invite you to join us in a tour of the kitchens of these countries. Since the break-up of the Soviet Union, Russia's neighbors have once again had their own culture in the forefront of their minds, and this has revealed an amazing individuality in their history, their stories, in customs that had almost been forgotten—and of course in their diverse culinary traditions.

We have chosen these particular five countries, because—due to their very different geographical, climatic, and cultural situations—they offer a breathtaking variety of ways of preparing food. After all, the area covered stretches from Europe to the Far East and from the eternal snows to the subtropical. So it is easy to understand that in Siberia, where there are only three months between seedtime and harvest, nature titillates the palate in a very different way from south of the Caucasus, where the magic of the sun fills the kitchens with a kaleidoscope of colors and oriental spices.

However, we must not forget to mention that even now, in times of upheaval, large parts of the population still live in difficult conditions. Many traditional dishes only appear on the table on feast days. To prevent the recipes that have been handed down from vanishing into oblivion, we have also included specialties that are hardly ever made today and have almost become a part of history. We have selected and classified our recipes as even-handedly as possible. Each country has its own special features, even if some of them are shared with other lands and it is not always possible to determine where a particular dish was "invented."

As a personal calling card, each nation presents its own feast days. Even though many families have to save up for a festive meal, the people of each of these countries know how to celebrate. Then the tables groan under the weight of the food and the hospitality is unparalleled. Join in the celebration and the enjoyment, because people in Russia, the Ukraine, Georgia, Armenia, and Azerbaijan will always find reasons to celebrate.

Marion Trutter

Hartmut Moreike
Alexey Kozlachkov

РОССИЯ

Russia

Russia – a multiracial state of vast expanses that the eye can never get enough of. When a Russian family in an apartment block in Kaliningrad sits down at sunrise to a breakfast of croissants, fresh butter, jam and eggs, in the dark polar night on the shores of the Bering Sea, the Chukchens' traditional evening meal of dried fish and raw seals' liver is on the table. A blizzard howls around the wooden house, forcing the mercury down to minus 40 degrees. Between the enclave of Kaliningrad—surrounded by Lithuania and Poland—far to the west and Chukotka in the distant east, lie over 6,000 miles (10,000 km), 12 time zones, and several climate zones. In the Volga Delta, fishermen take a break from catching sturgeon and, on an island in the mighty river, they prepare the popular fish soup *ukha*. Over 2,000 miles (3,500 km) to the northeast, in the little town of Norilsk, the pale sun awakens the spring in the frost-bound taiga. It hangs crystal icicles on the artistic carving of the log cabins. On the lunch table are filled pasta pockets called *pelmeni*, the Siberians' favorite dish.

The distances are breathtaking and the kaleidoscope of changing landscapes is fascinating. In central Russia, you find crystal clear rivers full of fish, birch woods and mixed forests, fields of fertile black soil, and gently rolling hills. In the north, snowy wastes, flat expanses of sparsely vegetated tundra, and the virgin forests of the taiga, rich in game, extend from the continent of Europe into Asia. The landscapes of the south are characterized by vast, herb-scented forests, grassy steppes, and barren deserts.

The Russian Federation is a country brought together by territory and history and a melting pot for more than 125 peoples and communities who are now rediscovering their traditions. Landscape and culture are always reflected in the cuisine of any region. The slow cooking methods of boiling, braising, stewing, and baking are determined by the warmth of a Russian stove. The liking for preserves such as pickled cucumbers and marinated mushrooms has its roots in the need to lay in stores for the long, cold winter. The Russians owe their wealth of traditional vegetarian recipes to their religion as, according to the Russian Orthodox Church, more than half the year must be spent in fasting. As a result, a strict separation developed between food for fast days—vegetables, mushrooms, berries, and a limited amount of fish—and dishes for feast days made from meat, dairy products, and eggs.

Over the course of history, Russian society has split into two classes, with the poor and peasant masses opposed to the rich minority. Similarly, Russian cooking is noted on the one hand for simple basic foods like rye bread and cabbage, and on the other hand for the development of *haute cuisine* in the 19th century. The latter is characterized by such culinary highlights as sturgeon, caviar, and Crimean champagne, and resulted from the magical transformation of

Previous page: At Susdal to the northeast of Moscow, in the open-air museum by the River Kamenka, stands the Church of Christ's Transfiguration from the village of Kozlatyevo in central Russia.

traditional dishes into refined creations like Salad Olivier and Charlotte Russe at the hands of the French chefs in the palaces of the tsars and the nobility. Only bread always appeared on the table in every home, be it Tsar's or peasant's. After all, Russians have long regarded bread and salt not merely as foodstuffs but also as symbols of hospitality and respect for the gifts of nature. Like the Trans-Siberian Railway today, for centuries the Silk Road and the Tea Route linked distant regions, allowing the various national cuisines to have a mutually inspirational effect on one another. Although many culinary traditions were simplified or completely lost during the 70 years of Soviet rule, since perestroika opened up the country people have shown interest not only in international specialties and American fast food, but also once again in the oft-forgotten variety of Russian cuisine and its regional and national features. Anyone who has sat down with the sensual, pleasure-loving Russians at a table laden with food knows that eating together creates a bond and contributes to better mutual understanding. Russian cuisine is an ambassador for the way of life, hospitality, temperament, customs, and character of a whole country and for the peoples and ethnic groups united within its vast territory.

Like many other rivers and lakes in Russia, "Little Mother Volga" provides her children with fish. Street traders in Saratov on the lower reaches of the Volga offer their freshly-caught wares with a smile, even at –13 °F (–25 °C).

The traditional Russian stove

In the villages of Russia, two things are greatly cherished: the samovar and the stove. As the old saying has it: "A house is only as much use as the stove inside it." This respect for the stove also appears in countless fairytales, in which stoves are even able to travel across country. It is almost impossible to imagine Russia without its wooden houses and its stoves. A Russian stove cannot be squeezed into a corner of the kitchen; it dominates the entire room. In the old days, the elderly, the children and the sick slept on its warm tiles. Guests found a bed for the night on the bench that formed part of the stove, beneath garlands of fish and mushrooms that were hanging there to dry. There is always a depression in the stove, where felt boots, furs, gloves, stockings or underwear can be put to dry. In front of the warming oven, in which the next day's porridge or cabbage soup slowly simmers and thickens, there is often a brightly-colored calico curtain. The poker,

The brick-built kitchen stove is still the focal point of every traditional Russian household.

pusher, and pot and pan forks have their place on the shelves at the front of the stove, with cast iron pots, pans, and containers in front of the mouth of the oven.

A meal cooked in a Russian oven is characterized by a distinctive aroma, because the meat and vegetables stew slowly in their own juices. The temperature either remains constant or falls slowly, without rising as it does in an electric oven. In the old days, there were three different heats for warming food: before bread-baking, immediately after bread-baking, and at your discretion. For example, you can test whether the temperature is right for baking pirogi by throwing a handful of flour into the oven. If it burns, you have to wait a little longer. If the correct temperature has been reached, food is not roasted in the direct heat of the fire but braised or stewed for a long time in clay pots. This gentle braising method preserves the flavors and nutrients in the soups, stews, and pot roasts. The slowly falling temperature in the oven is ideal for making porridge *(kasha)*. The cereal grains swell up and the vitamin content is preserved.

For country folk, the stove is still a symbol of warmth and food, health, wellbeing, and security. That is why they take particular care of this treasure. So it comes as no surprise that the stove builder is even more highly respected than the vil-

lage headman. In the old days, Russian stoves were usually decorated by being whitewashed by the stove builder, then painted with fairytale motifs or covered with tiles. The tiles, might be flat or decorated with reliefs, they were glazed and were either used as borders or put together decoratively to make up bigger pictures with all kinds of animal and hunting scenes. As well as stove builders, famous painters, including icon painters, and other artists were busy creating Russian stoves. One of the real masters was the symbolist painter Mikhail Vrubel (1856-1910), who invented a method for making the paint on the tiles shimmer like mother-of-pearl. His stove designs with fairytale motifs are particularly enchanting. However, this did not happen by chance. Because the stove is such an essential feature of life, it also plays a large part in Russian fairytales, for instance in "The Wicked Goat," who claimed the best seat on the stove, or in "Little Terenty," who was about to be roasted in the oven by the daughter of the wicked witch, but finally succeeded in pushing the witch girl herself into the oven. However, the most famous tale, in which a stove plays a role, is "By the Will of the Pike" by Alexey Tolstoy. In this story, the lazy peasant Emelya travels on a stove to the Tsar's court, and wins the heart of the Tsar's daughter.

The stove is not just for cooking and baking, the family also use it for heating and for drying the washing.

Main picture: Typical dishes from the oven are piroshki and various milk-based dishes cooked in clay pots.

Pirogi

There is an old Russian saying, which says that it is not the decoration that makes a house beautiful, it is the pirogi at the feast. These filled pockets of dough are a national dish with a place of honor at the Russian table. The name goes back to the Old Russian word *pir*, meaning banquet, probably because in the olden days they were only made on feast days. What is more, there were special pirogi for each feast day. They were filled with everything the garden, the barn the field, the forest, and the pond could provide. Until the 14th century, pirog dough was made only with rye flour; later wheat flour was added. Other traditional ingredients are milk and butter for poultry-filled pirogi, vegetable oil for vegetable and fish pirogi, and beef suet for meat-filled pirogi. The secret of light pies lies in the dough. It must always be "living," that is it must be leavened, prove several times, and be thoroughly kneaded in between. To ferment it they use yeast, sour milk, sour cream, must, beer or whey. You can find pirogi filled with white cabbage, peas, carrots, and cream, turnips, potatoes, onions, mushrooms, berries, eggs, quark, and poppy seeds, as well as porridge made from buckwheat or pearl barley, or with rice. Meat pirogi filled with ground meat, innards, poultry, or game are a particular delicacy. *Kulebyaki* have several layers of different fillings and are taller and narrower than classic pirogi. For instance, at the bottom there will be a firm layer of rice or *kasha* (see page 54), in the middle a juicy meat or fish filling, and on top you have hardcooked eggs. In the old days, these pirogi "towers" were given to the peasants out in the fields as an all-in-one midday meal, and they still make a filling snack for travelers to take with them. At a classic Russian meal, pirogi follow the fish course, and the second main course is served after them. In classy restaurants, they are served with soup. Sweet *piroshki*, filled with Quark, or well-drained fromage blanc, honey, or fruit, go well with tea.

Russkoye drozhzhevoye testo
Russian yeast dough
1 tray for 8-10 people or about 20 piroshki

1½ oz/40 g yeast
1 cup/250 ml milk
2 tsp sugar
Generous 1 lb/500 g all-purpose flour
2 egg yolks
8½ tbsp/125 g butter or margarine
1 pinch salt

Dissolve the yeast in 7 tablespoons/100 ml lukewarm milk, then add the sugar, cover, and leave in a warm place for about 15 minutes to start fermenting. Sift half the flour into a bowl, stir in the yeast mixture with a wooden spoon and make a pre-dough. Cover with a cloth and leave to prove in a warm place for about one hour. The pre-dough should roughly double in size.
Beat the egg and butter or margarine until frothy, add salt and the remaining milk and work into a smooth mass. Sift in the remaining flour and work in thoroughly. On a well-floured board, knead the dough until it no longer sticks, adding a little flour, water, or milk if necessary. Cover the finished dough again, and leave to prove in a warm place for a further 1–2 hours.
Tip: For the yeast to work, all the ingredients should be at room temperature.

Pirog
Pirog

Using a wooden rolling pin, roll the dough out to about ½ in/10 mm thick (keeping back a small amount for decoration). Cover the center of the dough with filling, fold the edges over the filling and press together firmly. Place the pirog on a well-greased baking sheet with the wrapped side underneath.
Roll the remaining dough out thin, cut out decorations and stick them to the pirog with egg yolk. Brush the pirog with egg, prick several times with a fork, leave to stand for 15–20 minutes, then bake in a pre-heated oven at 400-425 °F/200-220 °C for 30–50 minutes, depending on the filling.

The basis of pirog (plural: pirogi) is a yeast dough. It is best to stir the pre-dough with a wooden spoon.

Roll out the dough, cover with a savory or sweet filling, and then close firmly.

Then you can decorate the pirog with leftover dough as your fancy takes you—either simply or artistically.

Savory and sweet pirogi: the *kurnik* (1) is the wedding pirog which has several fillings, one of which must always be chicken; *vatrushki* (2) are small, circular, open pirogi made of rye and wheat flour, usually containing sweet Quark or fromage blanc, less often jam; *rastegay* (3) have an opening on top, and are usually filled with fish, though also often with meat, rice or mushrooms; *sochniki* (4) are folded into the shape of half-moons with their Quark filling showing.

Nachinka iz kapusty s yaytsom
White cabbage and egg filling

2¼ lbs/1 kg white cabbage, finely chopped or grated
3 tbsp/45 g butter
4 hardcooked eggs, finely chopped
2–3 tbsp each of finely chopped parsley and finely chopped dill
Salt and pepper
1 pinch sugar
2 eggs, beaten, for brushing

Make a yeast dough as described in the basic recipe and roll out (see instructions for pirogi).
Squeeze the white cabbage well, then sauté in butter until soft and a light golden brown. Add the hard-cooked eggs and herbs to the cabbage, mix well, and season with salt and pepper. Allow the filling to cool before use. It is suitable for both pirogi (bake for 30–40 minutes) and piroshki.

Rybniy pirog
Fish pirog

4 medium potatoes, coarsely grated
1¾ lb/750 g fish fillets (e.g. porgy, perch, sturgeon, sea bass), thinly sliced
2 medium onions, finely chopped
Salt and pepper
4 tbsp melted butter
2 eggs, beaten, for brushing

Make a yeast dough as described in the basic recipe and roll out (see instructions for pirogi).
In the centre of the dough base, arrange first the grated potatoes then the fish and onions, evenly distributed. Season well with salt and pepper and drizzle with melted butter.
Continue as for the basic pirogi recipe. Bake for 50–60 minutes.

Piroshki s yablokami i yagodami
Piroshki with apples and forest berries

Generous 1 lb/500 g cooking apples
⅔ cup/150 g sugar
Cinnamon to taste
Generous ½ lb/250 g forest berries (e.g. raspberries, strawberries, blueberries)
1 egg, beaten, for brushing

Make a yeast dough according to the basic recipe and roll out (see instructions for pirogi).
Peel the apples, remove the core, and grate the flesh (continue with preparation immediately, so that the apples do not go brown!). Mix the apples with sugar and cinnamon, leave to draw for about 20 minutes, then add the berries.
Make piroshki according to the instructions and fill with the fruit mixture. Brush the piroshki with egg and bake until golden brown.

Zakuska table

Because a table without hors d'oeuvres or appetizers is just a bare board to the Russians, and one bite leads to another, *zakuski* are the uncrowned kings of the table. Russians are not accustomed to hurrying, and certainly not over a meal. "If you spend a long time eating, you will have a long life," as the saying goes, and zakuski extend every meal by a few delicious moments. These little appetizers are as many and varied as the peoples and landscapes of Russia. They come hot and cold, pickled and marinated, salted, boiled, smoked and dried. Fish, particularly sturgeon, salmon and caviar, accompanied by jellied meats such as pig's trotters in aspic with horseradish, sturgeon or pike in aspic, and poultry. Meats such as ham, pork loin and boiled tongue are also popular. Zakuski are the prelude to a meal. The everyday choice is fairly modest, but on feast days or when guests are expected, the table threatens to collapse under the weight of the zakuski. Until the 17th century, the word *zakuska* was used to mean "something to eat with something else"—bread as a zakuska for meat, sugar as a zakuska for bitter medicine. In an alehouse, you usually get a portion of dried fish as a zakuska for your drink. Real Russians do not pull faces if they drink 100 g high-proof vodka in one go. However, the follow up bite of pickled cucumber is a must, though it can also be an onion, or a lemon, or a piece of bread with salt or fatty bacon. Quite simply, a zakuska.

Over the course of time, the range of zakuski became increasingly lavish. In the 19th century in particular, foreign dishes, such as stuffed eggs, goose liver pâté, cold marinades, sausages, butter, white bread, marinated vegetables, and preserved fruits have been added to the zakuska table. The Russians took over the word *(buterbrod)* from German cuisine, along with the slices of bread and butter, but they are always topped with egg, cheese, sausage, and especially with different kind of herring. These have become a number one hit on the zakuska table: herrings in mustard, in sour cream, with vegetables, with nuts, with eggs, in marinade, lightly salted, with onions, or as rollmops. Many salads also have herrings added to give them an extra touch of class. In modern day Russian cuisine, you also get hot appetizers, such as filled pirogi, stewed mushrooms in cream, blini, and occasionally French-inspired creations such as poultry livers and porcini with raspberry sauce and shrimp, which can be found on the menu of the elegant hotel Metropol in Moscow (see page 35).

A collection of culinary art works. A lavish zakuska table shows you at first glance the variety that Russian cuisine has to offer.

Russian meals and eating habits

Breakfast *(zavtrak)* is large and usually consists of tea, kefir (see glossary), yogurt, and sour cream, white or black bread with cheese and sausage, and buckwheat porridge *(kasha)* with meatballs or roast meat. Breakfast is commonly eaten as late as between 10 am and 1 pm. If it starts earlier, it may even be followed by a second breakfast. **Lunch** *(obed)* is traditionally eaten late, sometimes not until 5 pm. It is always made up of several courses and clearly divided portions. The variety and lavishness of the menu depend on the setting. On feast days and at the weekend, the Russians sit at the table for hours, whereas things have to move a bit faster in the works canteen. According to the classical menu order, various *zakuski* such as pickled vegetables and salads are served first. These are followed by a hot soup and the main course of fish, meat, or poultry, accompanied by potatoes, rice, or vegetables. For dessert there is usually stewed fruit or ice cream and tea or coffee. For reasons of time, **evening tea** *(vecherniy chai)*, a fixed element in the day in noble and bourgeois circles in the 19th century, now only happens at the weekend. Tea from the samovar is accompanied by cakes or cookies and chocolates. The **evening meal** *(ushin)*, eaten between 7 pm and 10 pm, is more modest, but like lunch, it consists of several courses, such as zakuski, soup, main course and dessert. It often ends with vodka and may continue far into the night.

The many varieties of zakuski

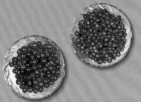

Cranberries from Russian forests stimulate the digestive system and go very well with substantial meat courses.

Kvass, a drink made from fermented bread, goes with almost all foods and can be found in typical earthenware jugs on many zakuska tables.

Russian cuisine includes countless varieties of vegetables pickled in brine or vinegar, such as cucumbers, garlic, and green beans.

The favorite accompaniment for delicate pink slices of boiled pork, and many other Russian foods, is horseradish.

Red caviar from the chum salmon may not be as classy as its black relative from the sturgeon, but the Russians enjoy it almost as much.

Along with a whole sturgeon, black caviar is the crowning glory of any zakuska table. People who take pride in their table serve these precious beads in vast quantities.

There are no limits to the uses made of salmon. Little rolls of smoked or marinated salmon garnished with olives are particularly decorative.

Colorful salads of fresh vegetables ensure people get plenty of vitamins. This mixture of grated carrots and horseradish has a sweet, tangy taste.

Classy vegetable salads with mayonnaise may contain potatoes, boiled carrots, mushrooms, pickled cucumbers, or hardcooked eggs.

Fine seafood comes mainly from the Pacific, though exquisite delicacies such as crabmeat also command a high price in Russia.

There are usually large numbers of herring dishes to be found on zakuska tables. Plain salt herring fillets are often served with onions.

Cocktail sauce with tomatoes and fresh parsley makes an excellent accompaniment to a delicate mushroom salad. Larger mushrooms are chopped fine; small ones are left whole.

Rollmops with pickled gherkins and onions may take a bit of effort but, decorated with dill, they attract admiring glances from the guests.

Small colorful canapés with smoked fish and caviar go down well. They are extremely delicious and are easy to eat with the fingers.

This salad of rice, shrimp, and pickled cucumbers is very tasty with a fresh dressing made from the brine from the cucumbers and vinegar, or with mayonnaise.

It could hardly be easier, but most guests still have room for simple pleasures like small new potatoes with melted butter.

Cooked red beet, prunes, walnuts and sour cream combine to make an unusual and delicious salad mixture.

Raw pickled cabbage is always a healthy pleasure. It is tasty on its own, or with finely chopped carrots, scallions and oil.

Slices of pressed ham can be filled in different ways, for instance with a vegetable and mayonnaise salad (see picture) or with asparagus.

These tasty fritters with a delicious filling of onions and parsley are fried in fat and taste best when hot.

This simple salad of finely grated carrots, lemon juice, and a little sunflower oil is often served with sour cream or mayonnaise.

Big fish in small strips: Russians are fond of smoked sturgeon. They like it best with mayonnaise or horseradish.

Despite its characteristic earthy taste, red beet combines well with other ingredients, for instance with apples and good quality sunflower oil.

Lampreys are now rarely seen on the starter table. They are primitive fish, with an eel-like body and a jawless mouth.

Tender, lightly cooked chicken meat can be eaten hot or cold. It is also served as a delicious chicken roulade in aspic.

Tomatoes, cucumbers, and bell peppers bring a scent of summer to the zakuska table. Suitable dressings are sour cream, or vinegar, oil, and herbs.

Finger food Russian style: *Buterbrody* are particularly popular for stand-up parties. Topped with salmon, herring, or caviar, sausage, ham, or cheese—these colorful open sandwiches always meet with approval, especially when they are attractively garnished.

Thinly sliced, tender boiled beef is hidden beneath a layer of sour cream and tart cranberries.

In Russia, mushrooms and other fungi are often stewed in sour cream with finely chopped onions.

Beans combine with chopped walnuts to make a particularly nourishing starter to take the edge off people's hunger before the main course.

To make "mushroom caviar," pickled wild mushrooms are finely chopped and then dressed with chopped onions, garlic, vinegar, oil, and herbs.

For the zakuska table, red and green tomatoes are often pickled in brine. In this form they go very well with meaty starters.

Braised quails are something of a rare delicacy. They taste particularly good with a filling of wild mushrooms or giblets.

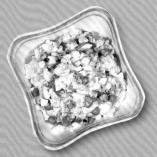

Russian "vinaigrette" is a vegetable salad in a herb dressing, often including meat or fish as well, and hardcooked eggs if desired.

Small fish dishes such as pike or perch in tomato sauce are often served hot, but can also be eaten cold some hours later.

A great combination of colors and flavors: red beet salad, perhaps with a little honey, is a perfect accompaniment to salt herring.

For "herrings in fur coats," you arrange layers of herring filets, potatoes, vegetables, chopped eggs and mayonnaise with sour cream one on top of the other.

A feast for the palate and the eye: crayfish and smoked salmon in delicious aspic is a product of the imagination of modern zakuska cuisine.

The consistency of goose meat in aspic and other Russian jellied meats is usually soft. They are not turned out on to a plate but served in the dish.

There are hardly any kinds of meat that cannot be served in aspic. It is also a practical way of using up leftovers such as roast beef.

Roast partridge with tropical fruits shows that international flavors have also found a place on the modern zakuska table.

Innards are also a popular starter in Russia. Delicate kidneys in tomato sauce should be eaten while warm and not stand for long.

Delicious pâtés, for instance chicken liver and herbs, are also among the most popular of cold starters, as are tasty sausages.

Egg salad appears in a number of different varieties in Russian cuisine, for example with mushrooms, scallions, sour cream, and/or mayonnaise.

Pickled green and black olives are imported and can look very attractive when served in flowers made from carved radishes.

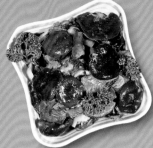

Mixed wild mushrooms are often pickled in brine. They are tasty on their own or with a dressing of onions, herbs, oil, and vinegar.

This simple potato salad is just dressed with oil and vinegar and sprinkled with fresh herbs. Dill and parsley are particularly good for this.

Red beet gives a Russian meat or fish "vinaigrette" its characteristic color and a slightly tart flavor.

The popular herring pâté comes in many varieties, for example with salt herring, grated apple, onions, butter, and sour cream.

The abundant riches of the Russian forests also appear on the zakuska table. There are countless delicious appetizers containing fresh or pickled mushrooms.

To make a herring pâté for spreading on bread, the salted fish is put through the grinder together with potatoes and onions, and plenty of butter is added.

Elegant little tartlets of mixed mushrooms add a note of modern Western European cuisine to the lavish Russian zakuska table.

As well as tender loin of beef, this particularly fine meat salad contains ham, potatoes, mushrooms, tomatoes and fresh herbs.

Tasty "eggplant caviar" is made with eggplant, onions and herbs that are first roasted in the oven and then finely chopped.

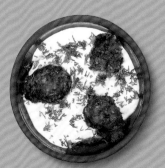

A favorite way of cooking meatballs, usually made of ground beef, is to braise them in sour cream. They taste best when hot.

Simple ingredients imaginatively presented. Salt herrings are cut in thick slices and arranged in a flower shape with boiled potatoes.

This delicious version of potato salad with radishes and hardcooked eggs is even more colorful and tasty than the straightforward version.

Fruit such as baked apple with prunes also appears on the zakuska table, not as a dessert but as a fruity appetizer.

Zakuski

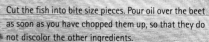

... vegetarian

Farshirovannye yaytsa
Stuffed eggs

6 hardcooked eggs
3 tbsp mayonnaise
1 tbsp mustard
3 small pickled gherkins, finely chopped
2 tbsp finely chopped scallions
Salt and freshly ground pepper
Lettuce leaves, capers, and pickled red bell peppers

Peel the eggs and cut in half lengthwise. Carefully remove the yolks and crush well. Mix with mayonnaise, mustard, gherkins, and scallions and season with salt and pepper. Using a spoon, fill the egg halves with the mixture, arrange them on lettuce leaves and garnish with capers and peppers before serving.

Pomidory, farshirovaniye gribami
Tomatoes with mushroom stuffing

2 onions, finely chopped
2 tbsp butter
Generous 1 lb/500 g assorted fresh mushrooms
7 tbsp/100 ml mushroom or vegetable stock
Salt and pepper
1/2 cup/125 g sour cream
1/2 bunch parsley, finely chopped
Generous 1 lb/500 g firm tomatoes
4 tbsp grated cheese (e.g. Gouda)

Sauté the onions in butter, add the mushrooms and sauté briefly. Add the stock, salt, and pepper, mix in the sour cream and parsley, and allow to cool. Cut lids off the tomatoes, and scoop out the flesh. Fill with the mushroom and onion mixture, sprinkle with cheese, and bake on a greased baking sheet in a pre-heated oven at 340 °F (175 °C) for about 15 minutes. Serve hot or cold.

Baklazhannaya ikra
"Eggplant caviar"
(Not illustrated)

3 medium eggplants
2 medium onions, finely chopped
3 tbsp oil
2 tbsp tomato paste
3-4 cloves garlic, finely chopped
Salt and pepper
2 tbsp finely chopped parsley
2 tbsp finely chopped chives

Bake the eggplant in the oven at 340 °C (175 °C) for about 20 minutes, rinse in cold water, peel, and chop the flesh fine. Lightly brown the onions in oil, stir in tomato paste, and cook for 2–3 minutes. Add eggplant flesh, garlic, salt, and pepper, bring briefly to a boil, then leave to cool. Sprinkle with parsley and chives before serving.

Vinegret s ryboy
Russian vinaigrette with fish

3/4lb/300 g boiled fish fillets
(e.g. herring, pike, perch, sturgeon)
2 medium beets, boiled and diced
3 tbsp oil
5 medium potatoes, boiled and diced
3 medium carrots, boiled and diced
3/4 cup/100 g steamed green peas
3 pickled gherkins, finely chopped
2 hardcooked eggs, finely chopped
1 apple, peeled and diced
1/2 bunch scallions, finely chopped
3 tbsp vinegar
Salt, pepper, and sugar
1 bunch parsley or dill, finely chopped

Cut the fish into bite size pieces. Pour oil over the beet as soon as you have chopped them up, so that they do not discolor the other ingredients.
Thoroughly mix together all ingredients, season with salt and pepper and garnish before serving with pieces of fish and freshly chopped herbs.

... with meat

Telyachi yazyk v zhele
Calf tongue in aspic
(Not illustrated)

1 calf tongue
1 onion
2 carrots, sliced
1 small head of celery and 1 parsley root
2 bay leaves
Salt and 5 black peppercorns
6 envelopes/1/3 oz/40 g gelatin
3 1/2 tbsp/50 ml dry white wine
1 bunch parsley
Hardcooked eggs and tomatoes for garnish

Wash the tongue and place in a large pan. Add vegetables, bay leaves, salt, pepper, cover with water, and bring to a boil. Allow the meat to simmer for 1 hour until tender, skimming occasionally.
Remove the tongue from the stock, skin, slice, and cover with the slices of carrot. Soften the gelatin in lukewarm water. Strain the stock, add the wine to 4 cups/1 liter of stock and bring to a boil. Stir in the gelatin. Pour the liquid over the slices of tongue and leave to set in a cool place. Garnish with parsley, slices of egg, and tomatoes. Horseradish sauce makes a good accompaniment (see also page 37).

Salad "Olivier"

Generous 1 lb/500 g poached chicken without skin or bone
3 hardcooked eggs
3 medium potatoes boiled in their skins
1 large carrot, boiled
2–3 pickled gherkins
¾ cup/100 g peas, boiled
10 tbsp/150 g mayonnaise
¾ cup/200 g sour cream
Salt
Pepper
2 tbsp capers
2 tbsp finely chopped dill

Cut the boiled chicken in thin strips. Peel the hard-cooked eggs and chop small. Peel and slice the cooked potatoes and slice the carrot. Chop the gherkins small. Mix together all the solid ingredients. Whisk the mayonnaise and sour cream together, season with salt and pepper, add the capers and the chopped dill, and carefully add to the solid ingredients.

Tip: For a vegetarian version, Salad Olivier can also be made without chicken. This version goes very well on the zakuska table with smoked ham and other kinds of smoke or boiled meat.

Bitochki s gribami
Meatballs with mushroom filling
(Not illustrated)

3–4 slices white bread without crusts
1 cup/¼ liter milk
1¾ lb/750 g mixed ground meat
3 eggs
Salt
Pepper
3½ oz/100 g porcini mushrooms
3½ oz/100 g streaky bacon, diced small
2 medium onions, finely chopped
7 tbsp/100 g butter
½ bunch parsley, finely chopped
50 g breadcrumbs

Soak the bread briefly in the milk and squeeze well. Mix with the ground meat, eggs, salt, and pepper and knead well.
Clean the mushrooms, blanch briefly with boiling water, chop, and sauté with the bacon and onion in 2 tbsp butter. Add salt, pepper, and parsley and mix thoroughly.
Form the meat into 8–12 flat cakes, put a little of the mushroom mixture in the center of each one, and form into meatballs. Roll the meatballs in bread-crumbs and fry on all sides in butter.

... with fish

Ryba s pomidorami
Fish with tomatoes
(Not illustrated)

2 tbsp oil
Juice of ½–1 lemon
2 cloves garlic, finely chopped
1 tsp salt
1¾ lb/750 g fish fillets (e.g. cod, porgy, perch, bass)
2 onions, sliced
3 medium tomatoes, sliced
1 tbsp finely chopped parsley
1 cup/250 ml fish stock

Make a marinade with oil, lemon juice, garlic, and salt. Divide the fish into bite-sized pieces, marinate for 1 hour, then place in an oven-proof dish.
Spread onions, tomatoes and parsley over the fish, pour over the fish stock, cover and bake for about 30 minutes at 340 °F/175 °C.

Selyodochny pashtet
Herring pâté
(Not illustrated)

500 g white bread without crusts
1 cup/250 ml milk
Fillets of 2 medium salted herrings, finely chopped
1 small tart apple, peeled and finely grated
1 medium onion
3½ tbsp/50 g butter
½ cup/125 g sour cream
Pepper
2 tbsp breadcrumbs

Soak the bread briefly in the milk and squeeze well. Mix the herring fillets with the softened bread, add the apple and onion and put the mixture through the grinder. Add butter and sour cream, season with pepper, and put the mixture into a greased oven-proof dish. Sprinkle with breadcrumbs and bake in the oven at 340 °F/175 °C until golden brown.

Marinovannye sardiny
Marinated sardines

1¼ lb/600 g fresh sardines, ready to cook
All-purpose flour
Oil

For the marinade:
3 medium onions, finely chopped
1 carrot, finely chopped
1 medium parsley root, finely chopped
3 tbsp oil
2 cups/500 ml fish stock
Salt and pepper
1 tsp sugar
1 bay leaf
4 tbsp vinegar
Parsley, dill, and onions for garnishing

Toss the sardines in flour and fry in oil until golden brown. Remove from pan and leave to cool. For the marinade: fry the vegetables in oil, pour over fish stock, season with salt and pepper, add the bay leaf, cover, and simmer for 20 minutes. Add vinegar to taste and leave to cool. Leave the sardines to draw in the marinade for 3–4 hours. Garnish with the herbs and onion rings.

The sardines are first tossed in flour, then fried in hot oil until they are a nice golden brown.

A marinade of vegetables, seasonings, vinegar and oil is prepared and poured over the fish.

Vodka

Some people say that vodka is a creator. The glass industry and foundries developed alongside it, and the building of roads and factories was financed with the taxes brought in by the sale of vodka. International peace agreements were sealed with vodka. Vodka makes people happy, kinder, more open, and helps them to confess their love. Russian history is full of great events, and vodka has often played a part in important discoveries and heroic deeds. However, it cannot be denied that vodka is also a great destroyer. It makes clever people stupid, and taken in excess is a cause of family quarrels and crime. So in Russia vodka is also known as the devil's drink, because it has always been accompanied by fear and misery and caused peace-loving people to lose control. Vodka first appeared in chronicles in 1386, though not as a drink, but as a medicament: "Squeeze out the wound and pour vodka on it to prevent gangrene." At the court of Ivan Grozny—Ivan the Terrible—vodka was regarded as a ceremonial drink and a "Russian weapon" that could be used to render foreign envoys mild and compliant when negotiating agreements. In the 16th century, drunkenness became rife, and even monks are said to have led a dissolute life. Peter the Great complained that more men were killed by vodka than by enemy bullets—and began his day with a quarter of a liter (about half a US pint) of the spirit, seasoned with black pepper. Anyone who was willing was allowed to drink with him. Peter's ability to hold his liquor inspired fear and amazement in everyone. He created a network of state vodka factories and bars, and the profits from them went into building the fleet and the war against Sweden. In the 18th century, the name *vodka*, meaning "little water," passed into general use. Vodka is still the Russians' elixir of life, in good times and bad, and a guarantee for the only business sector in the country that is safe from crisis.

According to official statistics, Russians spend 8.8 percent of their income on vodka. Information from the Ministry of Commerce says that on average every Russian drinks nine liters (about 18 US pints) of legal vodka a year; alcoholism associations talk of more than double that amount. There are 120 vodka factories producing 150 different brands of this high-proof spirit, but only 10 distilleries use the best raw materials—rye, wheat, and yeast to make crystal-clear, top quality vodka of at least 40 percent proof. In the country, the Russians distil their own vodka, which can be up to 70 percent proof, from sugar, corn, and potatoes. It is served mainly at christenings, weddings and funerals. So the range extends from fine vodka to the illicitly distilled *samogon* (see also page 192f).

To make both kinds, grain is put into warm water. As soon as the corn has germinated, it is dried and ground. The meal is put into boiling water and constantly stirred until it is creamy. Then this mash must be covered and left to stand for 10 to 12 hours. Yeast is added at room temperature. It ferments for five days, as haste is said to spoil the vodka. After this rest period, the brew is heated, causing the alcohol to rise. It is then cooled in the snake pipe, collected, and filtered through active carbon.

The majority of Russians like pure vodka; only a few people also like flavored vodkas such as *pertsovka*, which is flavored with bell peppers, or vodka with lemon, berries or herbs. In Velikiy Ustyug, the home of the Russian equivalent of Father Christmas, the liqueur and vodka factory based in the town sells *Ded Moros* (Father Frost) vodka, which is actually flavored with fresh pine needles. In Russia, toasts are part of the vodka culture, like the little *zakusk* of a good bite of pickled cucumber, a piece of dry bread with a slice of bacon or the popular dried fish *vobla*. So vodka is often drunk before the main courses of a meal. The magazine *Ruskaya Vodka* (Russian Vodka) recommends that you drink vodka until your 50th year, then beer, but do not forget the old customs. For instance, at a wedding, there is a cry of *gorko!* (bitter!), whereupon glasses are raised and the couple have to kiss to sweeten the bitter food for the guests. Throwing the glasses at the wall brings the newlyweds good luck. And when saying goodbye at the station, you smash vodka glasses under the oncoming train for a safe journey. At the graveside, they often drink to the health of the deceased—but never clink glasses.

Right: Russians often drink their vodka from tumblers.

Below: A worker at the vodka factory in Kostroma examines a freshly labeled bottle.

Vodka as a sophisticated home remedy

Vodka is always ordered in grams in restaurants and bars and Russians usually drink it in its pure form. However, they do add herbs or fruits to their "little water" to make liqueurs and elixirs (see page 124). Wrapping the chest with cloths soaked in vodka is an ancient Russian home remedy for influenza or wrapped around the neck it is effective against tonsillitis. High-proof vodka (60–70 percent proof) is used externally to prevent infection in wounds. Russian beekeepers rub themselves with vodka to prevent being stung. This is also said to work for mosquito bites. When added to the natural hair dye henna, it gives a bright chestnut color and the Siberians swear that, if the hair and scalp are massaged regularly with the local hooch *samogon* (see page 192 f), it can help to prevent dandruff.

If shoes are too tight, vodka is poured onto the seams to make them stretch. Hard leather is supposed to become softer and more pliable if rubbed with the spirit. Housewives reckon vodka mixed with sunflower oil makes an excellent polish for dull or scratched walnut or jacaranda wood furniture. It also restores the shine to marble. Glasses and car windscreens are wiped over with vodka to protect them from chipping and freezing up. This gives rise to the Siberian joke that people who wear glasses can go to the front of the queue for vodka, because for them it is a matter of an optical emergency rather than alcoholism. On television, there was a famous long-running commercial for a Russian vodka firm that said, "Take our *Kristal*, for your glasses as well, if necessary— for absolute clarity of vision."

Sturgeon

It is one of nature's miracles that a huge sturgeon more than 25 feet/8 m long and weighing over 3,300 lb/1,500 kg can grow from a tiny caviar egg the size of a pinhead. Russia is one of the homes of this boneless fish with its typical bony plates, a very ancient species that goes back to the age of the dinosaurs. In the 5th century BC, the Greek historian Herodotus wrote of the river Dnieper, "it also produces a very large spineless fish, good for pickling and known locally as antacaeus." In the 12th century, at the court of the rulers of Novgorod, there was an official known as the *osyotrennik*, a tax collector for sturgeon-fishing. However, fine sturgeon caviar was reserved for the prince's table. Most sturgeon live and are caught in the Caspian Sea, the Black Sea and the Volga with its tributaries and delta. In the past, the number of fish in the Volga was so great that, according to chronicles dating from the 15th to the 17th centuries, up to 10,000 fishermen would come to the middle reaches of the river each year for the season.

Sturgeon are among the biggest, most valuable fish in Russia. The species includes the sturgeon *(osyotr)* that has given its name to the entire genus, the *beluga*, *sevruga*, river sturgeon, kaluga and sterlet. Their delicious flesh is firm, tender, and slightly oily. Although the flesh is white, the sturgeon is also called *krasnaya ryba* ("red fish" or "noble fish"), because in the old days in Russia everything rare, beautiful and expensive was described as *krasniy*, which at that time was used to mean "beautiful."

In Russia and the CIS, the sturgeon is still the most highly prized fish. However, as a result of the pollution of the seas, overfishing and uncontrolled black market trading—especially in Turkmenistan, Kazakhstan and Azerbaijan—stocks have drastically decreased. Since April 1 1998, the sturgeons of the Caspian Sea have come under the Washington Agreement on the Protection of Endangered Species. The quotas for Russia and Iran, the two major countries bordering the Caspian Sea, were restricted in order to promote the recovery of stocks. Since spring 1999, every tin of caviar over 8 oz/250 g must be accompanied by the appropriate papers, in order to make illegal trading more difficult.

Nowadays this noble fish is caught by fishery companies and joint stock companies, and also by the caviar Mafia and fish poachers. Poaching is a serious problem, especially in the Russian Republic of Dagestan, where almost the entire coastal population is engaged in the illegal catching and processing of sturgeon and involved in endless corruption scandals.

According to official Russian estimates, in spring almost 10 metric tonnes of illegally caught sturgeon are delivered to Moscow every day—three and a half times as much as permitted by the quota. Every year at the sturgeons' spawning time under the codename "Fish train," special units from the Ministry of the Interior carry out successful operations against poachers and the organized "Caviar Mafia" in the lower reaches of the Volga and the northern part of the Caspian Sea. The sturgeon is caught at spawning time in the early summer using hand nets and trawls, and occasionally also with fishing lines. In the winter, when the sturgeons lie still with their heads buried in the mud, the stiff bodies are pulled out of the deep mud on to the ice with hooks. The fish is frozen when freshly caught, cut into fillets, dried in the southern sun, or smoked as a delicacy. Preserving by pickling is out of the question, because the sturgeon loses its delicious taste during the process.

Fresh sturgeon is most often served in aspic as a starter, but it is also popular as a main course. In addition, it is the highlight of every good fish soup (see page 92 f). Its delicious and individual flavor comes out best if it is cooked on its own, steamed or fried in butter. This means that most sturgeon recipes have few other ingredients. However, the sturgeon is loved most of all for its "black gold"—caviar (see pages 32 ff).

Right: a successful catch in Astrakhan. The *osyotr* can yield over 33 lb/15 kg of caviar.

Osetrina tushonaya s sousom iz khrena
Braised sturgeon with horseradish sauce

1 cup/250 ml brine from pickled cucumbers
7 tbsp/100 g butter
1 onion, halved
1/2 small celeriac, coarsely chopped
1 bunch parsley, chopped
2 bay leaves
Salt
1 3/4 lb (750 g) sturgeon, ready to cook

For the sauce:
5 1/2 oz/150 g horseradish root
Salt and sugar
3/4 cup/125 g sour cream

Mix the brine from pickled cucumbers with 1 cup/250 ml water, add the butter, vegetables, parsley, bay leaves, and a little salt. Place the fish in the liquid, cover, and cook over low heat for about 30 minutes. Keep warm on a preheated dish. Grate the horseradish finely, pour over 3/4 cup/200 ml boiling water, season to taste with salt and sugar, allow to cool to room temperature, and mix with the sour cream. Pour the sauce over the cooked fish and serve with a side dish of boiled potatoes.

Isinglass

In former times, sturgeon were not only caught for their delicious flesh and caviar. They were used in so many ways that, when defending the Stoic philosophy against the Epicurean, Cicero was moved to ask: "If you find any of your relatives broken down by grief, will you give him a sturgeon rather than a Socratic treatise?" The bony plates of this fish have long been used to make buttons. In the Volga delta the skin was made into balers and the big swim bladder was boiled down to produce isinglass and was even used in the building of fishing boats and mixed into the paint for mural paintings in churches.

Caviar production

In Russia caviar reigns supreme on the zakuska table. For centuries, sturgeon caught in the Volga Delta and the Caspian Sea have been the main source of supply. Until the 1860s, this fine roe was only traded within Russia, because it did not keep very long. Even this inland trade was difficult before the coming of the railroads. Russian caviar did not come on to the European market until around the end of the 19th century. It made its first appearance in 1900 at the great World Exhibition in Paris. Since then, this treat for the palate has become the epitome of epicurean pleasure throughout the world. In Soviet times, caviar was a food of the people. Black Sea fishermen ate it for breakfast; it was even fed to soldiers, and in the 1960s large quantities of black and red caviar were on sale in ordinary food stores and inns. Recently the price of the best blue-black roe has risen considerably. The Caspian Sea, which is home to the most important caviar-producing species of sturgeon, is an inland sea. The shallow northern part is suffering increasing pollution caused by extensive oil extraction. As a result, the sturgeon that produce the best quality caviar are caught in the deeper southern part of the sea off the coast of Iran. Moreover, stocks of this noblest of edible fish have drastically decreased as a result of overfishing and poaching, and that too is driving up the price of caviar. In the Volga Delta, with its 70 branches and hundreds of islands, bands of poachers take huge amounts of sturgeon at spawning time. Even greater damage to sturgeon stocks is caused by illegal fishing on a professional scale in the Caspian Sea. The greed for the "black treasure of the sea," as caviar is sometimes known, and the ever increasing prices encourage gangs of criminals and smugglers with the latest technical equipment on to the scene.

The main route for caviar from illegally caught fish runs through Azerbaijan and Turkey to western Europe. International gangs organize the catching, processing, transport and sale of this delicacy with profits matching those of the drug trade. In the season, 2 ¼ lb/1 kg of caviar can be bought from a poacher for between $5 and $10. In New York's Nobel Restaurant it ends up costing up to $2,000. With the aid of false papers, large quantities of the "hot" merchandise also reach the major Russian cities; almost all of the Moscow market is supplied with illegal caviar.

In the Russian Federation, the legal export of caviar and other sturgeon products requires a license from the Ministry of Foreign Trade, which only brings a few million dollars a year into the treasury. The Caviar Mafia's profits from illegal exports amount to many times that sum.

Because the processing centers on the lower reaches of the Volga and the Caspian Sea are hopelessly antiquated, Russia has the majority of its caviar processed to international standards in Iran. Immediately after the sturgeon is caught, the egg-sack is taken from the female and the membrane surrounding the eggs is removed. The caviar is washed, sorted by size and color, and mixed with about 12 percent dry sea salt. Then the eggs mature for 8 to 12 days in a dry, airtight wooden chest. After that, all that remains is for the salt to be washed out of the caviar, giving it that typical pearly sheen. Then it is vacuum packed in cans or jars and stored at a temperature of 32–37 °F/0–3 °C.

Malossol is a particularly good quality caviar. As its Russian name suggests, it is only lightly salted, and it keeps for about a year. There are also modern processes, during which the eggs are pasteurized at 140–150 °F/60–65 °C and therefore keep for longer. Less valuable roe is more strongly salted and processed into pressed caviar.

Above left: Export-class caviar in cans.

Caviar from the bottling plant in Astrakhan in the Volga Delta is the region's biggest foreign currency earner.

A specialist tests by feeling whether the female sturgeon has already produced enough eggs.

The roe is removed through a slit in the belly. Part of it is kept for breeding.

The fresh roe is carefully cleaned, sorted by size, and then mixed with sea salt.

Women workers supervise the smooth running of the mechanized process of filling the jars.

1 "German" caviar (lumpfish), 2 Chum salmon, 3 Beluga, 4 Trout caviar, 5 Osyotr, 6 Sevruga.

Types of caviar

True caviar

Beluga: the most expensive caviar with the biggest grains. Bead-sized, silver-gray eggs ⅛ inch (3–4 mm) in diameter and extremely thin skin. Beluga caviar is an exclusive rarity and comes from the biggest of the sturgeon, Russian name *beluga*, which is found in the Caspian Sea, the Black Sea, and the rivers Dnieper and Dniester. It grows up to 13 feet/4 m long, weighs over 2,640 lb/1,200 kg and produces up to 440 lb/200 kg of caviar—that is about 7 million eggs.

Osyotr: caviar from the sturgeon (Russian *osyotr*), highly prized for its slightly nutty flavor. The egg size is 1¹⁄₁₆ inch/2–3 mm, and the color varies from blue-black through dark green to silver. *Royal Black Caviar* is an osyotr specialty. It comes from young fish, is deep black, delicately flavored and has a thin shell. The sturgeon weighs up to 440 lb/200 kg and produces about 450,000 eggs.

Sevruga: the caviar with the smallest grains, a hard shell, about the size of a pin head (maximum 2 mm), aromatic, slightly tangy taste. It varies from mid to dark gray in color. This caviar comes from the *sevruga*, a sturgeon that has its home in the Black Sea, the Caspian Sea, the Aral Sea, the rivers Don and Kuban, the Syr Darya and the Amu Darya. Sevruga grow up to 6½ feet/2 m in length and weigh up to 176 lb/80 kg.

False caviar

Cheaper, but very popular in Russia, is red salmon caviar. It is mainly harvested from the chum salmon of the eastern Pacific and the amur or the king salmon (chinook) and has a grain size of about ¼ in/7 mm. Pink caviar from whitefish, muksun, or sea trout is a Siberian delicacy. The yellow-orange, coarse-grained caviar of the Lake Baikal salmon (see page 104) is delicately flavored. The roe of food fish such as hake and cod, as well as pike and zander is mainly processed into pressed caviar. False or "German" caviar, often dyed red or black, and popularly used as a garnish, comes from the lumpfish, which is not sold for its flesh because of its high water content. In Moscow and St. Petersburg, they sell so-called tsars' caviar, a dyed false caviar made from sturgeon flesh.

How to recognize fresh caviar

Except in the case of pressed caviar, the grains should fall apart. The egg skins should be easy to squeeze between the tongue and the palate, releasing their delicious contents. When spooning or dividing into portions, no smearing should appear between the grains. Gray or black, from sturgeon or salmon, the caviar eggs must shine and not be dull. Well-chilled caviar hardly tastes of fish at all but has more of a nutty flavor. Caviar that is too salty or flavored with lemon juice mostly indicates poor processing or storage. Another sure sign of this is eggs with tough skins that cannot be squeezed when eaten.

How caviar should be eaten

Caviar is the high spot of every zakuska table. Gourmets set a high value on this appetizer and know how it should be presented. Firstly, it must be in a glass bowl and on crushed ice, as caviar must always be served cold but never frozen. Secondly, it is best served using a small mother-of-pearl spoon, because silver tarnishes. And because all good things come in threes, it is accompanied by fresh herbs and half a lemon. The pleasure is completed by a good dry white wine or Crimean champagne. Bread and other additions are frowned on by gourmets, even though toast and butter are served in many restaurants.

Fresh oysters in their shells with a little cocktail sauce and caviar and garnished with a sprig of dill or lemon thyme, is said to have been the last Tsarina's favorite appetizer. At receptions, events, and openings in the capital Moscow, the organizers often serve white baguettes with caviar. The "noble roe" is also attractive and eye-catching, for instance on crackers with goat cheese, garnished with a little black or red caviar. In the national cuisine, eggs stuffed with caviar are a special favorite. Fresh eggs are hardcooked, plunged in cold water, halved, and the yolks removed. The yolks are seasoned with mayonnaise, salt, puréed onions, and mustard, and the mixture is piped back into the egg halves using a pastry bag. These creations are topped with red chum salmon caviar and a few grains of gray sturgeon caviar. However, if people want to make it very special, they simply fill the egg halves with black caviar. Caviar is also served as a delicious addition to hot dishes. Above all, the Russians adore *blini*—small buckwheat pancakes—with red salmon caviar. Another creation of fine cuisine is *blini* with smoked wild salmon, garnished with fresh dill and red salmon caviar. Vodka goes well with these tasty dishes. A traditional dish that has been rediscovered is "Pushkin" potatoes (see page 65), whole roast potatoes with butter and both black and red caviar.

Caviar is very healthy and highly nutritious. It is rich in vitamins A and B12 and contains iron, sodium, potassium and calcium. Because of its high protein content it is generally thought to be an aphrodisiac.

Caviar is served on ice. The best accompaniments are golden yellow *blini* and (left to right) sour cream, chopped capers, onions, parsley, the chopped white and yolks of hardcooked eggs, and champagne or sparkling wine.

The legendary Hotel Metropol in Moscow is both the best hotel in town and a gourmet temple.

Hotel Metropol

In Moscow there is one address for genuine Russian cuisine and hospitality. The art nouveau perfection of the Hotel Metropol welcomes travelers and gourmets. The elegant building, the flavor of old Russian culture and history, and its unique position by the Kremlin wall in the heart of Moscow attracted many famous people, including the writers Leo Tolstoy and George Bernard Shaw. The 333 luxury rooms are furnished with countless treasures. In 1999, a whole team of experts from the Hermitage Museum in St. Petersburg spent months working on the restoration of this luxury hotel that first opened in 1905.

The wealthy merchant and patron of the arts Savva Morosov had originally planned the Metropol as a grandiose cultural center. There is a famous majolica panel on the facade by Mikhail Vrubel depicting the "Princess of Dreams" from a very popular romantic legend of tragic love. The vaulted ceiling of the Boyarsky restaurant, until 1916 a favorite haunt of the miraculous healer Rasputin who had such great influence at the Russian court, was decorated entirely in red and gold, like the chambers of the Tsar's palace. The fanciful shapes of the hotel disguised the fact that inside it housed the latest technology. The Metropol was the first building in the whole of Russia to have electric elevators, there was hot water in every room, a cold store in the cellar, and a ventilation system. The "Babylonian church of the 20th century," as the hotel was labeled in the press, cost over seven million Russian rubles, an unimaginably large sum at the time.

Since its opening, the Metropol has been a favorite meeting place for artists. The composers Sergei Rachmaninov and Sergei Prokofiev and the world famous bass Fyodor Chaliapin loved the cuisine and the atmosphere of the hotel. Exhibitions by famous painters, meetings of important companies, unforgettable concerts, royal weddings, state receptions and splendid banquets all took place in its halls. After the October Revolution of 1917, the head of state of Soviet Russia lived in the hotel. Later the hotel also housed illustrious guests from the world of politics, including the American President John F Kennedy in the 1960s and, more recently, the French president Jacques Chirac. The Metropol has always been a focus of culture in Moscow—and a temple for culinary feasting. In February 1945, the chef of the Metropol Vassily Tarakhanov was summoned to Yalta, where he cooked for Stalin, Churchill, and Roosevelt to their immense satisfaction. Tarakhanov lived to the proud age of 102, probably thanks in no small measure to his excellent cooking. Since 1998, the head chef of the restaurant Metropol Andrei Makhov has more than once been chosen as Russia's foremost chef. The jury declared Natalia Nazarova, the doyenne of the in-house cake store, to be the best confectioner. Under her regime, 13 different kinds of bread, fancy filled pirogi, and splendid gateaux are baked every day.

Healthy natural products from the farmers' market: garlic and honey are not only favorite ingredients in Russian cuisine, they also play an important part in folk medicine, as they strengthen the immune system.

Farmers' markets

In Russian towns, the market is still a picturesque subject for writers and painters, the setting for passions and curiosities, a haunt of beggars, a place to exchange news, and of course a trading place, where even in times of famine there was always something to be had. Markets traditionally constituted the center of the town. Typically Russian market halls were found around the edges of the central squares, alongside citadels, churches, monasteries, and barracks. These small stores, usually linked by arcades, are still a characteristic feature of the townscape in many places in central Russia.

In old Russia, as well as the peasants and fishermen, potters, woodcarvers, and weavers of raffia shoes would come from the surrounding villages to sell their wares from wagons and carts. According to ancient chronicles, there was a market in the Moscow Kremlin in the middle ages, which developed into the famous halls of the department store GUM in the 19th century. Boyars drove past in their richly decorated sleighs, and the Muscovites drank the Tsars' health in mead and kvass. Only a few steps away was a fish market, selling giant sturgeon, Solovets herrings and fish from the river Moskva, and in the *okhotny ryad* (hunters' row) they sold duck, black grouse and hare.

As well as the daily market, in the bigger towns there were annual fairs—cattle and trade fairs, which were often held before high church festivals. A famous one was the annual fair in Rostov on Don, which is mentioned in sources as long ago as the 11th century. Rostov supplied vegetables to Moscow and St. Petersburg. In this city in the south of Russia, they were particularly skilled at growing onions and making delicious pickled cucumbers, and they knew the secret of keeping tomatoes fresh into the depths of winter.

In Soviet times, the Kolkhos markets offered an opportunity to buy fresh but expensive foods that were not obtainable in the state stores. They were supplied by individual smallholdings run by Kolkhos members, who had been allowed to sell their agricultural produce freely since 1935. Kolkhoses (farmers' cooperatives) and Sovkhoses (state agricultural collectives) could also sell here what they had produced over and above their target. Today there are 25 markets in Moscow, where you can find everything from live carp from Klin, pomegranates from Abkhasia, melons and bacon from the Ukraine, through to mushrooms and pickled garlic. The Muscovites love their bazaars,

because they always offer an extensive selection, unlike the dreary state stores. In addition, you can haggle in the market and the scales are correct to the gram, since they are installed and calibrated by the market office. One of the most popular markets in Moscow is the *Tyshinskiy rynok* near the Belorussia station, which is famous for its fresh fruit, its selection of vegetables, pickled cucumbers and pickled cabbage as well as the many different kinds of honey. The farmers' markets in smaller towns are equally popular. Everywhere, the fruit, vegetable, and flower stalls are firmly in Caucasian hands. Meat, eggs, and dairy produce often come from the surrounding countryside. Produce from private supplementary farms and small farms is on sale almost everywhere—in stations and subway stations, in the streets and on the bridges, even if the Dacha owners only have a couple of buckets of berries to sell, or a few cabbages harvested from their small gardens.

Horseradish

Khren, as horseradish is known in many Slavic countries, and also in Austria, was originally an import. German settlers had horseradish in their baggage when they migrated eastwards in the 15th century, and they did not want to be without their favorite seasoning for sucking pig and pork in aspic. Nowadays, Russian cuisine without this tangy vegetable is also unthinkable. It is used both fresh and dried. Horseradish is especially popular in appetizers and sauces. It adds a pleasing sharpness to boiled ham, jellied fish, or tongue in aspic, and whets the appetite. The older the root, the sharper it is. The intense taste is kept in check by mixing horseradish with apple or sour cream. Its healing properties are used in folk medicine and its enzymes are a proven household remedy for colds. Russian women also swear by horseradish facemasks, which are good for stimulating the circulation.

A lot of haggling goes on in Russian markets.

Vegetables

White turnips *(repy)* are often used in soups and stews for their delicate flavor.

Red beet *(svyokla)* tastes good raw or boiled, in salads and savory stews.

Cauliflower *(tsvetnaya kapusta)* is good in soups, salads, and also in savory puddings.

Rutabaga *(bryukvy)* have more flavor than turnips and their flesh is yellowish.

Tomatoes *(pomidory)* are stuffed for the zakuska table or add flavor to soups, sauces, and salads.

Onions *(luky)* are found in many varieties in the markets—from mild to strong.

Parsley root *(petrushka)* is mainly used to give soups and stews a strong earthy taste.

Cucumbers *(ogurtsy)* are usually pickled in Russia and stored for the winter.

Carrots *(morkovy)* are extremely versatile and are used in salads, soups and vegetable dishes.

The Russians like to carve radishes *(rediski)* into artistic table decorations.

Eggplant *(baklazhany)* is very popular in Russia today, and is often combined with tomatoes.

White cabbage *(belokochannaya kapusta)* is used in soups, stews, salads and for fine sauerkraut.

Garlic *(chesnok)* is frequently used in Russian cuisine, but not in large quantities.

Countless varieties of potatoes *(kartofel)*, or in everyday speech *(kartoshka)* are found in Russian markets.

Pumpkin *(tykva)* tastes good in stews, but is often preserved as a sweet or savory pickle.

Peppers *(perets)* of different shapes and colors are used for pickles and garnishes.

Broad-leaved garlic *(dikiy chesnok)* is picked in spring as a wild plant for use in salads, soups and pirogi.

The tasty shoots of ferns *(paporotnik)* are most often used as a vegetable in Siberia.

Vegetable dishes

Cheremsha
Siberian wild onion salad
(Illustration in background)

9 oz/250 g fresh wild onion shoots or wild garlic
2–3 hardcooked eggs
3 tbsp sour cream
2 tbsp mayonnaise
Salt and pepper

Wash the green onion shoots under running water
and cut across into small pieces. Chop the eggs and
mix with the wild onion. Thoroughly mix the sour
cream and mayonnaise and season with salt and
pepper. Pour over the salad as a dressing.
Tip: This mixture—but without mayonnaise—is also
a suitable filling for piroshki.

Bryukva s belymi gribami
White turnips with porcini
(Not illustrated)

2¼ lbs/1 kg white turnips
2 onions, finely chopped
6 tbsp/90 g butter
6–7 oz/200 g pickled porcini, cut in small pieces
Scant 1¼ cups/300 g sour cream

Bake the turnips in a preheated oven at 400 °F/
180 °C for 10–12 minutes depending on size. Peel
and cut off a lid, then hollow out, leaving a rim
about ⅜ in/1 cm thick. Chop the turnip flesh finely.

Sauté the onions in 2 tablespoons butter, add the
mushrooms and turnip flesh, and sauté for 5–10
minutes. Fill the turnips with this mixture and place
in an ovenproof dish. Melt the remaining butter, pour
over the filled turnips, and bake in the preheated
oven at 400 °F/200 °C for 20–30 minutes depending
on size. Lastly, pour over sour cream and allow to
brown.

Golubtsy
Russian cabbage rolls
(Illustration below)

10 prunes, pitted
1 tbsp raisins
1 large white cabbage
¾ lb/350 g mixed ground meat
2 cups/300 g rice boiled "al dente"
Salt and pepper
3 tbsp/45 g butter
1½–2 cups/400 g sour cream
2 tbsp all-purpose flour
3 tbsp chopped dill

Soak the prunes and raisins in lukewarm water for
at least 30 minutes. Separate the cabbage leaves,
blanch in a little water, drain, and leave to cool. Mix
the ground meat with the rice, salt and pepper. Place
3–4 tablespoons of the mixture on each cabbage
leaf, roll up, tie with kitchen string, and fry the rolls
briefly in the butter on all sides. Then place the rolls
in a flameproof dish. Beat 1 cup/250 g of the sour
cream with the flour, and add with the drained
raisins and prunes to the pan juices, boil briefly, and
pour over the rolls. Cover and simmer gently for 35
minutes. Remove the string from the rolls before
serving. Serve the cabbage rolls with dill and the
remaining sour cream.

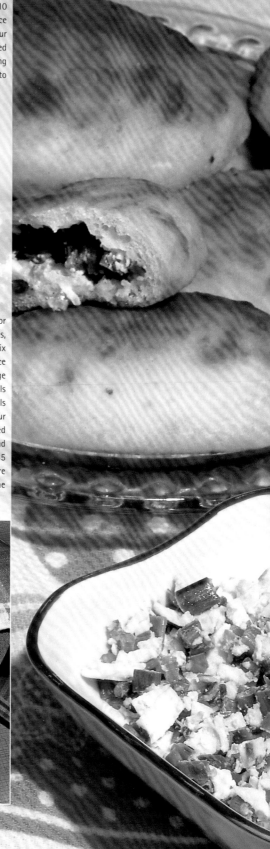

Zapekanka iz tsvetnoy kapusty
Baked cauliflower cheese
(Not illustrated)

1 medium cauliflower
Salt
3–4 tbsp all-purpose flour
7 tbsp/100g butter
2 cups/500 ml milk
2 cups/500 g sour cream
Salt
Pepper
³/₄ cup/100 g grated hard cheese

Wash the cauliflower and split into florets, boil in lightly salted water for about 5 minutes, then leave to drain in a colander.

Meantime, sauté the flour for the sauce in 2 tablespoons of the butter until golden brown, add another 2 tablespoons butter and the milk, stirring continuously with a whisk. Allow to thicken a little, then stir in the sour cream. Season with salt and pepper and simmer for about 5 more minutes, stirring regularly.

Tip the cauliflower florets into a greased pudding basin (or, if desired, divide into individual bowls), pour over the hot sauce, sprinkle with grated cheese and drizzle over the remaining—melted—butter. Bake in a preheated oven at 400 °F/200 °C until golden brown.

Puding iz morkovi
Carrot pudding
(Illustration below right)

2 tbsp raisins
Generous 1 lb/500 g carrots, diced
1 cup/250 ml milk
¹/₃ cup/50 g semolina
1 scant cup/200 g Quark
3 eggs, separated
2–2¹/₂ tbsp sugar
Few drops of vanilla essence or to taste
Salt
Melted butter or sour cream

Soak the raisins in lukewarm water for about 30 minutes, drain, and pat dry with paper towels. Boil the carrots in half the milk until tender, then purée. Add the remaining milk and the semolina, reheat, and thicken, stirring continuously. Allow to cool a little, then stir in the Quark and egg yolks. Season with sugar, vanilla extract, and salt, add the raisins, and fold in the stiffly-beaten egg whites. Pour the mixture into a greased pudding basin or small ovenproof bowls and bake for 20–30 minutes at 400 °F/200 °C. Serve with melted butter or sour cream.

Kartoshka po-moskovsky
Moscow potatoes
(Illustration below)

2¹/₄ lb/1 kg medium potatoes
4 tbsp melted butter
1 small onion, very finely chopped
5 tbsp/75 g sour cream
Salt
2 oz/50 g red caviar (chum salmon caviar)

Peel the potatoes (washed new potatoes can be used with their skins on). Bake in the oven at 350 °F/180 °C until they are almost soft. Cut lids off the potatoes while still hot, and hollow out the potatoes. Mash the potato with butter, add the onion and sour cream, season with salt, and mix well. Fill the potatoes with the mixture, sprinkle with caviar, and serve immediately.

Cabbage

Cabbage is the most popular vegetable in Russia. The Slavs adopted it from the Greek and Roman settlers along the Black Sea coast and soon began filling pirogi with cabbage. The Russian name *kapusta* can be traced back to the Celtic word *kap*, meaning "head". When talking about *kapusta*, Russians usually mean white cabbage. This is harvested from April to October and keeps all winter. Cabbage must be "planted under the sign of the manure and cooked under the constellation of bacon," runs a saying about how to handle it. This useful plant has always thrived in the fields around Ryasan, Tamboz, and Tula, where the cabbage harvest would bring the whole village community together and girls in festive costumes would fetch the peasant families to the harvest. At first, cabbage dishes were the prerogative of the wealthy, but once cabbage had begun to flourish even in the raw climate of northern Russia, it began its triumphal progress toward becoming the favorite vegetable of the people. Now it is grown almost everywhere in Russia, and varieties have been bred that can stand temperatures as low as 23 °F/ –5 °C. In the south, record yields of up to 900 metric hundredweight per hectare are harvested in the Volga area, and in southern Russia there are cabbage varieties with heads weighing more than 33 lb/15 kg. In that part of the world, they put good health in old age down to eating a lot of cabbage. White cabbage is an important source of vitamin C, containing as much as oranges and lemons. In addition, it protects against stomach ulcers. Russian researchers discovered that white cabbage contains substances that bind free radicals and can help to prevent cancer. Cabbage is also considered to be a remedy for the effects of vodka. Cabbage soup *shchi*, see page 44) taken before a binge is said to help you hold your drink, and after you have got drunk it quickly clears your head.

Sauerkraut

There is no market in Russia without sauerkraut, because for lack of cold storage facilities, up to two thirds of white cabbage ends up in barrels of sauerkraut. Every farmer's wife has her special secret recipe, so tasting when buying is a must. For every 220 lb/100 kg of white cabbage, 4 ½ to 5 ½ lb/2 to 2 ½ kg of salt are usually spread over it in layers. The cabbage is firmly pounded and must sour for two to three weeks, until the gas has escaped. Various additions determine the flavor. Carrots, apples, beet, raisins, celery, juniper berries, cranberries, and blackberries are added to the cabbage, and sometimes also red pepper, vine or currant leaves and dill seeds. As well as vitamin C, sauerkraut contains iron, calcium, lactic acid, which stimulates the intestinal flora, and easily digestible protein.

White cabbage has always been the king of Russian vegetables and the farmers' pride and joy.

Kapusta kvashenaya "provansal"
Sauerkraut Provençal style

For each 2¼ lb/1 kg sliced cabbage:
About 2 tbsp/20–25 g salt
1 carrot, grated
1 medium apple, grated
¼ cup/20 g cranberries
Pinch of dill seeds

Give a wooden barrel a thorough wash and line it with cabbage leaves (alternatively use a large stoneware pot that will hold at least 3 quarts/3 liters). Put the shredded cabbage in another container, salting, mixing and pressing firmly with your hands, and adding the other ingredients as you go. Transfer this mixture into the barrel or pot in layers, pounding it down firmly after adding each layer. Make a few holes in the mixture with the handle of a wooden spoon, to allow the gases that form during fermentation to escape. Cover the top layer with one or two large cabbage leaves and a clean cloth, place a plate with a weight (a stone or some cans) on top of it and leave it to stand at room temperature for 3–4 days, then store in a cool place. It is important for the fermentation of lactic acid that the cabbage is always covered in its own juices. The sauerkraut is ready to be eaten after 3–4 weeks.

To serve, dress the sauerkraut with cold pressed sunflower oil.

Tip: Late varieties of white cabbage are best for pickling. They must be fresh, tightly closed, and mild.

For home made sauerkraut, you can use vegetables and fruits as well as cabbage.

The white cabbage must first be thinly shredded.

The sliced cabbage is put into a big barrel, salted, and the other ingredients thoroughly mixed in.

Then the cabbage mixture is tipped into a stoneware pot or a wooden barrel and firmly pounded.

Sauerkraut is produced by the fermentation of lactic acid. It contains a lot of vitamin C and is therefore best eaten raw. It tastes good on its own, but you can also dress it with sunflower oil and fresh berries.

Dill—not just a herb

Dill seeds are a very popular seasoning, as they are said to be both calming and appetizing. They are used in not only sauerkraut but also in baking, for instance in crackers and rolls, and in marinades and soups, such as the famous fish soup *ukha* (see page 92 f). Dill flowers and sprigs of fresh dill, which flourishes in northern latitudes, also add an unmistakable flavor to many Russian dishes.

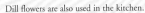
Dill flowers are also used in the kitchen.

From the soup pot

For a quick, everyday shchi, first sauté onions, carrots and tomatoes.

Boil the white cabbage in the meat stock until tender and then add the other vegetables.

Cut the meat up small and add that and the mushrooms to the soup.

The finished shchi is always served with a dollop of sour cream, and fresh herbs if desired.

Soups undoubtedly belong among the culinary delights of the Russian Kitchen. Dinner begins with *shchi*, borscht, (see page 144) or solyanka on ordinary days as well as feast days. In winter, body and soul are warmed by the cabbage soup *shchi*, or *rassolnik*, a soup soured with the juice from pickled cucumbers. In spring, soups made with fresh herbs such as nettles and sorrel, or with dried mushrooms, are particularly popular. In the late spring, when flooding allows the fish to stray into the meadows, there is *ukha* (see page 92) and in the heat of summer, cold soups like *okroshka, kholodnik,* and *botvinya* are refreshing. These are based on kvass (see page 80) with cucumbers and herbs, and served with ice cubes. *Okroshka* also contains beef or smoked fish, while *kholodnik* contains hardcooked egg and dried fish. *Botvinya* is especially fine, as it is served with cold poached trout or salmon.

The cabbage soup shchi goes back over 1,000 years. It came from ancient Byzantium to Kievan Rus (see page 350), where its triumphal progress began. There are cookbooks containing 60 different recipes for shchi. It can be made with fresh white cabbage or sauerkraut, with nettles, sorrel, spinach, apples, beef, pork, or fish. Traditional shchi cooks slowly in a Russian stove, a gentle cooking method that gives the soup its full flavor and ensures it will keep for a long time. In peasants' huts, there was always cabbage soup standing in the oven waiting for unexpected guests. Enriched with a spoonful of sour cream and eaten with solid, aromatic rye bread, shchi is an unforgettable delight.

Lenivye shchi
"Lazy" shchi using fresh cabbage
(Illustration left)

2 oz or about 2 cups/50 g dried mushrooms
2 medium onions
2 medium carrots
2 tomatoes
2 tbsp/30 g butter
Generous 1 lb/500 g fresh white cabbage, shredded
2 quarts/2 liters strong meat stock
salt
Pepper
11–12 oz/300 g smoked pork loin or other meat, boiled
1/2 bunch each of dill and parsley, chopped
4 tbsp sour cream

Soak the dried mushrooms in lukewarm water for at least 30 minutes.
Cut the onions into half rings, the carrots into thin strips, and dice the tomatoes. Sauté the onions and carrots in the butter. Add the tomatoes after about 5 minutes, and sauté everything together for approximately another 10 minutes.
Heat up the stock, add the shredded cabbage, and boil over medium heat until tender. Then add the sautéed vegetables, season with salt and pepper, and allow the whole mixture to draw for another 10–15 minutes over low heat. Cut the meat and reconstituted mushrooms in thin strips and divide between soup bowls or plates. Ladle the finished soup over them, and serve with herbs and sour cream.
Tip: For the Lenten version, use vegetable stock and leave out the meat and tomatoes.

Okroshka
Okroshka
(Not illustrated)

2 hardcooked eggs
8–9 oz/250 g boiled or roast meat (beef, pork, smoked tongue, ham, game or poultry) or assorted fish
3 medium red beets, boiled and diced
3 pickled cucumbers, diced
1 bunch scallions, chopped
1 tsp mustard
Sugar
1 tbsp grated horseradish
1 1/4 quarts/1.5 liter kvass (see page 80), can be replaced with dry apple juice
Salt
Pepper
1 bunch parsley, finely chopped
1 bunch chives, finely chopped
1/2 cup/125 g sour cream

Separate the egg yolks and whites, and cut the whites in small pieces. Cut the meat or fish into bite-sized pieces, then mix with the egg whites, red beet, pickled cucumbers, and scallions.
Crush the egg yolks and mix with mustard, sugar and horseradish. Add a little kvass and stir well. Pour over 2 cups/500 ml kvass and stir to form a smooth stock. Season with salt and pepper.
Pour this stock over the mixed ingredients, stir in carefully and leave to draw in the refrigerator for 2–3 hours. Before serving, add the remaining kvass, and the parsley and chives. Serve with ice cubes and sour cream.

Rybnaya solyanka
Fish solyanka (1)

1³/₄ lb/750 g assorted fish, e.g. sturgeon, porgy,
perch, salmon
Salt
2 bay leaves
4–6 peppercorns
1 onion, chopped
2 tbsp/30 g butter
1 tbsp all-purpose flour
1 parsley root, chopped small
1 carrot, chopped small
4–5 pickled cucumbers, chopped small
2 tbsp black olives
1 tbsp capers
1 untreated lemon
¹/₂ bunch dill
4 tbsp sour cream

Clean the fish. Use the tails, bones and heads, with
about 3 quarts/3 liters water, a little salt, bay
leaves, and peppercorns, to make stock. Strain the
stock. Cut the fish into bite-sized pieces. Pour half
the stock over the pieces of fish, bring to a boil, and
poach gently over low heat for about 15 minutes
(the fish must not fall apart). In the meantime,
sauté the onion in the butter, dust with flour, and
pour over the remaining stock while stirring continuously. Add the vegetables and pickled cucumbers and simmer, then add the fish and its stock,
and season with salt. Bring it all gently to a boil
again, and add the olives and capers. Serve in deep
plates with a thin slice of lemon, a sprig of dill, and
a dollop of sour cream in each one.

Shchi sborniye
Mixed shchi with sauerkraut (2)
(Serves 6 to 8)

8–9 oz/200 g each of stewing beef, lamb and
chicken
11–12 oz/300 g smoked loin of pork, boned, and
cut in pieces
2 bay leaves
1³/₄ lb/750 g sauerkraut
4 tbsp/60 g butter
1 large onion, chopped
1 parsley root, chopped small
1 carrot, chopped small
2 tbsp tomato paste
3–4 cloves garlic, crushed
Salt and pepper
1 bunch dill, finely chopped
4 tbsp sour cream

Cover the meat ingredients with water, add the bay
leaves, and boil for stock until the meat is tender.
Meantime, lightly sauté the sauerkraut in 2 tablespoons of butter and allow to simmer for 1 hour,
adding a little water or stock as necessary. Sauté
the other vegetables in the remaining butter, and
add the tomato paste. Then add it all to the cabbage, add the garlic and simmer for a further
15 minutes.
Remove the meat from the stock and cut into bite-
sized pieces. Strain the stock. Tip the sautéed vegetables into the stock, season with salt and pepper,
and add the meat. Heat it all up together once
more. Serve with dill and sour cream.

Perlovy sup
Pearl barley soup (3)

1 onion, chopped
2 tbsp oil
2 red bell peppers, cut small
2 carrots, cut small
1 bunch parsley, finely chopped
1 ¹/₂ quarts/1.5 liter meat stock
3 potatoes, diced
³/₄ cup/150 g pearl barley, boiled until almost soft
Salt and pepper
5¹/₂ oz/150 g chicken breast, poached
4 tbsp sour cream
¹/₄ cup/25 g grated Parmesan cheese

Sauté the onion in the oil until transparent, then
add the bell peppers, carrots, and half the parsley,
and fry briefly. Pour over boiling stock. Add the
potatoes and pearl barley and boil for about 15
minutes. Season with salt and pepper.
To serve, cut the chicken breast into small pieces
and divide between the soup plates. Pour over the
soup. Top with sour cream and the remaining parsley and serve with the cheese.

The dacha

When flying into Moscow, the dacha belt begins long before the city skyline is visible. Plots are arranged in dead straight lines, squares with almost identical houses. Back in the 19th century, dachas were originally country houses, which the officers, teachers, doctors and civil servants rented for the summer in the area surrounding Moscow and St Petersburg in order to escape from the stifling cities. World culture is indebted to this fresh summer air for immortal works of literature, music, and painting. Patrons of the arts invited artists to their dachas, where they could devote themselves entirely to their creative work and find themselves the center of attraction at many parties. Boris Pasternak's *Doctor Zhivago* was written in a green idyll. Many of Anton Chekhov's dramas are set in dachas, and the most famous painter of Russian Realism, Ilya Repin (1844–1930) painted numerous works in the summer residence of the patron of the arts, Savva Mamontov.

After the October Revolution, the Bolsheviks confiscated the dachas and allotted them to civil servants and functionaries, army and secret service officers, writers, actors and theater directors. Workers were not given dachas, and the Kolkhos farmers were not allowed to run small farms for their own needs until 1935. However, the war, and the famine that overshadowed the after-war years, soon made the towns take possession of unoccupied plots of land and turn them into allotments. The authorities did not forbid these sidelines, because without them, many towns would have starved. Later, the trade unions took over the acquisition of land and shared the lots out among their members. So the dacha and its harvest came to represent freedom in socialist times, a refuge for individuality in the over-organized collective life. People escaped from city apartments that were far too small and busied themselves with the physical activity of gardening, thereby easing the burden on the state budget. The majority of city-dwellers still have such gardens where they grow fruit and vegetables, often simply in order to survive. What is more, the dacha is also a holiday resort for families who cannot afford to travel.

As for a long time there were very few building materials available, many dacha colonies have a colorful, almost fairytale look—with added gables and small rooms built of different kinds of planks, corrugated iron and sheets of veneer. With the reforms that followed the end of the Soviet Union, there was a twofold increase in the number of allotments that were supposed to ensure the survival of ordinary people in times of crisis. Even at the start of the 21st century, dachas are still a necessity for many Russians if they are to survive the winter, especially for keeping them supplied with potatoes, cabbage and carrots. Summer and autumn is the time to harvest apples, pears, plums, cherries, sea buckthorn, blackcurrants, and raspberries. The allotments bloom and flourish. This distinguishes these colonies from the villages, often almost empty of people, whose vegetable gardens are overrun by weeds. In today's Russia, the townspeople are among the most hardworking farmers. In early February, vegetables are already being sown in pots in city apartments. Seedlings are grown for planting out in late spring. Then in autumn, the suburban trains are full of happy dacha owners carrying home their harvest in boxes and buckets, so they can work on it. Many families live on their preserved garden produce until the start of the following summer.

In the dacha, they enjoy plain country food such as fresh forest fruits with Quark and sour cream.

Right: Typical dacha colonies represent an idyllic holiday and allotments for millions of Russians.

In Russian gardens you find varieties of bell pepper that can bear rich fruits even in a harsh climate.

If you sow early, you reap early. Protected early beds are essential in the north, where the snow lies until May.

Tomatoes can often only be grown in a greenhouse, because of cold nights and drought.

Storing food

Russia has always been a land of farmers. There is a long tradition of pickling and marinating fish, cucumbers, cabbage, and mushrooms, bottling fruit, and drying mushrooms, berries, and fish. Such stores help many Russians to survive the winter, above all in remote areas and hamlets, where preserving food is a matter of vital importance. In the villages, there are cellars under the kitchens; in the south, they are under the front steps. In Siberia and the north, food is stored in outbuildings and pits in the permafrost. Even in Moscow, chickens, pig heads, half a sheep, half a salmon, and bags of pelmeni hang from the windows of apartment blocks in the harsh winter. Nowadays, of course, many products can be stored in freezers.

Methods of Preserving

Salting preserves meat, fish, vegetables, mushrooms, fruits, and berries such as cornelian cherries and rose hips, because salt draws out water and inhibits the growth of bacteria. Wooden barrels made of oak, birch or lime are suitable for salting, as are ceramic pots, glass jars, and enamel containers. The salt must always be distributed evenly and cover the vegetables completely. This method produces lactic acid and fermentations that preserve the food. Salted products like crisp Russian cucumbers and green tomatoes belong on every zakuska table.

For **marinating**, cucumbers, tomatoes or apples are preserved in vinegar or alcohol, which acts as a disinfectant and inhibits the growth of bacteria. Salt, sugar and herbs are also added, according to taste.

Blackberries, cranberries, peaches, cherries, and apples are preserved by **bottling**. To prevent the fruit from fermenting, raw fruit is put in jars with sugar and pasteurized or sterilized in a double boiler at 185–212 °F/85–100 °C. In Russia, they also bottle meat, cucumbers, bell peppers, and tomatoes. Jars with a capacity of over 2 gallons/ up to 10 liters are often used for this.

For **sugaring**, fruits and berries are briefly blanched or just thoroughly washed, patted dry, sugared and then placed in the oven for a few hours at a low heat. The amount of sugar added depends on the ripeness of the fruit and how much sugar it contains. Homemade jams and conserves *(varenye)* made from raspberries, cher-

ries, yellow plums, green walnuts, honey melons, rowan berries, and even green tomatoes, are particularly popular with tea (see page 122 f).

During the hot continental summer, berries and fruit, fish and vegetables are mostly preserved by **drying**. Houses in southern Russia are decorated with garlands of peppers and corn. Strings of mushrooms twine around the big Russian stoves or hang ornamentally in windows. Apricots, pears, and apples are usually blanched briefly before drying.

Traditionally, villagers store cabbage for the winter near the house in a dry ditch lined with plenty of straw. The cabbages are laid on a bed of straw and covered with more straw, then boards are laid on top, earth is tipped over them and the cabbage clamp is finished.

Over the centuries, the Russians became very experienced in the preservation of milk and dairy products. For example, milk was lowered into cold streams in closed containers attached to ropes—the easiest way of keeping it before the age of refrigeration. Milk that had previously been boiled and then slowly heated in the oven (*varenets* see page 125), a typical delicacy from southern Russia, not only keeps longer than fresh milk, it is also delicious with honey or sugar.

Solyonye ogurtsy
Pickled cucumbers

Oak leaves for lining the barrel
2¹/₂ oz/75 g dill flowers
1 oz/25 g currant or sour cherry leaves
If desired, a handful of marigold flowers
1 oz/25 g horseradish root, thinly sliced
5 cloves garlic, sliced
11–12 lb/5 kg small unblemished garden cucumbers for pickling
Brine (2 heaping tbsp/50–60 g salt per 4 cups/1 liter water)

Thoroughly wash a 2 gallon/10 liter wooden barrel or a stoneware pot, and line the bottom with oak leaves. Carefully clean the herbs, mix with horseradish and garlic, and fill the barrel with alternate layers of cucumbers and herb mixture, starting and ending with a layer of herbs.

Cover everything generously with brine and cover the barrel with a loose lid or a cloth. Store at room temperature for 2–3 days for the lactic acid fermentation, then store in a cool place. The ingredients must always be well covered with brine. The first cucumbers may be eaten after 2–3 weeks.

Harvest time is preserving time. Glass jars holding three or five quarts/3 or 5 liters are the favorite for storing food for long winters.

Garlic, salt and various herbs give crisp cucumbers the right flavor.

For a version of pickled cucumbers without lactic acid fermentation, the herbs are put into the jar first.

These are followed by the cucumbers and the remaining herbs and hot brine is poured in.

The jars are closed and briefly placed upside down. These cucumbers should be eaten soon.

Mushroom hunting

With 7½ acres/3 hectares of woodland per inhabitant, the Russian Federation is particularly rich in forests. The green coniferous belt of the Taiga stretches from the Urals to the Pacific, whereas mixed and deciduous forests predominate in European Russia. The forest has always been both a protection and a source of food. It provides wood for huts and the fire in the hearth. Game and fish enrich the present table, because nature is generous with her gifts of berries, nuts, resins, roots, medicinal herbs, and mushrooms.

The "silent hunt" for mushrooms is one of the Russians' favorite hobbies. It is recreational and useful, and they also find it exciting. Collecting mushrooms requires a knowledge of the landscape and of mushrooms, because these sought-after fungi like to hide and disguise themselves or lie in wait as dangerous poisonous look-alikes.

Although pirogi were filled with mushrooms way back in the past, and mushrooms baked in sour cream are now a popular Russian appetizer, no research was done about them until the 18th century. Instead they fired the imagination that finds expression in fairytales and superstitions, because the way they appeared from nowhere, their swift growth, forming fairy rings, and their many different forms—with a cap, like a coral, a pagoda, or a flower, bowl or goblet-shaped, like pipes or balls—everything about them was eerie, supernatural, inexplicable. Moreover, people were frightened of being poisoned. There is an old proverb, which advises, "Take every mushroom in your hand, but do not put every mushroom in your basket."

In Russia there are about 300 kinds of mushroom, of which 30 are collected and used in the kitchen. Ninety percent of these mushrooms grow in woodland, the rest in meadows, on field edges, in gardens, and in greenhouses. The varieties chiefly cultivated in Russia are field mushrooms, oyster mushrooms, honey agaric, and morels.

There are no limits to the ways of cooking mushrooms. They are used in soups, sauces, and puddings, served in salads with herbs and onions, fried, put in pirogi or on *blini*, and accompany roasts. They can be fried in breadcrumbs, stuffed with cheese and baked, or made into rissoles. One specialty is *kundyumi*, a 16th century dish consisting of pockets of dough filled with mushrooms, semolina and herbs, which are steamed rather than boiled. As mushrooms whet the appetite, they have a permanent place on the zakuska table. Russian housewives pickle mushrooms for the winter in marinade or brine. Mushrooms contain a lot of water. Their protein content varies between 2 and 5 percent, most of it in the cap. They contain very little fat, but they do contain lecithin, which lowers cholesterol levels, as well as potassium, magnesium, phosphorus and iron. In addition, they have traces of copper, iodine, manganese, zinc, and vitamins B and D. Unfortunately another property of mushrooms is that they fix heavy metals and radioactive substances. After the Chernobyl disaster in 1986, radiation levels in the southeast European part of Russia remain worryingly high.

Gribnye kotlety
Mushroom rissoles

Generous 1 lb/500 g mushrooms, ready to cook
2 slices stale white bread without crusts
1 large onion, chopped
6 tbsp sunflower oil
Salt
Pepper
2 eggs
2–3 tbsp all-purpose flour
1 tbsp chopped parsley
Breadcrumbs for frying
½ cup/125 g sour cream

Blanch the mushrooms in boiling water for about 10 minutes. Soak the bread in cold water. Sauté the onions in 1 tablespoon sunflower oil until transparent. Drain the mushrooms, squeeze out all the liquid, and chop finely. Squeeze the liquid from the bread, mix with the mushrooms and onions, and season with salt and pepper. Beat the eggs and mix well with the flour and parsley, adding enough flour to make a "dough". Set aside to firm up for one hour in the refrigerator. Shape the mixture into 10–12 round or oval rissoles and roll them in breadcrumbs. Fry on both sides in the remaining sunflower oil until golden brown. Serve with sour cream.

Farshirovannye shampinony
Stuffed mushrooms

12 large mushrooms or porcini
1 slice white bread
1 large onion, chopped
3 tbsp oil
1 tbsp chopped parsley
¾ cup/200 g sour cream
1 tbsp grated cheese
Salt and pepper
Breadcrumbs
1–2 tbsp/15–30 g butter

Clean the mushrooms thoroughly, remove the stalks, and chop these very finely. Cover the mushroom caps with water and blanch briefly.

Soak the bread in cold water. Sauté the onion and chopped mushroom stalks in 2 tablespoons oil, add the parsley, and sauté for a further 5 minutes. Squeeze the bread thoroughly and mix it into the mushroom stalk mixture together with 1–2 tablespoons sour cream and the cheese. Season with salt and pepper.

Drain the blanched mushrooms and pat dry with paper towels. Fill with the mushroom stalk mixture.

Grease a baking pan with the last of the oil, place the filled mushrooms in it, and sprinkle with breadcrumbs and flakes of butter. Bake in a preheated oven at 400 °F/200 °C for about 15 minutes. Serve with the remaining sour cream.

Background: In autumn, the Russians take to the woods to collect mushrooms and reap rich rewards.

Porcino *(bely grib,* Lat. *Boletus edulis),* expensive mushrooms, often dried or marinated.

Chanterelle *(lisichka,* Lat. *Cantharellus cibarius),* a favorite accompaniment or in sweet-sour marinades.

Field mushroom *(shampinon,* Lat. *Agaricus campestris),* eaten raw in salad or sautéed with sour cream.

Honey agaric *(opyonok osenniy,* Lat. *Armillaria ostoyae),* boiled; only the caps are marinated.

Bay bolete *(polskiy grib,* Lat. *Xerocomus badius),* steamed and used as pirog filling in Central Russia.

Red-capped Scaber Stalk *(podozinovik,* Lat. *Leccinum rufum),* used in mushroom solyanka and dark sauces; turns black when fried.

Saffron milk cap *(ryzhik,* Lat. *Lactarius deliciosus),* valuable mushroom, caps fried or in salad.

Red-tinted Russula *(siroyeshka bolotnaya,* Lat. *Russula paludosa),* good mushroom for fried mixtures, sweet-sour marinade.

Pelmeni are often eaten as a main course with butter, sour cream or bouillon.

The *pelmenitsa* makes it easier to produce the dough pockets, and can be found in every good kitchen.

Pelmeni

When the Russians invite guests to a pelmeni feast, they like to keep up an old custom. The housewife hides a button or a ring in the pocket of dough, along with the filling. It is said to bring good luck to whoever finds it on their plate. In the Tsars' kitchens, it was even standard practice to put a precious stone in one of the pelmeni. The Russians took over pelmeni from the peoples of the east, the Permaks, Komi, Nentsen, Udmurts and the Siberian Tatars. These little pockets of noodle dough are usually filled with meat. According to the traditional recipe, there should be three kinds of meat: mutton, beef and pork. The Siberians even insist on having eight kinds, and like to add moose, reindeer, wild boar, bear and poultry. The Yakuts and Buryats swear by wild pony meat.

Pelmeni come in the shape of half-moons or "little ears." The Buryats eat *manty*, rice pelmeni, which have an opening on top so you can drink the gravy.

Fish pelmeni are a special delicacy with a filling of finely chopped cod, chum salmon, humpback salmon and blueback salmon (also known as red salmon or sockeye salmon). To make the filling more juicy, they add small pieces of ice when cutting up the fish. For fast days or vegetarian ver-

sions, pelmeni can also be filled with mushrooms, herbs or kasha (see page 54). The Siberians eat pelmeni with vinegar and pepper, in other regions they are eaten with bouillon, butter or just with a dollop of sour cream.

It used to be the custom in Siberia to give travelers, hunters, or fishermen a linen bag of frozen pelmeni to take with them for food, since all you need to prepare them is a fire and a cauldron of water. What is more, they are said to taste especially good when they have been exposed to the bitter frost for a while. In winter, bags of their beloved "little ears" still hang outside many windows in Moscow apartment blocks.

You can have pelmeni on both working days and holidays. Often all the members of the family and even the guests take part in the time-consuming preparation. After all, pelmeni only taste right if they have been made by hand. The difficulty lies in making the thinnest possible dough and making sure that the pelmeni do not split during cooking or stick to one another.

Many modern housewives use a *pelmenitsa*, a special plate of cast aluminum with hexagonal gaps in it. The rolled-out dough is pulled onto it, small portions of filling are placed in the hollows, with a second sheet of dough on top. The pelmeni are

then pressed through the openings with a rolling pin. Rolling over the sharp edges of the hexagons closes the pelmeni so tightly that they will certainly not come apart again in the cooking. Pelmeni are also served in small specialist restaurants called *pelmennaya*. Young families often buy frozen pelmeni to save time and for ease of preparation. They come in many different versions, filled with meat, fish, or vegetables.

Pelmeni come in different shapes and with various fillings: top with meat, left with mashed potato and mushrooms, and right with steamed cabbage.

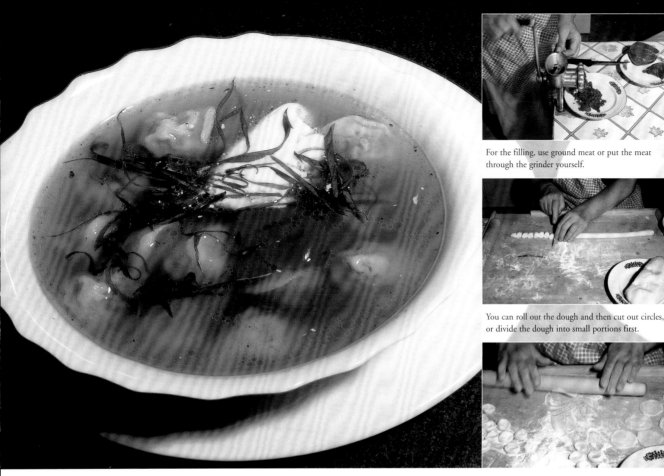

For the filling, use ground meat or put the meat through the grinder yourself.

You can roll out the dough and then cut out circles, or divide the dough into small portions first.

Here the dough is being rolled into pieces the size of the palm of your hand with a rolling pin.

Now you use a spoon to put a small amount of the prepared meat filling on each circle of dough.

It takes a little patience to fold the pelmeni into their typical shape and close them.

Pelmeni
Filled dough pockets

For the dough:
Generous 2¹/₃ cups/350 g all-purpose flour
1 egg
¹/₂ tsp salt
For each plate, 4 tbsp sour cream and melted butter.

Knead flour, egg, salt and about ¹/₂ cup/125 ml water into a firm smooth dough. Allow to rest for 20–30 minutes.

On a floured board, roll the dough out as thin as you can and cut out circles using a 3-inch/8 cm-cookie cutter or a glass. Place a teaspoonful of filling in the center of each one. Fold the dough over and press the edges together firmly.

Place the pelmeni in a pan of lightly salted boiling water and boil for about 5 minutes. When they rise to the surface, leave them to draw for a further 2–3 minutes over low heat. Lift them out of the water with a slotted spoon and serve with butter and sour cream.

Tip: Instead of cooking the pelmeni in salt water, if you prefer, you can cook them in meat or vegetable stock (see illustration above.)

Meat filling:
Generous 1 lb/500 g mixed ground meat
(beef and pork, possibly also lamb or poultry)
1–2 onions, finely chopped
2 cloves garlic, finely chopped
Salt and pepper

Mix the ground meat with the onions, garlic, salt, and pepper.

Fish and mushroom filling:
1 cup/25 g dried mushrooms
Generous 1 lb/500 g fish fillets (e.g. sturgeon, salmon, sea bass)
2 onions
2 tbsp/30 g butter
Salt and pepper

Soak the mushrooms in water, then boil until tender and cut in small pieces.

Put the fish and onions through a grinder, add the softened butter and stir to a smooth filling, mix in the mushrooms and season with salt and pepper.

Kasha

Kasha is one of the oldest and most popular Russian national dishes. This porridge is eaten as a main course on its own, but often as an accompaniment. In old Russia, it was almost exclusively served as a special treat on festive occasions, such as victory celebrations, weddings, and baptisms. From the 12th to 14th centuries, the term *kasha* was synonymous with the word *pir*, banquet.

Kasha was traditionally prepared in the Russian oven. Semolina, millet or buckwheat, and also rice from the 14th century on, were put in an earthenware pot with water and left to stew slowly for several hours. Kasha is still made from a wide variety of different cereals, but most commonly from buckwheat semolina. Porridges made from whole buckwheat, durum wheat, spelt, barley, millet or oats are also quite widespread, as is green porridge made from young unripe rye. Kasha usually has other nutritious ingredients added to it. Butter, buttermilk, sour and sweet cream, and Quark, are all used to make the porridge smooth. It can be flavored with pepper, herbs, garlic, vanilla, nutmeg or cinnamon. Meat, fish or peas go well with thin porridge, eggs and mushrooms are added to thick kasha, pumpkin purée livens up millet porridge, and poppy seeds add the finishing touch to barley porridge. To flavor sweet porridges they use sugar, *varenye* (see page 126 f), honey, raisins, nuts, chocolate, and fresh or dried fruit.

Kasha
Buckwheat porridge
(Serves 8)

1³/₄ lb/750 g buckwheat grits
8¹/₂ tbsp/125 g butter
Salt

Put the buckwheat with twice the quantity of water in an earthenware pot or other heatproof container and bring to a boil. Remove the lid and allow the kasha to swell for about one hour in a preheated oven at 340–350 °F/175 °C without stirring. Stir in the butter and salt.

This simplest form of kasha tastes good on its own as a main course or as an accompaniment to meat and fish dishes. In addition it goes very well with sucking pig, poultry or fish.

Kasha, Russia's favorite side dish, is made from whole or shredded buckwheat.

Buckwheat

Botanically speaking, buckwheat (*grechikha*, Lat., *Fagopyrum*) is a member of the knotgrass family and is related to sorrel and rhubarb. Because its small triangular seeds resemble wheat in the way they are arranged and they can be processed in the same way, it is often assigned to the cereals. This herbaceous plant with its narrow heart-shaped leaves and pink flowers came to Russia from Asia minor very early on, and is mostly grown in the plains of Central Russia. The Russians value buckwheat highly, because it is tasty, easily digestible, cheap, healthy, and very filling. The seeds contain a lot of protein with useful amino-acids. They are rich in lecithin, which explains why buckwheat porridge is often cooked in hospitals and prescribed as a regime for liver, neural and cardiovascular diseases. Buckwheat also contains vitamins of the B group, rutin (vitamin P), as well as minerals, iron, calcium, and phosphorus.

Buckwheat is distinguished by a strong, slightly bitter taste, and is served as an accompaniment to meat dishes. Buckwheat semolina is often added to the cabbage soup *shchi* during fast times, and in many regions coarse buckwheat grits are added to pork sausages. Buckwheat *blini* (see page 56) with caviar, sour cream and Matjes fillets are the secret tip of Russian gourmets.

Sucking pig

Sucking pig is one of the pleasure-loving Russians' festive dishes. It is an old country tradition to spit-roast a young pig that must not weigh more than 22 lb/10 kg, in the snow on New Year's Day. So a sucking pig must not be more than eight weeks old, and they love it for its sweet, delicate, nutritious, juicy meat. It is rubbed with salt, pepper and garlic, impaled on a spit and barbecued slowly over charcoal. The skin must be basted with beer or kvass from time to time, to produce crisp crackling.

In many regions, sucking pig is also thought of as a wedding meal. For this celebration, the bones are taken out from the inside except for the head and feet, to make room for the stuffing of buckwheat kasha and fried pig liver. Before roasting, the piglet is rubbed with vegetable oil and brushed with melted butter. As a finishing touch, cranberries add a fruity, slightly sour or bitter note to the delicate meat.

Porosyonok s grechnevoy kashey
Sucking pig with buckwheat stuffing

1 small sucking pig weighing about 6 ½ lb/3 kg,
with innards, ready to cook
Salt
Pepper
2 cloves garlic
1–2 onions, finely chopped
4 tbsp/60 g butter
Buckwheat grits as per recipe (facing page)
250 g sour cream

Lightly rub the sucking pig inside and out with salt, pepper, and garlic.

Cut the innards up small, sauté in butter with the onion, mix with the stewed buckwheat and season the stuffing with salt and pepper. Stuff the piglet and sew up, brush with sour cream, place on a deep baking sheet and roast in the oven at 400 °F/200 °C for 1–2 hours, basting continually with the juices to produce crackling. Remove the thread from the piglet, slice and reassemble the meat before serving.

Serve on a bed of buckwheat kasha.

Blini grechnevye
Buckwheat pancakes

3 tsp dry yeast
3 tbsp sugar
2 cups/500 ml lukewarm milk
1½ tbsp/25 g butter, softened
2 cups/300 g buckwheat flour
1⅓ cups/200 g all-purpose flour
2 eggs, separated
1 tsp salt
Generous ⅔ cup/175 g sour cream
Butter for frying

Place 6–7 tablespoons lukewarm water in a small bowl, stir in the yeast and 2 tablespoons of the sugar and leave to stand in a warm place until the volume has doubled and the liquid is frothy.
Stir half of the milk into the yeast mixture together with the rest of the sugar and the butter, add the buckwheat flour; stir well for about 10 minutes and leave to rest for approximately 30 minutes. Then add the rest of the milk, the wheat flour, egg yolks, salt, and sour cream to the batter and stir for about 1 minute. Cover and leave to rest for a further hour until the mixture is frothy and the volume has doubled again. Beat the egg whites until stiff and carefully fold into the batter. Heat a skillet over medium heat, brush lightly with butter and fry pancakes with a diameter of 3–4 inches/8–10 cm using about 3 tablespoons of batter for each. Serve hot. They are particularly good with chilled caviar and sour cream.

Blini with a variety of fillings have been a feature of abundant Russian feasts for centuries. The most popular varieties include mini buckwheat pancakes with sour cream, cranberries, caviar, salmon, or with salted herring.

Blini

"Round is the blin, yellow gold and hot like the sun, the symbol of sublime days, rich harvests, harmonious marriages and healthy children," is how the Russian poet Alexander Kuprin (1870–1938) extolled the virtues of these delectably light pancakes. Even in pre-Christian Russia blini (pancakes) were eaten on feast days in honor of Wolos, patron saint of fertility, cattle, and the arts. The original form of the word "blin" was "mlin," deriving from the Russian word for milling and referring to a dish made from the ground grains.

As blini are inexpensive, tasty, and filling they remain one of the favorite foods in Russia today. On every corner in Moscow and elsewhere there is a kiosk selling blini. Yet the true Muscovite gets together with friends and family for a blini feast. As a guest at a blini meal it is an honor to be allowed to sit in the kitchen next to the stove where the housewife conjures up delicate, wafer-thin pancakes in her little cast-iron skillet. The skillet must be absolutely clean and is therefore rubbed with salt while it is hot and greased with bacon fat. According to the original recipe, blini are made from one-third wheat flour and two-thirds buckwheat flour and are refined with rich cream and frothy beaten egg whites. Sour cream

lends a heartier note to the batter. Blini made solely from buckwheat flour are called *krasnyje blini*, red pancakes, due to their dark color. Real yeast pancakes are soft and porous with almost transparent bubbles. They soak up melted butter and cream like a sponge making them wonderfully shiny and moist.

The cooked pancakes are eaten hot. They are served with butter, sour cream, honey, cranberry jelly, pickled herring, smoked salmon, or caviar, according to taste. On feast days they can also be served with innards (offal) or beef. Several blini piled on top of one another and baked with a variety of fillings in a Russian oven result in a delicious blini cake. Blini are served in every home during Butter Week (see page 58). Such is their popularity, however, that they are made not only for celebratory occasions but also on an everyday basis. Many retailers now also sell deep frozen mini-blini with fillings varying from mushroom or potato, ham, liver, cream cheese with raisins, raspberries, and cheese. These earn no more than a disapproving glance from the older, more traditional Russians, however.

The national dish gourmet style—in Moscow's fine dining restaurant "Imperial" blini are served with Royal Black Caviar. True to form, this delectable dish is of course served on a silver platter.

Butter Week

Butter Week (or *maslenitsa* from the Russian *maslo* meaning butter), originally a Slavic pagan feast ushering out the winter and welcoming in the spring, is the Russian carnival time during which Christians prepare themselves for Lent. No more meat may be eaten from now on and so they particularly enjoy buttery blini with sweet or savory fillings, sweet bread rolls, and meat-free *zakuski*, hors d'oeuvres and appetizers. Butter Week falls in the last week of February and therefore comes at the end of the old and the start of the new year, which began on March 1 in Russia up until the adoption of the Julian calendar in the 13th century. According to ancient chronicles, people used to dress up at this time with fearsome masks and go rampaging through the streets. The townspeople and the villagers held troika rides and raucous toboggan parties. Even today, the Shrovetide week in Moscow and in St. Petersburg is characterized by public entertainment, theater premieres, and balls. Following the end of the Soviet era, during which the carnival customs had become almost extinct, these were revived in the countryside as well. Stalls are set up and children in fancy dress are to be seen ice skating on the frozen lakes. The "Maslenitsa," the figure of a witch made of straw and with skillet and blini in her hand, is burnt as a symbol of the winter. The vodka flows freely during this time and the men from neighboring villages stage a large would-be brawl, followed by brotherly salutations and toasts. As a time of rebirth and fertility, Butter Week is a popular time to begin a new life and get married. Each day has its own name and own meaning and these are gaining in significance again. On the eve of *Maslenitsa* the people remember their forefathers and gather at their graves for a celebratory meal. Monday is the day of encounters and the first butter blini are given to the poor in remembrance of the dead. Tuesday is all about teasing and flirting. Wednesday, when the mothers-in-law spoil their daughters and sons-in-law with blini, is called the sweet tooth day. Thursday is a day of carousing and brawling; Friday evening belongs to the mothers-in-law and the Saturday evening is reserved for the gathering of the daughters-in-law. Finally, Sunday is a day of forgiveness and of farewell to exuberance. No more butter blini and no more cheese may be eaten on this last day before Lent.

Background: The highlight of Butter Week is the burning of a straw figure symbolizing the winter.

Blini and Butter Week go together like the Russian winter and vodka. The charcoal samovar provides hot tea for the feast.

Fasting times

For millions of believers in Russia the Russian Orthodox Church is the only institution in this vast land, plagued by corruption and misgovernment, providing any credible representation of moral values. With its 7,500 churches and monasteries it inspires confidence and gives hope and solace. Russian Orthodoxy went through a renaissance after the end of the Soviet Union following 70 years of persecution and suppression and more and more Russians are reverting to a religious lifestyle, of which fasting is part. Devout Orthodox Christians often fast for more than 200 days spread throughout the year. The Great Lent fast, lasts for 48 days and begins seven weeks prior to Easter. The Apostles' fast and Dormition fast are observed in summer and the long Christmas fast lasts from the end of November until January 7, the Russian Orthodox Christmas. In accordance with the strict rules no meat, bacon, animal fat, butter, eggs, or milk may be eaten during the fast. Strictly speaking fish is allowed only on Saturdays and Sundays. Similarly, all red-colored foods reminiscent of blood are forbidden: beetroot, tomatoes, red bell peppers, even carrots. Sticking to these rules is not easy, especially for farmers who need a great deal of energy for their hard labor in the fields and the harsh climate. It was therefore an ongoing challenge for house-wives and cooks to provide as diverse a meal as possible during the frugal fasting time. Popular fasting dishes include mushroom soups such as cep bouillon with vegetables as well as fasting *shchi*, the meat-free variety of the famous Russian cabbage soup (see page 44). During fasting times pirogi are filled with cabbage, mushrooms, peas, turnips, berries, and on those days when it is allowed, various types of fish. The range of fasting dishes also includes *kasha*, (a dish made of confectioners' buckwheat), blini, and onion tart or pumpkin pancakes which are made without any eggs.

The imaginations of the vegetable chefs know practically no limits. Cabbage is filled with vegetables and made into delicious meatballs or juicy fritters. There is eggplant stuffed with mushrooms or turnips filled with currants, rice cutlets and numerous bakes and pudding varieties made from mushrooms, onions, pumpkin, and many other types of vegetables.

A change of flavor is also achieved through serving hot or cold, by using different fats (primarily vegetable oils such as hemp, nut, and poppy seed oil, as well as by using herbs such as nettles, sorrel, dandelions, orache, and ground elder. Flavorings such as onion, garlic, horseradish, dill, parsley, aniseed, cilantro, bay leaves, black pepper, and cloves round off the aroma of what, from a culinary perspective, is really not a very frugal fasting time.

The Monastery Renaissance

An open-air museum outside the walls of the idyllically situated *Ipatiev* Monastery on the Volga River is testimony to the country's traditions.

Russian monastery buildings have been integrated within towns and villages since time immemorial. Sequestrated during the 70 years of Soviet rule for use as movie houses, warehouses, coal bunkers, barracks, or prisons, they have now been returned to the faithful who are restoring and rejuvenating them. The most significant centers of the Orthodox Renaissance include the Sergiyev Posad Monastery of the Holy Trinity near Moscow with the famous tomb of the holy Sergey von Radonesch, the Solowezki monastery situated on the archipelago of the same name in the White Sea, and the Pskov Cave Monastery. These are not just pilgrimage destinations for devout Russians; the monks and nuns also perform important social services in keeping with their vows of humility and charity. They run hospitals, soup kitchens, and homes for the aged. The monastery gardens and cottage industries provide all of their daily subsistence requirements as well as herbs and medicines. They tend to the gardens and fields and see this as a means of self-communion. The monasteries bake Holy Communion bread, engage in the painting of frescoes and icons as well as the embroidery of vestments and make a valuable contribution to the compilation of Russian history. Excerpts from their monastery records have provided the basis for a number of Russian recipe books.

Kartofelny gribnoy sup
Mushroom soup with potatoes

9 oz/250 g fresh mushrooms (porcini, chanterelles, button) cut into bite-sized pieces
1 onion, finely chopped
1 carrot, finely chopped (according to taste)
2 tbsp oil
1 lb 2 oz/500 g potatoes boiled in their skins, peeled and finely diced
1 tbsp finely chopped parsley
1 tbsp finely chopped dill
1½ quarts/1.5 liters water or vegetable stock
Salt and pepper

Fry the mushrooms with the onion and carrot in the oil; add the potatoes and herbs; pour over the water or vegetable stock and leave the soup to simmer for 10–15 minutes, stirring occasionally. Season to taste with salt and pepper.

The Russian Easter

Easter is the most important celebration for Orthodox Christians. The belief is widespread that, on this day, the Savior mingles among the Russian people dressed as an ordinary person while the devil lazes about in hell. *Paskha*, Easter, is celebrated as the feast of charity and so the poor and the sick are continually invited by the better off to a generous Easter meal. Today as in the past, the bells ring throughout Easter Sunday heralding Christ's resurrection. Celebratory church services reach their culmination on Easter Sunday with processions of icons and holy banners. During Easter goodwill visits are paid to relatives and friends. In Perm the custom remains that families get together after morning prayers on the first day of Easter to prepare *pelmeni* (see page 52 ff) Throughout Russia the preparations for the Easter meal begin the day before the Feast of the Resurrection. In the past, well-to-do families symbolically served 48 hors d'oeuvres and main dishes on the day after the long 48-day fast with everybody tucking in eagerly after seven weeks of going without, at least in part. In addition to the colored eggs on the Easter table decorated with flowers, branches, and candles, there are gingerbread in the shape of lambs, rabbits, and doves, blini, and rich cakes, particularly the traditional *kulich* which the faithful carry to the church the night before Easter to have it blessed. The preparation of this Easter cake is very elaborate as it requires so many ingredients—particularly raisins, candied fruit, saffron, almonds, and vanilla in addition to the flour, butter, eggs, and yeast (see page 63.) Once baked the *kulich* is covered with sugar or chocolate frosting and is often decorated with fruit or nuts. The culinary highlight of the Easter meal is the cream cheese dish *paskha*, named for the occasion and traditionally prepared in a pyramid-shaped wooden mold with a flattened top and which has holes through which the liquid can drain. If possible one should use a dry cream cheese or a cottage cheese (see page 62.) One can have *paskha* with almonds, candied fruit, or chocolate. *Paskha krasnaya*, red *paskha*, with candied orange peel and raisins, is baked. Warm *paskha*, of which there are numerous varieties, is also very popular.

The patriarchs from the Cathedral of the Assumption in Vladimir bless the Easter bread, *kulich*, and eggs.

Easter eggs

Eggs are the symbol of new life in Russia at Easter. It was the custom then for members of the Russian royal family to give each other valuable, decorative eggs made from gold and silver, adorned with precious stones and which could be opened, revealing ornate miniatures. These noble gems were made by the jeweler Peter Carl Fabergé since 1885. Even today the farmers in the villages around Moscow carve wooden eggs which, painted with church motifs and the images of saints, are sold at the markets. Each egg carries the two Cyrillic letters X.B.—the first two letters of the Russian Easter greeting *Khristos voskres!— Voistinu voskres!*, Christ has risen! Christ has truly risen! In the past, wooden eggs or hardcooked eggs were placed in the bed of newly weds, "with the wish that children be born to them." This custom used eggs as a symbol of fertility and the renewal of life. Colored eggs are made everywhere at Easter—grass, onion skins, and berry juice were traditionally used to make colorings but nowadays synthetic colors are used. They are frequently painted as well and some of them turn into true works of art. The eggs are the first things to be eaten from the Easter table. Boiled, colored eggs are also given to relatives and friends as well as being brought to church. The first fresh eggs to be laid on the first day of Easter are holy and are not eaten; they are kept for a year instead. Children today still play the egg game in which they bash their boiled eggs against another's. Whoever's egg remains undamaged also gets the opponent's egg. They call out "Christ is risen!" when bashing the eggs together.

The little ones, too, look forward to the colorful eggs and the dishes decorated with candles at Easter.

Romanovskaya paskha
Romanov cream cheese pudding
(Illustration above)

²/₃ cup/150 g butter, softened
4 egg yolks
2 ¹/₄ cups/250 g confectioners' sugar
1 vanilla bean and 1 pinch salt
1¹/₂ tbsp Cognac
3 cups/750 g Quark or soft curd cheese, strained
6 tbsp/50 g each of finely chopped candied fruit and almonds
6 tbsp/50 g currants
2 cups/500 g whipping cream

Beat the butter, egg yolks, confectioners' sugar, vanilla seeds, and salt together until light and fluffy. Add the Cognac and blend everything with the Quark or curd cheese. Stir in the fruit and almonds, lastly folding in the stiffly whipped cream. Place in a mold and leave to chill overnight. You can decorate the *paskha* with cream, chocolate, almonds, and fruit, as you wish.

Sweet Easter excess

Kulich
Easter cake
(Illustration large picture left)

9 tbsp/75 g sultanas
4 tbsp rum
¹/₂ tsp saffron powder
1 cup/1/4 liter milk, lukewarm
3 envelopes dried yeast
1 tsp sugar
2¹/₄ cups/250 g confectioners' sugar
About 6 ¹/₂ cups/900 g all-purpose flour
2 tsp salt
1 tsp vanilla extract
10 egg yolks, beaten lightly
1 cup + 2 tbsp/250 g butter, softened and cut into pieces
²/₃ cup/75 g roasted almonds, finely chopped
¹/₂ cup/100 g mixed candied fruit
About 3 ¹/₂ tbsp/50 g butter, softened, for greasing

For the frosting:
2¹/₄ cups/250 g confectioners' sugar
Juice of 1 lemon

Soak the sultanas in the rum for at least 10 minutes, drain and leave to dry on a paper towel. Dissolve the saffron in the rum and set aside. For the dough, mix the milk with the yeast and sugar, leave to rest for 3 minutes, then stir well and leave to rise in a warm place for about 10 minutes until the quantity has doubled. Sift the confectioners' sugar, about 4¹/₂ cups/700 g flour and the salt into a large bowl, make a well in the center and pour in the yeast mixture, vanilla, egg yolks, and the rum/saffron mixture. Work into a smooth dough using a wooden spoon; work in the butter pieces, then roll the dough into a ball and knead well on a lightly floured surface. Gradually add more and more flour until the dough no longer sticks. Knead for a further 10 minutes until it is smooth, shiny, and elastic. Grease a bowl with the softened butter, place the lightly floured dough in it, cover and leave to rise for about 1 hour until the dough has doubled in quantity. Dust the almonds, candied fruit, and soaked sultanas with 1 tablespoon flour and work into the dough. Grease the bottom of an empty, clean canister (e.g. 4 ¹/₂-lb/2-kg catering-pack conserves or fruit container, about 6 inches/15 cm in diameter and 7 inches/18 cm in height.) Cut a piece of baking parchment to fit, grease on one side and line the side of the canister (greased side inward.) Place the dough in the canister, cover and leave to rise for a further 30 minutes. Preheat the oven to 400 °F/200 °C and bake the cake on the lower shelf for about 75 minutes, lowering the temperature to 350 °F/180 °C after 15 minutes. During baking the dough rises up over the edge of the

canister forming a decorative, mushroom-shaped top. In order to remove the cake from the canister without damaging it, leave the canister to cool slightly at first. Then lay it on its side, remove the bottom with a can opener, run a knife between the paper and the canister, turn the cake the right way up, carefully prize the top of the cake away from the edge of the canister. Lift the cake out, place on a wire rack and then remove the paper.

For the frosting, mix the confectioners' sugar with 4 tablespoons cold water and the lemon juice and drizzle over the cake while still warm. The frosting should drizzle down the side of the cake.

The basis of the *kulich* is a rich yeast dough. Saffron dissolved in rum provides the color and the delicate aroma.

Once the yeast dough has risen, the almonds, candied fruit, and sultanas are kneaded in.

The Russians bake their Easter cake in a large canister rather than a baking pan.

Last but not least the frosting is spread over the *kulich* which is then decorated with religious Easter motifs.

Pushkin: culinary poetry

Alexander Pushkin (1799–1837), said to be more than any other the embodiment of the Russian-ness, of the "Russian soul," the Russian character, and the Russian language, loved the simple, country life and, like the peasant farmers, he liked to eat the solid meals served in wooden bowls with carved wooden spoons.

Pushkin's favorite dishes were blini, buckwheat *kasha*, cabbage soup, *bitochki*, meatballs made with spinach or celeriac, baked potatoes, baked apples, rose hip jelly, and lingonberry compote.

Even as a regular at the Tsar's court and a recognized poet Pushkin was no gourmet who gave up much of his time for food. Friends' accounts from 1828, when he wrote the poem *Poltava* in just three weeks, tell us "The verses even pursued him in his dreams such that he would spring out of bed and write them down in the dark. When he was hungry he went to the nearest tavern but even there he could not escape the verses. He would eat quickly, whatever was on offer, and hurried back home to write down the verses which had come to him on the way and while he had been eating." Nevertheless, the poet knew how to produce an ironic portrayal of the culinary debauchery of the

Pushkin delivers a lecture to a literary society in 1825, the year in which he worked on *Eugen Onegin*.

nobility. The Russian upper class had been devoted to the select French dishes and delicacies of their chefs from Western Europe since the start of the 18th century (see page 67.) With his poem *Eugen Onegin* 1825 Pushkin recaptured an evening of excess in the highest circles in verse: *Before him roast beef, red and gory, / and truffles, which have ever been / youth's choice, the flower of French cuisine: / and pâté, Strasbourg's deathless glory, / sits with Limburg's vivacious cheese / and ananas, the gold of trees.*

Such delicacies were not to be found on the table of the debt-ridden poet. The meager fee from the

publisher of his works was often not even enough for his daily bread. Tsar Nicholas I, whose fascination with the legendary beauty of Pushkin's young wife, Natalya Goncharova, was well known, knew this and supported the family of the impoverished poet. In a letter to a good friend Pushkin wrote "The Tsar took me into his service. He said that, as I am married and not wealthy, one needs to make sure that I have some porridge on my plate." Pushkin's exceptionally

The poet Pushkin's parlor in his Moscow apartment on the Old Arbat, today the Pushkin Museum.

Russian wine

Pushkin loved French wine and champagne but wine was also produced in Russia then as now. The most important producing areas, with around 28 thousand acres (70 thousand ha) of vineyards, lie along the lower stretches of the Don river, in the area around Krasnodar, on the floodplains of the Kuma and Terek rivers and in the northern Caucasus. The climate in these areas is dominated by a continental influence whereby the winters are often so cold that the vines are only able to survive due to complicated protective measures such as piling earth around the individual stalks. The most widely grown grape variety is the white Rkaziteli, covering almost half of the vineyards. Aligoté, Riesling, Clairette, Cabernet Sauvignon, and Saperavi are also cultivated, together with different indigenous varieties.

beautiful wife is said to have taken as little interest in the household as she took in the children. Balls, dinners, dressmakers, and fashion houses took up all of her time and Pushkin was left to his own devices. When he came home late at night and the servants were already asleep, he would go into the kitchen, peel some boiled potatoes and roast them whole. To this day whole roast potatoes are known as *pushkinskiye* (Pushkins).

When it came to beverages Pushkin emerged as a true connoisseur. Like many Russians he was somewhat fond of drinking whereby rather than vodka, his favorites were rum, champagne, and French red wine. A verse from *Eugen Onegin* is testimony to this:

Yet hissing froth deals a malicious, / perfidious blow to my inside, / and now it's Bordeaux the Judicious / that I prefer to Champagne's tide; / to Aÿ's vintage in the sequel / I find myself no longer equal; / for, mistress-like, it's brilliant, vain, / lively, capricious, and inane… / But in misfortune or displeasure, / Bordeaux, you're like a faithful friend, / a true companion to the end, / ready to share our quiet leisure / with your good offices, and so / long life to our dear friend, Bordeaux!

Even though he himself ate frugal meals, Pushkin's works feature the culinary delights of the Russian nobility who were served many other extravagant dishes besides roast partridge with roast apple and good wine.

Porcelain manufacture

St. Petersburg porcelain from the Lomonosov factory with its blue-gold net pattern is among the finest made from the "white gold." It was founded under the patronage of none other than Tsarina Elisabeth Petrovna (1709–1762). European porcelain fever also took hold in Russia in the 18th century. The Tsarina planned to recruit craftsmen from Meissen but the first to arrive turned out to be a fraudster. Elisabeth therefore commissioned the chemist Dmitry Vinogradov, a student of the Russian University professor Michail Lomonosov (1711–1765), with the manufacture of porcelain. In 1744 Winogradov founded the royal porcelain factory in a series of blockhouses on the banks of the Neva River. Three years later the craftsman presented the Tsarina with the first Russian porcelain: an unimposing platter with a lid for serving chocolates. This was soon followed by buttons, cane knobs, pipe bowls, knife and fork handles, and the very popular snuff boxes. Tsarina Catherine II later demanded more of the porcelain makers and new, larger kilns made the firing of elaborate dinner services possible for which fine, white clays from Gschel, near Moscow, were used. This porcelain was in no way inferior to the Meissen porcelain from Germany.

The royal porcelain factory was named after Lomonosov following the October Revolution in 1917. From 1920 the factory exhibited at numerous international exhibitions and won a gold medal in Paris in 1937. The fine tea and coffee services as well as the crockery in historical, traditional, and modern designs continue to enjoy great popularity today.

Fine porcelain is manufactured by first pouring the liquid porcelain mixture into the plaster molds.

Once the mixture has dried properly it is carefully removed from the molds.

Some plaster molds comprise a number of parts which can be reused later.

Any surplus porcelain remaining on the edges or joins is carefully removed before the first firing.

At the Lomonosov Porcelain Factory in St. Petersburg every single piece is meticulously hand painted.

Royal cuisine

The Russian tsars were in no way inferior to their subjects when it came to hospitality and their dinner tables were an every day feature of diplomatic life. Up until the 17th century the royal cuisine was not vastly different from that of the ordinary people. It was simply the quantity which set it apart. The Tsar's table was always characterized by a tremendous excess of courses; a meal comprised up to 200 different dishes. The largest pigs, geese, and turkeys, the fattest sturgeon or catfish were selected—some of them so large that they had to be carried to the table by three or four men. Ivan the Terrible (1530–1584) gave banquets for up to 700 guests and once invited 2,000 soldiers to join him at the table. From the 18th century on there was an obligatory order for the menu at the royal courts. Eight courses were served one after the other: first there were soups such as *shchi* or *ukha*, followed by hors d'oeuvres such as brawn, fish in aspic, and pickled vegetables. After roast meat and poultry came boiled or baked fish. Then came the pirogi, followed by *kasha* and then finally cakes, tarts, and pastries. Compotes, ice cream, *kisel* (see page 122), or chocolate were served to end the meal. The dishes were always consumed in great quantity and many were served in the form of imaginary animals or even whole palaces. Peter the Great (1672–1725) liked to eat solid, Russian food but was not averse to German or Dutch dishes. The nobility also increasingly hired chefs from western Europe. The tsars adopted French cuisine under the rule of Catherine the Great (1729–1796). Cabbage and cucumbers were replaced by cauliflower and artichokes. The Tsarina based her bacchanalia on the example of Greek revelry. The handwritten menu alone, decorated by renowned artists, was a book in itself. There were soups and consommés, turkeys, black and hazel grouse, rabbit, venison, with truffles, quails and poultry, turtles, pies, salads, oysters, oranges, gingerbread, pirogi, exquisite desserts, sugar loaves, and ice cream. Following the war in defense of the Russian homeland against Napoleon in 1812 the Russians began to take more of an interest in local specialties and refined these with a French touch. The last Tsar, Nicholas II, loved Russian cuisine, particularly cabbage soup and suckling pig with radish. In the evenings the royal family would get together for a typically Russian meal comprising five courses.

Background: The banquet room in the Catherine Palace at Tsarskoe Selo (Pushkin in the Soviet era), one of the Tsar's three summer residences near St Petersburg.

A Romanov menu

The recipes on this page are from the book *Le Tsar et la Tsarina, Le Journal*, Paris 1896.

Sterlyad potsarsky
Sturgeon à la Tsarina (1)

1³/₄ lb/750 g sturgeon, gutted, cleaned, and ready for cooking
Salt
Butter for greasing
1–2 parsley roots, finely chopped
1 bay leaf
1 clove garlic, finely chopped
2 cups/500 ml Chablis (dry white wine)
¹/₂ cup/125 ml pickled gherkin brine
Juice of 1 lemon
2–4 tbsp black caviar
1 tbsp butter

Slice the sturgeon diagonally and season with salt. Place in a buttered flameproof pan, add the parsley roots, bay leaf, and garlic. Pour over the wine, pickled gherkin brine, and lemon juice, cover and cook gently over a low heat for about 35 minutes. Pour the stock through a strainer, add the caviar, bring to a boil and stir in the butter. Pour the caviar sauce over the sturgeon and serve the remainder separately. Serve with potato croquettes.

Rakovy sup
Light crayfish soup (2)

For the mirepoix:
2 small onions, finely chopped
1 large carrot, finely chopped
2 tbsp butter
1 sprig thyme
1 small bay leaf
1 sprig parsley, chopped finely
1 tbsp wine

20 crayfish
2 tbsp Cognac
Salt and pepper
Cayenne pepper
¹/₂ cup/100 g rice
1 tbsp butter
¹/₂ cup/125 g cream

First prepare the mirepoix: in a deep pan sauté the onion and carrot in butter, add the herbs, cover and sauté over a low heat for about 15 minutes. Slake with the wine.
Place the crayfish in boiling water and leave to simmer for about 10 minutes. Remove, place in the pan with the mirepoix, pour over the cognac and flambé. Then cover with water, season with salt, pepper, and cayenne pepper and leave to simmer gently for about a further 15 minutes.
Bring the rice to a boil in double the amount of water, season with salt and pepper and boil for 15–20 minutes until softened.
In the meantime remove the crayfish from the stock, drain, and leave to cool. Remove the shells and set the tails aside.
Crush the heads with a pestle and mortar, place in a sieve, add the cooked rice and pass both through the sieve with a wooden spoon, gradually adding the stock so that everything is well mixed.
Bring the soup to a boil for 1 minute while stirring continuously; cut the crayfish tails into cubes and add to the soup. Remove the pan from the heat, stir in the butter, thin the soup with the cream, reheat, and serve immediately.

Krem iz vina
Wine cream (3)

4 eggs, separated
1 cup/250 ml dry white wine, preferably Côteau
Champenois
10 sugar lumps
Grated peel of 1 organic lemon
1 tbsp kirsch

Whisk the egg yolks with the wine. Crumble the
sugar lumps over the lemon peel, add to the wine
and egg mixture, beat well and add the kirsch.
Stir over a low heat for 10 minutes (do not allow
to boil) and leave to cool. Immediately before serving, whip the egg whites until stiff and carefully
fold into the cream.

Orlovsky farshirovanny fazan
"Prince Orloff" stuffed pheasant (4)

2 young pheasants, plucked and dressed
1 small glass Cognac
Salt and pepper
3 1/2 oz/100 g fatty bacon, finely sliced
9 oz/250 g ground veal
5 1/2 oz/150 g liver sausage with truffles
2 egg yolks
14 tbsp/200 g butter
2/3 cup/150 ml red wine
8 thin slices smoked ham

Wipe out the insides of the pheasants with Cognac
and rub in the salt and pepper mixed together.
Layer the breasts with the bacon slices.
Mix the ground veal, liver sausage with truffles,
egg yolks, and the remaining Cognac together well.
Stuff the pheasants with this mixture and stitch up
the opening. Roast in 7 tablespoons/100 g butter,
basting frequently, at 425 °F/220 °C for about
35–40 minutes; remove and keep warm. Pour the
juices and residues from the roasting pan into a
saucepan, add the red wine and reduce over a high
heat. Stir in the remaining butter and season with
salt and pepper.
Carve the pheasants, remove the stuffing and place
spoonfuls on the ham slices. Arrange with the
pheasant on a warm platter and serve with the
wine sauce. Serve with creamy mashed potatoes,
carrot purée, and Brussels sprouts.

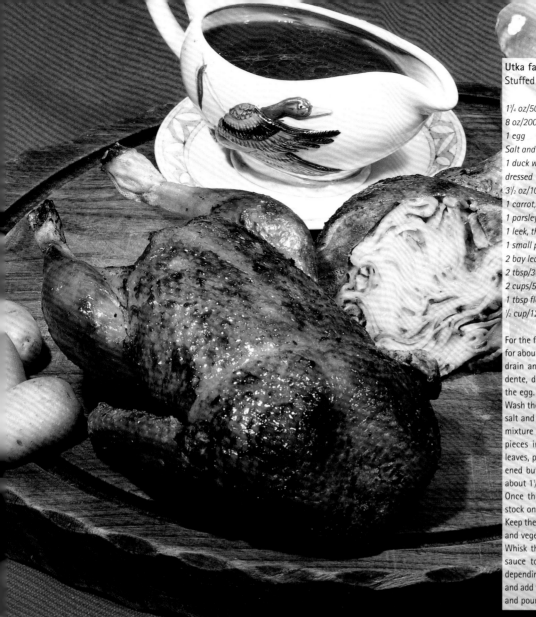

Utka farshirovannaya
Stuffed duck

1³/₄ oz/50 g dried ceps
8 oz/200 g ribbon noodles
1 egg
Salt and pepper
1 duck weighing about 4 ¹/₂ lb/2 kg, plucked and
dressed
3¹/₂ oz/100 g fatty bacon, thinly sliced
1 carrot, finely chopped
1 parsley root, finely chopped
1 leek, thinly sliced
1 small piece celeriac, finely chopped
2 bay leaves
2 tbsp/30 g butter
2 cups/500 ml meat stock
1 tbsp flour
¹/₂ cup/125 ml Madeira

For the filling soak the mushrooms in lukewarm water for about 30 minutes; simmer in fresh water until soft, drain and cut into strips. Cook the noodles until al dente, drain well and mix with the mushrooms and the egg. Season with salt and pepper.

Wash the duck and pat dry, season inside and out with salt and pepper, stuff with the mushroom and noodle mixture and stitch up the opening. Place the bacon pieces in a casserole, add the vegetables and bay leaves, place the duck on top, smeared with the softened butter. Roast in the oven at 400 °F/200 °C for about 1¹/₂ hours, basting regularly with the pan juices. Once the flesh has become browned add the meat stock one tablespoon at a time.

Keep the duck warm once cooked. Strain the pan juices and vegetables through a sieve into a small saucepan. Whisk the flour with a little water and stir into the sauce to bind it. Add the rest of the meat stock, depending on the desired consistency, bring to a boil, and add the Madeira according to taste. Carve the duck and pour over the sauce. Serve with boiled potatoes.

Poultry in the Kitchen

Kotlety pozharskiye
Russian chicken fritters

5 slices white bread, crusts removed
¹/₂ cup/125 ml milk
1¹/₄ lb/600 g chicken meat skinned and boned
7 tbsp/100 g butter
Salt and white pepper
2 cups breadcrumbs
6 tbsp/90 g ghee
Generous ³/₄ cup/200 g sour cream

Soak the bread in the milk for about 15 minutes and squeeze well. Pass the chicken meat twice through the grinder or food processor, mix with the bread and pass through the grinder again. Mix with the softened butter, salt, and pepper and work into a smooth stuffing. Cool your hands under cold water and shape the meat mixture into fritters about 1¹/₂ inches/4 cm thick. Coat with breadcrumbs and fry in the melted ghee for about 5 minutes on each side. Arrange on a plate and drizzle with the frying fat and the sour cream before serving.

Gus s yablokami
Goose with apples

1 small goose, plucked and dressed
4–5 sharp apples, peeled, cored, and quartered
Salt and pepper
3 ¹/₂ tbsp/50 g butter
2 tbsp honey
Preserved apples, cucumbers, and sauerkraut for gar-
nishing

Clean the goose and pat dry, stuff with the apples, stitch up the opening, rub with salt and pepper and place on a rack in a roasting pan with the butter. Pierce the skin in several places so that fat can run out while cooking (especially between the wing joints and the breast.) Cover the goose with honey. Roast in a preheated oven at approx. 400 °F/200 °C for 2–2¹/₂ hours, basting regularly with the pan juices. Once cooked, carve the goose, garnish with preserved apples, cucumbers, and sauerkraut. Serve with buckwheat *kasha* (see page 54).

Kuritsa tushonaya s chernoslivom
Chicken with prunes

3¹/₄ lb/1.5 kg chicken pieces
Salt and black pepper
2 tbsp oil
4 tbsp/60 g butter
1 carrot, sliced
1 celery stalk, finely chopped
2 medium size onions, finely chopped
1 tbsp chopped parsley
1 bay leaf
1 cup/250 ml chicken stock
8–9 oz/250 g prunes (pitted)
1 tbsp lemon juice
1 tbsp sugar
1 tbsp all-purpose flour

Clean the chicken pieces, rub with salt and pepper, fry in the oil and half the butter for 5–6 minutes on each side until crispy. Remove from the skillet and keep warm. Sauté the vegetables in the frying fat for about 5 minutes. Add the chicken pieces, parsley, and bay leaf, pour over the chicken stock with 1 cup/250 ml water. Bring to a boil, cover and simmer over a medium heat for 30 minutes, basting with the sauce from time to time. In the meantime, simmer the prunes in the lemon juice and the sugar in a covered saucepan for about 15 minutes; drain and set aside. Preheat the oven to 260 °F/125 °C. Arrange the meat on a platter, spread the prunes over the meat, cover and keep warm in the oven. Pass the cooking juices through a sieve. Cook the flour in the remaining butter for 2–3 minutes, add the cooking juices, stir until smooth and bring to a boil. Season to taste with salt and pepper and pour over the meat.
Serve immediately.

Meat recipes

Bitochki v smetane
Fritters with sour cream
(Not illustrated)

4 slices/100 g stale white bread, crusts removed
½ cup/125 ml milk
1¾ lb/750 g ground beef or mixed beef and pork
1 egg
Salt
Pepper
3 tbsp/45 g butter
1 tbsp flour
7 tbsp/100 ml meat stock (instant)
Generous ¾ cup/200 g sour cream

Leave the bread to soak in the milk for about 15 minutes and squeeze well. Combine the ground meat with the bread and egg, season with salt and pepper. Shape into fritters about ¾ inch/2 cm thick and fry in butter until crispy on both sides. Keep warm.
Stir the flour into the cooking fat, slake with a little stock and add the sour cream. Bring the sauce to a boil, allow to simmer for about 5 minutes and pour over the fritters. Serve with potatoes and pickled gherkins.

Okorok v teste
Ham in a bread crust

2 tsp/8 g dry yeast
1 pinch sugar
2–3 tbsp caraway seeds
2 tbsp sorghum molasses or corn syrup
2⅔ cups/400 g rye flour
3¼ lb/1.5 kg boiled or lightly cured smoked ham, in a piece

Dissolve the yeast in 3 tbsp of lukewarm water, add the sugar and leave to rise in a warm place for 10 minutes or until it has doubled in volume.
Gradually stir in about ⅔ cup/150 ml cold water, the molasses or corn syrup, and half of the flour. Place the dough on a lightly floured surface, knead in the remaining flour, adding a little water or more flour as required to obtain a smooth, firm dough. Cover the dough and leave to rest for about 30 minutes. Roll out into a rectangle about ⅖ inch/1 cm thick and large enough to contain the ham. Place on a well-greased baking sheet. Rinse the ham, pat dry and lay on top of the dough. Wrap the dough around the ham and press the edges firmly together. Bake in a preheated oven at 350 °F/180 °C for about 2 hours until golden brown. Leave to cool and then slice the ham in the crust before serving.

How Beef Stroganoff got its name

Even though all over the world Beef Stroganoff is considered to be a Russian dish, it in no way originates from traditional Russian cuisine. The preparation of the thinly sliced beef is more typical of French cuisine, not surprisingly, since the dish is thought to have been invented by the French cook employed by Count Alexander Stroganov (1795–1891), the General Governor of Southern Russia based in Odessa and after whom it is named. Stroganov himself has no particular culinary claim to fame; in fact, he was not even much of a gourmet. Nevertheless, he was a well-known, very wealthy statesman and proponent of enlightenment at the close of the 19th century who did much for national education. As was the wont of Russian magnates at the time he entertained at home on an "open house" basis. Any arbitrary, even halfway decently dressed individual got a free meal at his house. It was for these open house meals that the dish was invented because the finely shredded meat is particularly easy to serve in portions.

Bef Stroganov
Beef Stroganoff

1¾ lb/750 g beef fillet steak, sliced into thin strips
2–3 tbsp/25–30 g all-purpose flour
3 tbsp oil
Salt and black pepper
1 large onion, finely chopped
9 oz/50 g button mushrooms, sliced
Generous ¾ cup/200 g sour cream
1 tsp mustard
2 tbsp finely chopped parsley

Coat the strips of steak in flour and fry quickly in hot
oil on both sides, one portion at a time. Remove from
the skillet, season with salt and pepper.
Sauté the onions in the same fat, add the mushrooms
and sauté until soft. Add the sour cream and mustard.
Add the steak to the sauce, bring to a boil briefly and
sprinkle with parsley.
Serve with fried grated potato and pickled gherkins.

Telyatina tushonaya s solyonimy ogurtsami
Roast veal with pickled gherkins

2 medium-sized onions, sliced
2 tbsp/30 g butter
1 carrot, sliced
2 celery stalks, sliced diagonally
2 tbsp finely chopped parsley
2 bay leaves
3 cloves
1 veal roast about 2¼ lb kg in weight (boneless sirloin
or rump veal)
4 tbsp oil
1 cup/250 ml dry white wine
Salt and pepper
4–5 pickled gherkins, sliced
Pickled gherkins as accompaniment

Sauté the onions in the butter, add the vegetables,
herbs, and spices and sauté over a low heat for about
15 minutes until soft (do not allow them to start turning brown).
Fry the meat in very hot oil for about 10 minutes or
until it is equally browned on all sides.
Place the vegetables in an ovenproof dish. Place the
meat on top, pour over the wine, season with salt and
pepper, cover and roast in a preheated oven for 1½ to
2 hours at 350 °F/180 °C. After 45 minutes turn the
meat over and add the pickled gherkins. Slice the roast
and arrange on a warmed platter.
Serve with boiled potatoes and pickled gherkins.

Innards

Russian cuisine makes particularly diverse use of innards, also known as organ meat—offal in the UK. Almost all parts are used: the tongue, liver, kidneys, heart, lungs, stomach, udder, intestines, and brains. This meat can be prepared very simply by roasting or boiling. When in the past animals were slaughtered in the village the special delicacies such as fried heart and liver were kept especially for the children.

Other dishes, however, require a certain degree of skill due to their diverse ingredients. Boiled ox tongue or tongue in aspic—both of which must always be served with horseradish—are classic Russian *zakuski* with vodka. In the famous Moscow taverns of the tsarist era one could also order ox and sheep's brains as a particularly tasty appetizer.

The classic organ meat dishes also include steamed kidneys with vegetables as well as *rassol-nik*, a soup based on pickled gherkins and kidneys. Also popular are pirogi with a stuffing made from a variety of innards. For this stuffing heart,

liver, and lungs are first boiled, then fried with spices and finally baked in dough in the oven. The preparation of the old Russian dish *niania*, "child woman", is very complicated: a sheep's stomach is stuffed with buckwheat porridge, meat, brains, and vegetables and slowly braised in a clay pot in the oven.

Farshirovanny yazyk
Stuffed ox tongue

1 ox tongue
3 onions
1 carrot, roughly chopped
1 parsley root, roughly chopped
1 bay leaf
5 black peppercorns
2 slices white bread, crusts removed
5 tbsp milk
2 tbsp/30 g butter
1 egg
Pepper and salt
1 bunch parsley, chopped
10 tbsp/50 g sour cream
2 tbsp all-purpose flour

Wash the tongue well; place in a saucepan of cold water together with 2 onions halved, the vegetables, and the spices and boil until soft. Drain and keep the stock. Blanch the tongue with cold water and remove the skin. On one side leave one end not completely cut open and remove enough meat from the inside so that a casing about ¾ inch/2 cm thick remains. Soak the bread in the milk and squeeze well. Finely chop the remaining onion and sauté in 1 tablespoon butter until transparent.

Put the tongue meat and the soaked bread through a grinder. Mix well with the sautéed onion, 1 tablespoon softened butter, the egg, pepper, salt, and the parsley. Fill the tongue with the stuffing and bind with cooking twine. Place in an ovenproof dish, pour over 1 cup/250 ml of the tongue stock and cook in a preheated oven at 350 °F/180 °C for about 30 minutes, basting with the stock from time to time. Remove the tongue and leave to cool; remove the twine.

Stir the sour cream and the flour into ¾ cup/200 ml stock and use to bind the cooking juices, bring back to a boil and stir to thicken.

Slice the stuffed tongue and arrange on a platter so that the shape of the tongue is recognizable. Serve the sauce separately.

Mozgi v limonnom souse
Calf brains in lemon sauce
(Not illustrated)

4 calf brain halves, prepared ready to cook
Salt
2 eggs
Breadcrumbs
Butter for frying

For the sauce:
1 medium-sized onion, finely chopped
2 tbsp/30 g butter, plus extra for frying
2 tbsp all-purpose flour
About 1¼ cups/300 ml meat stock
1 organic lemon

Briefly boil the calf brains in salted water then drain and allow to cool.

In the meantime sauté the onions for the sauce in the butter, sprinkle with the flour, slake with the stock and bring to a boil. Slice one half of the lemon into very thin slices, add to the sauce and leave to infuse for a few minutes.

Pass the sauce through a strainer. Squeeze the remaining half of the lemon and season the sauce to taste with the juice.

Pat the brains dry and slice thickly. Whisk the egg and breadcrumbs together, coat the brain slices and fry in butter until golden brown on both sides. Serve the fried calves brains with the lemon sauce.

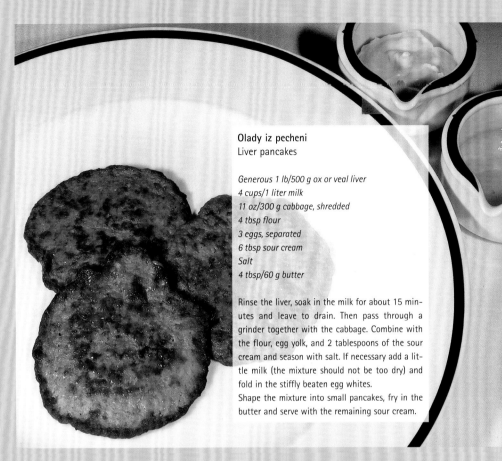

Olady iz pecheni
Liver pancakes

Generous 1 lb/500 g ox or veal liver
4 cups/1 liter milk
11 oz/300 g cabbage, shredded
4 tbsp flour
3 eggs, separated
6 tbsp sour cream
Salt
4 tbsp/60 g butter

Rinse the liver, soak in the milk for about 15 minutes and leave to drain. Then pass through a grinder together with the cabbage. Combine with the flour, egg yolk, and 2 tablespoons of the sour cream and season with salt. If necessary add a little milk (the mixture should not be too dry) and fold in the stiffly beaten egg whites.

Shape the mixture into small pancakes, fry in the butter and serve with the remaining sour cream.

Pochki v gorshochkakh
Stewed kidneys with potatoes

1¾ lb/750 g kidneys
Salt
Oil for frying
Generous 1 lb/500 g potatoes, sliced
2 medium-sized carrots, sliced
2 onions, sliced
1 parsley root, sliced
2 tbsp tomato paste
Generous ¾ cup/200 g sour cream
2 pickled gherkins, diced
4 cloves garlic, finely chopped
Pepper

Slice the kidneys lengthwise and discard the core, rinse well. Leave to soak in lightly salted water for 1–2 hours. Pat dry thoroughly, cut into slices and fry on all sides in oil in a deep skillet. Lift the kidneys out and set aside to drain.

Fry the potatoes and other vegetables in the oil, adding more if needed, stir in the tomato paste and fry for a few moments. Add the kidneys, sour cream, pickled gherkins, and garlic; season with salt and pepper. Cover and simmer over low heat for about 30 minutes. Serve with a rich rye bread.

Provisions through the ages

In the 9th century the princes of the Kiev empire, the predecessor of the Russian nation, used to invite soldiers and comrades-in-arms to their table, one which differed from that of the peasant farmers only in the quantity of food on it. The Mongolian incursions at the start of the 13th century and those that followed into the 15th century during foreign rule under the Tatars saw the ransacking of many villages and fields reverting to steppe. In the 16th century the policies of the Moscow Empire led to a social rift between the Tsar and the nobility on the one hand and the peasant farmers on the other. Since 1649, the nobility had been owners of the land upon which the peasant farmers were settled.

The inequality was also reflected in the availability of foodstuffs. While the ordinary people's menu was constantly diminishing and consisted of little more than bread, cabbage soup, and watery porridge, the cuisine of the nobility

became more and more sophisticated. The serfs in the countryside had to make do with the most meager of meals as a result of failed harvests, droughts, and famine. Famine gave rise to peasant revolts such as that led by Stefan Razin and which spread through the whole of southern Russia between 1667 and 1671.

The town populations obtained their provisions from special markets which differed considerably in quality, variety, and freshness depending on location. Traders had set up shop around the Kremlin in Moscow from the 17th century and their cellars contained all manner of delicacies. Cheaper markets for servants and coachmen, artisans, waiters and for down-and-outs were widespread in the outlying areas. As a result of industrialization, which only took hold in Russia at the end of the 18th century, a small middle class developed in the towns and more and more shops arose. By the end of the 19th century they

had attained an impressive grandeur in terms of both décor and their range of goods. Today the former gourmet temples of the Yeliseyev family in Moscow and St. Petersburg remain a testimony to that.

World War I and the October Revolution of 1917 put an end to this well-to-do era for the upper classes. When production was disrupted due to the takeover of the factories by the workers and the towns were no longer able to provide the country folk with any more industrially produced wares, the exchange of goods between town and countryside came to a halt. Bread was available in the towns only upon production of coupons. The civil war which lasted until 1921, together with the disastrous harvests caused by drought, brought hunger and epidemics to this vast country. Nettle or sorrel soup and bark tea were the order of the day, a frozen potato was a delicacy. In order to check the famine the Soviet powers often

confiscated the seed grain as a nature tax. Uprisings by the peasant farmers and other sectors of the population demanding the restitution of free trade led to an initial liberalization of the economy. Yet time and again there were phases where the state confiscated the grain. The end of the 1920s saw the start of enforced mass collectivization which led to the destruction of the economy. A disastrous famine occurred again, costing millions of lives. One of the consequences thereof was the establishment of the free *kolkhoz* (collective farm) markets where the prices, however, were often one hundred times higher than those for state produced goods. Yet they brought no surplus for the peasant farmers, only the means with which to acquire the most essential industrial goods.

Due to the enforced industrialization, the efficiency of which, was achieved only through the relentless exploitation of human and natural resources, the rationing of consumer goods could finally be lifted in 1935. A low level of food supply was made possible by state shops, the kolkhoz markets, and the public feeding schemes intended to ensure that the desperately needed workers received a nutritional minimum. However, World War II again brought death and unimaginable destruction to the European part of Russia. Millions of field acreage were mined, the farm implements destroyed, and there were hardly any crops to speak of.

In the decades following the war the majority of the population took their meals in the public canteens which usually served standard dishes such as kefir, eggs, soups, *kasha*, boiled beef, fritters, or fish. Due to time pressure, more and more mass-produced ready meals were consumed. Women working full time often stood patiently in line for hours after work in order to buy their family's evening meal from the limited and monotonous selection on offer in the state stores. Since the 1970s, party officials, on the other hand, had been secretly setting up luxury stores offering even imported groceries at giveaway prices. Following the collapse of the Soviet Union and the introduction of the market economy the early 1990s were a time of tremendous inflation. Time and again there were very dramatic shortages in the years that followed and standing in line overnight for even the most basic of commodities was not unusual.

At the start of the 21st century the range of local and imported goods is superabundant even if the majority of the population has to make do with basic foodstuffs because the state often delays for several months paying its modest salaries and pensions. Young people in particular often resort to criminal measures in order to be able to enjoy the new range of goods on offer. The high prices are largely attributable to the Mafioso structures in control of both the wholesale sector and the markets. Russian housewives deserve all the more respect for still being able to conjure up delicious menus out of nothing but relying on a great deal of resourcefulness.

Background: Waiting in line outside one of the public *stolovaya*, or canteens, in 1912—canteens that are still in existence today.

American fast food restaurants are very popular with the young but it is only the minority who can afford the trendy food.

Even in the monastery bakeries the ingredients for the bread dough are kneaded by machine today.

The dough is divided into portions and carefully weighed to obtain exactly the same sized loaves.

The loaves are placed in rectangular tins and then baked in the preheated oven.

Bread tradition

Moscow's *Tverskaya* shopping and amusement mile has seen a lot of changes in the past. "But *Filippov* is still the same," claim the capital's residents. This is where bread is baked today as it was a hundred years ago. Russian rye bread made from sourdough is bought fresh every day and is always on the table. It is eaten not only with soups but also with main dishes which are also served with accompaniments such as cabbage, potatoes, or rice. One takes a sniff before biting into it in order to relish the unmistakable aroma of this local rye bread with its century-old tradition. Wheat has only been grown in Russia since the 14th century. The combination of wheat and rye flour led to new types of bread; *kalachi*, their shape resembling a padlock, are made from pure wheat flour.

Fillipov's is always full. Bankers are there at lunchtime, passersby are there for the fresh *vatruchki*, cheese puffs, housewives gather there to gossip and to argue about which of the 27 types of bread is the best, gaggles of schoolgirls are feasting on the delicious *pluchki*, yeast pastries filled with poppy seeds. The bakery's founder was famous especially for his rye bread well beyond the city limits of Moscow. He described the secret behind the flavor as follows: "The bread needs love. Baking alone is not enough, the strength is in the flour. I buy specially selected rye from the countryside around Koslovo, near Tambov, and at the mill I have my people who make sure that not a speck of dust gets into it." In addition to his rye bread, Filippov's raisin buns also saw his fame spread throughout the land. Legend has it that one day a temperamental Moscow governor found a cockroach in a bread roll from the famous bakery. Filippov is alleged to have claimed that it was a raisin and invented his specialty promptly thereafter.

Filippov's rye bread and his famous *kalachi* used to be delivered to the Tsar's court in St Petersburg on a daily basis. An attempt was once made to bake them there but it was unsuccessful because, according to Filippov, the water from the Neva is not good enough. In winter whole wagon loads full of his rusks, *kalachi*, and bread rolls traveled as far as Siberia. A method had been invented for freezing them as soon as they came hot out of the oven. They were transported over thousands of miles before being defrosted in moist cloths immediately before being served. Thus Filippov's bread was served fresh for breakfast even in faraway Irkutsk.

The Martha and Mary Convent in Moscow still supplies bread specialties from its own bakery today.

Bread and salt

It is customary among the Slavs to provide an honorary welcome for highly valued guests: "For you, dear guests, bread and salt." The guest then breaks off a piece of the proffered bread, seasons it with the salt and eats it. Bread is considered to be the measure of all things and salt to be a valuable possession which, in the Middle Ages, was obtained during raids on the south, bartered in exchange for sable and arctic fox fur and was literally weighed out with gold. The symbolic combination of bread and salt still plays a significant role today. For example, on their wedding day brides are welcomed into the home of their parents-in-law with salt. The custom is an expression of the proverbial generosity and hospitality of the Russians which in the past knew no limits even in the face of the enemy, as is reflected in sources such as *Domostroy* (see page 65). Even the enemy, once defeated, found shelter, bread, and salt in a Russian house, "Bread and salt conquer even the robbers," according to a Russian saying. In other words, being charitable and accommodating pays for itself. The word *khlebosol* is derived from the words *khleb*, bread, and *sol*, salt and means a "hospitable person."

It has something to do with the vastness of the country, the inhospitable climate, and the mentality of this sentimental, peace-loving, and hospitable people that travelers and foreigners are always invited into even the poorest of households and fed a hearty meal. The Russians lavishly serve whatever the kitchen and the cellar yield for they live intensively and make the most of the moment.

A decorated celebration bread is given to special guests, newly weds, or on official occasions to bring luck. The motifs vary from region to region but the little well in the center with the salt remains the same.

There were over a thousand small bakeries in Moscow at the beginning of the 1920s. Today the capital's residents are mostly catered for by 20 large concerns in which the baking of bread has undergone many changes. The aromatic *baton*, tin loaf, reaches the shop shelf without having been in contact with a human hand. Yet the taste and aroma remain unchanged—thanks to old, traditional recipes going back several centuries and which are characterized by the use of malt, kvass, honey, nuts, and herbs.

Today Russia, a nation of bread lovers, has more than 10,000 bakeries producing 25 million tons of baked goods annually using 700 recipes. According to recent statistics, every Russian consumes an average of more than 110 lb (50 kilograms) of bread annually. The first bread museum in St. Petersburg is also testimony to this love of bread, established in a former state bakery which was founded in the 17th century.

Kvass

Kvass is the tsar of thirst quenchers in Russia—refreshing, full of vitamins, caffeine-free, delicious, and easy on the digestion. It is indispensable in the kitchen as this low-alcohol, beer-like drink is used in the about 50 recipes. It forms the basis of borscht and cold soups or as a sauce for beef and venison. In Russia the preparation of kvass is typically a man's task. Traditionally, a liquid batter, the so-called mash, is made from rye flour or rye malt, water, sugar, and peppermint. Water and yeast are then added later to start the fermentation process. Today kvass is made at home using brewer's yeast.

There are around 150 different kvass recipes. In the north, ground iceland moss (Lat *Cetaria islandica*) and blackcurrant leaves are added to the kvass. In central Russia caraway and even horseradish make their way into the drink, where carrot kvass is also considered a delicacy. In the south the kvass contains apples, pears, rosehips, strawberries, and lemon juice. A favorite in Moscow is a bitter-sweet kvass made from cranberries to which only a few raisins are added in addition to the yeast and sugar.

Kvass is also available as a ready-made concentrate and in summer it is sold from large barrels on wheels. The long lines in front of the kvass van are testimony to the popularity of this ancient brew varying in color from honey-colored to dark brown and more than about 250,000 gallons (1 million liters) are drunk by the Muscovites in the summer. In the capital alone there are three kvass factories producing hundreds of hectoliters daily. The vast consumption of kvass is proof of its health benefits. Experts have found vitamins and amino acids as well as an array of minerals in kvass. This pleasant, tasty drink is an excellent thirst quencher, stimulates the circulation, and keeps the intestines healthy.

Khlebny kvas
Kvass

Generous 1 lb/500 g rye bread
2 tbsp/25 g yeast
Generous 1¼ cups/300 g white or brown sugar
Sprig of mint and black currant leaves as preferred
6 tbsp/50 g raisins

Slice the bread and bake brown in the oven. Place in a large pan and cover with 4¼ quarts/4 liters boiling water, cover and leave to soak for about 24 hours. Then add the yeast, sugar, and the mint or blackcurrant leaves according to taste, stir well and leave to ferment in a warm place for 10 to 12 hours. Strain everything through a fine strainer or a cheesecloth. Pour into bottles, add the raisins and seal well. Leave to chill and rest for about 4 days.

For the kvass, slices of rye bread are soaked in water before the yeast is added.

Sugar is then added. Either white or brown sugar is used depending on preference.

Everything is left to ferment for around 12 hours and the kvass is then strained through a strainer or a cheesecloth.

Filling up on hot summer days: kvass, the most popular refreshment in Russia, is sold by the liter on the streets from mobile tanks with a tap.

Limonny kvas
Lemon kvass

3 organic lemons
6–7 tbsp/200 g honey
¾ cup + 2 tbsp/200 g sugar
5 tsp/20 g yeast
6 tbsp/50 g raisins

Slice the lemon thinly and remove the pips. Cover with 4¼ quarts/4 liters boiling water, add the honey and sugar, and leave to cool to room temperature. Add the yeast and leave to ferment in a warm place for 24 hours. Strain and pour into bottles together with the raisins, seal well and leave the lemon kvass to rest for about 4 days.

Vishnyovy kvas
Cherry kvass

3¼ lb/1.5 kg cherries, stoned
5 tsp/20 g yeast
¾ cup + 2 tbsp/200 g sugar
6 tbsp/50 g raisins

Cook the cherries in 4¼ quarts/4 liters of water for about 1 hour and leave to cool to room temperature. Strain the juice, add the yeast and sugar, leave to ferment for about 24 hours. Pour into bottles together with the raisins, seal well and leave the kvass to rest for a further 3–4 days.

Yablochny kvas
Apple kvass

2¼ lb/1 kg apples, peeled, cored and thinly sliced
7 tbsp/100 g sugar
6–7 tbsp/200 g honey
1 cinnamon stick
5 tsp/20 g yeast
6 tbsp/50 g raisins

Bring the apples, sugar, honey, and cinnamon to a boil in 4¼ quarts/4 liters of water, leave to cool to room temperature. Add the yeast, cover and leave to ferment for 24 hours. Strain the liquid, pour into bottles adding a few raisins to each bottle, seal well and leave to stand for 3–4 days.

Beer

The Chuvash know how beer should be: "As blond as a young woman from the north, as light as the conscience of a diplomat, as lustrous as the Tsar's promises and as foamy as the talk of a drunkard." In Russia, *pivo*, beer, is one of the most popular alcoholic beverages. Through the import of Western beers and the cooperation between local and West European breweries the foamy beverage enjoys increasingly good quality. Some 150 light and dark beers are brewed in Russia at present, not only for local consumption but also for connoisseurs in Poland, Finland, and the Ukraine. During the Soviet era beer was a seasonal product brewed according to schedule and all of the state breweries produced the same inferior beer—without a head of foam, cloudy, and yellowy green in color. The Russians have now reverted to the old traditions of beer brewing which came to Russia with the German and Dutch artisans in the 16th century. Former state concerns such as *Baltika* in St. Petersburg or *Donskoye Pivo* in south Russian Rostov on the Don

river were privatized in the 1990s and are today among the biggest and best breweries in Eastern Europe. Around 2,000 million (70 million hectoliters) of beer are produced in Russia annually; according to statistics every resident of the country drinks 13 gallons (50 liters) annually.

St. Petersburg is considered to be the cradle and the capital of Russian beer. In 1795 Catherine II founded the oldest brewery in the country there which, following the October Revolution, was named *Stepan Razin* in honor of the rebel farmer. The beer was initially brewed according to English recipes and delivered to the Tsar's court. In 1848 Bavarian brewing methods were adopted and in 1862 Alexander II granted the brewery the status of royal brewery. At the end of the 19th century the brewery was the largest in St. Petersburg. Since its reprivatization in 1992 it has remained true to its tradition and is among the most successful beer producers in Russia. Moscow, too, has developed into a city of beer drinkers. Once the metropolis starts wilting under the dry heat of summer the beer van season has arrived with the vans supplying the refreshing drink from tanks. The brew from these vans, however, as with the street stalls, is often so

In Irkutsk it is high season for the beer bars when the mercury rises above 86 °F/30 °C in the summer. Siberia's beer drinkers are particularly fond of their local beer *Rosar* from the Omsker Brewery, which brews more than 65 million gallons (260 million liters) annually.

diluted that it hardly tastes like beer anymore. One of the most popular brands in the capital is *Klinskoye*, a luxury beer from a small town with astoundingly clean and clear water.

A specialist state food institute provides support for the breweries in bringing local beers brewed according to the old recipes onto the market. Yet most of the small local breweries supply less than 10 percent of overall consumption—too little to be profitable and competitive. Their equipment is also often obsolete.

In Russia *vobla*, stockfish, are eaten with beer, as are crayfish or shrimp. The beverage is also a popular thirst quencher in the *banya* (see page 84). The salting of beer is a Russian specialty. Every table in the *pivnushki*, beer bars, has a little barrel full of salt that is sprinkled on the thick glass rims of the 2-cup size (500 ml) beer mugs.

Hops from Chuvashia

Hops give beer its bitter taste. The best are from the Chuvash Republic.

Chuvashia lies on the right bank of the Volga river at the confluence of the Sura and Svijaga rivers, around 470 miles (750 km) east of Moscow (see map on page 4). The country is one of the most stable republics in Russia. Its coat of arms is framed by the plant for which this small region is famed: hops. The century-old specialization in this perennial, high-altitude climber which needs little space is attributable to the limited cultivable land in the country. The climate and growth conditions are also ideal for hops that prefer limey and loamy humus soils.

Cheboksary, capital of the republic is the headquarters of the Association of Hop Growers of Russia. Overall there are more than 70 hop farms in Chuvashia. This region contributes about 70 percent to overall Russian production. 3,500 metric tonnes of dried hops are produced here annually and which are highly valued not only in Russia but also in the neighboring countries. Although the natural conditions for Chuvashian beer production are good, foreign breweries have not yet invested in modern production units here because the transportation to the consumer centers would be too expensive due to the poor infrastructure.

On celebration days the Chuvash proudly wear their richly embroidered traditional costumes comprising a top decorated with token coins, boots, belt, and wide sleeves. Tablecloths and runners, napkins, and towels all made of hand-embroidered linen are to be found in all of the bars and restaurants. Of course the embroidered motifs often portray stylized hop tendrils.

A typical and popular hangover breakfast after a long night is dried fish and beer.

In the more up market Russian beer bars boiled crayfish are a popular accompaniment to freshly poured beer.

A happy apple seller—in winter fresh fruit provides vitamins and top prices!

Facing page: When the rivers and lakes are frozen over the anglers spend their time ice fishing.

The Russian winter

The Russians are proud of their iron will and their hardy constitution which is necessary in a country where the temperatures at the earth's cold pole can sink to below minus 94 °F (-70 °C) and the grim winter can last for up to nine months. That is when *Ded moroz*, Father Frost, takes over with snow and ice. He also determines the menu while energy requirements increase despite the thick furs. During the cold months a samovar simmers in every household and preserves are the order of the day. Meals are made from what the kitchen and the larder provide: especially hearty soups made from sauerkraut, dried or marinated mushrooms, and stockfish, together with pirogi and pelmeni. A traditionally popular hot drink on cold winter days is *sbiten*. This drink made from honey and spices used to be offered for sale by street sellers who carried it in big barrels wrapped up against the cold on their backs.

The Russians make the most of winter's positive aspects wherever they can. In Moscow and St. Petersburg people flock out of the city in special trains to indulge in their cold weather pastimes. Some have cross country skis over their shoulders, others their fishing boxes and ice drills. Ice fishing is a national pastime in Russia. For hours at a time the fishermen, wrapped up in thick fur coats, sit motionless on their boxes which contain their supplies, vodka, and their fishing equipment. Untiringly they dangle a thin fishing line through a hole in the ice, until they finally have a fish floundering on the ice. Winter fish is a spe-

cialty in Russia: the catch is cut up, dipped in water and rolled in snow until it is frozen white. When it is prepared later it is just as delicious as fresh fish.

In the parks of the larger towns there is hardly a pond which is safe from the "walruses," as the devotees of ice swimming are known, who warm themselves up in thick sports clothes playing volley ball only to then jump into the bitterly cold water.

The white months are also fun for the children who play outside wrapped up warmly. While the little ones are tobogganing down snowy slopes the older children are chasing the puck across frozen fields playing hockey or throwing snowballs at each other. And if they have been good they get an ice cream, despite the below zero temperatures. In some parks one can go ice skating to waltz music and sometimes you can meet a troika while walking through the forest in winter. Ice skating with the sound of the harness bells from the three horses is a longstanding tradition which is kept alive in the country's tourist centers. Here the old winter festivals are also celebrated with folklore programs, jesters, and public entertainment. Particularly popular is the "tree climbing" where young boys try to climb up a smooth, icy tree trunk to reach a sausage or piece of ham on a wheel at the top.

The highlight of the Russian winter is *Novyi god*, the New Year celebration with the dance under the fir tree. On this occasion Father Frost and *Snegurochka*, Snow Maiden, his fairy-like assistant, bring the children presents and sweets. For the adults the most important part of *Novyi god* is the sparkling wine which, during the Soviet era, was hoarded for months in advance. Even in hard times, wherever possible the table should be laden with rich *zakuski* and main courses, even though it is fasting time for the very devout. In general it is believed that the New Year will resemble the celebration with which it is welcomed.

Banya

Not only is strong schnapps good for warming up in the winter, even more important is the Russian *banya*, "the peoples' doctor" as it is called in jest. In addition to a small front room for storing clothing, the small bathroom in country houses also includes a sauna with an oven which can be heated from outside. The visit to the *banya* is a Russian ritual. One does not just laze on a wooden bench, adding water or kvass to the hot stones with a wooden ladle from time to time. Instead one whips oneself and one's companion with birch branches to stimulate the circulation. *Banya* have been public establishments in the towns since the 11th century, a steamy place for socializing and refreshment. One goes to the sauna with good friends and business partners and Moscow's upmarket *banyas* have even seen the making of ministers. During and after the sauna there is plenty of relaxation as well as plenty to eat and

The sauna makes you hungry and thirsty. A meal is set up in the front room of a country *banya*.

drink in order to replace the lost salt and fluids. At the top of the list of classic *banya* foods are beer and stockfish whereas more well-heeled Russians make do with champagne and caviar. In the countryside one also jumps from the sauna directly into a lake, river, or simply into the ice cold snow.

Moskovsky sbiten
Moscow sbiten

5–6 tbsp/150–200 g honey
1 bay leaf
2–3 cloves
1 tsp ground cinnamon
1 tsp ground cardamom
1 pinch ground nutmeg
1 tbsp dried hop leaves

Bring ingredients to a boil with 4 cups/1 liter water,
leave to simmer for 30 minutes, strain and serve hot.

Like the Pomors, the Korjak in Kamchatka dry salmon and other fish as provisions for the winter.

The salmon harvest

The salmon family can be divided into two groups: salmon from the Atlantic and from the Pacific. The oceans of the Far East are home to the chum salmon, humpbacked salmon, silver salmon, and the quinnat salmon. The noble European salmon, known as *syomga* in the Russian north, is found in the Baltic Sea, White Sea, and Barents Sea. The *syomga* is a large predatory fish feeding primarily on small herring and which, when fully grown, can be up to 5 feet (1.5 m) long and up to 101 lb (46 kg) in weight.

In the Karelian oceans as well as in the Ladoga and Onega Lakes and their tributaries there are also salmon types which are related to the *syomga* but which mostly weigh only 6 to 11 lb (3–5 kg). At the start of spring through to autumn the salmon migrate out of the oceans to spawn in the rivers where hordes of amateur fishermen are waiting for them, despite the fact that there are strict licensing requirements for salmon fishing and the licenses are very expensive. On the Kamchatka peninsula salmon are still caught today using traps which are set in the rivers. The fresh fish are dried on wooden racks or else are smoked.

Here as with the Pomors on the White Sea, the fish harvest has been a communal task for the whole family for centuries.

The Pomors are descendants of Russians from Central Russia who mixed with the Nenz and Karelian peoples settled along the White Sea coast and who, up until the 18th century, constituted a north Russian ethnic group with a special dialect. Their stubborn character is attributable to the very hard living and working conditions on these northern oceans. In the past, when a single clan lacked a means of subsistence, several Pomor families would join forces and form together a fishing community, a commune. The strictest of rules applied to the distribution of the catch and to the reciprocal help. Anybody who infringed these rules would be outlawed along the entire coastline. During the Soviet era the traditional Pomor communes more or less transformed themselves into collective fishing farms while in

Salmon as a health food

To a much greater extent than freshwater fish sea fish contain valuable elements such as iodine, minerals, and protein, and especially zinc, selenium, vitamin D, and omega-3 fatty acids, which the human body is not able to produce for itself. These acids are not only very important for the body's own defenses but they also reduce the cholesterol and fat levels in the blood, strengthen the heart, and protect it against disease. They are also considered to be an ideal supplement in the treatment of inflammatory conditions such as chronic digestive diseases, psoriasis, or neurodermatitis. They have also shown positive effects in the treatment of rheumatism and arthritis.

In order to ensure sufficient intake of omega-3 fatty acids it is recommended that salmon or other sea fish be eaten at least three times a week in portions of up to 8 oz (250 g). Omega-3 fatty acids are particularly highly concentrated in salmon oil, a form of cod liver oil from this family of fish. Coming from the very cold and oxygen-rich polar seas, salmon is particularly well suited to the production of omega-3 fatty acids.

Large illustration left: Fishing for salmon is hard work. In the past members of a clan got together to fish, later it was done as a collective. Today salmon fishing is often handled by interregional companies.

Above right: A fisherman in Kamchatka proudly displays a quinnat salmon. This is the largest of the Pacific salmon and weighs an average of 11 to 22 lb (5–10 kg). The flesh is very low in fat and full of flavor.

Center right: On the Kamchatka peninsula and in other parts of Russia salmon is also bred in fish farms. The roe is removed from a fully grown female quinnat salmon in order to breed the young fish.

Below right: Russian red salmon (also known as blue-back salmon) is a relatively small pacific salmon that is also popular internationally. The salmon are filleted and packed for export in a Kamchatka fish factory.

the post-Soviet era they are frequently joint stock companies.

The north has its own rules for the preparation of salmon. The noble salmon is never baked, but always grilled over the fire. It is also boiled, salted, pickled, or smoked. When preparing *balyk* various spices and sugar are rubbed into the salmon before it is smoked. In the past the residents of the north pickled salmon heads in holes in the ground which were layered with twigs and soil.

Partaking of this strong smelling specialty is, however, something of an acquired taste and requires a robust stomach. A particular delicacy is the red caviar from salmon that ought not to be missing at any Russian celebration. It is processed on site directly after the catch and then shipped to all regions of the country.

Herring rollmops as *zakuski*

Herring

A small fishing boat chugs bravely across the stormy Baltic Sea. Ivan Semzov is at the helm of the *Chayka*, "The Seagull," and rolls himself a cigarette with one hand. His weathered face shows the signs of hard work at sea. The fisherman looks anxiously at the barometer which is dropping all the time. The cutter is lying low in the water, full to the brim with fat Atlantic herrings. However, there are still 3 or 4 hours to go before reaching his fishing cooperative's small harbor. The "Seagull" took on fuel in Sweden, as it is expensive in Russia, and paid for it with fish. On the way home he then found another herring shoal.

For centuries the *selyodk* has been the most impor-

tant fish in Russian cuisine next to cod. Russian fishermen catch about 175, 000 tons every year in the Pacific Ocean, Atlantic, Baltic Sea, Black Sea, and Caspian Sea. Wars have been fought over it, such as that of the Russians against the Livonians in the 15th century, and it has kept many people from starvation after failed harvests. In the Middle Ages fish was the most important foodstuff in Russia next to bread; salted and marinated herring was considered the food of the poor people. In about 1700 the Baltic Sea fishermen caught herring with long lines, called festoons. Yard-long lines with a baited hook were attached to these *yarusy* at regular intervals. In 1721 Peter the Great decreed that merchants and fishermen should also be allowed to fish for herring with nets, something which had previously been the privilege of his favorite, Prince Menschikov. Now, however, the army and the navy needed to be fed economically. As a result herring became one of the most widespread foodstuffs in the Russian empire in the 18th century. In winter it was delivered frozen by sled to Moscow and as far as Astrakan on the Caspian Sea.

The herrings from the Solovezki monastery on the White Sea coast were famous well beyond the borders of Russia. The fish was placed whole in

barrels immediately after being caught and sprinkled with coarse salt, they were then seasoned with pepper and bay leaves.

Even today herring has a special place especially among Russian appetizers. It is truly delicious with sour cream, with vegetables, nuts, as rollmops, with eggs, in marinades, and with raw onion. Fresh herrings are baked and served with a variety of sauces. Particular delicacies include the herring pie *forshmak*, herring fritters with vegetables, herring in beer batter, *sapekanka*, a herring bake with ground beef and potatoes, and broiled herring. Preserved salted herring is served with horseradish, vinegar, cabbage, radish, or beetroot salad. In Russian cuisine herring dishes play a major role at family celebrations such as christenings, weddings, and funerals. Fasting times are also herring time. All in all, Ivan Semzov does not need to worry about being able to sell his catch.

Fresh herring arrive daily at the Russian markets. The majority of them are preserved in salt for keeping.

Sea fish

Herring *(selyodka)*, the most popular eating fish in Russia with very flavorsome flesh and numerous ways of preparation, particularly salted for *zakuski*.

While large-scale fishing takes place on the high seas, the fishermen on the coast lay smaller nets that are more than capable of providing a rich bounty.

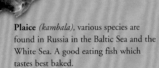

Plaice *(kambala)*, various species are found in Russia in the Baltic Sea and the White Sea. A good eating fish which tastes best baked.

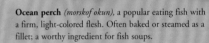

Ocean perch *(morskof okun)*, a popular eating fish with a firm, light-colored flesh. Often baked or steamed as a fillet; a worthy ingredient for fish soups.

Mackerel *(skumbriya)*, a fish with several subspecies and with flavorsome flesh; is usually smoked or preserved.

Sprats *(sprotes)*, small but with a delicate flesh; usually preserved or smoked, also tastes good fresh but is baked whole.

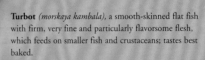

Turbot *(morskaya kambala)*, a smooth-skinned flat fish with firm, very fine and particularly flavorsome flesh, which feeds on smaller fish and crustaceans; tastes best baked.

Cod *(treska)*, a very fine tasting and valued fish; it is baked, steamed or used for fish soups and provides a liver oil full of vitamins.

Angling

Anyone who stands at the railroad station of any large Russian town at the weekend will get an impression of how large the country's army of hobby anglers is. In summer there are long fishing rods sticking out of the rucksack of every third passenger. In winter shoulders are laden with the fishing boxes. Even in Moscow you can see people with fishing rods on the banks of the Moskva river in the summer. It is the cat back home who looks forward to the fish caught in the city.

For millions of Russians angling is a passion which overshadows even the love of football and the widespread enthusiasm for which is comparable only to that for gathering mushrooms. According to the Russian Amateur Angling Society there are some 20 million anglers in the country. Every medium-sized Russian department store has an angling department and a basic knowledge of the various kinds of fishing rods,

hooks, and bait is almost part of general knowledge from childhood on. Despite environmental pollution in some areas, Russia's lakes and rivers today still provide the amateur angler with rich fishing grounds and the angling regulations are extremely liberal in comparison with Western Europe. Both converts to the pastime and psychologists maintain that there is nothing better than fishing for combating stress. Not to mention the culinary benefits, for freshwater fish is hard to come by in Russian shops.

Some enjoy the solitude when fishing, others prefer to fish in small groups. Angling is not just about pulling a fish out of the water every now and again; it involves a complicated social ritual, the journey together to the fishing spot and the discussions about legendary fishing trips of the past and those of the future. And of course such joint outings also mean the joint preparation of the *ukha*, the fish bouillon (see page 92 ff).

Shining scales, clear eyes, firm flesh, red skin behind the gills, and the smell of algae and of the ocean are the signs of a fresh fish.

Handling fish

The classic method for telling whether a fish is really fresh is to take a look behind the gills: with deep-water fish this skin must be red, for fish from shallower waters it must be pink. Brown or gray coloring are signs of the fish having been kept for a long time. The scales of fresh fish are shiny, the eyes are still clear, firm and sparkling—not cloudy and sunken. Furthermore, the fish must be nice and firm; press the fish with your finger and the depression disappears, that is the sign of a particularly fresh fish.

A trusted Russian method for testing fish is as follows: squeeze the fish tail in your hand for about 30 seconds and then smell your hand. The smell should not be unpleasant or repellant. Fresh fish from lakes and rivers smell of algae and mud, fresh sea fish smell of salt.

To keep fish fresh while out fishing they need to be kept alive for as long as possible by placing them in a net in a deep, shady part of the river. Freshly killed fish are kept in the shade, wrapped and transported in nettles, blackcurrant leaves, or other herbs. You can also bury the fish in damp sand or else wrap it in a damp cloth after sprinkling the gills lightly with salt.

To keep the fish fresh for several days it is recommended that you remove the head, gills, and innards, rub it inside and out with salt or ascorbic acid and then to place it in ice. Large fish also receive two slits along the backbone in which salt or ascorbic acid are also sprinkled. If you want to keep the fish for a longer period then it is better to freeze it.

Angling techniques

A wide range of lures are used for spinning, the majority of them shiny metal disks and small dead bait fish. In the rivers around St. Petersburg mainly reflective lead weights are still used with great success for catching salmon. This is fishing gear that cannot be bought anywhere—the angler makes his own. They comprise a lead weight attached to the metal disk which is dragged along the bottom of the river. A small dead fish is impaled on the hook of the double fishing line just above the weight as bait.

Wobbler fishing is becoming more and more popular along the rivers to the north. A wobbler is a small synthetic fish made of a lightweight material. Unlike the metal disks and lead balls, the wobbler moves like a fish underwater. There are innumerable varieties of wobblers in a wide range of shapes, sizes, colors, and "wobble frequencies." The wobbling movement of the baitfish is caused by the movement of the water and attracts larger fish looking for prey. This fishing gear is expensive, however, and in Russia wobbler fishing is still considered to be particularly elitist.

Fly fishing requires great skill. One also needs a special flexible rod fitted with tapered fishing line and which is very expensive. The fishing rod is fitted with an artificial fly made to imitate an insect sitting on the water. This fly is cast out as far as possible into the water with a striking, whipping movement. The angler then starts to slowly reel the lure in toward him, cleverly moving the fly about, sometimes just under the water's surface, sometimes just above, in order to catch a fish's attention.

Once the fish has taken the bait, it is solely up to the skill of the angler to land his catch—or not.

Background: Angling is a popular sport and in the areas around towns like Rostov on the Don, one seldom fishes alone.

The Moscow fishing equipment shops sell fishing lures in a variety of shapes and materials.

Wobblers are lures that swim in the water and appear as easy prey to predatory fish.

Ukha

The preparation of *ukha* is an art which has developed over the centuries. It is a dish comprising fish, fresh herbs, and spices as well as an absolute minimum of vegetables, mostly just carrots, leeks, and onions. It is important to obtain a transparent bouillon with a gluey consistency.

Ukha contains at least two and a maximum of four types of fish. The classic white *ukha* is prepared from pike, perch, kaulbarsch (a species of perch), and whitefish. Black *ukha* contains different types of carp as well as ocean perch. If salmon, sturgeon, or other noble fish are used, together with high quality saffron, then this is known as red or amber *ukha*.

The "fourfold" *ukha* is considered a culinary masterpiece and here it is not just a case of the four different types of fish but also of the protracted preparation with the cooking of the soup being repeated four times. The general rule is that the smallest types of fish are cooked first and the largest and best quality last. So, for example, one would cook the kaulbarsch first, then the ocean perch and the sturgeon last. The most exquisite and the oldest variation of the fourfold *ukha* is made with chicken bouillon and champagne. It originates from the 18th century and here the heated champagne replaces the fourth bouillon. There are also other varieties using heated vodka.

For the simple but elegant fish soup *ukha* you really need fresh fish and some vegetables and spices.

The *ukha* tastes best when the fish is absolutely fresh. Russian anglers usually observe the following tried and tested rule: if the fish is still alive when you start preparing the soup then you only need onions and spices for a tasty *ukha*. If, on the other hand, the fish is already dead, then the flavor needs to be rounded off with vegetables. The *ukha* is only ever cooked over a small fire in open enamel or ceramic dishes which give it a more intense flavor. The fishermen also resort to an old method for making the *ukha* transparent: a glowing log from the fire is dipped into the bouillon

The crowning glory of any fishing trip: the whole family prepares an *ukha* over the open fire.

and all of the cloudy particles then adhere to it. The preferred accompaniment to *ukha* is rye bread or else pirogi filled with fish, rice, or egg. Vodka is also served around the campfire.

Troynaya ili chetvernaya ukha
Threefold or fourfold ukha
(Serves 6)

3¹/₄ lb/1.5 kg fish (3 or 4 different types, e.g. cod, ocean perch, pike, perch, kaulbarsch, tench, carp, burbot), gutted and cleaned but not scaled
Generous 1 lb/500 g omul (see page 104) or sturgeon, gutted and cleaned (keep the head and scraps)
2 onions, chopped
2 potatoes, diced
1 carrot, sliced thinly
1 parsley root, finely chopped
1 celery stalk, finely chopped
2 bay leaves
Salt and 5–6 peppercorns
¹/₂ bunch each parsley and dill
2 tbsp/30 g butter

Place about 1 lb/500 g of the fish and the scraps from the omul or sturgeon in 3 quarts/3 liters of boiling water and boil until they are falling apart. Strain the stock, discard the fish and then repeat this process with the rest of the fish (excluding the omul or sturgeon) another two or three times. Add the vegetables and spices to the recooked fish stock, simmer for about 20 minutes, add the omul or sturgeon, bring to a boil and simmer for a further 15 minutes. Remove the soup from the heat and leave to infuse for another 5 minutes. Add the butter and herbs before serving. For a very sophisticated variation: work 1 oz/25 g of red or black caviar to a paste with a little cold water, add about ³/₄ cup/200 ml of the hot fish stock, stir and add to the soup 15 minutes before the end of the cooking time.

The omul or sturgeon is gutted and cut into portions. These are later eaten with the soup, the other fish are simply for flavor.

A mixed fish stock is prepared and is cooked two or three times. The stock is then strained and used to cook the vegetables and the omul or sturgeon.

The *ukha* should be left to infuse for a short while before serving. Fresh herbs and butter are then added before enjoying this fine fish soup.

From the rivers and oceans

Onions and potatoes are grated over the fish pieces for Herring in a Fur Coat.

These are followed by the carrots alternately with a layer of smooth cream mayonnaise sauce.

Freshly grated beetroot gives this fish and vegetable dish an interesting color.

To serve, the dish is garnished with a top layer of chopped eggs and a few pieces of herring.

Selyodka pod shuboy
Herring in a fur coat

10 tbsp/150 g sour cream
10 tbsp/150 g mayonnaise
Freshly ground black pepper
Generous 1 lb/500 g salted herring fillets, diced
1 large onion, finely sliced
3 medium-sized potatoes, boiled and finely grated
3 medium-sized carrots, boiled and finely grated
3 medium-sized beetroot, boiled and finely grated
2 hardcooked eggs, finely chopped

Stir the sour cream, mayonnaise, and black pepper together. Layer the fish and vegetable ingredients in a deep dish with a few spoonfuls of the cream and mayonnaise sauce between each layer. It is recommended that you keep to the following order: herring (retain a few pieces for garnishing), onion, potato, carrot, beetroot. Garnish with chopped egg and herring pieces.

Lososina tushonaya s sousom iz petrushki
Steamed salmon with parsley sauce
(Not illustrated)

1 salmon weighing about 3¼ lb/1.5 kg, gutted and cleaned
7 tbsp/100 g butter
1 cup/250 ml dry white wine
½ cup/125 ml pickled gherkin brine
1 bunch parsley
1 bay leaf

For the sauce:
1 bunch parsley
1 shallot, finely chopped
7 tbsp/100 ml dry white wine
¾ cup/200 ml fish stock
⅔ cup/150 g butter, cut into pieces
Salt and pepper

Cut the salmon into portion-sized pieces. Melt the butter, add the white wine, pickled gherkin brine, parsley, and bay leaf, bring to a boil, add the salmon pieces, cover and steam over low heat. Strain the stock and set aside. Place the fish on a plate and keep warm.
For the sauce, blanch the parsley and chop finely. Steam the shallot in the white wine until the liquid has almost all evaporated, add the fish stock and boil until reduced by about a half. Remove from the heat, add the butter piece by piece, season with salt and pepper and add the parsley shortly before serving.
Pour the sauce over the salmon pieces and serve with boiled potatoes.

Treska zapechonnaya v moloke
Cod in milk
(Not illustrated)

2 medium-sized onions, sliced
1¾ lb/750 g cod fillet
Salt and pepper
1¼ cups/300 ml hot milk
2 tbsp/30 g butter

For the sauce:
1¼ cups/300 ml milk
½ cup/75 g all-purpose flour
1 tbsp sugar
Salt
1 egg yolk

Blanch the onions briefly in a little water. Cut the fish fillets into portions and place in a saucepan layering them alternately with the onion, season with salt and pepper. Pour over the hot milk, add the butter and steam for 20–25 minutes.
In the meantime, whisk the flour for the sauce with the milk, slowly bring to a boil while stirring continuously and allow to simmer for 10 to 15 minutes, stirring all the time. Add the sugar and salt, then add the beaten egg yolk. Pour the milk sauce over the steamed fish and bring everything to a boil briefly.
Serve with mashed or boiled potatoes and green beans.

Som s beloy fasolyu
Catfish with white beans
(Not illustrated)

1 cup/200 g dried white beans
Salt
1¾ lb/750 g catfish fillets
4 onions, sliced
1 small parsley root
1 carrot
3 sprigs parsley
3 garlic cloves
1 tbs/15 g butter
2 tbsp oil
Pepper
8 slices white crusty bread, toasted

Leave the beans to soak overnight and then cook in boiling salted water until soft, then drain. Cook the fish with 1 onion, the vegetables, and parsley in lightly salted water until just becoming soft and then remove from the stock. Leave to cool and cut into bite-sized pieces. Sauté the rest of the onion and garlic in the butter and oil. Mash 3 tablespoons of the cooked beans and mix into the onions. Place the fish and the remaining beans in a saucepan. Season with salt and pepper and steam over medium heat for 15 minutes. Serve with toasted bread.

Kharius s pivnym sousom
Grayling with beer sauce

1¾ lb/750 g grayling fillets or other fish
Salt and pepper
Juice of 1–2 lemons
4 tbsp/30 g all-purpose flour
4 tbsp oil
4 large onions
3 tbsp/45 g butter
3 cups/750 ml light beer
½–1 tsp sugar
Scallion tops to garnish

Season the fish fillets with salt and pepper, drizzle with lemon juice and leave to marinate for 15 minutes. Coat the fillets in 3 tablespoons of the flour and fry in the oil until golden brown on both sides.

In the meantime prepare the sauce: slice the onions into half rings and sauté in butter until transparent (do not allow them to become brown.) Add the beer and simmer over low heat until the liquid has reduced by about a third. Blend the remaining flour in a little cold water, stir into the sauce and thicken over low heat. Season with salt, pepper, and sugar. Place the fish in the sauce and reheat gently. Serve garnished with shredded scallion tops. Best served with boiled potatoes.

Ryba s kartoshkoy, gribami i yaytsami
Fish with potatoes, mushrooms, and eggs

1¼ lb/600 g fish fillets (e.g. pike, catfish, perch, or sea fish such as cod, bass)
Salt and pepper
Juice of 1–2 lemons
1¾ lb/750 g potatoes
Generous 1 lb/500 g mushrooms (preferably wild)
Oil
4 tbsp/30 g all-purpose flour
4 eggs
½ bunch each parsley, dill, scallions, chopped

Cut the fish diagonally into slices, season with salt and pepper and drizzle with the lemon juice. Leave to stand for about ½ hour. Boil the potatoes in salted water until just soft, drain and slice. Clean the mushrooms, blanch in lightly salted water, leave to drain, and then chop finely. Sauté in 2 tablespoons oil. Coat the fish fillets in flour and fry in plenty of oil until golden brown on all sides. Place the fried fish fillets in a greased baking dish, surround them with potato slices and sprinkle over the mushrooms. Beat the eggs, season with salt and pepper and pour over the fish and vegetable mixture. Bake in a preheated oven at 400° F/200 °C until the egg is firm.
Serve sprinkled with the herbs.

Multiethnic cuisine on the Volga

Even today women belonging to the different population groups along the Volga River like to dress up in their traditional costumes on celebratory occasions.

The Volga region was and is a diverse catchment basin for peoples and cultures. Generally considered as a territory comprising the Russian regions of Astrakan, Volgograd, Saratov, Samara, Simbirsk, and Nizhniy Novgorod, as well as the national republics of Mari, Chuvash, Tatar, and Kalmykia, historically and ethnically there are another two peoples and regions that belong to this area, but whose borders no longer extend directly to the Volga: the republics of Mordova

and Udmurtia. The present-day borders of all of these national territories were drawn up around the conference table during the Soviet era and are only an approximate reflection of the actual settlement patterns. The colorful mixture of peoples along "Russia's river of destiny" which, with a length of 2,460 miles (3,960 km), is the longest river in Europe, has taken shape over the course of centuries. The original Finno-Ugric tribes intermingled with the nomadic Turkic tribes and established the highly developed state of Volga Bulgaria in the 10th century. In the 16th century Russia annexed the Volga area with its very fertile black soils. The Volga peoples can be divided into the Turkic language groups—the Tatars, Bachkiri, and the Chuvash (the latter are of the Russian Orthodox faith unlike the first two groups which are Muslim), the members of the Finno-Ugric language group, the Orthodox Christian Mordovians, Mari, and Udmurtians and the Mongolian language group comprising the Buddhist Kalmykians. In each of the republics Russians make up about one third to almost a half of all residents. The close cohabitation of the various population groups has brought about a merger of their culinary specialties and customs which are

also influenced by the natural surroundings of the Volga region. All of the peoples in this region, with the exception of the Kalmykians who arrived from Mongolia in the 17th century (see page 100 ff), are agriculturalists and also engage in hunting and fishing in the forests and steppes. Staple foods comprise milk and meat, grains, freshwater fish, wild birds, and a lot of honey. Beekeeping has a long and important tradition among the peoples of the forested steppe regions. The forests also provide them with berries which are included in many of their traditional dishes.

All of the Volga peoples have a penchant for sour milk products. Every nationality has its own recipe for a refreshing drink made from sour milk either thinned with water or fermented. Both the Finno-Ugric and the Turkic peoples are fond of mutton. The nomadic Turkic peoples introduced horsemeat dishes such as *kasylyk* (see page 98) to the Volga region.

Of the Finno-Ugric peoples along the Volga the Mari and the Udmurtians in particular maintained their original, pagan religions that even today still coexist with Christianity which was adopted in the 18th century. This twin faith characterized by shamanistic and animalistic beliefs results in special customs and taboos when it

In the agricultural regions along the Volga river several generations often still live and work together.

comes to food. Accordingly, the Mari hunters and gatherers never kill or eat geese, swans, herons, or doves, but traditionally they do eat squirrels, owls, hedgehogs, otters, and even vipers.

Modern everyday food among the Volga people is less exotic, however. As is the case all over Russia, a variety of meat and dough combinations are popular, such as pirogi and *pelmeni*, while porridges and soups are often made. The Finno-Ugric culinary heritage includes a clear, dumpling soup derived from White Russian and before that German influences and which has been changed only slightly. The name *sup s klyutskami* appears to derive from the German *Suppe mit Kloesschen*, soup with dumplings. Among the Chuvash it is called *samach* or *salmach*.

For a sophisticated fish stew of Chuvash origin fish fillets are cut into pieces, coated in seasoned flour and then fried in hot oil until golden brown.

Sup s klyutskami
Clear dumpling soup
(Not illustrated)

2 quarts/2 liters meat or vegetable stock
2 tbsp/30 g butter
⅔ cup/100 g wheat flour or semolina
1–2 eggs
Salt

For the dumplings bring 1 cup/250 ml stock to a boil. Quickly whisk in the flour or semolina using a hand whisk and allow to simmer for 1–2 minutes for flour dumplings and 5–6 minutes for semolina dumplings, stirring all the time. Allow to cool slightly and then mix the beaten eggs in well and season the dumpling batter with salt.

Bring the rest of the stock to a boil. Use two teaspoons to form dumplings from the batter and allow them to swell in the slightly simmering stock for about 5 minutes.

Variation: For special occasions you can enhance the soup with meat and/or vegetables according to preference.

Muss medovy
Honey foam
(Tatar, Chuvash, Bachkiri; not illustrated)

10 egg yolks
6 tbsp/200 g honey
2 cups/500 g whipping cream

Beat the egg yolks, pour into a heavy-bottomed saucepan placed over low heat and gradually fold in the honey, stirring continuously. Simmer over low heat until the mixture thickens. Allow to cool. Beat the cream to soft peaks and carefully fold in. Serve well chilled in individual dishes.

Ryba s morkovyu
Fish stew with carrots
(Chuvash)

1¾ lb/800 g fish fillets, (cod, haddock ...)
About ⅔ cup/100 g all-purpose flour or ½ flour/
½ breadcrumbs
Salt and black pepper
½ cup/125 ml sunflower oil
4 large onions, sliced into half rings
Generous 1 lb/500 g carrots
10 tbsp/150 g sour cream
6 tbsp/100 g mayonnaise
About ½ cup/125 ml fish stock
2–3 bay leaves

Slice the fish fillets into pieces about 2 x 2 inches/5 x 5 cm. Season the flour with salt and pepper. Coat the fish pieces with the flour and fry in hot oil until golden brown and then remove to drain on paper towels. Sauté the onion slices in the same oil, add the grated carrot and fry together briefly. Combine the sour cream and mayonnaise. Layer the fish and carrot mixture in a flameproof casserole, adding some of the cream and mayonnaise mixture to each fish layer. Stir any remaining seasoned flour into the fish stock and add together with the bay leaves, bring to a boil and cook over low heat for about 20 minutes. Serve either hot or cold.

Onion and grated carrot are sautéed in the same oil and the vegetables are then layered with the fish in a saucepan.

Small quantities of a cream and mayonnaise sauce are added between the layers to make a rich and flavorsome dish.

Finally the rest of the flour is mixed with the fish stock and poured into the casserole. Bay leaves are added and the fish stew is ready for a final cooking.

The life of the Tatars

The traditional religion in Tatarstan is Sunni Islam, adopted by the ancestors of the Russian Tatars, the Volga Bulgars, in the 10th century. After 70 years of communist suppression in Tatarstan, Islam is experiencing a true rebirth at the start of the 21st century, which has repercussions in all areas of life. Thus the standard Islamic bans on alcohol and pork apply to Tatar cuisine. Islamic festivals are official holidays.

The Volga Tatars were always a settled people, and the use of horsemeat in their cuisine can be traced back to the influence of the Golden Horde nomads, some of which were also the ancestors of the Volga Tatars. Products from agriculture and cattle breeding form the basis of Tatar cuisine, and one delicacy is *kasylyk*, a sausage made from dried horsemeat.

The most popular meat is mutton, which is also used in the Tataric *plov* (see page 314). Rice is cooked with mutton and beef, carrots, onions, and raisins. Poultry such as chicken, geese, and duck are also frequently served. Particularly typical are soups based on meat broth and numerous variants of meat in pastry. The best known is *zur balish*, a large meat pudding in a pastry case. *Gubadiya* is a round pastry made from yeast dough, or a milk puff pastry without yeast, with a multilayered filling made from dried curd cheese, cooked rice, chopped egg, soaked raisins or plums, ground beef, and puréed onions.

Although the Tatars always used food from the forest such as honey and berries as a basis for their cuisine, the mushrooms that are so loved by the Russians are not traditionally part of their menu. Typical are milk products such as curd cheese and soft cheeses based on scalded sour milk *(katyk)*. Diluted with water, *katyk* becomes the tasty thirst-quencher *ayran*.

Tea plays a significant role in Tatar culture. Frequently, a sumptuous tea-table covered with sweet dishes will replace breakfast or supper. The tea is hot and strong, often drunk with milk or cream, and virtually every meal is concluded with a cup of tea. A wealth of honey pastries are served alongside. A culinary calling card from Tatarstan is *chek-chek*, pieces of dough fried in butter and drenched in honey, and strewn with rose petals for celebratory events such as weddings. Many drinks also contain honey, some in association with lemon or herbs. Much loved is a weak alcoholic drink known as "sour honey."

Eating with the family and with friends is still a cornerstone of Tatar culture. Indeed, at their most important festival, the *Sabantuy*, which translates roughly as "the festival to honor the summer sowing," the Tatars do not just serve up enormous amounts of food. At *Sabantuy*, the Tatar "Olympic Games" also take place, and the men compete in wrestling, running races, horseback races, tug-of-war, and pole climbing. The victor wins the honorary title of the strongest fighter, the *batyr*, and thus achieves national fame.

The sugar festival

The ninth month of the lunar calendar, Ramadan, is the time of the great fast for all Muslim believers. Food may only be eaten after sunset. Only water is allowed during the day. Each evening before sunset, the faithful are called to prayer in the mosques, where the mullah offers dates and raisins at the end of the ceremony, as permission to eat at night. At the end of the fast is the famous festival of *urasu bayram*, which is also called the sugar festival. On each of the three days of the festival, numerous traditional Tataric and oriental sweets are the main items served. These include *chek-chek, rachat lukum*, small cubes of thickened fruit-juice tossed in icing sugar, originating from the Iranian-Turkish region, and *chalva*, many different sorts of sweet pastries and delicious honey.

Zur balish
Tataric meat pie

For the pastry:
²⁄₃ cup/150 g butter or margarine
1 egg, beaten
10 tbsp/150 g kefir
3½ tbsp/50 ml oil
2 tbsp mayonnaise
2 tbsp sour cream
Dash of vinegar
½ tsp salt
About 2²⁄₃ cups/400 g whole wheat flour

For the filling:
1 lb 2 oz/500 g mutton with fat, chopped small
2 potatoes, cut into small dice
3–4 onions, chopped
1 bay leaf, finely shredded
Salt and pepper

To make the dough, beat the butter or margarine until fluffy. Mix in the beaten egg, kefir, oil, mayonnaise, sour cream, vinegar, and salt. Knead in sufficient flour until the dough no longer sticks to your hands. Place the dough, wrapped, in the refrigerator while preparing the filling.

For the filling, mix together the meat, potatoes, onions, shredded bay leaf, and seasoning. Roll out two thirds of the dough and use it to line a fairly shallow casserole dish, allowing the dough to hang over the edges. Brush the dough with oil and add the filling. Roll out the remaining dough, cover the filling, pinching the edges firmly together. Cut an opening in the center and pour in 7 tablespoons water or meat stock. Cover the opening loosely with the cut-out piece of dough. Bake in an oven preheated to 350–400 °F/180–200 °C. Reduce the heat to 250 °F/120 °C as soon as the Zur Balish starts to brown. After baking for about 1 hour, pour in about 7 tablespoons water or stock through the opening, and re-cover. Bake for a further 30 minutes. If the Balish is browning too quickly, cover with aluminum foil.

To serve, first remove the top layer of pastry, cut it into portions, lay these on individual plates and place the filling on top. Finally, the pastry base—the tastiest part—is cut into pieces and served.

Top left: There is no festival without *chek-chek*. The macaroni-shaped individual pieces of these fine pastries are made from yeast dough and generously drenched with honey after baking. Then they can be easily formed into little pointed hats.

Above: Once a year, the Tatars get together in Kazan, their capital, for the *Sabantuy* agricultural festival. There are boisterous celebrations, and the men take part in competitions, watched by excited spectators.

Left: The winner of the competitions does not just receive a sheep as a prize for his achievements. He may now use the honorary title of *batyr* and is thus a highly honored man among his people.

Bottom left: The Tatars put up their tents for the agricultural festival. Horses and carts are richly decorated because it is summer, and at *Sabantuy* the sowing is the main focus of celebrations, with people full of hope for a good harvest.

Below: The Tatars uphold their traditions. Families wear classic headgear on many occasions, and they like to serve typical Tatar sweets, such as rose-scented pastries, with their tea.

With the Kalmyks

The Kalmyks, who originated in central Asia, still lived as nomads in the 19th century. Their ancestors, the Oirats, an important Mongolian tribe, served as guards in the main quarters of the Mongol leader, Genghis Khan, and in the advance guard of his army in the 13th century. After the fall of the Mongolian-Tatar empire in the 15th century, some of the Oirats voluntarily placed themselves under Russian rule. In 1609, they were contractually granted areas of land by the Tsar on the lower reaches of the Volga where they maintained their traditional way of life as nomadic stock breeders. Today, most Kalmyks live in the Kalmyk Republic (called *Khal'mg Tanghch* in their own language), which is part of the Russian Federation.

The Kalmyk nomads primarily ate meat and milk products. In addition to the plants of the steppes, important sources of food were sheep, horses, camels, and yaks; beef was also eaten at a later date. To preserve it for long journeys across the steppes, the Kalmyks used to cut raw meat into long thin strips and then dry it in the wind, sun or frost.

Meat was traditionally prepared in the largest possible pieces in an underground oven, for this is the simplest way to cook meat during a rest stop without having to fiddle about with spits, pans, pots or baking sheets. One can even see whole castrated rams or suckling lambs being cooked in underground ovens by the Kalmyks today: the animal is slaughtered and dressed. While this is going on, a large fire is lit and brought up to the highest possible temperature. When sufficient embers are available and the ground has become hot, the embers are pushed apart and a pit is dug in the position of the fire. The lamb is placed in the hot earth. The embers are layered over the top and the fire rekindled. The meat, sometimes also packed in clay, is left to cook in the ground for a whole day. When it is ready, it is taken out of the pit. If it was cooked in clay, the fire-baked clay shell is carefully knocked off in pieces. The wool and skin stick to the clay. The Kalmyks eat the meat from this clay shell, using it like a type of disposable crockery. They generally just use their hands for this, but nowadays also use forks.

This traditional type of food preparation is the result of centuries of nomadic life. Today it is almost impossible, as the Kalmyks now cook under the conditions of a settled way of life. However, sheep and cattle are still the most important basis of food and income. Kalmyk-style tea preparation *(dzhomba)*, which is almost like a soup, has

also survived the centuries. It is prepared from pressed green tea, to which milk, butter, salt and spices, particularly nutmeg, are added during preparation. Every meal started with this tea. Today, in villages, *dzhomba* is still an important part of everyday life. The first mouthful is frequently offered to the home's statue of Buddha.

As with most nomadic people, breads and pastries originally played almost no part in the Kalmyk diet and are due to more recent influences, primarily that of Russian cuisine.

The cooking of non-traditional pastries is, however, often combined with Kalmyk culinary habits that have been handed down over time. For example, the Kalmyks are in the habit of frying small dough balls or patties in large quantities of mutton fat, which can be traced back to the days when sheep raising was their traditional food

Healthy mare's milk

Milk products are particularly important in Kalmuck cuisine. The principal role is played by fermented milk, as in former times it could be prepared in nomadic camps and then kept for some time. The Kalmyks thus produced butter and products similar to curd cheese from their sheep, mares, camels, yaks, and cows.

Traditionally recognized as a curative is *kumiss*, a slightly alcoholic drink, similar to kefir, made from mare's milk. It was formerly produced by the fresh milk being whipped with rennet in animal skins, later in wooden barrels, and then left to ferment. Today, *kumiss* is made both at home and on an industrial scale.

The slightly sparkling beverage can contain up to 3 percent alcohol. It tastes sweetish yet sharp and is extremely refreshing—especially on hot summer days on the steppe. Containing antibacterial enzymes, lactic acid and vitamins (mainly vitamin C), it supports the function of the gastrointestinal tract, the kidneys and the nerves; it strengthens the immune system and is also supposed to cure tuberculosis.

Even in the 19th century, people traveled to the Kalmuck steppes to take *kumiss* as a cure. In the

Soviet era, special sanatoria were set up for this purpose with stud farms and their own *kumiss* production. The sanatorium at Lola, to the south of the Kalmuck capital city of Elista, is still operational.

Not just for the foals! Mare's milk is a popular and healthy thirst-quencher for the Kalmyks.

Asiatic inheritance—the Kalmyks are descended from the Mongols and still maintain their traditional music and dances today, as here in a performance in the capital city, Elista. Colorful festivals carry spectators into another world.

base. This food is called *borzogi* (patties) and consists of a plain dough of flour and water, which is only salted and/or sweetened for special events; it is made as a yeast dough even less frequently.

Buddhism in Russia

In Buddhist Kalmykia, people make the Buddha offerings of fruit and food.

Since the 16th century, the northern branch of Buddhism, Lamaism, has been the national religion in Kalmykia. The Kalmyks who came to Russia brought "portable" monasteries with them, *chiruly*, consisting of three or more specially worked nomad tents *(kibitki)*. Soon permanent monasteries were also founded, but these were closed in 1917 just like the theological academies in the course of communist secularization. Since perestroika, Buddhism in Kalmykia has experienced a gradual rebirth. In 1989, the first Buddhist community was registered in the capital city of Elista, and in the 1990s, several Buddhist monasteries were founded. The fourteenth Dalai Lama visited Kalmykia in 1991 and 1992. In Elista, an institute was opened for the renaissance of Kalmyk language and Buddhism in its Kalmyk form. Currently, Buddhism in Kalmykia is finding an entry in all areas of life. Young people are turning with great enthusiasm to religious customs and in many situations request the presence of Buddhist monks—whether at the birth of a child, at weddings or before examinations.

Dzhomba
Kalmyk tea

3 heaping tbsp green or black tea
1 tsp salt
2 bay leaves
1¹/₂ quarts/1.5 liters milk
3¹/₂ tbsp/50 g butter
¹/₂ tsp ground nutmeg

Bring the tea leaves, salt and bay leaves to a boil in 4 cups/1 liter of water, then simmer for 15–20 minutes on a low heat. Skim off the tea leaves that float to the surface. Add the milk and simmer for about 5 minutes, then strain, stir in the butter and nutmeg, cover, and leave to infuse for 10–15 minutes.

The Kalmyks are again taking time for their traditions and for their tea with milk and spices.

First, the tea leaves are boiled with spices and then removed with a skimmer.

The tea is then boiled for a few minutes with milk and strained.

Finally, nutmeg and a little butter are added and the tea is left to brew briefly before serving.

An experience for young and old—the Russians love traveling in beds on wheels, enjoying the landscape and making friends.

Background: By Lake Baikal, the Trans-Siberian railway crosses one of the most beautiful landscapes in Russia—an unforgettable sight.

The Trans-Siberian railroad:
Food on the right track

A couple of men in pilot's uniforms, still drinking vodka and saying goodbye to friends, fling their glasses against the wheels of the train. That's supposed to bring luck—and you'll need it on the 5,800-mile/9,300-km journey on the Trans-Siberian railway from Moscow to Vladivostok. The Trans-Siberian railway is the longest rail connection in the world and the most varied—an eight day adventure on wheels. It passes light birch forests, villages with picturesque white churches in a rolling landscape, surrounded by fertile fields. It crosses the "mother" of all Russian rivers, the Volga, before it starts climbing into the Urals beyond Perm. At the transition between Europe and Asia in Vershina, the train driver gives a signal so that the tourists in particular can get their cameras ready for the white obelisk, which at this point symbolizes the border between the continents. Then the train moves on to West Siberia, where the apparently endless taiga starts just past Omsk and Novosibirsk. Mighty bridges cross the rivers Irtysh and Ob, before reaching Krasnoyarsk on the Yenisay. On the third day, the train stops at Irkutsk, the oldest and most beautiful city in Siberia. Many people break their journey here for one or two days to continue it in the form of long tours around the town and a picnic in the taiga. On the fourth day, the high point of the landscape awaits the travelers: a stop of one hour on an open section of the line at the sparklingly clear Lake Baikal, the largest freshwater reservoir in the world. The "Siberian Sea" is framed by the endless taiga and snow-covered mountains. Then the train passes 600-year-old trees at Ulan-Ude and Chita. After a week, the express reaches Khabarovsk, and on the morning of the eighth day it pulls into Vladivostok—with a whistle and on time after a good 163 hours. Obviously, for the well-being of the travelers, there is an on-board restaurant, which opens at eight o'clock in the morning for breakfast and does not close after dinner until past midnight. But most Russians prefer to go for the cheaper self-catering option. The compartments smell of dried fish and smoked meat, of robust cheeses and fresh bread; they are fragrant with apples, apricots, and melons, and soon also with vodka, because a toast must be drunk to a traveling acquaintance. Conviviality is always a passenger here, along with the samovar of the carriage steward, which she heats up with hard coal for tea in the morning, at noon, in the evening and at night. Whilst savoring the strong *chay* from glasses held in chased metal holders with handles,

you are initiated by your fellow travelers into life histories, family relationships and philosophical ideas about God and the world, and learn the correct way to drink vodka, eat dried fish *(vobla)*, and suffer defeats at chess.

The train travels east at 35–60 miles per hour/60–100 km/h, and it is worth staying awake for each stop, even at the smallest stations. After all, the frequent stops provide a good opportunity to get to know the country and its people, to stretch your legs, to watch the colorful hustle and bustle, to try out specialties on offer, and to buy provisions. The Trans-Siberian railway is not only refreshing for the soul, but also for the stomach, because the journey is designed as an expedition through the cuisine of the Russian state of four different peoples.

In Yekaterinburg, old grandmothers sell wonderful hot *pirogi*, yeast dough pastries, and delicious sour cream *(smetana)* in paper cups for a couple of rubles. Like everywhere else, red-cheeked apples are held up to the windows, as well as *kvass*, a beer made from bread, and marinated mushrooms. In Tyumen, you must try the shanga pirogi made from cream, eggs and buckwheat, cooked in lamb fat and eaten hot with tea. *Klyukvy*, bitter-sweet cranberries, are sold by the jar. In Novosibirsk, you can select *pelmeni*, filled dumplings, because Siberia is the home of these "bread ears"; fine ice cream made with cedar pine-nuts is also made here. Continuing on your journey through the endless taiga to Irkutsk, women continue to stand on the platforms, offering hot *piroshki, smetana,* giant blueberries, roast chicken and small, sweet-sour pickled melons. The daily menu in the dining car, aimed at foreigners and business people at a price of 25 dollars, is, however, competitive. There is *shchi* (see page 44 f) and störsülze (diced sturgeon in aspic), with *pelmeni*, meatballs, as a main course, and ice cream. In Ulan-Ude, Buryat women bring *manty* to the train, fist-sized pastry pockets twisted together at the top, and deliciously filled with lamb or wild pony mince, peas and green herbs. In Nerchinsk, it is worthwhile eating in spite of your fatigue, because fishermen are lured to the station with *yukola*, salmon cut into strips and dried. Tea and home-made jam *(varenye)* from your neighbor conclude the multicultural treat for the tastebuds on the train. Now the culinary specialties of Vladivostok, Russia's gateway to the Pacific, await (see page 106 f).

Travelers like to supply themselves with regional specialties when stopping at stations.

Russians are self-sufficient people even on the train: they all bring something to eat, which is then shared hospitably.

Freshly smoked omul is a true delicacy.

Air-dried fish, pinned with wooden sticks.

Treasures of Lake Baikal

Lake Baikal, the "blue eye of Siberia," attracts the viewer as it reflects the changing play of clouds.

"Even we, who live on Lake Baikal, cannot boast of knowing it, because it is impossible to know everything about it, Lake Baikal being what it is." This is how the Siberian-born novelist Valentin Rasputin, born in 1937, put it. The "blue eye of Siberia" is one of the most immense lakes on earth. It extends 395 miles/636 km from east to west and covers an area of 12,165 square miles/ 31,500 square km. At up to 5,370 feet/1,637 m deep, Lake Baikal is the deepest and largest fresh water reservoir on earth.

Its name comes from the Tatar language and means "rich lake." In fact, there is a wealth of fish in its waters, including many endemic types, including the omul. Traveling along the shores of Lake Baikal by train in the winter, a remarkable sight can often be seen: thickly muffled-up forms lying face down and unmoving on the ice, their heads sunk deep into ice holes. Anglers lie in wait here with fishing lines and bait for the omul,

which is much more than just a fish for the Siberians. For example, one proverb states: "If a Siberian is seriously ill, it is enough to stroke his lips with the tail of an omul—and he'll be revived."
The silver-colored, beautiful fish from the whitefish family is Lake Baikal's calling card. It lives only here, spawning in the tributaries of the lake; it is about 15 inches/40 cm long and weighs up to 2¼ lb/1 kg. The commercial catch is restricted by the state to 10,000 metric tonnes each year, in order to prevent a rapid decline in stocks, as was caused in the 1960s by over-fishing. While the omul was hard to obtain commercially in the Soviet era even on the shores of Lake Baikal, today there are stalls on the beach where locals offer for sale the treasures of Baikal, fresh or smoked, and at an extremely moderate price for such a fine delicacy.

There is hardly any other fish from which so many delicious dishes can be prepared. It can be

eaten pickled as *zakuska*, baked in pirogi, or one can enjoy the mild, almost sweet flavor that it develops when smoked. To smoke, fresh omul is hung for three days over smoldering alder wood, and then consumed along with its innards. To air-dry the fish, on the other hand, it is gutted, cut up, and salted. Connoisseurs also prize the exceedingly tender flesh of the omul when it has gone off slightly. To the inexperienced, it seems that the fish has gone bad, but the characteristic piquant aroma is part of this delicacy.

Right page: Omul is the finest delicacy of Lake Baikal. It is tasty raw, smoked or gently cooked.

For *stroganina*, fine raw fish fillet, a whitefish is scaled and then skinned.

The fish fillet can then be cut. A very sharp knife is used for this.

Some dexterity is needed to cut the fish fillet into thin and even slices.

Stroganina is seasoned with pepper and salt and served with cranberries, onion, dill, and bread.

Vladivostok fishing harbor

Vladivostok lies 5,775 miles/9,300 km south east of Moscow on the Pacific and has about 650,000 inhabitants. The city, called "ruler of the east," was founded in the mid-19th century as a military settlement in an area common to Russia and China. As it is favorably placed on the shores of the "Golden Horn" bay in the Sea of Japan, it soon became an important international harbor. With the start of regular traffic on the Trans-Siberian railway between St. Petersburg and Vladivostok in 1903, the town developed into a base for the Russian fishing and whaling fleet, and in the Soviet era became an important center for the fishing and fish processing industries. Due to its significance as a base for the Russian Pacific fleet, from 1958 to 1991 Vladivostok was barred to foreigners and could only be accessed by Soviet citizens with special permission.

As the Black Sea was lost to Russia after the decline of the USSR, and as the fishing grounds in the north, based in Murmansk, are almost exhausted, today Vladivostok remains the state's principal fishing city. However, there are many signs of decline. The fall in fish stocks in the world's oceans has resulted in strict fishing quotas, and the outlay on ship maintenance often costs more than the gain from any possible profit. In addition, many ships no longer call into Vladivostok because they have to pay heavy taxes there. They therefore prefer to sell about 90 percent of their catch on the open sea to the Japanese, Chinese, Koreans or Americans. So the harbor of Vladivostok generally only contains small, elderly, rusted boats—a true ships' graveyard. The harbor with its fish factories and cold stores is the center for storing and processing the remaining ten percent or so of the actual catch. Of this, about one half is exported to the USA and Japan, and the other half enters the Russian market. The most important export product is cod, but crabs, halibut, plaice, sea cucumbers and squid are also exported. The Pacific salmon and its red caviar, on the other hand, mainly enter the Russian market.

In the Soviet era, there was no market for fresh fish in Vladivostok. However, freshly landed catches were sold unofficially in the harbor directly from the ships. In the 1990s, a decision was made to legalize this black market trade. Even though the fishermen are unwilling to hand over their catch for the new fish market—it is much more profitable to sell it on the open sea to the Americans for dollars—the market on Sundays can provide up to 100 different types of fish and seafood. Here you can buy both the economical

Vladivostok on the Pacific Ocean continues to be Russia's most important fishing harbor.

Here you can get many different types of shrimp.

Nautiluses are often sold shelled.

There is even a large selection of squid.

Crayfish are some of the finest products.

A fish seller in Vladivostok presents fresh squid from the Pacific.

and much loved Pacific herring, as well as expensive and exclusive products such as king crabs, sea cucumbers, razor clams and—primarily red—caviar. In addition, there are mountains of fresh sea kale *(Crambe maritima L.)* and sea kale salads in all their possible variants. The Russian Far East can mainly thank the influence of Chinese and Japanese cuisine for the enjoyment of this vegetable and the consumption of mollusks such as calamares *(Teuthida)*, blue mussels *(Mytilus edulis)*, sea cucumber *(Stichopus japonicus)* or squid *(Octopoda)*. However, in Russia the culinary finesse of Asian cookery is seldom given to the preparation of these products. They are preferably eaten raw and with a glass of vodka—how could it be any other way?

Squid is also prepared as a range of fine preserves in the fish factories in the city.

Sea cucumber

Live sea cucumbers are almost the epitome of national culinary pride in the Far East, and they are also a certain test of courage for foreigners. Like sea urchins, they belong to the echinoderms, and only some members of this family are edible. The Japanese sea cucumber *(Stichopus japonicus)* found near Vladivostok can only be caught through laborious work by individual divers close to the coast—ideally at night from a ship equipped with search lights. The thick, leathery skin is opened immediately on board with a knife, then ketchup is poured onto the live sea cucumber and it is consumed raw. However, beginners are best to indulge in a well-filled glass of vodka before first enjoying this strange type of delicacy—then the sea cucumber slips down almost like a little oyster. Locals advise drinking another glass of vodka afterward.

In China and Japan, sea cucumbers are considered one of the greatest pleasures and apparently have an aphrodisiac effect. Dried sea cucumbers are sold as so called trepang and are also produced today in Southeast Asia and the Caribbean for the Chinese market.

Pilengas zapechonny v dukhovke
Baked mullet

4 tbsp oil
1³/₄ lb/750 g potatoes, peeled and sliced
Salt
1 whole mullet or other fish (e.g. gilthead sea bream
or other bream), weighing about 2¹/₄ lb/1 kg, prepared
5¹/₂ oz/150 g bacon fat for larding
4 tbsp/60 g soft butter
2 tbsp all-purpose flour
6 black peppercorns
10 tbsp/150 g sour cream

Brush roasting pan with oil. Distribute the potatoes
evenly over the pan and salt lightly. Make cuts across
the fish and lard with bacon fat. Spread butter all over
the fish and place on a rack.
Place the rack in an oven preheated to 400 °F/200 °C
directly above the pan so that the fish juices can drip
onto the potatoes. After about 10 minutes, sprinkle
the fish with the flour and peppercorns and cook for
a further 10 minutes. When a crust has formed, pour
over the sour cream and cook for about 10 minutes to
finish. Serve the fish together with the potatoes.

Fine seafood of the Far East

Salat iz morskoy kapusty i midy
Salad of mussels and sea kale

Generous 1 lb/500 g sea kale
1 tbsp vinegar
2 cloves of garlic, finely chopped
2 carrots, cut into fine strips
2 tbsp oil
1 large beefsteak tomato, finely diced
8 oz/200 g mussels, weight cooked and shelled
Salt, pepper and caraway seeds
Salad leaves and cooked shrimp to garnish

Wash the sea kale, just cover with water, add the
vinegar and simmer to soften. Leave to cool and cut
into strips.
Brown the garlic and carrots in the oil, then add the
diced tomato and simmer for a few minutes. Add the
cooked mussels and sea kale, season to taste with salt,
pepper and caraway seeds. Continue to cook for a further 5 minutes or so.
Arrange on salad leaves and garnish with cooked
shrimp.

Makarony po dalnevostochnomu
Far Eastern-style spaghetti

3½ oz/100 g squid, cooked
3½ oz/100 g crab meat, cooked
3½ oz/100 g sea cucumber, cooked (to taste)
3½ oz/100 g salmon fillet
3½ oz/100 g turbot fillet
3½ oz/100 g shrimp, cooked
Generous 1 lb/500 g spaghetti or other noodles (e.g. linguine)
Salt
2 small onions, finely diced
2 tbsp/30 g butter
2 garlic cloves, finely diced
½ red bell pepper and ½ green bell pepper, cut into strips
¾–1 cup/200 ml white wine
Freshly ground black pepper
½ bunch parsley
Sesame seeds for garnishing

Cut the squid into square pieces about 1–1½ inches/ 3–4 cm in size. Cut the crab meat, sea cucumber, salmon, and turbot into dice. Peel the shrimp.
Cook the pasta till al dente in lightly salted water.
Fry the onions in the butter until transparent. Add the garlic and peppers and cook together briefly, then pour on the wine and bring to a boil, stirring constantly. Season with salt and pepper. Place the fish pieces in the sauce and simmer for about 5 minutes, then add the seafood and bring back to a boil briefly.
Drain the spaghetti and arrange on plates. Pour over the seafood sauce and garnish with parsley and sesame seeds.
Tip: the sauce can also be enriched with cream.

Crabs from Kamchatka

Whoever sees live Kamchatka crabs for the first time, pulled on board a ship in a fish trap, is fascinated by their size. King crabs are the largest crustaceans of all. The shell of a male can reach a diameter of 10 inches/25 cm, and the width of the whole creature with its legs extended can be up to 5 feet/1.5 m. On the scales, a crab can weigh up to 22 lb/10 kg. The kingdom of the Kamchatka crabs (Paralithodes camtschaticus) off the coast of the northern peninsula of Kamchatka extends for over 435 miles/700 km from north to south. The catch is of great commercial importance and brought both Russia and the US unimaginable profits up until the 1980s. Even an ordinary crew member on a crab trawler could earn about $100,000 in one season. But eventually the stock of these large crustaceans fell so dramatically that crabbing was recently banned in the US and severely restricted in Russia. Of the crabs still being caught, more than 95 percent are exported, mainly to Japan. Most king crabs are still caught just off the western coast of Kamchatka, where they push toward the shoreline in droves to spawn in spring. The males help the females, weighed down with ripe eggs, by carrying them on their backs to the shoreline. This is the best time to make a catch. For this, people build special net fish traps on the bed of the sea, which are linked together to form long rows, like garlands. Fish bait is placed in each trap. The traps fill up with crabs over one to three days. On board the fishing boat, the crabs are sorted immediately by size and sex. The females and young males are then put back into the sea to ensure the survival of the next generation and thus the future of the crab fishermen. Only fully grown males with a shell width of at least 5 inches/13 cm are processed. As the Kamchatka crabs are threatened with extinction, smaller crab types (such as Paralithodes platypus and Lithodes aequispina) from the Far East are starting to be marketed and exported, primarily to Japan.

The king crab from the waters off the Kamchatka peninsula is one of the world's largest crustaceans and provides tasty, exceedingly tender meat. In the West, it is also known as king crab meat.

Zapechonnye kamchatskiye kraby
King crab au gratin
(Not illustrated)

Generous 8 oz/250 g fresh king crab meat (or canned crab meat)
2½ tbsp/40 g butter
6 tbsp/100 g mayonnaise
7 tbsp/50 g grated hard cheese

Divide the crab meat between 4 small, greased, ovenproof ramekins. Baste with melted butter and mayonnaise and sprinkle over the cheese. Bake in an oven preheated to 440 °F/225 °C until golden brown. Serve hot in the ramekins as a first course.

The legs of the Kamchatka crab contain more meat than one would expect at first glance. They are cracked open and enjoyed simply with mayonnaise and lemon.

The people of the north

Twenty-six different ethnic groups, comprising just 160,000 to 170,000 people, live in the extreme north of Russia. They live scattered across an enormous territory—from the Kola peninsula in the west to Chukotka in the east. Due to geographical conditions, their ways of life, however, are similar. About one half of these people live as nomads and roam with herds of reindeer through the tundra and tundra woodland. The other half is settled and catches fish and hunts marine mammals. Before the Americans started to build up their whaling industry in the mid 19th century, the northern waters teemed with whales. Their hunting was one of the most important foundations of existence for the inhabitants of the Chukotka and Kamchatka peninsulas. An average-sized whale brought in about 120 to 150 metric tonnes of high-quality meat. In addition, it provided valuable whalebone as well as fat and innards, from which the Chukchen produced tableware and clothing. One such catch was sufficient to supply a whole settlement with food for two to three months.

If one does not primarily eat marine animals, then raising reindeer is a must for surviving the hard northern climate. The reindeer is the "food that runs along behind you," as they say in these polar zones. Reindeer raising is only compatible with a nomadic way of life, as the animals are continually on the move, tugging food from the ground here and there. In the spring, the reindeer roam from their winter pastures, where they feed on lichen, to their calving and summer pastures, which also offer food in the form of grasses and shrubs. If a herd was kept on a restricted pasture, their hooves would destroy the ground for new lichen when they searched for food.

Enormous meat and fish consumption is typical of the diet of the northern people of Russia. In autumn and winter, one adult will eat about 6 to 8 lb/3–4 kg per day. Flour from grain has only been known since the 19th century, and the northern people still use it to bake unsalted round, flat loaves using water or deer's blood. In summer, many berries enhance the menu, including cranberries and cloudberries. Roots, moss, lichen, green sapwood, and seaweed are also a supplement to meals.

All of the people of the north are amazingly competent in using the slaughtered animals to the full. Practically everything is eaten apart from the skin, including all the innards, marrow and spinal cord, eyes, tendons, and cartilage. A particular delicacy is the semi-digested tundra lichen from reindeer stomachs. It is roasted over the fire, dried, or eaten with berries in a frozen state. The bones are ground and processed into flour; fat is rendered down. The animal's blood is drunk fresh or is kept in leather sacks, pickled with leaves. Such an efficient exploitation of the food base is necessary because finding food in the frozen north is extremely difficult. In addition, the calories required by a person under these extreme conditions are about two to three times higher than that required by a person in a temperate climate. This will also explain the high consumption of animal fat.

The methods of storing food and its rapid consumption are also determined by the climate. Blood, brain, liver, and the heart of reindeer; the heads, cartilage and the liver of fish; as well as the flippers, tails and cartilage of marine mammals are eaten raw immediately on being caught.

In the icy cold of the northern winter, everything is flash-frozen in moments, which means the food retains its nutritional value. Meat and fish are shaved into thin slices when frozen. They are stored this way and are seasoned with salt, seaweed and herbs before eating. Another form of preservation is to first air-dry meat and fish and then to freeze it. The whole of the north knows frozen dried fish as *yukola*.

How healthy it is for people to eat raw animals is evaluated differently by doctors and nutritional experts. On the one hand, the people of the north seldom suffer from the illnesses of the more sophisticated societies widespread in Europe. On the other hand, the former average life expectancy of 30 to 35 years was extremely low, and a surprising number of people died of infections and intestinal diseases. While the traditional way of life and eating has still changed very little in remote areas, people in the towns and settlements of the north have to a large extent gone over to Russian-influenced cuisine.

Large illustration: Nomads in the Russian north are still drawn through the tundra on reindeer sledges.

Top right: In the coastal regions, seal ribs and innards are also on the menu.

Centre right: The Itelmens prepare a fortifying soup made from bears' paws, potatoes, and noodles.

Below right: Nomadic tribes of the north, such as the Hanti and Mansi, often eat meat raw.

Alkhalalalay—the ritual festival of the Itelmens

"Alkhalalalay!" With this joyful cry, the Itelmens rid themselves of evil spirits and prepare themselves for the long northern winter. The cry was heard back in the 18th century by explorers who first described the customs of these northern people, and it continues to be heard to this day. The festival is deeply rooted in the old pagan traditions of the Itelmens, but it had fallen into oblivion after the conversion of the region to Christianity about 300 years ago. Only in 1988 did this small group of people bring its ancient ritual festival back to life.

The Itelmens are a palaeoasiatic people and inhabit the western part of the Kamchatka peninsula, the eastern tip of Russia. Many of them continue to live primarily from catching fish and raising reindeer—just like the Chukchens, Koryaken, Aleutians, and Evens. The food base is mainly provided by salmon, red fish roe, herring, and cod. In addition, they hunt seals and the Kamchatka bear, one of the largest brown bears in the world. As winter lasts almost nine months in the far north, the Itelmens collect herbs and berries during their short summer, and preserve fish and meat by salting and drying. Following the Russian example, today they also grow some simple and fast-growing types of vegetables such as potatoes and carrots which flourish in their fertile volcanic soil.

To round off the crop year, to give thanks for protection and food, and to request forgiveness from the animals and plants for killing them, the Itelmens celebrate their *Alkhalalalay* ritual festival each year in mid-September. At this time, Kovran, the principal town of these people, is bursting at the seams. Friends and relations come from far away to Kamchatka to celebrate together and to say thank-you together with the locals for abundant food in the previous year.

At the start of the celebrations, the young men from Kovran make the arduous hike to sacred Mount Elvel. They lug a hand-carved totem pole for over 20 miles/30 km to raise it on the peak to exorcise the spirits of the volcano.

The Itelmens lived close to rivers in the summer, and in the winter they built earth huts that also had to be cleansed of evil spirits: the women swept the floor with grasses and then, under the guidance of a shaman, they performed a dance with fierce grimaces and songs, to drive out illness, grief and everything bad. The men covered themselves in furs and performed the bear dance—they symbolically offered their fierce companions something to eat in order to put them in a gentle mood and to ask them for food for the next year. In the dance of the Kamuli, the volcano spirits, they beseeched mother nature not to treat the people too hard in the winter and to keep them from storms and cold.

Today, the one-week festival is traditionally opened by dance offerings by children. In ritual dances around the fire, men and women then follow the call of the drum all night long. Dancers and singers imitate animals according to shamanic tradition: either the loveplay of the seals, the lumbering of the Kamchatka bear or the chirruping of birds. With drums and song, they ask the spirits of the volcano for leniency.

Finally, everybody celebrates the ritual of liberation and cleansing—the men bind a large wreath of young birch wood and hold it for the people to walk through. All of the village inhabitants step through this circle. Then the men shout *alkhalalalay!* and the women *alulu!* —onomatopoeic calls without meaning. When all of the evil of the previous months has been left behind in this way, a totem figure is set up as the female protector of

In the ritual dance at Alkhalalalay, the Itelmen woman embodies a seagull and the man a bear.

No life without fire. A shaman calls up the flames at the Alkhalalalay festival in the far north.

the village for the coming year. With the Alkhalalalay festival being brought back to life, a cooking competition has also been introduced to make people, the younger ones in particular, enthusiastic about traditional Itelmen cuisine and to lead them back to the old customs. The cuisine is centered on numerous variations made from

Dishes are prettily decorated at the cooking competition during the festival.

fish, potatoes, herbs, berries, and animal fat. *Kirilka* is a combination of fish and crowberries with seal or bear fat. For *baraban*, fish roe is pounded with potatoes and then fried in fat. Also acceptable to west European stomachs are *chuprik*, fish baked whole, stuffed with wild garlic and potatoes, or little fish pockets stuffed with the same ingredients *(telno)*. The high point of the culinary festivities at Alkhalalalay is the slaughtering of a seal, whose fat and meat is shared among those present and can thus form a food base for the hard months ahead. Winter can now arrive.

Shamanism in Siberia

Shamanism, banned during the Soviet era, is again widespread in many groups in Siberia. It is based on the mystic idea of the great mother, the world soul, to whom the shamans turn. As religious agents between people and the other side, they need a higher calling, and often come from a line of shamans or are marked by an earlier, serious and possibly psychic illness, or by an external mark, such as a birthmark. The fundamental ritual of the shamans is the *kamlaniye*, a shamanic nighttime journey. In this, he will carry out a ritual dance, bang a drum, ring a little bell and fall into an ecstasy. He imitates the calls of animals and appeals to the spirits. This ritual is used to cure illness. His journey takes him to the underworld, where he seeks out the soul of the sick person in order to bring it back. People ask for his help when animals are ill or have disappeared, or when luck and success in hunting or in an examination need to be conjured up.

The Yakuts

Yakutia, *Sakha* in the language of its people, is the coldest country on earth, an enormous area of over 1,158,300 square miles/3,000,000 sq km in the north of Siberia, which covers 2.5 percent of the surface of the globe. Forty percent of the country lies above the Arctic Circle, about 80 percent is covered with taiga woodland, and the rest is characterized by tundra. One of the poles of cold of the northern hemisphere is located here, with lowest temperatures reaching minus 94 °F/ –70 °C.

Even before the Russians penetrated the area in the 17th century, two tribes had joined to form the Yakut ethnic group with its unique language and way of life —the hunters and reindeer herders of the north, originally indigenous to this area, and nomadic Turkic cattle herders who migrated in from the south. Today, about 350,000 Yakuts live in a Republic of just over one million people: over 50 percent of its inhabitants are Russian and the others are of numerous other nationalities.

Yakut cuisine, just like the Yakut language, reflects these influences. The culinary customs of the Turkic people have been adapted to the conditions of the north; very many Mongol and Russian elements have been adapted and many have been absorbed from other people of the north. The traditional customs have been maintained by and large by the Yakuts who live outside the towns. Their way of life does not essentially differ from that of their forefathers.

The northern Yakuts raise reindeer and hunt animals for their fur, such as sable, the arctic fox and squirrels, but for food they prefer elk, wild reindeer, bears, and birds. The Yakuts have developed special techniques for hunting wild reindeer. Even today, they hunt using a tame reindeer as a decoy. The hunter sends the specially trained animal toward the wild herd on a long rope, and then pulls it slowly back. A wild animal will generally follow the tame one, and the hunter will catch it with a lasso.

Formerly, very arduous forms of hunting whole herds of elk and reindeer were widespread; they were banned in 1917 for reasons of nature con-servancy but were still practiced illegally until just after World War II. Giant barricades, 3 to 6 miles/ 6–10 km long and made from felled trees, were set up in the taiga and the herds were guided directly into the hands of the hunters.

As the majority of the area is covered in permafrost, and the soil only thaws to a depth of 8 to 10 inches/20–25 cm in the summer, after a successful hunt the meat is stored by removing the upper layers of the soil, placing the skinned animal onto the frozen ground and covering it with the removed skins and soil.

The northern Yakuts feed themselves like all the people of the north — they primarily eat lots of raw meat, fish and fat (see also page 110). A particular Yakut delicacy is also prepared for children: dried elk noses and lips. These are finely grated and processed into a type of hearty "confectionery". Widespread semi-luxuries also include tobacco, obtained from the Russians by bartering furs. The women and children also smoke, not just the men.

Dogs have always had a particular status in the life of the people of the north. They are indispensable as sledge dogs on the tundra, as hunting dogs, and as protectors of the reindeer herds against wolves. Therefore much of the meat and fish preserved for the winter is fed to the dogs, and in the late winter when stocks are low, the people often go hungry along with their four-legged friends.

The Yakuts in the south are primarily cattle and horse raisers, which also leaves its mark on their cuisine, in which horse meat and mare's milk is used. Many milk products enrich the menu, principally in summer. The ways of preserving milk products as stores for the winter (see facing page) are characteristic of Yakut cuisine and unique, as is the combination of milk, fish and meat products with berries, roots and tree bark.

Background: Reindeer provide transport and milk, meat, and warming skins.

Yakut specialties

Tar: for this unique traditional Yakut milk dish, all of the milk product residues over the course of a summer are poured into large barrels made from birch bark. The mixture then undergoes an acidification process and the liquid that collects on the top is siphoned off. Berries, roots, and sap wood are then added to the *tar* in the barrel. When the frosts arrive, the *tar* freezes. Lumps of the frozen mixture are chopped off with a hatchet as required, and are used with meat, fish, and flour to make stews and different types of porridge.

Chokhoon: fresh, soft creamery butter is mixed alternately with warm and cold milk. Then fresh berries and sugar are added. Finally, the food is shared out into small dishes, placed in the frost or in the freezer box to be frozen, and then served in small crushed pieces.

Suorat: 4 cups/1 liter whole milk is brought to a boil and then cooled to room temperature. Six tbsp/100 g sour cream is then added and the mixture is whisked up hard until lots of foam forms. Then the pot is covered and placed in a warm spot. After two to three hours, it develops a kefir-like consistency and the pot is put in the refrigerator. Traditionally, this sour milk is prepared in barrels made from birch bark.

Kulnin: blueberries are boiled down with fresh, crushed fish roe. Patties are made from this mixture, which is dried either in the sun or over a fire. Cut into small pieces, *kulnin* is enjoyed with tea.

Khaan: this blood sausage is made from fresh cattle or horse blood. When the animal is slaughtered, the blood is collected and it is left to stand. The upper, liquid part is used for top-quality blood sausage and the lower "black" part is used for "black" blood sausages. Intestines are filled with the blood and the sausages are cooked in salt water. They are ready to serve when they are firm.

Dried fish has always been a practical and protein-rich food for the people of the north.

The hunt

The hunt, which at one time was an important source of food in Russia, is now a luxury at the start of the 21st century. The pleasures of the huntsman are not cheap and are strictly regulated by law. On the other hand, commercial hunting exists, which is enormously significant in eastern Siberia and in the north in particular. Professional hunters are combined into businesses that not only process animals caught for their fur, and birds and marine mammals obtained through hunting, but also everything that the woods and tundra can provide, including mushrooms, herbs, and berries.

In Russia there are many climatically different hunting areas, each with their characteristic fauna (see map). Within the legal framework, hunting is permitted everywhere—apart from in nature conservancy areas, national parks, and recreational areas. However, you must join a hunting association first and obtain shooting licenses for the individual animals. The exact dates of the respective hunting seasons are determined each year by the local communities.

Amateur hunting is always on foot and traditional techniques are generally used: hunting courting capercaillies in spring is one of the oldest forms of Russian hunting. It enjoys high prestige, and requires some skill as well as rapid reactions, endurance, and cunning. The hunter must hide close to the creature before sunrise. As soon as the capercaillie starts its courtship display, it is deaf to everything around it. During this phase, the huntsman can creep up and shoot. If the bird interrupts its courtship display, the hunter must remain immobile so that he remains unobserved. Hazel grouse are generally hunted using a birding whistle that imitates the call of a female. It all depends on how genuine the call sounds, which requires a lot of practice. The best birding whistles are carved from the hip bones of hares, capercaillies, or geese.

For hunting duck, the old technique of duck decoys is frequently used. The success of the hunt depends to a large extent on the particular talent and character of the decoys— generally a mixture of wild and domestic ducks. It is said that the ideal duck decoy must be "bold and communicative." In many areas, duck hunting in spring is completely forbidden without duck decoys, in order to restrict it to the few owners of carefully trained creatures.

When hunting birds with dogs, pointers or spaniels flush out the birds and the hunters shoot them on the wing.

Hare hunting normally uses coursing by dogs that drive the hare in a circle and finally toward the hunter. Ideally, hunting takes place after the first snow when the tracks are easier to find.

Today, about 60,000 brown bears still live on the taiga. You need a special permit for bear hunting; it is completely banned in some communities. As in former times when spears were used, people still like to hunt bears today in their dens—but with rifles. Hunters generally start this in the second half of the winter when the animal is sleeping deeply. The hunters position themselves around the den at a distance of up to 30 feet/ 10 m and let their dogs loose. The dogs force the bear from its den with their barking. The hunters must be accurate shooters with rapid reactions because the first shot must be lightning fast and result in a kill. A miss or an injury to the bear means a furious animal and this can easily mean the death of one or more hunters. Even more dangerous is hunting a bear that has been wakened from hibernation, and is wandering around, irritated. In this case, the hunters form a ring, and they continually draw in closer. The hunters place themselves where the bear will probably try to break through the circle. However, these animals are unpredictable—and hunting them always carries a risk.

Right: Bear hunting in Siberia is subject to strict conditions and is extremely dangerous for the hunters. It requires courage and high-precision shooting.

Due to its wide range of climatic and geographical conditions, Russia can be divided into several different hunting zones.

The elk *(los)* and other types of deer provide lean red meat that is good for braising.

Wild boar *(kaban)* sometimes tastes rather strong and is therefore best marinated before cooking.

The meat of the young hare *(zayats)* is tender with a fine gamy flavor. It is suitable for roasting and braising.

Even in the days of the Tsar, roasted pheasant *(fazan)* was valued as a particular treat for special occasions.

Duck *(utka)* is loved in Russian cuisine stuffed and roasted, and also in aspic or in pies.

The capercaillie *(glukhar)* often provides tough, rather tasteless meat and is hunted primarily as a trophy.

Hunter's cuisine

Kuropatka v smetana
Partridge in sour cream

4 small partridges, prepared for cooking
Salt
Pepper
5 tbsp/70 g butter
2 onions, finely chopped
4 large carrots, finely diced
1 small parsley root, finely diced
1½ cups/400 g sour cream
2 tbsp all-purpose flour
½ bunch parsley, finely chopped

Cut the partridges in half along their length, rub liberally with salt and pepper and fry in portions on all sides in 3 tablespoons of the butter. Lift the partridge halves out and set aside.
In a deep, ovenproof casserole, fry the onions, carrots, and parsley root in the remaining butter. Season with salt and pepper.
Place the partridge halves on the fried vegetables. Add ½ cup/125 ml water and the flour to the sour cream and stir well to mix. Pour over the partridges, cover, and braise over low heat for about 1 hour.
Sprinkle with chopped parsley before serving.

Pirog s zaichatinoy i gribami
Pirogi with hare and mushrooms

Generous 1 lb/500 g of pirogi dough, prepared as
described on page 18

For the filling:
1¾ lb/750 g joints of hare, bones removed
1–2 onions, finely chopped
Oil for frying
5½ oz/150 g fresh mushrooms, any type
2 hardcooked eggs, chopped
½ bunch each of dill and parsley, chopped
Salt
Pepper

First prepare the pirogi dough as described on page 18.
Cut the hare meat into 1–1½ inch/3–4 cm cubes. Fry the onions with the meat to brown in hot oil. Pour on some water and gently cook the meat, covered, until it is tender.
Meanwhile, clean and slice the mushrooms, and fry in the oil.
Grind the cooked meat, add the fried mushrooms, the chopped egg and the herbs. Season with salt and pepper and mix well.
Prepare one large pirogi or small *piroshki* according to the instructions on page 18, and bake.

Kabanina s gribami i kartofelyem
Wild boar stew

For the marinade:

1 small parsley root
1/2 head of celery
1 carrot
1 onion
3/4 cup/200 ml vinegar
4 bay leaves
4 cloves
1 tbsp salt
6 garlic cloves, halved

1 3/4 lb/750 g wild boar meat, boned
9 oz/250 g fresh or 1 oz/25 g dried wild mushrooms
3 tbsp/45 g lard (preferably not shortening)
2 onions, chopped
4 large potatoes, diced
1/2 cup/125 ml meat or vegetable stock
Salt and pepper
2 large carrots, cut into pieces
3/4 cup/200 g sour cream

To make the marinade, roughly chop the vegetables, bring to a boil in 2 cups/500 ml water with the vinegar, spices, and salt, then leave to cool. Add the garlic. Cut the meat into bite-sized pieces and leave to marinate overnight in the marinade.

Clean the fresh mushrooms well; or soak the dried mushrooms in tepid water. Cut them into small pieces. Take the meat from the marinade and pat dry, then brown quickly on all sides over high heat in the lard. Add the onions and fry briefly, then add the mushrooms and potatoes. Pour on the stock and any water used for soaking the mushrooms, season with salt and pepper and cook gently for about 1 1/2 hours, adding more water if necessary. Half way through the cooking time, add the carrots, and stir in the sour cream just before the end.

Olenina pod yagodnom sousom
Venison with cranberries

2 1/4 lb/1 kg venison fillet
Salt
Pepper
Oil for frying
14 oz/400 g fresh berries (e.g. cranberries, blueberries)
1 onion, chopped finely
2 tbsp/30 g butter
1 tbsp all-purpose flour
1 tbsp cornstarch
1/2 cup/125 ml dry white wine
1 tbsp sugar
2 cloves

Cut the meat across the grain into slices about 1/4 inch/5 mm thick and season with salt and pepper. Fry on both sides in hot oil and put to one side.

To make the sauce, cook half of the berries in about 3/4 cup/200 ml water until soft and then drain, retaining the liquid. Push the cooked berries through a sieve with a wooden spoon.

Cook the onion in the butter, then sprinkle over the flour and add the berry liquid. Dissolve the cornstarch in the wine, add to the berry sauce with the remaining berries and sugar, season the sauce with salt and pepper to taste and stir to thicken over low heat. Add the venison slices to the sauce and heat through.

Serve the meat slices with the berry sauce. Boiled potatoes, peeled or in their skins, go well with this dish.

Alcohol from the forest

Almost as soon as the Russians had discovered vodka itself, they found out that they could produce infusions and liqueurs from almost any raw vegetable material to provide different flavors, fragrances, and even medicinal effect. Even poisonous vegetable ingredients thus became components of effective medicinal liquids.

While liqueurs (*nalivki*) are made using sugar or sugar syrup, herb and berry vodkas (*nastoyki*) have either a bitter or dry flavor. As domestic production at home is widespread, there are numerous individual recipe variants with the widest possible range of ingredients from the garden, forest, and meadows.

The most famous herb vodka of old Russia is known as "Yerofeyich" and its fame is due to its medicinal effectiveness. About 1768, the barber Yerofeyich cured Count Grigoriy Orlov, lover of Catherine II, of a serious stomach complaint using this special infusion of roots and herbs. As thanks for this, he was given permission to manufacture and sell his herb infusion for commercial use. Today, an infusion is available commercially called "Yerofeyich," but this has nothing to do with the original "Yerofeyich." Aromatic drops still have their place in local remedies. Some of the traditional infusions are produced exclusively for medicinal purposes, such as vodka with garlic, juniper, birch buds, propolis, and sea buckthorn. Sweet liqueurs are traditionally drunk with tea and dessert, and the bitter or neutral flavored herb vodkas with the zakuska.

Liqueur and vodka recipes

"Yerofeyich" (herb infusion)

Add ½ oz/15 g each of St. John's wort, yarrow, mint, wild thyme, dill, and anise, plus 1 oz/25 g of red boronia root (*Boronia heterophylla*) to 3 quarts/3 liters of vodka and leave the whole to infuse for at least two weeks. Then strain and bottle. The more ingredients the "Yerofeyich" has, the more efficacious it is supposed to be.

Simple herb vodka

Fill a bottle half full with vodka and hang a little bunch of dried herbs in it. Wrap the bottle in an opaque cloth and place in the sun for at least one month. Then remove the herbs and top up with the rest of the vodka.

Wormwood infusion

Fill a bottle one quarter full with fresh wormwood plants and then fill up with vodka. Add lemon peel to enhance the flavor and leave to infuse for 2–3 weeks.

Mint infusion

Put ¾–1 oz/20–25 g of dried mint in a bottle, top up with vodka and leave to stand in a warm place for at least 20 days.

Liqueurs

You need fresh, ripe fruit for all types of liqueur. Fill a glass bottle ⅔ full with fresh berries or other fruit and top up with vodka. Then wrap the bottle in an opaque cloth and place in a warm spot.

Vigorously shake the bottle every 4–5 days over the next 2–3 months. At the end of this process, strain the liquid and add water, depending on the desired alcohol content. In a large pan, bring a thick syrup to a boil, made from 1 scant cup/200 g sugar per 4 cups/1 liter of liqueur and a little water, stirring continually. Add the strained liquid to this sugar syrup and bring the whole to a boil. Then leave to cool—and your fruity, aromatic liqueur is ready.

Birch sap

The endless birch forest with its rustling, silvery leaves is typical of the Russian landscape. Freshly budding birch in the spring is considered a symbol of awakening life. When "Father Frost" has slowly withdrawn his sharp claws in April, and nature starts to defy the cold and is filled again with new life, then it is time to tap birch sap.

To make the sap flow, a hole is scratched through the bark and a small wooden pipe is inserted. The sap now drips slowly into a large bucket. When this is full after a few days, the drink, full of vitamins and minerals, can be enjoyed fresh. It is supposed to cleanse the blood and strengthen the kidneys, bladder, and skin. The wound on the trunk is painted with resin to allow it to heal. Traditionally, to stimulate a slight fermentation process, fried peas and warm rye bread are added to the fresh juice. Ten days later, the slightly sour, full-bodied birch kvass is ready to drink.

Birch trees yield a healthy and tasty juice.

Fruit and berries

Moscow was once the currant city. The River Moskva was once called Smorodinka (from the Russian *smorodina*, meaning currant), because of a wealth of currant bushes along its banks.

The endless Russian forests are still rich in fruit, and the Russians gather about three million metric tonnes of berries each year, of which the majority ends up at farmer's markets. In late summer, blueberries, European cranberries, currants, cranberries and sea buckthorn are piled high on the stalls. They play a larger role in the kitchen and in natural medicine than garden-grown fruit, which is hard to come by in the raw Russian climate.

European cranberries are the red gold of the Russian forests, where they ripen like a glowing carpet. The best-loved berry type in northern and central Russia, it is picked from September until the first snow and is one of the delicacies of Russian cuisine. Good collectors can pick up to 65 lb/30 kg per day, in competition with black grouse and capercaillie. In recent times, there have also been successful attempts to cultivate European cranberries. The fruit is processed into jams and conserves, marmalades, and juice. It is considered a universal remedy in folk medicine and promotes an active stomach and bowel. With its phenol content, European cranberries improve capillary elasticity, promote the absorption of vitamin C in the body and strengthen the effects of antibiotics. Cranberry juice is a household remedy against coughs and colds, helps combat kidney infections, and is applied, mixed with honey, against cramps.

Russia's different climatic zones mean that the apple is available all year round; it is the most widespread and widely used garden fruit. Pears are one of the less frequent culinary fruits, as they can only be stored and transported to a limited extent due to their high sugar content. Quinces, on the other hand, last longer, are stewed and give all types of fruit cakes a fresh and fruity aroma.

In the south of this enormous country, even melons ripen. On the Volga delta and in the south of the Black Earth area, fodder melons are primarily grown. Honeydew melons *(dynya)* are available in round, oval or pear shapes. Watermelons *(arbusy)*, whose juice is sometimes made into *nardek*, a type of melon honey, are a popular dessert in Russia. Sweet cherries only thrive in the south of the country and are only regionally significant as a seasonal fruit. On the other hand, plums, mirabelles, peaches, and apricots from the Caucasus or the Crimean peninsula are always widely available.

Mors

A rediscovered beverage from ancient times is for sale in Russia: mors, a juice made from fruit and berries. Berry drinks were known even in the chronicles of Yaroslav the Wise in the 11th century. According to *Domostroy*, the ancient Russian book of the household from the 16th century, a good housewife should be able to produce "blueberry water and cranberry water as well as sweetmeats made from cherries, raspberry beverages, and other delicacies" as desserts. Before the reforms of Peter the Great and the introduction of tea to Russia, most Russians drank raspberry and cranberry mors. Today, this vitamin-rich berry juice is again being made on an industrial scale and can only just meet demand.

Background: Currants *smorodiny* have a fine, sharp taste and always need sweetening.

European cranberries *(klyukvy)*, as well as being delicacies, are vitamin-providers and medicine.

Sweet wild strawberries *(semlyaniki)* are enjoyed fresh, in milk drinks and in jams.

Raspberries *(maliny)* are used in gingerbread, jams and conserves, and fruit tea.

Blackberries *(yezheviki)* are popular eaten raw or in jams, or as stewed fruit or juice.

In Russia, tart European cranberries are popular eaten as a dessert, sweetened with icing sugar.

Fruit desserts and conserves

Russian cuisine is characterized by its particular love of sour flavors. This is the taste of *kisel*: fruit soups available in thick, medium-thick, and liquid forms. They are cooked up from potato flour and fresh, frozen or dried berries. Kisel is served with cold milk, sweet cream, and light fatless sponges or rusks—an exquisite meal on a hot summer day. Popular fruits for making kisel are cranberries, redcurrants, strawberries and wild strawberries, raspberries, and blueberries. The south has its very refreshing kisel made from sour cherries, enriched with sweet almonds and crowned with a cap of cream with roasted flaked walnuts. Each housewife will swear by her home-made *varenye*. For this, whole fruit, generally berries, are cooked down, with or without sugar. Varenye is not only eaten on bread but also eaten on its own with tea. Particularly popular is varenye made from raspberries, cherries, yellow plums, green walnuts, muskmelons, rowan berries or even from green tomatoes.

Jelly is also made from many fruits by cooking it up with juice, gelatin and sugar. One specialty is milk jelly with almonds. For this dessert, sweetened milk is brought to a boil, thickened with gelatin, and peeled and crushed almonds are added. The jelly must cool for about one hour.

In Russia, *kompot* is diluted fruit juices with fruit. The fruit is cooked briefly in water with sugar, the juice obtained is flavored with lemon and cloves, and poured over the fruit—a fine dessert.

Kholodets iz yagod
Cold sweet berry soup

Generous 1 lb/500 g fresh berries, e.g. raspberries, cranberries, currants (or cherries)
$^{2}/_{3}$–$^{3}/_{4}$ cup/150–200 g sugar
2–3 tbsp cornstarch
1 cup/250 ml cream or milk to serve

Cover the berries with water and cook until soft. Push through a sieve, add sugar and briefly bring back to a boil. Dissolve the cornstarch in cold water and mix into the hot berry syrup, stirring continually. Do not allow it to boil. Serve with cream or milk as desired.

Yabochny kompot
Apple compote

Generous 1 lb/500 g apples, peeled, cored and quartered
¾ cup/175 g sugar
1 cinnamon stick
4–6 cloves

Bring the apples to a boil in a small amount of water, with 2 tablespoons of the sugar, the cinnamon stick and the cloves. Pour off the juice and place to one side. Put the apples into a dish. Stir the remaining sugar into the juice, bring to a boil, pour over the apples and leave the compote to cool before serving.

Varenye iz kryzhovnika
Gooseberry jam

2¼ lb/1 kg gooseberries
2 tbsp vodka or rum
6 cups/1 kg sugar
2 tbsp lemon juice
½ an unwaxed lemon, cut into thin slices

Wash the gooseberries, and carefully top and tail (the gooseberries should remain whole). Sprinkle with the vodka or rum and leave for about 2 hours to be absorbed.
Make a syrup from 3½ cups/¾ liter of water and the sugar in an enamel pan. Add the berries carefully, bring to a boil and simmer for about 5 minutes.
Leave to cool, then bring back to a boil. Add the lemon slices, stirring very carefully so that the berries do not disintegrate. This jam does not have to be kept to develop a flavor but, if required, pour it hot into jars and seal well to keep.

Fine *kompot* made from fruit, water, and sugar is stored in large preserving jars and generally served as a refreshing drink.

Milk

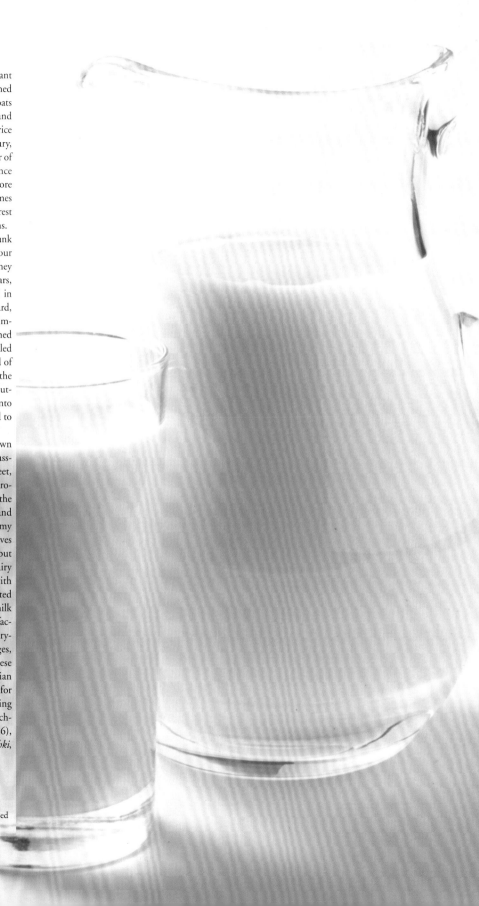

Milk has always been considered an important and healthy food in Russia. It is mainly obtained from cows, but also from mares, ewes, and goats in the Buryat and Kalmyk Republics and Tatarstan. However, fodder has increased in price enormously since the end of the 20th century, and livestock has fallen drastically. The number of ewes and goats has fallen by 50 percent since 1991, and the number of dairy cows by more than 25 percent. Today, one third of milk comes from domestic and ancillary production, the rest from medium and large agricultural operations.

At the time of the Kievan Rus, milk was drunk raw, boiled or soured. Curd cheese and sour cream were made from any excess, and the whey given to the livestock. Through the Tatars, numerous new milk products were included in Russian cuisine from the 13th century onward, such as soured soups, yogurt, and kefir. The simplest type of milk processing has been maintained in villages to this day: fresh, strained milk is sealed tightly in barrels and hung in wells on the end of ropes. Over time, the fat collects and forms the cream. Once skimmed, this is churned into butter, the skimmed milk is drunk and processed into blancmanges and curd cheese. The whey is fed to the calves.

Sweet cream and butter were mainly unknown until the 16th century. *Smetana* is typical of Russian cuisine, made from buttermilk. Its sweet, creamy flavor is very different from west European sour cream. Natural *smetana* is eaten by the spoonful at breakfast, is added to borshch and *shchi*, and gives *blini* and *pelmeni* their creamy smoothness. In the Soviet era, many housewives made their own yogurt, kefir, and cream, but since the 1990s the farmer's markets and dairy businesses in the cities have been swollen with homemade cream and butter, as well as imported cheese and ready-made yogurt. Traditional milk products such as *prostokvash* or *varenets* (see facing page) are still primarily made in the countryside. Milk forms the basis of sweet porridges, blancmanges, and innumerable curd cheese dishes. When preparing curd cheese, Russian housewives do not discard the whey, but use it for chilled soups *(kisel)* with berries, for making kvass, or for jellies. Curd cheese is also a much-loved filling for *varenyky* (see also page 166), pirogi and loose curd cheese *piroshki* (*vatrushki*, see page 127).

Milk is enjoyed as a cold or warm drink and is also used in numerous dishes.

Milk products

Butter *(maslo):* skimmed cream is inoculated with lactic acid bacteria, generally in the form of buttermilk, to sour. In about 24 hours at 53°–65 °F/12–18 °C, the cream becomes thick and sour. Then it is churned in tall wooden barrels to allow the fat globules to clump into butter. Russia's best butter comes from the Vologda area. It is quince yellow, contains 82.5 percent fat, and is well salted.

Kefir *(kefir):* pasteurized milk (generally cows' milk) is charged with kefir mold. Depending on the duration of fermentation, the beverage effervesces with a fresh and tangy flavor and can contain up to 2 percent alcohol in addition to 3 percent fat.

Sour cream *(smetana):* fresh milk is placed in a flat dish for 12–15 hours to allow the fat to rise. Buttermilk is added to the skimmed cream to sour it. Then the mixture is put into a slow oven at about 195 °F/90 °C, and cream is added continually. When the jug is full, the cream is whipped, heated briefly, the container then rinsed with cold water and put in a cool place. The higher the fat content, the creamier and more full bodied the flavor.

Yogurt *(yogurt):* high fat milk is heated to 195 °F/90 °C for about 10 minutes in order to kill off any bacteria. Then it has to cool to between 104–113 °F/40–45 °C. Yogurt cultures are added whilst stirring. The batch is placed in an oven preheated to 120°F/50 °C for about 30 minutes. The yogurt cultures then have to mature for at least 8 hours.

Soft curd cheese *(tvorog):* milk must stand covered in a dish for at least two days until it is thick. Then the thickened milk is placed in an oven heated to 85 °F/30 °C for 30 minutes. This encourages the formation of curds and whey. The curds are drained through cheesecloth for 2 hours. What is left are loose, damp curds. To form a dry mass, damp curds are clamped in a bag between two little boards and weighed down. For rapid production of curd cheese, raw milk is heated to 95 °F/ 35 °C with buttermilk and rennet.

Varenets, prostokvasha and *ryashenka:* boiled milk is placed in the oven in a clay pot for 2–3 hours at a low temperature or left in a warm place overnight and often mixed with *smetana*. *Varenets* and *prostokvasha* are thickened milk products greatly reduced over heat and with a very high fat content. *Ryashenka* is just the light cocoa-colored cream that forms below the skin and is carefully skimmed off. These typical Russian milk dishes have a slightly nutty, smoked flavor and are popular for breakfast.

The Russian market has a wealth of different milk products: curd cheese is much loved, as are soured and salted butter, whole and skimmed milk, fine kefir, and sweet and sour creams, some with a high fat content.

Curd cheese delicacies

Blinchiki s tvorogom i yablokami
Pancakes with soft curd cheese and apple

For the batter:
1⅓–1⅔ cups/250 g wheat flour
2 cups/500 ml milk
2 eggs
1 tsp sugar
1 pinch salt
Oil for frying

For the filling:
11 oz/300 g apples, peeled, cored, and chopped small
2 tbsp/30 g butter
3½ cups/750 g soft curd cheese
1 egg
100 g sugar
1 pinch salt

Mix a smooth pancake batter using all of the batter ingredients apart from the oil.
To make the filling, cook the apples in the butter until golden. Add the egg, sugar, and salt to the cheese and stir well. Mix into the apples.
Use the batter to cook thin pancakes in a hot skillet, cover with the filling, and roll up.
Tip: you can also drizzle the filled pancakes with butter and honey and then heat through under the broiler.

Tvorozhniki (Syrniki)
Sweet curd cheese cakes

2¼ cups/500 g soft curd cheese
¾ cup/200 g sour cream
1 egg
3–4 tbsp all-purpose flour
5 tbsp/60 g sugar
Few drops of vanilla extract, or to taste
1 pinch salt
Oil for frying
Sour cream and jam for serving

Mix all the ingredients together thoroughly apart from the oil. Roll out the dough about ½ inch/1½ cm thick onto a floured board and cut out round cakes using a cookie cutter or glass. Fry in butter on both sides and serve with sour cream and jam to taste.
Variation: *syrniki* taste particularly good if 9 tbsp/75 g of raisins soaked in water or rum are stirred into the mixture before frying.

Ice-cold pleasure

Foreign visitors always wonder why Russians love eating ice cream on the streets even in deepest winter—even at temperatures of 30 degrees below freezing. Muscovites argue over the best place to eat this cold delicacy. Many people go to the ZUM department store on Bolshoi Theater just for the homemade treats there.

Centuries ago, crushed glacier ice was served with fruit and nuts in Georgian courts and even brought to Moscow and St. Petersburg in winter. However, it soon stood no chance against the competition from France: The name of the Russian *plombir*— ice cream with chocolate, nuts, and candied fruit—comes from the town of Plombières on the edge of the Vosges, from which French cooks brought this cold treat to the court of the Tsar in the 18th century. In 1845, the businessman Ivan Isler obtained a patent for a machine for making ice cream, which started the triumphal march of this cold delicacy in Russia.

At the start of the 21st century, Russian companies produce almost 1 million metric tonnes of ice cream each year—often in cooperation with global brands. Moscow's Institute of Refrigeration Technology monitors the quality. More than 160 ingredients are used for ice cream, primarily milk, cream, eggs, sugar and salt, as well as vanilla, chocolate, fruit, and nuts. Only natural additives can be used, even for the colors and flavors. Chocolate and vanilla ice creams are favorites, along with ice creams made with cranberries, raspberries, wild strawberries, and nuts. Vanilla ice cream with cedar nuts from Siberia is a delicacy. The range is supplemented by different types of diet ice creams.

Simple treats as a snack: curd cheese or Quark with sour cream and forest fruits.

Vatrushki
Open curd cheese cakes

Yeast dough according to the recipe on page 18

For the filling:
2¼ cups/500 g soft curd cheese
9½ tbsp/125 g sugar
1 egg
1 tbsp wheat flour
Few drops of vanilla extract, or to taste
1 pinch salt
¾ cup/100 g raisins to taste
Butter for spreading

Prepare the dough according to the recipe. Roll out into a sausage and cut into 20 even-sized pieces. Shape the pieces into balls and place on a greased baking sheet about 2 inches/5 cm apart. Leave to rest for about 15 minutes.
Meanwhile, mix the filling ingredients together well. Press hollows into the dough balls and fill with the curd cheese filling. Leave to rest for another 10 minutes, then bake in an oven pre-heated to 430 °F/220 °C until golden brown. Spread the edges of the baked *vatrushki* with butter.
Variation: *vatrushki* can also be filled with spoonfuls of a jam of your choice, or with fruit.

The way to heaven is through the samovar. Tea with good friends means warmth and security.

Below: Cross-section of a traditional charcoal samovar, still in frequent use today.

sugar, honey, different conserves and jams (*varenye*, see page 122 f.) and jellies. As the Russians swear by sweetmeats, there are also waffle gateaux filled with nut nougat or vanilla cream, delicate sponges, oat cookies, yeast dough *piroshki* (see page 18), cracknel, gingerbread, or confectionery.

In Russia, tea is a true drink of the masses. It is enjoyed all day; it is the first thing offered to a guest and concludes the meal in restaurants. And whoever has traveled on Russian trains will remember with warm affection the many glasses of hot tea that can be ordered from the carriage steward at almost any time of the day or night.

Tea from the samovar

"A table that is set but not crowned with a samovar is not a table but a thing without worth, a manger as for birds and animals; there is no pleasure here, no comeliness," wrote the Siberian novelist and tea connoisseur Valentin Rasputin. The tea boiler is the most typical utensil in a Russian household and the samovar has a place of honor in every family. In former times it provided boiling water for breakfast tea without the large oven having to be heated.

The precursor of the samovar ("self-boiler") was the *sbitennik*, a type of kettle with a pipe for glowing coals and an air hole. It was used for cooking or warming the much-loved honey drink *sbiten* (see page 85).

The first samovar factory was founded in 1778 in Tula. This town, with its rich supplies of ore and high-quality metal processing, became famous as the center of Russian samovar production. In 1826 there were eight samovar factories, and 70 by 1886, some of which produced very elaborate devices. The materials used were copper, brass, tinplate and, less frequently, silver. In the armory in the Kremlin, a golden samovar belonging to Tsar Paul I (1754–1801) is on display, decorated

with ivory, enamel, and precious stones. Standard samovars were made from so-called Polish silver, an alloy made from nickel with iron and copper, and these were always tin-plated on the inside. They were often adorned with epigrams such as: "Drink tea and you'll live for one hundred years!" Today's samovars are generally made in the "Schtamp" factory in Tula and are affordable mass goods. There are also wonderfully painted souvenir samovars.

The traditional samovar is heated using charcoal placed on a grid in the fire tube within the vessel. Modern samovars heat the water using an electric coil, which does, however, impair the flavor and quality.

While the water boils in the samovar, a strong black tea is brewing on a small teapot placed on top. Thus everyone can mix their tea to the desired strength.

For tea preparation, simmering water should always be used, not water at a rolling boil, as there is otherwise a risk that the volatile flavors of the tea will evaporate. When the water in the samovar starts to sing, it is just about to boil and is at the right temperature. The tea is sweetened with

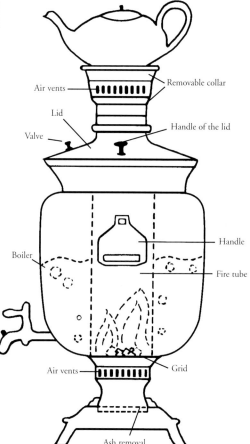

Air vents

Removable collar

Lid

Handle of the lid

Valve

Boiler

Handle

Fire tube

Air vents

Grid

Ash removal

Little Russian tea stories

In Russia, tea is not only the favorite national drink and part of life, it is also an expression of hospitality, peace, and refreshment. The Siberians learned about tea from the Mongols—long before it came to Europe. In 1638, a boyar brought tea as a gift to the Tsar's court in Moscow from a west Mongolian khan, which was the start of a success story beyond compare. From then on, tea was brewed not only in the kitchens of the Tsar but also quickly became generally loved in the rest of Moscow and its environs. Healers additionally discovered that tea is a superb remedy for colds, stomach disorders, and headaches.

In 1679, contracts were signed with China for its supply. The arduous journey to Moscow took three months, and the cost of transportation increased the price from 50 to 130 rubles per case. Two packets of tea cost as much as a sable skin. Later, the sea route from Canton to Odessa made tea more economical. It first became a drink of the people on the construction of the Trans-Siberian railway, which was finally completed in full in 1916.

Muscovites have always been particular lovers of tea. In the mid-19th century, there were already a hundred specialist businesses on the Moskva and no food was served without this leaf infusion. Hot tea was an indispensable accompaniment when traveling along Russia's endless roads. In the mail offices there were samovars as tall as a person. Tea was brewed in the bitter frost during coach journeys. There was a special chest to carry the travel samovar, crockery, coal, and sugar.

Georgia, Azerbaijan and even Russia have been growing tea since the mid-19th century. Botanists cultivated cold-resistant types, suitable for the Russian climate. Russian tea comes from the region around Krasnodar on the Black Sea, the most northerly area of cultivation in the world. It is soft, almost sweet, aromatic, fragrant, and therefore much loved.

Tea, which contains 2–3 percent caffeine, stimulates the circulation and fortifies the nervous system. Its etheric oils, tanning agents, and tannin promote digestion and have an antibacterial effect. Tea refreshes the body, stimulates the mind, and lowers blood pressure and the risk of heart attacks. In addition, it strengthens respiration, protects against infection, and maintains the teeth through its fluoride content.

Rich businessmen partake of tea at the Trade Fair in the city of Nizhniy Novgorod in 1905.

Tea types

Black tea is particularly widespread in the European part of Russia and is generally imported from areas of cultivation such as Sri Lanka, India, and China. It gets its name from the dark color that is produced through the natural fermentation and subsequent drying of the freshly harvested leaves. Black tea provides an intense infusion with a fresh flavor. **Green tea** is the most widespread after black tea. It is mainly imported from China. The best sorts are silvery-green when harvested and light green when dried. After harvesting, green tea is heated briefly in iron pans or steam in order to stop fermentation. In Russia, it is drunk in the south and primarily in the summer, because it is a good thirst-quencher. **Red tea** is a fermented particularly slowly and incompletely, and is similar to black tea in flavor and fragrance. It used to come to Russia over the land route from China and is still obtained from there, but is now only available in selected delis. **Yellow tea** is derived from buds and young shoots. It is similar to green tea, but unlike this is no longer drunk in Russia.

If you want to enjoy Russian tea in true style, then you need typical tea glasses. The finely polished glass is placed in a metal holder. In the case of very fine glasses, these are naturally made of silver—just like the teaspoons.

Baking gingerbread

Gingerbread is baked and eaten in Russia all year round. Its precursors existed back in the time of the Kievan Rus. The simple rectangular cakes were made from rye flour, honey, and berry juice. From the 11th century, bakers also used cinnamon, cloves, cardamom, bitter orange and lemon peels, Jamaica pepper, nutmeg, star anise, mint, and aniseed for the dough, spices that had found their way along the Silk Road (see page 328 f.) and through the south to Russia. Thus the name *pryaniki* (from the Russian *pryanosti*, spices) became established for gingerbread. It obtains its distinctive flavor from ginger, which is absolutely indispensable in the gingerbread dough.

More dried than baked, gingerbread was always cooked in Russian ovens at a low heat after the bread was baked. Over centuries, each town built up its own gingerbread bakery. The residents of Tula have the tastiest gingerbread in their opinion, which is filled with jam. Gingerbread from Arkhangelsk can be distinguished by its figures in colored sugar glaze, and Muscovites are proud of their fine gingerbread that includes honey or dark syrup. St. Petersburg promotes its fine chocolate gingerbread, baked using mineral water. Vyazma, Gorodez near Nizhniy Novgorod, and Voronezh specialize in raspberry gingerbread and black gingerbread made from rye biscuit crumbs, sweetened with cranberry syrup and honey. In almost every region of the country, *pryaniki* are covered with a sugar glaze, usually white. Gingerbread from Tula, Gorodez, and Vyasma additionally carry a relief pattern. For this, special molds are made from limewood. Popular motifs are names, initials, coats of arms, tendrils, flowers, and animals. The most original gingerbread must be the so-called *kovrishki* ("little rugs") from the Volga near Nizhniy Novgorod. They are up to 6 ½ feet/ 2 m long, about 3 feet/1 m wide and 2 ½– 4 inches/6–10 cm high. The dough for these giants is beaten and broken up using large sticks. Then two layers are placed one on top of the other, with a filling of jelly or jam, almonds, and raisins. Finally, the gingerbread is covered with a pale pink sugar glaze. The famous *kovrishki* have entered colloquial language in a saying: *ne sa kakiye kovrishki* is what you say when you would not do anything for the world, not even for this great delicacy.

Tula gingerbread carries the name of its city.

Russian gingerbread molds are traditionally carved from limewood. It is relatively soft and is easy to work.

The finished wooden shapes, often laboriously decorated with flowers, animals or coats of arms, are finally oiled using a small cloth.

Flour, honey, and spices are the most important ingredients for making gingerbread dough. The baker divides this up into portions.

For the famous gingerbread from Tula, a piece of gingerbread is rolled out quite thick, some jam is placed on top and it is covered with a second piece of dough.

This gingerbread "sandwich" is now given its characteristic pattern using the wooden mold and is then baked golden brown on a baking sheet in the oven.

The cooked Tula gingerbread is given a final polish and a beautiful white shine with a sugar glaze applied by hand at the finish.

From the cake shop

Tort ptiche molochko
Bird's milk cake

For the sponge:
3 eggs, separated
½ cup/100 g sugar
1 pinch baking powder
⅔ cup/100 g all-purpose flour

For the filling:
2 tsp/10 g agar-agar or other gelling agent
(see Glossary)
¾ cup/175 g butter
⅓ cup/75 ml evaporated milk
1½ cups/300 g superfine sugar
2 egg whites

To decorate:
5½ oz/150 g dark bittersweet chocolate
½ cup/125 g cream
2 tbsp/20 g toasted slivered almonds

For the sponge, whisk the egg yolks with 3 tablespoons of luke-warm water and half of the sugar until foamy. Whisk the egg whites until stiff, stir in the remaining sugar, and place onto the egg yolk mix. Sift over the flour and the baking powder and mix everything together carefully with a balloon whisk. Line a 10½–11 inch/26–28 cm spring-form baking pan with baking parchment, add the batter and bake in an oven pre-heated to 400 °F/200 °C for 15–20 minutes. Loosen the cake pan and leave the cake to cool thoroughly. Then cut through the cake horizontally using a thread or a large sharp knife to produce two bases.

For the filling, soften the agar-agar in some cold water for about 3 hours or as packet instructions. Beat the butter with the evaporated milk until foamy, and place to one side. Bring ½ cup/125 ml water to a boil with the sugar, add the softened agar-agar and simmer on a low heat for 15 minutes. Remove from the heat.

Whisk the egg whites until very stiff, then add gradually to the hot agar-agar syrup, stirring continually and carefully. Slowly stir this mixture into the beaten butter-evaporated milk mixture and mix together well. Place one of the sponge bases into a flan ring, add half of the mixture, place the second base on top and add the remaining mixture. Place the cake in the refrigerator for 2 hours to chill.

Melt the chocolate in a basin set over a pan of barely simmering water and spread on the cake. Decorate the cake to choice and add the slivered almonds. Serve with whipped cream if desired.

Whether for anniversaries, weddings, children's birthdays or other family celebration—no important event in Russia should be without a cake from the baker. These sweet works of art are often elaborately decorated with figures made from colorful almond paste.

Sharlotka s yablokami
Stirred apple cake

Generous 1 lb/500 g cooking apples
6 eggs
Generous 1 cup/200 g sugar
1¹⁄₃ cups/200 g all-purpose flour
1 pinch baking powder
Butter/margarine and dry breadcrumbs for lining the pan

Peel and core the apples, cut into small dice. Beat the eggs with the sugar until foamy and the sugar has dissolved. Sift in the flour and baking powder one spoonful at a time, then mix in the apples. Grease a baking pan and line with dry breadcrumbs. Fill with apple batter and bake in an oven preheated to 340 °F/170 °C for about 1 hour (test with a skewer to make sure it is cooked). If the cake browns too quickly, cover with aluminum foil or damp greaseproof paper.

Russian chocolate

In the center of Moscow, a pleasantly sweet fragrance penetrates the traffic fumes. It comes from the largest chocolate factory in the world, called "Krasny Oktyabr" ("Red October"). It was founded by Theodor von Eimen, a master pastry cook from Würtemberg in Germany, who came to Moscow in 1850 to try his luck as an entrepreneur. After making cube sugar, he ran a chocolate and praline factory on the old Arbat, which at that time was the most important commercial street in Moscow, and a cake shop in the Theater Square. He invested the profits in the most modern machinery for a new factory on the Moskva river opposite the city castle of the Kremlin. The entry in the *Yearbook of Factories and Works of the Russian Empire* states: "One. Steam factory company for making chocolates and tea cakes. Founded in 1867."

The company was successful against the competition, thanks in particular to its wide assortment and the high quality of the chocolates, toffees, pralines, confectionery, biscuits, gingerbread, and sponges. They received a Grand Prix at the World Exhibition in Paris in 1900 for their range and quality. The company placed particular value on packaging: the confectionery boxes were made using silk, velvet, and even leather to meet the very highest standards.

Soon a branch was opened in Simferopol on the Crimean Peninsula. Its specialty was chocolate-coated fruit, such as plums, cherries, and pears, as well as conserves. After the October Revolution, the factory was expropriated and declared "the first state pastry factory," and given its current name of "Red October" in 1922. In subsequent years, pralines with fantastic names such as "Clumsy Mishka" *(Mishka kosolapy)*, "Southern Night" *(Yuzhnaya noch)*, and "Stratosphere" *(Stratosfera)* carried the fame of the chocolate factory across the whole of the Soviet Empire.

Today, the 2,500 employees of the chocolate giant, now converted into a joint-stock company, each year produce 60,000 metric tonnes of bonbons, pralines, chocolate, toffees, nut products, cocoa powder, and semi-finished goods made of chocolate in their eight factories, located in St. Petersburg and the Ukrainian cities of Kharkiv, Simferopol, and Odessa, in addition to Moscow.

They meet over one third of the demand in Moscow and 20 percent of chocolate consumption in the whole of Russia. The much loved candy type "Clumsy Mishka," which accompanied the first cosmonaut Yuri Gagarin into space in 1961, is characteristic of Russian full-milk pralines, which include no artificial ingredients or chemical additives. Waffle-nut fillings are very popular. Only select raw materials, such as cocoa powder, sugar, milk powder, glucose, vanilla, nuts, fruit, natural syrups, and domestically grown berries are used for all the types produced.

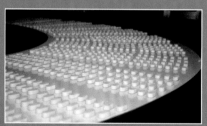

For delicious chocolate pralines with fine fillings, the sweet centers are made first, using machines.

The shaped confectionery on the conveyor belt approaches the coating bath at almost 104 °F/40 °C.

The chocolate coating solidifies immediately on the cool pralines, which can then be packed.

The "Red October" factory's own museum presents its range of confectionery products.

Chocolate types

Russia imports about 80,000 metric tonnes of cocoa beans each year, which is about 3 percent of global production, a large proportion of which comes from African countries such as Ghana and the Ivory Coast. Consumption per head of cocoa products has increased in the last 20 years from 1 lb/0.5 kg per year to almost 5 lb/2.5 kg. The use of chemical additives and substitute fats, artificial colorings, and flavorings is banned.

Russian chocolate comes in three different types, depending on the composition:

Pure chocolate: this keeps for 12 months because it is made of only cocoa powder, cocoa butter, and sugar. There are three types:
1. Bitter chocolate: 40 to 55 percent cocoa, up to 47 percent sugar
2. Semi-sweet chocolate: 29 to 33 percent cocoa, 48 to 52 percent sugar
3. Sweet chocolate: 22 to 28 percent cocoa, 53 to 57 percent sugar

Chocolate with additives: this chocolate has a lower proportion of cocoa and some are mixed with milk, nuts, coffee, raisins, cream, and candied fruits. This chocolate is less solid and only keeps for about 6 months (at 64 °F/ 18 °C and less than 75 percent air humidity).

Chocolate with fillings: sweet chocolate is frequently used for this, and it is filled with nougat, fruit creams and liqueur jellies, brandy, coconut, and vanilla, for example.

Background: Not only small cakes but also pralines, confectionery, and bonbons, some in multicolored wrappings, are also enjoyed with tea.

BELARUS

RUSSIAN
FEDERATION

POLAND

Schoska

Chernivitsi

Shayskiy
Osera   Kovel

Chernobyl

Korosten

Sumy

Lutsk   Rivne

KIEV

Pryluky

Okhtyrka

Kharkiv

Schytomyr

Dnieper

Veliki
Sorochintsi

Myrhorod   Poltava

Lviv

Ternopil

Khmelnitski

Cherkassy

Donets

Truskavets

Vinnytsya

UKRAINE

Krementschuk

Kramatorsk

Artemovsk

Luhansk

Ivano-
Frankivsk

Dnipropetrovsk

Dniester

SLOVAKIA

Uzhhorod

Carpathian Mountains

Uman

Kirovohrad

Zaporizhzhya

Donetsk

HUNGARY

Howerja
2058 m

Chernivtsi

Bug

Pervomaysk

Kryvyy Rih

Nikopol

Melitopol

Mariupol

Dnieper

Mykolayiv

MOLDOVA

Kherson

Sea of Azov

ROMANIA

Dniester

Odessa

Ismail   Danube

Crimea

Simferopol

BLACK

SEA

Sebastopol   Yalta

N
60 miles/
100 km
0

Beate Blaha

УКРАЇНА

Ukraine

Even though the word Ukraine means "land on the edge" or "borderland" this region has played a central role in the development of European culture, with "Mother Russia" having its origins in Kiev, the present day capital of Ukraine. In the 9th century the state of Kievan Rus was founded as an east Slavic empire extending from the Baltic to the Black Sea and including the region which today forms the European part of Russia. Its capital was Kiev which, even today, is still considered to be the mother of all Russian towns. Trade routes from Scandinavia through to the Caucasus crossed this region and were also thoroughfares for religions, art, and cuisine. The breakup of the Kievan Rus state in the 13th century was followed by the arrival of the Mongolians and over the centuries individual areas of present day Ukraine came under Lithuanian, Polish, Turkish, Austro-Hungarian, Russian, and after 1922, Soviet, rule. Today, however, Ukraine enjoys a newly found identity. At the end of 1991, 90 percent of the population voted for withdrawal from the Soviet Union and for independence. Europe's second largest country now has to overcome numerous political, social, and ecological problems but it is a country richly blessed by Mother Nature: most regions of the country have a mild continental climate while the Crimean peninsula is considered to be Mediterranean to subtropical. The majority of Ukraine is flat land characterized by forest, forested steppe and steppe areas with a wealth of berries, mushrooms, and venison. Potatoes, rye, oats, and barley are grown in the north. In central and southern Ukraine more demanding grain, vegetable, and fruit varieties are grown throughout this extremely fertile belt of black soils. In the west the Carpathian Mountains rise to more than 6,560 feet/2,000 m above sea level. The climate is harsher here and sheep farming plays an important economic role. In the south the wine and tropical fruit of the Black Sea area and the Crimea give the cuisine a Mediterranean touch and are a source of eggplants, herbs, and fish for the markets.

Typical of Ukrainian cuisine are roasted and slow cooked meat dishes as well as homemade sausages. Nourishing porridges are made from grains, vegetables serve as ingredients for soups, stews, hors d'oeuvres, and main dishes. Egg dishes are also just as popular as are filled pastries such as the favored staple *varenyky*. Steaming bowls of borscht, strong flavored bacon, and homemade schnapps all serve to provide warmth on icy winter days. Pastries and desserts are the link between the Ukrainian sweet tooth and the Austro-Hungarian traditions. Last but not least the southern Ukraine in particular has a long tradition of producing wines and sparkling wines which ought to be part of any celebratory meal.

Previous page: Sunflowers bloom in southern Ukraine in the summer for as far as the eye can see.

Whether its fresh ingredients for the kitchen or provisions for the winter, the range on offer at the markets is extensive.

Blessed by the southern sun the dark red Yalta or Crimea onions from the Crimean Peninsula in the Black Sea are mild and almost sweet. They taste best peeled and sliced with rye bread and dipped in unrefined sunflower oil and salt. They are also the perfect accompaniment to bacon and herring, baked potatoes, or salads.

A stroll through the market

We are tramping through the mud and deep puddles of an unpaved pavement along an arterial road in Kiev, wet and freezing. One hundred and sixty five feet/50 m farther on, however, we will find the best bread in the whole market, so Lyusya, a friend in Kiev, tells me. And she knows the farmer at the end of the row of stalls, the one on the stool under the canopy. One can buy really good sausage from him. The black market in Ukraine is booming, everyone tries to make ends meet with some kind of small business deal. There are dozens of street markets such as this in Kiev alone. Here you really can get everything you need: fruit and vegetables, roasted sunflower seeds and deliciously fragrant pieces of cake, as well as boots and safety pins. The lady with the Siberian fur hat and the fingerless gloves in her rickety wooden stall is glad to have our unexpected custom for her poppy seed pastries and her happy smile sets her gold teeth twinkling.

The two large, official markets in the Ukrainian capital are also full of life and full of everything one's heart could desire—Saturdays and Sundays are particularly busy days at these markets. The most expensive and, by virtue of its Art Nouveau ambience, the most upmarket is the *Bessarabsky* market right in the center of Kiev, known to the people of Kiev simply as *Bessarabka*. There has been a fruit and vegetable market on the present-day *Bessarabska Ploshcha*, Bessarabia Square, since the end of the 18th century. Between 1910 and 1912 an Art Nouveau style market hall was built on part of the square based on the plans of the architect H. Haj and using the latest technology of the day. The glass and metal roof covered 31,200 square feet/2896 sq m and almost 600 stalls. Kiev's oldest market, the rye market in the Podil area of the old town, was a market place for honey, wax, furs, grain, and raw amber even back in the Kievan Rus era. Today both markets provide ingredients for the capital's kitchens.

"*Shynochka*, madam, try a piece. Everything homemade and completely natural." In front of me is a piece of green bacon, perched on the tip of a sharp knife. You can and should test and buy something from practically every stand in the huge market hall. The market stalls offer homemade sausage and ham, smoked chicken which is eaten with horseradish, a wide range of milk products in huge preserving jars, eggs, geese, sauerkraut, and nuts or smoked plums which taste slightly bitter and are popular as a dessert with cream or in a pot roast. There is also fish and meat for sale, innards as well as boiled and preserved goods, carefully displayed on platters, a variety of trays, in plastic bowls and on wooden boards—horseradish with beet juice, stuffed cabbage leaves, eggplant rolls, and peppers, marinated mushrooms, garlic or mixed vegetables. And of course there are stands with mountains of fresh vegetables of all descriptions and which are served at Ukrainian tables primarily as cooked accompaniments to meat, as purées or as a stew with bacon.

The market computer

The predecessor of the high-tech computer, the abacus, is alleged to have been invented by a Babylonian centuries ago. The word is said to derive from the Phoenician *abak*, meaning an area spread with sand where one can write. Stones and wooden boards where the stones were moved around within carved lines were probably used as the first aids to calculation. Further refined and still in use today the abacus usually has a wooden frame fitted with rods along which the beads are moved to add, subtract, and even to multiply. In the countries of the former Soviet Union the abacus was still part of everyday life as a calculator up until a few years ago, just as it was in China or Japan. In Russia it is called *shchyoty*, in Ukraine *rachivnytsya*, from *rachuvaty* meaning to count, calculate. The board with the beads could be found in every shop and at every market, but nowadays the manually operated apparatus has been largely replaced by electronic tills almost throughout the country.

Ready to cook cabbage leaves stuffed with vegetables or meat are available at the market.

Ukrainian fast food—the delicious eggplants are filled with meat, vegetables, and nuts.

You can also buy eggplants like this at the market: layered with mayonnaise salad.

Left: Shopping at the *Bessarabsky* Market in Kiev.

Buryakovy salat z kvsoleyu i yablokamy
Salad of beets with apple and beans

3 medium-sized beets
2 medium-sized apples
1 cup/200 g white beans, cooked
3 tbsp oil
2 tbsp white wine vinegar
Salt
Pepper
Salad leaves for serving

Boil the beets for about 1 hour and peel. Chop the beets and apples into small dice. Combine with the cooked white beans, the oil, and the white wine vinegar, season with salt and pepper and arrange on the salad leaves.

Beets: the favorite vegetable

Beets ought to be a feature of every Ukrainian garden—
many people grow the red tuber themselves.

Buryak, beets, have been considered the undisputed queen of Ukrainian vegetables for centuries. Its skin is rough, a dirty red or gray color and is anything but attractive. But that doesn't bother anybody and the unattractive looking root tuber seems to be more of a "frog princess"—once kissed, that is cooked and peeled, she shows her noble side in rich crimson.

There is hardly a dacha, a piece of land or a garden in Ukraine where beets are not grown. Its parent plant is the wild beet that grows wild in the Mediterranean countries in particular. It was cultivated as a vegetable by the Ancient Greeks, Romans, and Egyptians.

The tuber reaches maturity at the end of the summer and can be kept raw in the refrigerator for up to two weeks. As the juice contains most of the aromatic properties beets should be cooked in their skins if possible. They take about an hour before they are soft and then they are delicious as a salad, with mayonnaise for example, grated cheese, and chopped walnuts. Also stuffed, baked, puréed, or as an accompaniment to grated horseradish they are an enrichment not only to country cooking. One is unlikely to find a zakuska menu without beets in the Ukraine and they appear in the forms of salads, with pickled cucumbers or with beans and apple for example, as well as raw combined with horseradish to accompany meat dishes. And almost every larder has large jars of preserved beets in store. The beet leaves are also used in a variety of ways such as in soups, hors d'oeuvres, or also rolled with a meat, rice, or corn filling. A beet kvass is also made from the tuber whereby the beets are peeled, quartered and then left to ferment with water and a piece of rye bread for about two weeks at room temperature. It is also popularly used as an ingredient for borscht.

The Ukrainians, among others, swear by the healthy attributes of the beet and the tuber has therefore played a significant role in popular medicine since time immemorial, such as an appetite stimulant, for example. Despite its high sugar content it is actually recommended for diabetics because it primarily contains the slow metabolizing fructose. With a great deal of vitamin C and the minerals potassium, sodium, calcium, magnesium, iron, and especially folic acid it also helps to prevent cancer. Folic acid also stimulates hematopoiesis and the immune system, fat levels in the liver are controlled by betaine, and the cellulose content stimulates the digestion. A combination of fresh beet and carrot juice is considered a real tonic against fatigue, amnesia, or high blood pressure. Beets do contain oxalic acid, however, which inhibits the absorption of calcium in the body and can lead to kidney stones. Consequently it should not be eaten on a daily basis.

One thing is for sure, though and can only be avoided by wearing gloves when peeling or slicing beets: red fingers. The tuber's color does stain and even adept Ukrainian housewives do not have any special tips for dealing with the red pigment belonging to the so-called beta cyan group. The only thing that really helps is the good old lemon. This is the only way to get your fingers clean again afterward.

Zavyvantsy z buryachynia
Stuffed beet leaves

Generous 1 lb/500 g beet leaves
Salt
1 carrot, grated
½ portion corn porridge (see recipe page 185)
5½ oz/150 g fatty bacon, diced
2 onions, sliced

Blanche the beet leaves in salted water and leave to drain, setting the stock aside. For the filling stir the grated carrot into the corn porridge. Place 2 tablespoons of the filling on each of the leaves, fold in the sides and roll up. Place the stuffed leaves in a baking dish and add about a finger's depth of the blanching stock. Bake in a preheated oven at 350–400 °F/180–200 °C for about 30 minutes. Shortly before the end of the cooking time fry the bacon in a dry skillet and sauté the onions until soft. Serve together with the stuffed beet leaves.

Buryakovy dyruny
Beet pancakes

¾ cup/150 g millet (see Glossary)
1½ cups/375 ml vegetable stock (cube or granules)
3 medium-sized beets
1¼ cups/300 g Quark, or soft curd cheese
½ cup/125 ml milk
1 egg
1 heaped tbsp sugar
Salt
Butter or oil for frying
¾ cup/200 g sour cream

Bring the millet and the vegetable stock to a boil, allow to simmer for about 10 minutes and then cover and leave to swell for about 20 minutes.

In the meantime boil the beets but do not allow them to become too soft, peel them and then grate finely. Mix the grated beets well with the millet, Quark or cheese, milk, egg, sugar, and salt. Shape small pancakes from the dough and fry in hot fat on both sides. Serve the beet pancakes with a dollop of sour cream on each.

Borscht

For borscht beets are sautéed in fat before tomato paste and vinegar are added.

The other vegetables are sautéed separately and then added to the meat stock together with the beets.

Fatty bacon, garlic, and salt are ground in a pestle and mortar before being added to the soup.

Generous quantities of fresh dill and parsley provide the finishing touches to the borscht, plus a dose of vitamins.

In Ukraine you just have to pose the question about the original borscht recipe and the conversation becomes heated. There are as many answers as there are housewives because each of them has her own recipe. However, there is one thing that they all have in common: the indignation at the fact that, abroad, borscht is attributed to Russian cuisine. The hearty stew is as Ukrainian and as old as the Kievan Rus empire itself. It takes its name from the old Slavic word *brsh* for beet. Originally, however, the dish was made from wild plants or from oats, only later did the beet become the heart and soul of borscht. There are only a few examples where it is lacking, such as green borscht with sorrel. The borscht ingredients vary according to the seasonal vegetables on offer. In the spring beet leaves and sorrel are available, in the summer carrots, green beans, and tomatoes, for example, in the autumn and winter mushrooms, cabbage, and root vegetables. There are numerous borscht variations in each of the 25 Ukraine administrative areas. In central and eastern Ukraine there are fish varieties, the borscht from Poltava contains poultry and in the *sakarpazky borschtsh* from the Carpathians the potatoes are replaced by sauerkraut and broad, or fava, beans. The rule for all borschts is that the beets should be cooked separately from the other vegetables. *Salo* or lard is usually used for frying the ingredients and the fatty bacon, which is ground with garlic and salt in a pestle and mortar, is added

shortly before the borscht is ready. For everyday purposes housewives usually use well-marbled pork. For celebratory occasions such as weddings and christenings, as well as funerals and wakes, the borscht is often prepared with several types of meat and poultry. During fasting times, on the other hand, mushrooms or smoked fish are used in addition to sorrel.

Once cooked every borscht should be left to stand for at least 40 minutes, better still overnight. The soup is served in a typical Ukrainian *horshchyk* or soup tureen. It is preferably served with *pampushky*, savory yeast doughnuts which are doused in a sauce made from sunflower oil, garlic, and parsley. Some varieties are also served with accompaniments such as *halushky* made from an egg batter (see page 164), small pancakes, and buckwheat or millet porridge.

Kyivsky Borshch
Kiev borscht

¾ cup/150 g dried white beans
1½ lb/600 g pork ribs, cut into pieces (optional: mixed pork, beef, chicken, or lamb)
1 whole onion
3 carrots
1 medium-sized parsley root
Salt
3 medium-sized beets, sliced into strips
2 tbsp lard
3 tbsp tomato paste
1–2 tbsp wine vinegar
½ celeriac root, sliced into fine strips
2 bell peppers, cut into strips
2 large tomatoes, sliced
3 medium-sized potatoes, diced
8–9 oz/250 g white cabbage, shredded
1 bay leaf
4 cloves garlic
2 oz/50 g fatty bacon (salo)
Pepper
About 1 tbsp sugar
½ bunch each dill and parsley, finely chopped
4 tbsp sour cream

Soak the dried white beans in cold water overnight, then drain and boil in unsalted water until just soft. Set aside.

Wipe the meat and cook together with the onion, one whole carrot, and the parsley root in about 3 quarts/3 liters salted water until just soft, skimming off the

There are innumerable variations of borscht, many of which can be made with or without meat. The traditional ingredient is beets; green borscht (left) contains sorrel or spinach.

foam from time to time. Remove the cooked vegetables from the meat stock.

Sauté the peeled and sliced beets in 1 tablespoon lard, add the tomato paste and vinegar and sweat for 10–15 minutes.

In another saucepan lightly fry the celeriac and the remaining carrot, finely sliced, in 1 tablespoon of the lard. Add the peppers and tomatoes and sweat everything together for about 10 minutes. Add the beans, potatoes, the carrots, celeriac and vegetable mixture, and the cabbage to the meat stock, then add the sautéed beets and bay leaf.

Grind the garlic with the bacon and 1 pinch of salt in a pestle and mortar and add to the soup. Bring everything to a boil, season with salt, pepper, and sugar and leave the borscht to cook over a very low heat for about another 30 minutes. Sprinkle with the herbs and serve with *pampushky* and sour cream.

A spicy sauce made from parsley and garlic is drizzled over cooked *pampushky* which are served with the borscht.

Zeleny borshch
Green borscht
(Illustration left page, below)

Generous 1 lb/500 g veal (or chicken, skinned)
Salt
4 tbsp/60 g butter
1 tbsp all-purpose flour
4–5 medium-sized potatoes, diced
1 onion, finely chopped
1 carrot, sliced into fine strips
1 parsley root, sliced into fine strips
1½ lb/600 g sorrel (or ¾ lb/300 g each sorrel and spinach), shredded
1 bay leaf
Pepper
1 bunch each scallions, dill, and parsley, finely chopped
6 tbsp/100 g sour cream
1 hardcooked egg (optional)

Cover the veal or chicken with cold water, season lightly with salt and boil gently until soft. Remove the meat from the stock and keep warm. Bring the stock back up to a boil, combine 2 tablespoons butter with the flour, mix well and stir into the boiling stock. In the meantime fry the onion, carrot, and parsley root in 2 tablespoons butter. Add to the stock together with the sorrel (and spinach if using) and the bay leaf, season with salt and pepper and simmer briskly for a further 10 minutes. Remove the meat from the bones, cut into bite-sized cubes and place in warmed, deep bowls. Pour the borscht into the bowls and garnish with the fresh herbs and sour cream. Chopped, hardcooked egg can be added if desire.

For *pampushky*, a dough is made from yeast and milk with flour, sugar, salt, egg, and water.

Once the yeast dough has risen well in a warm place, it is shaped into small balls.

Before baking, the small doughnuts are brushed with a mixture of egg and sunflower oil.

Garlic, parsley, and salt are combined with unrefined sunflower oil and water for the sauce.

Pampushky
Savory doughnuts for borscht

2⅔ cups/400 g wheat flour
1 oz/25 g yeast (or dried yeast, follow maker's instructions)
1 tbsp sugar
Salt
2 eggs
2–3 tbsp sunflower oil

For the sauce:
1 whole head of garlic
1 bunch parsley, chopped
Salt and pepper
3 tbsp unrefined sunflower oil

Prepare a yeast dough (see page 18) from the flour, yeast, sugar, salt, 1 egg, and about ¾ cup/175 ml water and leave to rise in a warm place for 1½–2 hours. Then knead well, form balls measuring about 1 inch/3 cm in diameter from the dough with your hands and place on a baking sheet brushed with oil. Whisk the remaining egg with the sunflower oil and brush over the *pampushky*. Bake for about 10 minutes in a preheated oven at 350–400 °F/180–200 °C. Grind the peeled garlic cloves with the chopped parsley and salt in a pestle and mortar, then combine with the oil and 3 tablespoons water. Season the sauce with salt and pepper, pour over the oven fresh *pampushky* and serve warm with the borscht.

A rich variety of vegetables

Pissni holubtsi
Cabbage leaves with mushrooms

2¼ lb/1 kg white cabbage
Salt
½ cup (½ oz)/15 g dried mushrooms (e.g. porcini)
1 small parsley root
1 onion
2 tbsp/30 g butter
2 cups/300 g cooked rice
Pepper

For the sauce:
2 tbsp/30 g butter
3 tbsp/25 g all-purpose flour
2 cups/500 ml mushroom stock
1 cup/250 g sour cream
Salt and pepper

Remove the stalk from the cabbage and blanch the cabbage in boiling, slightly salted water for about 10 minutes, then rinse under cold water. Separate the leaves and cut out the thicker veins. Select 3–4 large cabbage leaves and set aside. Soak the dried mushrooms in lukewarm water for about 30 minutes, cook in the same water together with the parsley root. Strain and set aside. Finely chop both the mushrooms and the parsley root. Sauté the onions in the butter, combine with the cooked rice, the chopped mushrooms and parsley root, season with salt and pepper. Place 3–4 tablespoons of the mushroom and rice mixture on each of the 4 large cabbage leaves and roll up. For the sauce prepare a roux from the butter, flour, and mushroom and parsley root cooking liquid. Add all but a few tablespoons of the sour cream.
Line a saucepan or an ovenproof dish with the remaining cabbage leaves and place the filled leaves on top. Pour the sauce over the rolls and cook either over low heat on the stove or in the oven for about 1 hour. Serve with a dollop of sour cream on each rolled cabbage leaf together with a few cooked fresh mushrooms, if desired.

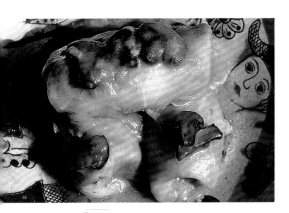

Rolled cabbage leaves without meat: the most important ingredients apart from cabbage are mushrooms and rice.

The cabbage leaves are blanched first of all and filled individually with the prepared mushroom and rice mix.

The sides of the cabbage leaf should be well folded in so that the filling does not spill out during cooking.

The rolled cabbage leaves are then laid in a saucepan or an ovenproof dish lined with cabbage leaves.

The rolled cabbage leaves are covered with a sauce made from mushroom stock and sour cream and then cooked.

Tusheni baklazhany
Stewed eggplant
(Not illustrated)

Generous 1 lb/500 g eggplant, diced
Salt
8 tbsp sunflower oil
2¼ lb/1 kg potatoes, diced
1 carrot, diced
1 parsley root, diced
1 medium-sized onion, diced
1 garlic clove, crushed
2 tomatoes, roughly chopped
Pepper
½ bunch each dill and parsley, finely chopped

Sprinkle the diced eggplant with salt, leave to draw for 15 minutes, drain, pat dry and sauté in 4 tbsp oil. Sauté the potatoes, carrot, and parsley root in the remaining oil with the onion and garlic. Add the eggplant and tomatoes, season with salt and pepper, cover, and cook over low heat for 20–30 minutes, adding a little water or vegetable stock if necessary. Serve garnished with the dill and parsley.

Tolchonka
Potato and bean purée
(Not illustrated)

⅔ cup/125 g white beans
5 medium-sized potatoes, diced
Salt
1 medium-sized onion, chopped very finely
1 tsp sugar
½ tsp freshly ground black pepper
Caraway seeds for garnishing

Soak the white beans overnight and then cook in unsalted water until soft, then drain. Cook the potatoes in lightly salted water and then purée together with the beans. Stir in the onion. Season the purée with salt, sugar, and pepper and sprinkle with caraway seeds before serving.

Cabbage is everybody's favorite in Ukraine, be it for soups, appetizers, or main dishes with vegetables. In addition to the classic white cabbage a number of other varieties are available at today's markets.

Nachyneny perets
Stuffed bell peppers
(Not illustrated)

4 large bell peppers
2 carrots
1 large onion, finely chopped
8–9 oz/250 g white cabbage
2 tbsp oil
1 cup/200 g cooked rice
Salt and pepper
1 cup/250 ml vegetable stock
Dill and parsley, according to preference

Wash the peppers, slice off the tops, and remove the seeds. For the filling wash the carrots, half cook them and pass through a grinder. Sauté the onion in the oil together with the cabbage. Combine the vegetables with the rice, season well with salt and pepper and fill the peppers with this mixture. Put the tops back on the peppers. Place the peppers in a greased dish, cover with vegetable stock and bake in a preheated oven at 350 °F/180 °C for about 30 minutes. Serve with dill and/or parsley and with a tomato sauce if desired.

Growing vegetables

Hot or mild? With some chiles and peperoncini types it is not easy to tell at first glance.

Ukraine was once one of the most fertile areas in Europe. However, the radical enforced collectivization under Stalin, the gigantic monocultures of the Soviet era and the far-reaching environmental destruction due to the one-sided exploitation of the soil, the excessive use of pesticides, and a rundown infrastructure have had noticeable effect on the country. The loess soils of the fertile black soil belt stretching from the forested steppe areas of the central *Dnieper* to the Black Sea steppe in the south are therefore in need of recovery. Nevertheless, Ukraine is considered to be an agricultural country with a future. Following the withdrawal from the Soviet Union the area of land under cultivation initially reduced considerably because the entire economy collapsed and the former socialist market outlets were no longer able to buy up the surpluses. In the meantime the fields lying fallow have been able to recover and fertilizers and pest control are usually too expensive anyway. Vegetable exports are also on the increase again and today Ukraine supplies Eastern Europe as before as well as supplying smaller quantities to new market outlets in the Middle East, for example. Cabbage, beets, potatoes, onions, garlic, cucumbers, peas, beans, bell peppers, and carrots are the main ingredients in the domestic kitchens. In addition, tomatoes, parsley roots, chiles or peperoncini round off the flavor of many dishes. Salads were first brought to Russia by Peter the Great and reached Ukraine in the first half of the 18th century. Forgotten vegetables like celeriac, parsnips, or lentils are now being grown again according to old traditions in order to repair the damage done by monoculture. Furthermore, products such as eggplant, artichokes, pineapples, or kiwi fruit have become very fashionable due to the increasing international trade.

Potatoes are often grown on smallholdings. Families harvest them by hand and a horse and cart help with the transport.

The versatile potato

The potato, originating from the Andes of South America, was brought to Europe by the Spanish. At the end of the 17th century it made its way across central Europe via Poland to Ukraine and was initially used here by the nobility and upper classes as a vegetable. In the Carpathian Mountains and in western Ukraine where grain did not grow well due to the poor soils, the solanaceous herb with the delicate leaves was initially grown as animal feed but soon became a foodstuff for the human population. The potato literally became the "second bread" or the "other bread" for the Carpathian people, the Huzul: *balabuchy* (also called *bulbyanyky* or *kartoplyanky*), a kind of potato puff, was made from cooked, ground potatoes and baked in cabbage leaves in a hot oven.

Ukrainians love potatoes but the markets are largely dominated by foreign varieties.

The end of the 18th century during the rule of the Habsburgs saw the arrival via Galicia of a great many immigrants from Germany where potatoes were already being widely eaten and the *kartoplya*, potato, permeated the whole of Ukraine. It was served with the main meal mornings, midday, and evenings, for example with sauerkraut or in *kulish*, the poor man's soup that is still served today in mining families, among others.

The first Ukrainian potato variety was grown at the beginning of the 19th century: *pyrishok maloshytzkoho*, the "little cake," which right from the start was often baked in the fire or the oven. Today the earlier variety *Nesabutka* is especially popular.

The potato crop is a hallmark of the Carpathian Mountains area as well of the entire north of the country. The *kartoplya* is one of the most important ingredients in Ukrainian cuisine; it is eaten as a side dish in the form of boiled or baked potatoes, as roast potatoes with onions, bacon, and caraway seeds, as a purée, also in hors d'oeuvre salads with eggs and pickled cucumbers for example, as well as rich potato puffs with sour cream. A popular main dish is *knyshi*, a potato dumpling filled with ground meat, mushrooms, or sauerkraut, which is crumbed and fried in a skillet. *Paltshyky*, "little fingers," are a kind of gnocchi made from potato dough and are served with melted butter and sour cream. Buttermilk or soured milk is also served as a drink to accompany them. Potatoes also taste good with sauerkraut or with *salamacha*, a sauce made from crushed garlic, water, and oil.

The potato is rich in vitamin B6 and vitamin C, in carbohydrates, fiber, potassium, and magnesium.

Kulish
"Poor man's soup"
(Not illustrated)

1 scant cup/175 g millet (see Glossary)
2 tsp salt
6 medium-sized potatoes
8–9 oz/250 g fatty bacon (salo), finely diced
3 medium-sized onions, finely chopped
½ bunch parsley, finely chopped

Wash the millet thoroughly and leave to drain in a fine sieve. Then place in a saucepan with 2 quarts/2 liters boiling salted water, cover, and leave to simmer over low heat for about 20 minutes. In the meantime peel and dice the potatoes, add to the millet. Cook together for a further 15 minutes. Lightly sauté the diced bacon in a skillet, add the chopped onion and sauté, add to the saucepan and allow everything to simmer together for a further 5 minutes. Sprinkle the soup with parsley and serve.

Dyruny z tsybuleyu
Potato puffs with onions

1¾ lb/750 g potatoes
2 eggs
1 onion, finely chopped
2–3 tbsp all-purpose flour
1 pinch baking powder
Salt and pepper
Lard or oil for frying
4 onions, sliced in rings
Sour cream (optional)

Peel the potatoes, grate coarsely, place in a sieve and press out the liquid using a wooden spoon. Whisk the eggs and combine with the chopped onion. Mix in the flour combined with the baking powder, season with salt and pepper. Heat a generous amount of oil in a skillet, add spoonfuls of the dough and cook the small pancakes on both sides until golden brown. Sauté the onion rings in the oil until transparent or crispy brown, depending on preference. Serve the potato puffs with the onion rings, and sour cream, if desired.

Above left: Earthenware containers, not just for water but also for sunflower oil and wine, were once to be found in every Ukrainian home. The vessels were made on the potter's wheel and were usually not glazed.

Above right: A traditional Ukrainian living room in the open air museum near Kiev. The floor used to be covered with straw. Icons and pictures are surrounded by a *rushnyk*, the richly embroidered traditional cloth.

Center: Country life was no bed of roses in the 19th century. The open air museum near Kiev brings the past alive and shows how Ukrainian farmers lived their modest lives.

Bottom left: In the days before electricity supplies Ukrainian housewives ground seeds, small quantities of grain, and dried herbs in a pestle and mortar. This is still the norm in many households today.

Bottom right: A variety of wild herbs gathered by hand were dried on ledges and beams in the living room, preferably close to the oven. Many were used as flavorings in the kitchen while others served as home remedies.

The writer Nikolai Gogol (1809–1852) immortalized the traditions of his hometown Poltava.

Life in Gogol's era

Nikolai Vassilyevitsh Gogol was born on April 1, 1809 in Sorochintsi in the Poltava area. His parents owned a small estate in the eastern Ukraine that was then part of the Russian Empire. Even though throughout Europe and also in Ukraine the first nationalist movements were making themselves felt at that time, as a Ukrainian of the orthodox faith the writer Gogol considered himself to belong to the tsarist empire and wrote in Russian all of his life. Despite his travels lasting many years, from St. Petersburg via Paris and Rome and then as far as Jerusalem, he remained closely connected to his Ukrainian homeland and its customs, dedicating some of his best works to his home country.

The Poltava region is one of the most fertile. The loess soils of this black earth area are considered among the best in the world and even in Gogol's time grain provided the livelihood for the people of the region. Cows and cattle, geese, chickens, or ducks supplemented the menu, pigs grunted in the straw covered stalls, the sound of goats came from the rooftops, bees hummed in the meadows, and the sun-blessed grain was waving in the wind. The houses in the village were simple, mostly made from aspen wood and the interior walls were plastered with clay. In summer the farmers spread hay over the living room floors, both to stop the dust and for its wonderful fragrance, and straw was used in the front rooms. The stove with its chimney for smoking meat and fish stood in the living room; there was a large wooden container with a large pestle for grinding poppy seeds and other ingredients needed in the kitchen, aromatic bunches of herbs hung from the roof beams, such as small wild marigolds for making tea, or camomile and calendula. Every house was decorated with several icons, always surrounded by an embroidered *rushnyk*, the traditional cloth. The crockery was mostly ceramic and the *makitra*, a colorful glazed bowl, is still used today together with the cast iron *kasan* for soups, roasts, porridge, or vegetable dishes. There was also a butter churn in almost every living room.

The regular markets were a source of social life and a change of scenery. People would meet there, transactions would be negotiated, goods would be bought and sold, primarily the produce of nature's bounty but also the loveliest and most colorful cloths and ribbons, clothes and fabrics, rings and bracelets. The annual fair in Sorochintsi, which has been held on the Feast of the Assumption since the 17th century, takes place every year on August 25 or 26 and is still associated with Gogol today. In his story, The Fair at Sorochintsi, the writer provides a colorful portrayal of the market: "An endless line of ox carts with salt and fish had been trundling across the countryside since the early morning. Whole mountains of pots wrapped in hay and harnesses were slowly moving forward, bored with being in their dark prisons; then here and there a garishly painted bowl or pot rose above the tightly spanned tracery of the cart and attracted the covetous glances of lovers of good living. …"

The ripe pods of the opium or garden poppy provide poppy seeds for use in the kitchen. The dark seeds lend a bitter-sweet taste to sweet and savory dishes.

Poppy seeds

Poppy seed cake with honey was a "paradisiacal dish" for Gogol. The flowering plant of the *papaver* genus is a legend not least as the source of opium which is extracted from the juice of the unripe pods of the opium poppy (*Papaver somniferum*). The ancient Greeks sacrificed poppy seeds to the fertility goddess Demeter as a symbol of the earth and of sleep. In Ukraine it has been used as a household remedy since time immemorial: babies who could not sleep used to be given a cloth sachet with poppy seeds soaked in sugared milk to suckle. With a fat content of up to 40% the little seeds are well suited to baking and in Ukraine they are used for *makovy tort*, poppy seed cake, for example, comprising a biscuit base made of poppy seeds, eggs, honey, and walnuts or almonds together with a butter cream. *Zavyvanets z makom*, poppy seed strudel (see page 209) or *pampushky z makom*, yeast doughnuts filled with poppy seeds, are also popular, as is sweet poppy seed sauce for desserts. The little seeds also have their place in the Christmas dish *kutya*, made from wheat grains, nuts, and honey (see page 175). The veneration for this plant is reflected in the annual *Makovey*, poppy seed festival, which takes place in August and which, since Ukraine's independence, has been increasingly celebrated in accordance with age old traditions. The seeds should be ripe by Seven Martyrs Day on August 14. The local residents bathe in the streams in rivers before sunset in order to cleanse themselves of any bad influences. In the church, water, flowers, and poppy seeds are blessed and then placed above the icon at home until sowing time the following year. Many people have happy childhood memories associated with *Makovey*, particularly of *shulyky*: these are pieces of pastry crumbled together with a mixture of poppy seeds and honey and eaten with a spoon (see page 206).

Pumpkin & Co.

At the markets in summer and autumn pumpkins, melons, zucchini, and cucumbers combine a blatant sensuousness and a sweet, delicate aroma to form a still life for connoisseurs. The pumpkin family is large and comprises more than 800 varieties. There is hardly any other vegetable or fruit plant that grows as quickly with the right soil and climate. A melon, for instance, needs a period of only four to six weeks from the planting of the seedling to harvesting. Most varieties cannot tolerate frost and they do not like cold, windy weather. It is therefore no wonder, that especially *kavun*, watermelons, and *dynya*, honey melons, are widespread in the southern areas of Ukraine, near Zaporizhzhya, Mykolayiv, and the Kherson area near the mouth of the *Dnieper* where it enters the Black Sea. Good soils and lots of sunshine make the fruit lovely and sweet.

The most popular and most widespread pumpkin variety in Ukraine is *kabathok*, the snakeskin pumpkin, which makes modest demands of the soil and grows almost everywhere. Pumpkin varieties such as the *harbus*, the normal garden pumpkin, or the small yellow *patissons*, and squashes are also popular. The ripening time for melons is primarily July and August and for pumpkins it is September. That's when the aromatic, stuffed, and roasted cucumber pumpkins, which are similar to zucchini, are served; then the watermelons are made into preserves or else simply cut open and eaten. Since they comprise up to 95 percent water and also contain vitamins and minerals, they are a great thirst quencher. Zucchini, cucumber pumpkins, and other related varieties also comprise mainly water. Before stuffing them, therefore, you should sprinkle them with salt and leave them to stand for half an hour in order to draw the liquid out.

According to Ukrainian custom pumpkins can sometimes also leave an unpleasant aftertaste: if a young man receives a pumpkin from the object of his desire rather than a colorfully embroidered *rushnyk* cloth then he should take to his heels—it means he has received a 'Dear John' letter.

Right hand page: The garden pumpkin *(harbus)* originates from Mexico and is available in a number of varieties in Ukraine. It is well suited to soups and preserves.

Nalysnky z harbusa
Pumpkin pancakes
(Not illustrated)

2¼ lb/1 kg pumpkin
Generous 1⅓ cup/200 g all-purpose flour
2 eggs
½ tsp baking powder
Salt
Butter for frying
¾ cup/200 g sour cream or melted butter

Peel the pumpkin, remove the seeds, and finely grate the flesh. Combine with the batter ingredients and fry as thin pancakes in hot butter. Serve with sour cream or melted butter.

Pechheny harbus z medom
Baked pumpkin with honey
(Not illustrated)

Generous 1 lb/500 g pumpkin
6–7 tbsp/200 g honey

Wash the pumpkin, cut into slices or cubes and scoop out the seeds. Bake the pieces on a greased baking sheet in a preheated oven at 350–400 °F/180–200 °C for about 30 minutes. Leave to cool and peel if preferred (not necessary for Hokkaido pumpkins). Drizzle the honey over the pumpkin pieces and serve with tea.

Nachyneny kabachok
Stuffed snakeskin pumpkin

1 large snakeskin pumpkin weighing about 2¼ lb/1 kg
¾ cup/200 g sour cream

For the stuffing:
¼ cup/50 g rice
Salt and pepper
2 medium-sized onions, finely chopped
3 tbsp sunflower oil
2 medium-sized carrots, finely chopped or grated
4 hardcooked eggs, finely chopped
Generous 1 lb/500 g ground meat (beef or pork or a mixture of both)

Slice the pumpkin into slices about 1 inch/2–3 cm thick and remove the flesh leaving an edge of about ½ inch/1.5 cm. Discard the seeds and finely chop the flesh. Cook the rice in double the amount of water. Sauté the onion in the oil, add the carrots and the diced pumpkin flesh and sauté everything until soft; then add the chopped eggs. Combine the ground meat with the cooked rice, vegetables, and salt and pepper to make the stuffing. Fill the pumpkin slices with the stuffing and pour over the sour cream. Place in a greased dish and bake in a preheated oven at about 350 °F/180 °C for about 45 minutes.

Orange colored flesh is to be found underneath the pale colored skin of the butternut squash. It is very flavorful, slightly sweet and is perfect for dishes such as soups, casseroles, and desserts.

The muscat pumpkin can weigh up to 22–26 lb/10–12 kg and the green skin turns browner with increasing ripeness. The flavorful flesh tastes good roasted or preserved, in soups, casseroles, or in desserts.

Watermelons contain up to 95 percent water and are therefore popular thirst quenchers in the summer. They are also eaten fresh as a fruit dessert but they can be preserved—either sweet or savory depending on preference.

Ukrainian zakuski

Salat z kapusty
Ukrainian cabbage salad
(Illustration below)

Generous 1 lb/500 g white cabbage, shredded
Salt
1 cooking apple, cut into fine strips
1 tbsp chopped scallion tops
Juice of 1 lemon
2 tbsp sunflower oil
Pepper
Sugar
Cranberries or lingonberries for garnishing (depending on preference and availability)

Sprinkle the cabbage strips with salt, pound them and leave them to draw for about 15 minutes. Then mix together with the apple strips and the scallion tops. Mix in the lemon juice and sunflower oil, season with salt, pepper, and sugar. Garnish with berries.

Salat z morkvy, z orikhamy i yablokamy
Carrot salad with walnuts and apple

Generous 1 lb/500 g carrots, grated
2 cooking apples, grated
1½ cups/150 g walnuts, chopped
Juice of 1 lemon
2–3 tbsp sunflower oil
Salt and pepper

Combine the carrots, apple, and nuts. Prepare a sauce from the remaining ingredients and fold into the salad.
Tip: Depending on preference you can add 3 tablespoons/25 g raisins soaked in water.

Myasny salat
Meat and vegetable salad
(Not illustrated)

9 oz/250 g each ox tongue and beef fillet, cooked
6 oz/175 g boiled ham
2 medium-sized beets, cooked
2 medium-sized potatoes, cooked
6 oz/175 g preserved mushrooms
1 tbsp white wine vinegar
6 tbsp mayonnaise
Salt and pepper
4 hardcooked eggs

Cut the meat and vegetable ingredients into bite-sized pieces and combine with the vinegar in a bowl. Fold in the mayonnaise, season with salt and pepper. Garnish with hardcooked egg quarters.

Nachynyuvani yaytsaya
Stuffed eggs with herring
(Not illustrated)

6 eggs, hardcooked and peeled
2–3 tbsp mayonnaise
1 tsp medium-strength mustard
1 tsp grated horseradish
Salt
Pepper
2 marinated herring fillets
½ bunch parsley

Halve the eggs, carefully remove the yolks, combine with the mayonnaise, mustard, horseradish, salt, and pepper and fill the egg halves with the mixture. Garnish each stuffed egg with herring pieces and a sprig of parsley.

Salat z krevetkamy
Shrimp salad
(Not illustrated)

Scant 1 lb/400 g shrimp tails, cooked and peeled
Juice of 1 lemon
3–4 potatoes, cooked
1½ cups/200 g green peas, cooked
5 tbsp mayonnaise
Salt and pepper
Salad leaves for serving
2 hardcooked eggs for garnishing
½ bunch parsley for garnishing

Drizzle the lemon juice over the shrimp tails and leave them to stand for a short while. Slices the potatoes, carefully mix together with the shrimp and peas, fold in the mayonnaise, then season with salt and pepper. Place the shrimp salad on the salad leaves and garnish with sliced eggs and sprigs of parsley.

Zaskuska z buryakiv
Beet zakuska
(Illustration below right)

Generous 1 lb/500 g beets, cooked and sliced
3/4 lb/300 g pickled cucumbers, finely chopped
2 medium-sized onions, sliced into thin rings
3 1/2 tbsp/50 ml beets cooking water
3 1/2 tbsp/50 ml pickled cucumber brine
4 tbsp sunflower oil

Layer the slices of cooked beets alternatively with the sliced cucumbers and onion rings in a ceramic or glass dish. Make a marinade from the cooking water, pickled cucumber brine, and sunflower oil, pour over the layered vegetables and leave to stand in a cool place for one day.

Oseledtsi po kyivske
Kiev herring pâté
(Illustration below)

Large white loaf, crusts removed
1 cup/250 ml milk
3/4 lb/300 g pickled herring fillets
1 cup + 2 tbsp/250 g melted butter
1 1/4 cups/125 g grated cheese (Cheddar, Monterey Jack...)
1 tsp medium strength mustard
Salt and pepper
1/2 bunch parsley, finely chopped

Soak the bread in the milk briefly, squeeze out and pass through a grinder together with the herring. Fold in the butter, cheese, and mustard, season with salt and pepper. Mold the pâté into a shape (of a fish, for example) and garnish with parsley. The herring pâté is eaten as a spread on bread.

Marynovani hrybky
Marinated mushrooms

Generous 1 lb/500 g fresh mushrooms
3 tbsp well-flavored vinegar
2 carrots
Juice of 1 lemon
1 cup/250 ml oil
Salt
10 peppercorns
3 bay leaves
2 tbsp medium strength mustard
1 large onion, thinly sliced into rings
1/2 bunch each parsley and dill

Clean the mushrooms and blanch in 4 cups/1 liter water with 1 tablespoon vinegar essence, then drain. Slice the carrots thinly and blanch briefly. Bring 1 cup/250 ml water with the lemon juice, remaining vinegar essence, the oil, and spices to a boil, then leave to cool. Place the mushrooms, carrots, and onions in jars, fill with the marinade and leave to stand in a cool place for 1–2 days. Stir in the chopped herbs before serving.

Ivan Kupalo

It is a time when the spirits become restless, the earth seems to be bursting, the first ears of corn are ripening and medicinal herbs are building up their healing powers. The summer solstice is still celebrated in Ukraine on July 7 in accordance with the Julian calendar that the Soviets only replaced with the Gregorian calendar in 1918. The day belongs to the witches and healers, to the fortunetellers and the mystics. It is Ivan Kupalo day, an ancient pagan festival in honor of, and for the protection of, nature. Kupala was the Slavic goddess of fertility and of water. In the aftermath of Christianity the Orthodox Churches tried to suppress the festival but when this proved to be in vain it was promptly linked with John (Ivan) the Baptist's name day which falls in the same period and made it into the festival of Ivan Kupalo. During the Soviet era, when all regional customs were frowned upon, it could only be celebrated secretly at home but since Ukraine's independence St John's Day has again been celebrated publicly.

According to legend it is at midsummer that nature reveals her powers. In the past people used to bathe in dew and collect dewdrops. Herbs that were preserved in the dewdrops developed miraculous powers. It is the night of miracles and, according to oral tradition, in this the shortest of nights the trees talk to each other and seek out new, better places. The ferns are said to blossom only once a year, in these hours of darkness. Hidden treasures will be revealed to those who find the flowers—they will grow strong and will be able to talk to the birds and to other animals. Midsummer night is preferably celebrated near a stream, river, or lake. The young people dress up and today even traditional Ukrainian costumes are taken out of the closets and chests. In previous centuries when the pre-Christian myths were still deeply anchored in the population, the midsummer hours were for flirting and celebration, for singing, laughing, and dancing. The summer solstice fires would blaze once it got dark; the young people bathed in the streams, rivers, and lakes and gathered medicinal herbs and roots.

On the evening of July 6 young men in the countryside gather brushwood for the fires together as they once did in the past. Happy songs are to be heard everywhere, the young girls pick flowers, they make dolls out of straw and twigs and decorate these with flowers and ribbons. Or else they make flowered wreaths and hang them on a tree. Toward the end of the celebration these are then placed in the flowing current of the river. If they stay on the surface and travel farther downstream it means good times are coming; if they sink then ill health and bad luck are to be feared. If two wreaths bump into one another then there will be a wedding in the near future. The celebratory meal primarily comprises dishes made from buckwheat, such as small pancakes *(mlyntsi)* made from buckwheat flour, grain porridge *(kasha)*, or dark buckwheat honey. The women also conjure up a variety of filled pirogi *(pyrohy)* and *piroshki* (*pyrishky*, see page 18 ff), including sweet ones since berries and other fruit such as apples are in season. The fruit are combined with sugar or placed in the pirogi as jam and which are then also eaten filled with poppy seeds or with Quark or some other soft curd cheese, or with sugar and cinnamon. Savory pirogi do also have their place at the meal, for example with buckwheat porridge, diced bacon and roast onions, with beans or peas, meat and rice, or sauerkraut. *Varenyky* (see page 166) are also popular, filled with cottage cheese and buckwheat. As beverages bread kvass, buttermilk, sour milk, liquid compote made from fresh fruit *(kompot)*, met as well as beer made from buckwheat honey are served. Sweet pastries such as the so-called peaches *(persyky)* with a cream filling and yeast pastries *(bulochky)* supplement the range of festive delicacies.

Above: "Peaches" *(persyky)*, a type of doughnut with a cream filling

Below: *Bulochky*, slightly sweet yeast pastries

Above: Young girls make traditional flower wreaths for the summer solstice celebration Ivan Kupalo.

Center: Flower wreaths and candles are placed in the water. If they float then one can expect good luck.

Large picture: At the summer solstice celebration, anyone able to jump over the fire is cleansed of bad influences.

Wheat: one of the oldest cultivated plants from the sweet grass family with a high vitamin B1 content. Durum wheat is grown in warm regions; the flour is best suited to pastries and bread. Wheat can tolerate lower temperatures, is rich in gluten and is ideal for soft bread and baking.

Buckwheat: belongs to the knotgrass family (and strictly speaking is therefore not a grain) with small, dark, triangular grains. Very undemanding, it originates from the Caspian Sea coast. The gray-white flour has a low gluten content and is therefore not suited to baking bread but rather for making pancakes, porridge, grits, soups, and stuffings. The fields provide the best pasture for bees.

Barley: a very undemanding grass variety, known in Asia Minor up to 6,000 years ago; rich in silicic acid and B vitamins; the vitamin niacin is important for energy, for growth, and for the nerves. The related grain spelt is not good for baking and is mainly used for porridge.

Rye: a very undemanding grain variety tolerant of cold, from the sweet grass family, originating from the Caucasus region. Rye is rich in valuable protein and minerals and also contains iron, potassium, phosphorus, and magnesium. Rye flour is mostly used for baking bread.

The Ukrainian bread basket

Wheat has been known in the Ukrainian region since the Stone Age (up to about 4000 B.C.). In the 6th century B.C. it was already being exported from there to Rome and Greece. The "golden grain," as wheat is affectionately known in Ukraine, has made the country into the bread basket of Eastern Europe since the tsarist era. Ears of wheat also featured in the Ukrainian coat of arms under the Soviet Union. Almost 50 percent of the Soviet Union's entire agricultural produce was provided by the Ukrainian republic. Yet the reckless exploitation and contamination of the soil and the very slow adaptation to the new market conditions have led to crises. As a result grain production went into a steep decline after the declaration of independence but a recovery has been evident since 1995 due to the initial successes with the privatization of the agricultural sector.

In addition to wheat, the most important grain varieties are buckwheat, rye, and millet, while oats and barley have long been grown in Ukraine. Consequently the cuisine is enriched by a wide variety of grain dishes: *varenyky*, filled pastries, (see page 166) are especially popular as are the little egg batter dumplings, *halushky* (see page 164). *Satyrka*, a crumble made from cooked gruel, is delicious with bacon and parsley, or else sweet with milk or sour cream.

Kasha, the porridge popular in Russia and Ukraine, (see page 54), is traditionally made in a clay pot *horshchyk* in the oven or in a *kazan*, a large cast iron kettle. In the past the whole family ate from one pot with wooden spoons; today everybody gets their own ceramic bowl, just as they do for *lemishka*, wheat groats porridge. For this, water is boiled with milk and salt, ground wheat is then stirred in and allowed to thicken before serving with sugar or honey. *Mlyntsi*, sweet Ukrainian wheat pancakes, used to be served only on Sundays or holidays because their preparation for several people is very time consuming. Today they are extremely popular all over Ukraine and they can be enjoyed every day.

Rice: the rice plant is an annual grass variety. In comparison with other grain varieties rice has a particularly high starch content and the lowest protein content. Due to husking and polishing rice white rice also loses minerals and trace elements. Rice is suitable for pilaf dishes with meat and vegetables as well as for stuffings, soups, and as a side dish.

Oats: the grain richest in fat and protein grows best in temperate climates. Oats have high levels of B vitamins, of zinc, copper, calcium, iron, and manganese; they are believed to help prevent cancer and are easily digested. Today oats are often used as animal feed.

Above: Yellow gold wheat ears featured in the Ukrainian coat of arms under the Soviet Union.

Left: Wheat, as far as the eye can see—the grain grows particularly well in the black soils of Ukraine.

Korovay

The period leading up to a wedding is exciting and busy. The preparations for the *korovay*, the wedding bread, alone are enough! In days gone by it was a strict custom that seven virgins had to grind the wheat from seven fields on seven days in order to prepare the artistically decorated lucky bread, ensuring that the young married couple would be affluent and that they never run out of food. A sweet yeast dough made from lots of butter and eggs is shaped into a round loaf; pairs of little doves made from a stiffer dough and symbolizing love, or flowers, fir cones, or little trees as a symbol of life, are positioned on the loaf. The wedding celebration used to last for seven days and even today the celebrations often go on for days. The *korovay* is not allowed to run out during the celebrations, nor is the *horilka*, as the Ukrainians call their vodka. The bride and bridegroom are the first to take a pinch of salt and a piece of the wedding bread, then the parents and then the guests. Friends also give bread as gifts for a happy start in the new married home.

Background: Need some fresh rolls? A woman selling bread offers passersby oven-fresh bread and a smile.

A richly decorated wedding bread brings luck to the newly married couple.

1 *palyanytsya* (wheat flour)
2 *Borodyns'ky zavarny* (rye flour with poppy seeds)
3 *kyrpychyk* (wheat flour)
4 *Ukrayins'ky* (rye and wheat flour)
5 *Kyyivski bulochky* ("Kiev bread rolls")
6 *khlib z otrubyamy* (bran)
7 *bulka* (wheat flour)
8 *Chumats'ky* (rye and wheat flour)
9 *kolach* (wheat flour)
10 *babka* (wheat flour, here with raisins)
11 *kolach* (wheat flour, here with poppy seeds)
12 *baton* (wheat flour)
13 *bulochka* (with poppy seeds)

Bread

"I counted 77 ways of baking bread," enthused Honoré de Balzac in the middle of the 19th century, the French romantic novelist who was used to good cuisine, who lived in a village near Kiev from 1847 to 1850 and who loved freshly baked bread in addition to a Polish countess.

In days gone by sour dough made from rye flour or a mixture of barley, buckwheat, or oats was normally used for baking. Wheat or buckwheat pancakes *(palyanytsya)* were served for breakfast, sometimes baked with onion rings, salt, and poppy seeds. Pirogi were eaten during the day, filled with potato, sauerkraut, soft curd cheese or the equivalent of present-day Quark, ground meat, or fruit. And since bread has formed the staple diet of the Ukrainians since time immemorial and is indispensable, potatoes, peas, acorns, nettles, or even plantains were added to the flour in times of need.

Even today you will find innumerable kinds of bread in Ukrainian bakeries and there is hardly a meal where only one type of bread is to be found on the table. There is dark bread made from pure rye flour and white bread made from wheat, as well as mixed breads made from both grains. The names differ from region to region and the kind most sold is a long loaf *(ukrayins'ky khlib)* made from rye, wheat, and a mixed flour. *Bulka* is a kind of sweet bread similar to a French brioche; *balabushky* is the name for small, sour dough plaits made from wheat flour and brushed with egg yolk so that they shine appetizingly. The *kaiserky*, a star-shaped roll made from wheat flour, is also brushed with egg yolk (the name is reminiscent of the old Austrian "Emperor roll"). The three traditional bread types, *paskha*, *babka*, and *kolach* are made of wheat flour, yeast, eggs, butter, milk, and sugar but differ in the proportions

of the ingredients. No Easter meal should be without *paskha* a round, barrel-shaped wheat and yeast bread which is richly decorated, as well as the related *babka* which is much richer because it contains lots of eggs and often enhanced with raisins, vanilla, and lemon peel. Although *babka* and *paskha* are slightly sweet they are eaten for Easter breakfast with meat or sausage. The Christmas bread *kolach* (from *kolo* meaning ring) the wheat flour dough is plaited and shaped into a ring, although you can also find it as a long plait. Sour dough is still preferred for baking. Yeast is used more seldom, for example, only for *palyanytsya*, usually a white bread shaped like a pancake, or else for *pampushky*, the small yeast doughnuts, the savory version of which are eaten with a garlic and oil sauce with borscht (see page 145) and which are also available sweet with a jam or poppy seed filling.

Bread is eaten with all meals: with soup and with appetizers as well as buttered with ham, cheese, or sausage. At breakfast the latter is seldom placed on the bread but is eaten with it. *Kanapky* are popular in the western Ukraine: the small slices of bread covered with sausage, ham, cheese, caviar, smoked fish, or eggs are usually imaginatively decorated and are part of any celebratory reception. A simple but very important ingredient in the kitchen is breadcrumbs. They are used to loosen fillings and ground ingredients or for crumbing meat and fish.

"If there is bread and water then there is no hunger," is an old Ukrainian saying. Yet bread is much more than just a tummy filler. It is also considered a luxury article and a symbol which accompanies all stages of life, not just the every day. New-born babies are greeted with bread, and on St. Andrew's Night (November 29) a young girl whose freshly baked bread rolls *(balabushka)* are eaten first can rest assured that she will be married by the end of the year. As in Russia, officials and especially important guests are received

with bread and salt (also see page 79) which are also given as gifts to those who have moved into a new home.

Ukrainians today still consider bread to be almost holy. Before baking they make the sign of the cross and also before slicing the loaf. And should a piece of bread land on the floor by mistake it is not simply thrown away but kissed and given to the birds.

Flour for the daily bread is sold at the country markets directly from large, open sacks.

A meal with the dead

Many Ukrainian cemeteries are not in the least gloomy and many have an almost familial atmosphere. There are benches between the graves, sometimes even small tables. The cemeteries are often located on small hills in a meadow where no trees block the view, perhaps so that the recently deceased who, according to popular belief, are not yet in the afterlife but are still in this life, are able to wander freely between the worlds. Yet this state of limbo for the dead has always frightened the living. Death, which in Ukrainian is feminine, was feared and appears in popular custom and folklore as a toothless, haggard, old woman dressed in white and carrying a scythe. When a death occurred, then a mirror was hung in the house, a candle or a lamp was lit and any knots that one could find were undone in order to free the soul of the deceased. The front door and the garden gate were opened, animals were locked up in the barn so that they would not be taken on the journey through the lives and the ages. If a villager died, nothing was allowed to be sown or planted, neither seeds nor even the smallest seedling were allowed to be touched. It was believed that the dead had a damaging influence on nature. People also avoided preserving vegetables for the winter so that they did not become spoiled. Hens were no longer allowed to sit on their nests, as it was believed that there could not be any life in the eggs anyway. Even today the oldest women of the house and the neighborhood wash the deceased in a symbolic cleansing and dress the body in traditional clothes, for instance in eastern Ukraine a woman is dressed in a blouse embroidered with flowers. The body is then laid on a bench with the feet toward the door. During the vigil prayers are said, dirges are sung, and the happy events in the life of the deceased are narrated. Anybody who wishes to come to the burial can do so, there are no invitations. For the requiem in the church large *kolach* loaves are placed on the small altar in the nave, either three loaves as a symbol of the Holy Trinity or seven loaves symbolizing the seven blessings of the Holy Ghost. The bread is blessed after the service and distributed among the poor members of the community. In the church the ritual porridge *kolyva* is distributed during every prayer for the dead. It comprises rice or whole-wheat grains that have been boiled in sweetened milk and sprinkled with sugar and cinnamon, sometimes also with walnuts and raisins, and decorated with a cross made from candied cherries.

Ukrainians honor their dead in a tangible manner and celebrate with them as if they were still among the living. Generous meals are served on the graves: bread rolls with sausage, cake, fruit, vegetables, and eggs.

The porridge is blessed and eaten in the church as an expression of sympathy. The funeral procession then departs for the cemetery. Those who wish to pay special tribute to the deceased lay vegetables, baked goods, fruit, and bread at the grave and later distribute them to the needy. The relatives of the deceased distribute sweets, biscuits, and cake as a symbol of love and solidarity. Once the grave has been filled the mourners gather at the home of the deceased for the wake. This always includes a yeast bread as the conversion of the corn to bread symbolizes the rebirth into eternal life. The generous meal can comprise borscht, filled pastries *varenyky* (see page 166), rolled cabbage leaves, a roast, potatoes, and sweet dishes. Since, in accordance with pre-Christian beliefs, it is undesirable to let the deceased make their way alone from this life to the next, it is still very common to have breakfast with the deceased on the day after the funeral. A woven cloth is laid over the grave and bread, sausage, eggs, cucumbers, or cake are eaten. The wake and the picnic with the dead are repeated not only at the annual remembrance but also for *Provody* (literally meaning "accompanying on the way"), the traditional remembrance of the dead. In the two weeks after Easter millions of festively dressed people make a pilgrimage to the cemeteries. Colorfully painted eggs, cakes, and sweets are spread out on tables. Eggs, sausage, ham, fish, and pirogi filled with meat, liver, mushrooms, sauerkraut, potatoes, rice, or chopped egg are traditionally eaten at the graveside. A glass of *hotilka* (schnapps) also helps to keep alive memories of the deceased.

Left: Families in Kiev remember their dead.

Typical *Provody* alms on a grave.

Egg and flour dishes

The eggs are beaten with milk or water. The liquid is then combined with flour and salt.

The dough is rolled out to almost finger thickness and cut into equal-sized squares with a knife.

The *halushky* are cooked in lightly salted water and then removed with a slotted spoon.

Halushky
Ukrainian dumplings

2 eggs
½ cup/125 ml milk or water
4 cups/600 g all-purpose flour
Salt
3½ tbsp/50 g butter (melted), or 6 tbsp/100 g sour cream

Beat the eggs together with the milk or water and then work into a smooth dough with the flour and a pinch of salt. Roll the dough out thickly and cut into equal-sized squares of about ¾ inch/2 cm. Place the dough pieces in lightly salted, boiling water and allow them to simmer until the *halushky* rise to the surface. Now remove them with a slotted spoon and serve with either butter or sour cream.

Yayeshnya z horodynoyu
Vegetable omelet

4 medium-sized baked potatoes, diced
8–9 oz/250 g raw ham, sliced into strips
1½–2 cups/200 g cooked green beans, finely chopped
6 tbsp/90 g butter
8 eggs
Salt and pepper
1 scant cup/100 g grated cheese

Combine the potatoes, ham, and beans and add 2 tablespoons melted butter. Whisk the eggs and mix in with the vegetables. Season with salt and pepper. Divide the mixture into 4 and fry each portion on both sides in 1 tablespoon butter in a skillet. Sprinkle the cooked omelets with the cheese and serve hot.

Lvivski nalysnyky
Lemberg pancakes

For the batter:
Generous 1 cup/150 g all-purpose flour
1 pinch baking powder
2–3 eggs
½ cup/125 ml milk
Salt
Oil for frying

For the filling:
1 onion, chopped
2 tbs/30 g butter
1 small carrot, diced
1 scant ½ cup/75 g each sliced button and flat mushrooms
¾ lb/300 g cooked chicken meat, finely chopped
3 tbsp sour cream

Salt and pepper
1 pinch nutmeg
2 tbsp chopped parsley
3 tbsp/45 g butter for baking

Combine the flour, baking powder, eggs, milk, and salt to make a pancake batter and leave to stand for about half an hour. Sauté the onion in the butter, add the carrot and sliced mushrooms and cook together. Add the chicken meat and sauté together briefly. Add the sour cream, season with salt, pepper, and nutmeg and fold in the chopped parsley.

Heat the oil in a skillet and fry 4 large pancakes from the batter. Fill each with the chicken and mushroom filling, roll up, and arrange in a greased baking dish. Dot the rolled pancakes with butter and bake in a preheated oven at 350–400 °F/180–200 °C for about 15 minutes.

Ptasheni hnizda
"Birds nests"

4 eggs, separated
1 pinch salt
7 tbsp/110 g sugar
3¼ cups/750 ml milk
Few drops of vanilla extract, or to taste
1–2 tbsp cornstarch

Whisk the egg whites with the salt and 1 tablespoon sugar until stiff. Bring the milk to a boil with 2 tablespoons sugar and the vanilla extract. Reduce the heat and using a tablespoon to spoon "nests" out of the beaten egg whites, place in the milk. Once set, remove with a slotted spoon and leave to cool. Whisk the egg yolks with the remaining sugar and stir into the milk. Mix the cornstarch with cold water and stir into the custard. Bring to a boil, simmer for 3 minutes stirring continuously, leave to cool. Serve floating on the sauce.

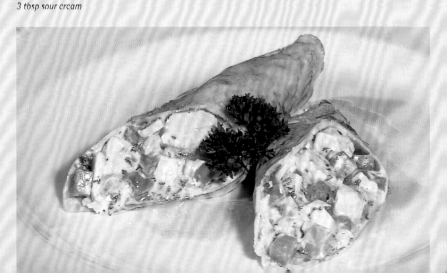

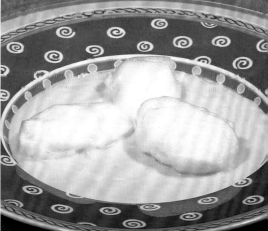

Varenyky

Varenyky ("cooked"), Ukrainian ravioli, are always a gourmet feast. Almost every Ukrainian adores the crescent-shaped dough pockets, filled with whatever the fields, forests, and gardens have to offer. And everyone has their favorite recipe. The savory versions have pâté de foie gras, potato, cabbage, bean, onion, pork crackling, or mushroom filling. The fans of sweet *varenyky* like them with poppy seeds, apples, plums, or prunes. And who can resist *varenyky* with fresh cherries or Quark? The preparation of this popular national dish may be a little time consuming as each one is filled by hand, but it is not difficult if you pay attention to a few basic rules: a superfine all-purpose flour which is not too dry should be used in order for the dough to work. This is combined with water, salt, and eggs if preferred. The dough should always be elastic. Once it has been rolled out, circles are pressed out of the dough using a glass, the filling is placed in the center of the circles which are then folded in half. The *varenyky* are cooked in lightly salted water at just under boiling point. Once they float to the surface they are removed from the water. The dough pockets should never be allowed to stick to one another during cooking, nor should they be allowed to break otherwise the delicious filling ends up in the water and not in the hungry mouths. These small delicacies are served hot. In order to prevent them from sticking together they are served with melted butter and are garnished with a big dollop of sour cream. They can be enjoyed as an appetizer, main dish, an entrée, or as a dessert. Some people like to eat *varenyky* the next day fried brown and crispy in butter.

Varenyky
Basic dough pocket recipe

For the basic dough:
3⅓ cups/500 g all-purpose flour
1 cup/250 ml water
2 eggs
1 tsp salt
Butter and sour cream

Make a dough from the flour, water, and eggs and leave to rest for 20 minutes. Roll out to about ¹⁄₁₆ inch/2 mm thick (double the thickness for *varenyky* with cherries). Use a thin-walled glass to press circles out of the dough. Place a teaspoonful of filling in the center of each circle, fold them in half and press the edges together well. Cook the filled dough pockets in a generous quantity of lightly salted, boiling water for about 10 minutes. When they float to the surface, add a glass of cold water, bring back up to a boil and remove with a slotted spoon. Drizzle with melted butter straightaway so that they do not stick together and serve with sour cream.

Savory cabbage filling
(Illustration below)

500 g cabbage, finely chopped
Oil for cooking
1 large onion, finely chopped
1 medium-sized carrot, finely chopped
1 medium-sized parsley root, finely chopped
Salt and pepper

Sauté the cabbage for 20 minutes. Sauté the other vegetables together and then add to the cabbage, season with salt and pepper. Cook everything together for about 15 minutes. These *varenyky* are usually served with chopped onions browned in a lot of butter.

Liver and bacon filling
(Not illustrated)

Generous 1 lb/500 g ox liver, prepared ready for cooking
4 tbsp/1/4 cup butter or oil
3 medium-sized onions, finely chopped
4 thick slices/100 g fatty bacon (salo)
Salt and pepper

Roughly chop the liver, fry in 2 tablespoons fat and cook until soft. Sauté the onions separately in 2 tablespoons fat. Put the liver and bacon through a grinder, combine with the onions, season with salt and pepper.

Cherry filling
(Illustration on facing page, below left)

1¾ lb/750 g cherries, pitted
⅔ cup/150 g sugar

For the sauce:
One handful of cherry pits
⅔ cup/150 g sugar

Combine the cherries with the sugar and leave to stand in a warm place for a couple of hours. Then drain and keep the juice. Fill the *varenyky* with the sugared cherries. For the sauce, crush the cherry pits in a pestle and mortar, bring to a boil in ¾ cup/200 ml water, simmer for about 10 minutes and then strain. Add the sugar to the liquid, bring to a boil again and reduce over high temperature. Combine the sugar syrup with the cherry juice and serve with the *varenyky*.

Varenyky with a meat filling can be prepared with ground beef, pork, or lamb. They are served with onions. Leftovers from the Sunday roast are also a good option for stuffing the delicious little dough pockets.

Sweet *varenyky* with Quark, or yogurt, and raisins are a treat for *varenyky* fans. They are filled with vanilla-flavored cream and lemon peel or, if preferred, are flavored with a little rum and are also served with sour cream.

The wealth of mushrooms in the Ukraine of course means that a wide variety of mushroom *varenyky* are served. For the filling the mushrooms are sautéed with onions and seasoned with herbs according to preference. Sour cream is also the best accompaniment for this variety of *varenyky*.

The filling for savory cabbage *varenyky* contains only chopped white cabbage, onion, salt, and pepper, as well as a little lemon juice if preferred. They are served with lots of melted butter or also with sour cream.

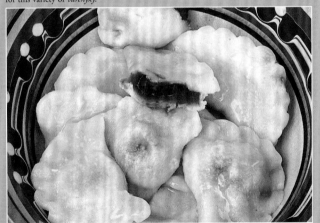

Varenyky with cherries are a welcome summer feast—whether as a sweet main dish or a warm, fruity dessert. They are filled with cherries and sugar and served with melted butter or also with cherry sauce.

Cherry *varenyky* are the top favorites among the fruity varieties, but the sweet dough pockets also taste good with blueberries. Other forest and garden berries, plums, jam, or poppy seeds also make for tasty fillings.

Sunshine for the kitchen

The climatic conditions and the fertile loess soils of the black earth area that covers almost half of Ukraine are particularly favorable for growing sunflowers. The plant originates from America and was brought to western Europe by the Spaniards in the middle of the 16th century. Its triumphant arrival in the region south of the *Dnieper* took place after it came back in Peter the Great's luggage following his return from western Europe. At first the ruler was simply enthusiastic about the large, attractive flower which is still considered the Ukrainian national flower today. Since the *soniashnyk*, sunflower, can be a lot more than mere decoration, however, it soon changed the eating habits in the Russian empire forever, only pork fat having been used for cooking in

Eastern Europe up until this point. The first oil mills in Ukraine went into production in about 1835. Ukraine now produces a variety of cooking oils from corn, mustard plants, flax, canola, linseed, soya, and hemp. However, the sunflower is by far the most important source of oil. Fifty-five percent of plant oils in the Soviet Union came from Ukraine, primarily from the Cherson, Saporishya areas, as well as Kirovohrad and Cherkassy.

Even today the sunflower crop is of significant value. Around one fifth of worldwide production comes from Ukraine. The Oil Institute of the Ukrainian Agricultural Academy, founded in 1989, is continually developing new, resistant, and high quality hybrids such as *Sustritish* or *Saporoshsky 9* which were patented in the 1990s. According to experts, however, the problems lie in the inadequate structures of the processing industry. Similarly to other areas of the food industry, the production and distribution of cooking oils are lagging behind, the conversion to a market economy having left behind deep wounds.

Sunflower oil is considered one of the healthiest cooking fats. Even today Ukrainian markets sell primarily cold pressed oil without chemical additives. The cold pressing of the seeds is a very gentle means of oil extraction because the mechanical grinding only involves temperatures of up to a maximum of 40 degrees. This means that the vitamins and valuable ingredients are retained. Unrefined sunflower oil contains polyunsaturated fatty acids that help to control the cholesterol levels in the blood, for example.

Due to its intense amber color and the characteristic aroma of roast sunflower seeds Ukrainians prefer to use unrefined oil for cold dishes such as salads. It is also delicious for simply dipping rye bread sprinkled with a little salt and eaten with raw onions. This aromatic, somewhat viscous specialty is also delicious with herring and baked potatoes. Refined sunflower oil is used for roasting and cooking. In Ukraine whole, roast sunflower seeds are among the most popular snacks. They are available wrapped in newspaper or the seller will also put them directly into your pocket.

Loose sunflowers seeds to snack on are available at the market in plastic beakers or wrapped in newspaper.

Sunflowers are able to display their golden glory to the full in the fertile black soils of Ukraine.

Top: The simplest old equipment is still used today for pressing the delicate sunflower oil.

Above: The solid residue, from the oil pressing, the so-called pomace, is collected in large sacks.

Mustard

The Ukrainians harbor a special affection for their mustard *(hirchytsya)*. It is spicy and has a healthy kick. It is eaten at all mealtimes, for example with dark rye bread and ham or sausage, with cold meat, with eggs or else in marinades. A sauce made from mayonnaise, egg yolk, mustard, and tomato paste or garlic goes well with shashlik, in modern cooking with roast zucchini or with eggplant slices which are spread with mustard and rolled up, filled with a walnut half if preferred. Mustard seeds from the mustard plants belonging to the cruciferous genus are used for making and flavoring the mustard. The milder white and hotter black mustard are the most common, but in Ukraine and other Eastern European countries brown mustard, the piquancy of which is between that of white and black mustard, is also frequently used. The mustard's piquancy comes from the ingredients, sinalbin and sinigrin. It is the grinding or crushing of the seeds which releases the aromatic ingredients that are then preserved by acids such as vinegar or lemon. The flavor of white mustard derives from the very durable sinalbin, while the sinigrin oil aroma in black mustard is more transient. Table mustard usually contains both white and black mustard, ground to a fine but slightly coarse-grained paste. Depending on the recipe there is also vinegar, wine, or lemon, as well as horseradish, sugar, cloves, cinnamon, herbs, salt, and pepper in varying proportions. The most piquant ready-made mustard available in Ukraine today is called *Moskovska hirchytsya* (Moscow Mustard). The milder mustard with horseradish *(Hirchytsya z khronom)* is also very popular.

Mustard as a natural remedy

At first it perhaps seems a little unlikely: as soon as they can feel a cold or the 'flu coming on the Ukrainians soak their feet in mustard, dissolving mustard powder in warm water. The dry alternative is: before going to bed in the evenings, place mustard seeds in a pair of socks and wear them overnight. The warmth of the bed then releases the healing effects of the seeds.

The healing properties of this century-old home remedy have long since been confirmed by scientists—mustard oils stimulate blood flow and have antibacterial properties. The well-known mustard plaster which helps with inflamed nerves, rheumatic complaints, lung infections as well as pleural infections is made from *Brassica nigra*, black mustard. *Sinapis alba*, white mustard, is used for stimulatory massages in order to alleviate tension or muscle pain. Used internally mustard overcomes digestion problems and is even thought to help prevent cancer. For poultices and mustard plasters the pulverized seeds are mixed with water heated to a maximum of 104 °F/40 °C. If the water is too hot it inhibits the effect of the enzymes which release the mustard oils and therefore the healing properties. For a mustard bath to relieve rheumatic complaints, about 2 cups/250 grams of freshly ground mustard flour are mixed with warm water and placed in a linen bag. After half an hour the bag can then be squeezed out in the bath water; its relaxant properties quickly take effect.

The seed grains of the mustard plant are ground to a paste and then seasoned to make mustard.

Vinegar

Otset, vinegar, is indispensable in the Ukrainian kitchen. It is needed for making mustard, it refines the flavor of salads and marinades as well as of casseroles and sauces. This sour companion gives borscht a final kick and it is also used for preserving fruit and vegetables such as sauerkraut with apples as well as cucumbers and tomatoes. It is also used in mayonnaise and sourdough. A zakuska menu without pickled herring would be an unforgivable culinary faux pas. Even hardcooked eggs are preserved in vinegar and while vinegar is not used for making aspic it is always served with the latter.

It is the bacterium *Acetobacter*, found in plants and in the air, which ensures that an alcoholic liquid, usually wine or fruit wine, turns to vinegar. The vinegar bacteria need oxygen to be able to transform the liquid. If supersaturation or acidity occurs the bacteria macerate and form a gelatinous mass, called the mother of vinegar. The bacteria become active again when dissolved in an alcoholic liquid. Fruit vinegar is obtained in the same way from fruit fermented into wine. In Ukraine vinegar is often made from basic, industrially produced vinegar essence. Many people swear by white wine vinegar for borscht and aspic, however. Red wine vinegar, on the other hand, is used less frequently because many Ukrainians find its stronger bouquet too intense. Some do use it for salads though. In the countryside apple vinegar continues to be very popular and is often made at home from leftover fruit. Where possible strongly flavored apples are pressed and the juice left to ferment. As with all types of vinegar the acid content is between 5 and 10 percent. As a rule homemade apple vinegar is naturally cloudy and especially aromatic. It is now known that this rediscovered age-old household remedy helps to keep the body's acid/base balance and, like apples themselves, contains secondary organic substances, vitamins and minerals, especially potassium, sodium, and calcium. Apple vinegar with honey and mineral water as an early morning drink has stimulating properties, especially in the case of a heavy head following excessive enjoyment of the Ukrainian schnapps *horilka*, and it also tastes good as a vinaigrette for salads. Ukrainians like to flavor their vinegar with tarragon or other herbs, with celery, garlic, blackcurrant leaves or else with horseradish or horseradish leaves. An age old marinade recipe recommends a mixture of vinegar with any kind of fruit and berries, honey or sugar, cloves, cinnamon, allspice, bay leaves, and salt. All of the ingredients are combined and used as a dressing for salads.

Sour is super: Ukrainians use vinegar—often flavored with herbs such as tarragon—not just for making marinades but also in casseroles, soups, and preserves.

Kholodets z koropa
Carp in aspic

2 medium-sized carrots, sliced
1 parsley root, thinly sliced
1 onion, chopped
1 bay leaf
5 black peppercorns
4 pieces carp, sliced diagonally about ¾ inch/2 cm
thick, with skin
Salt
1 x ¼ oz envelope/8–10 g gelatin powder
½ glass dry white wine
1 lemon and parsley for garnishing

Place the vegetables in a saucepan with the bay leaf and the peppercorns and place the fish pieces on top. Cover with water, season with salt, and poach (do not boil!) over low heat until the fish is cooked but not too soft. Carefully remove the fish from the stock and leave to cool. Strain the stock through a fine linen cloth. Dissolve the gelatin in a little of the slightly cooled stock. Make the rest of the stock up to about 2 cups/500 ml with the wine, add the dissolved gelatin and reheat (do not boil otherwise the aspic will be cloudy). Pour a thin layer over the base of a fish dish and leave to set. Then lay the fish pieces on top, decorate with carrot slices, cover with the remaining aspic and chill for 5–6 hours. Serve garnished with lemon slices and sprigs of parsley.

For the noble carp in aspic you need fresh vegetables, spices, gelatin, and wine in addition to the fish.

The fish pieces are cooked in slightly salted water together with the finely chopped vegetables and the various spices.

The aspic is made from the stock, wine, and gelatin. A thin layer is first poured over the plate.

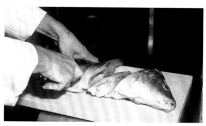

The carp is gutted and cleaned before being sliced into pieces about ¾ inch/2 cm thick.

Once the fish has been removed from the stock the latter is strained through a fine linen cloth.

The rest of the aspic is poured over the carp and the carrots once they have been arranged on the plate.

Artworks in aspic

Aspic was made long before there were refrigerators because the airtight conditions under the set jelly keep meat, fish, vegetables, and fruit fresh for longer—and it also looks attractive. On a walk through the markets the significance of jellied dishes in Ukraine becomes evident: everywhere there are containers with pig's head in aspic and a wide range of sausages in aspic. Since time immemorial the preparation of aspic dishes has been considered the best way of using up leftovers after the slaughter of an animal because they make use of the more inferior parts such as feet, ears, pig's head or oxtail. Pork or beef in aspic made from leg meat are the most common meals served as plain fare. Pig's feet, for example, cooked together with a piece of shoulder, are particularly good in aspic. They are preferably eaten with horseradish or mustard, vinegar, as well as bread or even roast potatoes. Ukrainians are particularly fond of fish in aspic for the Christmas meal. Preparing aspic is not difficult. The meat and spices are always placed in cold water together with onions or carrot which provide a bit of color. Once the water has come to a boil the liquid should no longer be boiled and the foam should be skimmed off from time to time so that the aspic is not cloudy. Glutin, a protein contained in bone marrow, is the magic ingredient which causes the liquid to set later. Traditionally it is considered a sacrilege to use commercial gelatin to make aspic. In the interests of saving time, however, or for jellying fruit or sweet ingredients, housewives do also use this neutral-tasting additive which is available either in powder form or as transparent leaves. The main component of gelatin is also glutin that is industrially extracted from bones and cartilage. You need 2 x ¼ oz envelopes of powdered gelatin (or 8 leaves) to set 4 cups/1 liter of liquid. More gelatin may be needed to support heavy ingredients if the dish is to be unmolded when set. For savory dishes crushed garlic, salt and imaginative garnishes are put into the almost set aspic. Colorful flowers made from egg shells and skillfully shaped carrot pieces as well as chives and parsley decorate the fish or meat as the main ingredient under the firm, transparent, and delicious aspic. Sweet jellies based on fruit juices are served as dessert especially in summer, with cherries, blackcurrants, gooseberries, and wild berries for example.

Kholodets z myasa
Meat in aspic
(Not illustrated)

3¼ lb/1.5 kg boiled beef
2 small, foreleg pork knuckles, prepared ready for cooking
1 onion, peeled
Bay leaves
5 black peppercorns
2 allspice corns
Salt
1–2 garlic cloves, crushed

Place the meat in 3 quarts/3 liters of water, briefly bring to a boil together with the onion and the spices (except the salt), skim off the foam and simmer (do not boil!) for about 3 hours. Once the liquid has reduced to at least a third, add the salt and simmer for about another 15 minutes. Remove the meat from the stock, remove the bones and cut into bite-sized pieces. Strain the bouillon, add the garlic, return to the heat to reduce. Place the meat in a large terrine or ovenproof dish, cover with the stock including the garlic and leave in a cool place to set. Serve with grated beets and horseradish.

Salyvani yahody
Berry jelly

2 cups/500 ml berry juice (raspberry, strawberry and/or blackcurrant)
2 scant cups/400 g sugar
2 cups/500 ml white wine
Juice of ½–1 lemon
2 x ¼ oz envelopes powdered gelatin or 8 leaves

Bring the fresh berry juice to a boil together with the sugar, white wine, and lemon juice. Dissolve the gelatin as indicated on the packaging, mix with the juice, and leave the liquid in a mold to cool and set. Before serving dip the mold briefly into hot water, loosen the edges with a knife, and turn out the fruit jelly onto the serving plate. Decorate with whipped cream or as desired.

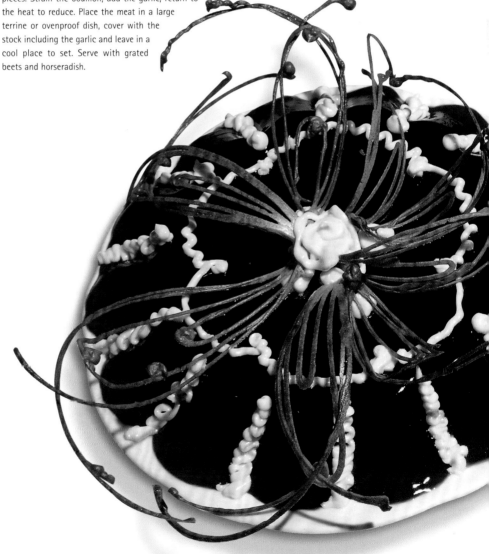

Christmas in Ukraine

According to Nikolai Gogol's tale of the same name, the night before Christmas belongs to the young people especially: "Droves of young people with sacks were thronging through the streets, there was the sound of song in the air, and there was hardly a single window without a group of carol singers beneath it. … Small windows were opened and the thin hands of old women (left alone at home with the worthy fathers) threw out sausages and pieces of cake. The boys and girls took turns at holding up their sacks to catch the bounty."

Christmas was not an official holiday in the Soviet Union and the faithful could only celebrate the festival with their families in private. The old traditions have since been revived however, as have the traditional costumes which Ukrainian families especially like to wear at Christmas. Many Ukrainians in exile, such as those in Canada, the US, or even Germany, do the same. The customs are a symbol of a revived self-confidence and sense of their own identity following so many years of Soviet egalitarianism. In addition to the Orthodox Church in Ukraine there is also the United Church which originated in the 16th century during a convergence of the Eastern Church with Rome. Followers of both faiths celebrate Christmas in the same way. Christian and pagan traditions—derived from the rhythms of nature—are gaining renewed significance and are often interwoven with each other. Thus Christmas celebrates not only the birth of Jesus Christ but also the spirits of the dead and people in the countryside pray for a good harvest. They also tap on the windows from inside imploring the frost to stay away from their gardens and fields. The days leading up to Christmas, which in Ukraine is celebrated according to the Julian calendar from December 6 to January 9, are today among the busiest in the year with shopping, baking, cooking, cleaning, and decorating. A Christmas tree, often a spruce, is part of the Christmas decorations in most parts of the country today. On Christmas Eve hay is spread in the corners of the room as well as on and underneath the tables.

The *diduch*, a bunch of wheat ears symbolizing the ancestors, is placed under the main icon. Dried fruit, a small container of salt, and the *knysh*, a cake sometime filled with white cabbage, also have their place. Garlic cloves are placed on the hay in the corners of the room in order to keep evil spirits away.

In the past when the cooking was done over a fire, it was customary to dry 12 logs 12 days before the celebration in memory of the 12 Apostles. This memorial also characterizes the meal on Christmas Eve in which traditionally 12 meat-free dishes are served, in the past prepared over the same fire in which the logs were burning. The family sits down at the table when the first evening star appears in the sky. *Kutya*, cooked wheat with honey, walnuts, chopped figs, and poppy seeds, is served first. Two cold fish dishes then follow, such as pike or carp in aspic and herring, then red borscht without meat and with *ushky*, cooked dough pockets with a mushroom or herring filling. Two different roulades made from fresh and pickled cabbage, mushroom sauce, and *varenyky* with potato and savory cabbage filling (see page 166) supplement the savory dishes. Finally there is *usvar*, a compote of dried fruit, and *pampushky* (see page 161), doughnuts baked in oil. *Kolach*, the traditional, slightly sweet, plaited Christmas bread made from wheat flour and yeast is always on the table. Since it also contains eggs that may not be eaten on Christmas Eve, it is only eaten the next day. Most Ukrainians today still forgo meat on Christmas Eve. The drinking of alcohol is also traditionally forbidden on Christmas Eve.

According to tradition in the country a little of every dish together with a little flour and salt is placed in a wooden bowl for the domestic animals so that they also partake in the evening meal. Since cattle are believed to be able to speak with God on Christmas Eve they receive especially good food. After the evening meal one is supposed to place the *kutya* dish under the icon, together with the *kolach* which symbolizes the baby Jesus, as well as glass of water for the ancestral spirits, who visit the house during this night. Christmas carols are sung together and after the meal one goes out into the cold winter night to bring Christmas food to neighbors, godparents, and relatives.

On Christmas Eve the *diduch* is placed under the main icon in the house. The bunch of wheat ears symbolizes the family's ancestors.

Usvar
Dried fruit compote

4–5 oz/125 g dried apple slices
4–5 oz/125 g dried pear slices
½ cup/75 g pitted prunes
½ cup/50 g dried blueberries
½ cup/50 g raisins
⅞ cup/200 g sugar
1 cinnamon stick
3 cloves
Rind and juice of 1 organic lemon
1 tbsp wildflower honey

Wash the dried fruit first in cold water and then in warm water. Bring 1½ quarts/1.5 liters of water to a boil with the sugar in a deep saucepan. Add the apples and pears and simmer briskly, add the prunes after about 5 minutes. After a further 5 minutes add the blueberries, raisins, cinnamon, cloves, and the lemon peel cut into spirals and leave to simmer for a further 5–10 minutes (add more water if necessary, the fruit must remain covered.) Remove from the heat and leave to cool slightly, then stir in the lemon juice and honey. Leave to stand in a cool place overnight to let the flavors develop. The fruit and juice are usually served separately. *Usvar* keeps for up to two weeks in the refrigerator.

Kutya
Christmas porridge

Generous 1 lb/500 g wheat grains (see Glossary)
½ tsp salt
1½ cups/200 g poppy seeds
6 tbsp/200 g honey
7 tbsp/100 g sugar
¾ cup/100 g chopped walnuts

In Ukraine a wide variety of dishes are served in traditional order at Christmas, such as the wheat porridge *kutya*, meat-free borscht, *varenyky*, fish dishes, and compote.

Wash the wheat grains and leave to soak overnight in a generous quantity of water. Bring to a boil in the soaking water and allow to swell over low heat for 3–4 hours. Add the salt ½ hour before the end of the cooking time. Drain the wheat grains through a strainer. Grind the poppy seeds in a coffee grinder or a blender. Dissolve the honey and the sugar in 1 cup/250 ml hot water then stir into the ground poppy seeds and leave it all to cool. Combine with the wheat grains and the walnuts.
Variation: Depending on taste *kutya* can also be enhanced with figs, soaked raisins and/or any other softened and chopped dried fruit.

Pike

"And then the snow began to melt again and the pike broke up the ice with its tail, as we liked to say," wrote Nikolai Gogol in his tale "St. John's Eve." The *shchuka*, pike, is one of the most popular fish in Ukraine and in Russia and is preferably enjoyed by connoisseurs between September and January. If the fish is not able to break through the ice on its own then the angler has to help. Bore a hole in the ice and then it is just patience, luck, and perhaps a little angling skill that are needed. Suspected exaggerations regarding the size and weight of the fish are, however, often not so far from the truth.

The female fish especially can weigh as much as 77 lb/35 kg, measure up to 60 to 63 inches/150–160 cm in length, and can be up to 30 years old. The smaller males weigh 17 to 19 lb/8–9 kg, with a length of 35 to 43 inches/90–110 cm. They live for 10 to 14 years. In the spawning season between February and May the female pike lays up to 50,000 eggs and the young fish can grow up to about 8 inches/20 cm in length during their first summer if conditions are favorable. The pike prefers slow-flowing streams and rivers, clear, still lakes or ponds and can be found throughout Ukraine; they are present in particularly large numbers in the Shazki Osera group of lakes in western Ukraine. As a static fish it is usually found near overgrown riverbanks. It is well camouflaged and waits among the water plants for other fish that it attacks with lightning speed. The largest predator among Europe's freshwater fish looks the part: the body is long and narrow, the mouth is similar to a duck's beak with lots of clearly visible teeth. Young pike are placed in carp ponds to control the number of feeding competitors for the carp. In their role as health policemen they also destroy weak and sick fish. The nobleman among the freshwater fish is a very popular culinary delicacy and is most tender when weighing under 6½ lb/3 kg. Then it is best suited to baking or sautéing. Older and heavier fish are used to make wonderful fillings, terrines, pies, and dumplings. The pike has been at home in Ukraine since time immemorial and, dressed in

Noble freshwater fish such as pike and perch used to be a simple food of the people as is shown in this wall painting in a Kiev restaurant: "Wife cook the perch so that there is also enough for a soup."

delicious aspic, is part of the Christmas meal. It also has its place in more simple dishes, crumbed or baked for example, or in a pike soup prepared simply with soup greens. As with carp and perch, pike is also very popular when skillfully and tastily stuffed, for example with a trout stuffing or with mushrooms and buckwheat. These specialties are eaten in slices as a cold appetizer. *Halushky z ryby*, fish dumplings made from three different fish such as carp, cod, and trout, are also popular cooked with onions, breadcrumbs, egg, and parsley. They are also served cold in aspic.

Background: Hobby anglers seek their fortunes in rivers everywhere, such as here on the banks of the *Dnieper* in Kiev.

Freshwater fish

Pike *(shchuka):* bony predatory fish. Firm white and lean meat with its own characteristic taste.

Carp *(korop):* a bony fish, lower in fat content than is often assumed. Flavorful, firm flesh, very good for fillings.

Eel *(vyun):* a snake-like fish with fatty meat, few bones, very well suited to smoking.

Zander *(sudak):* a freshwater fish with few bones, with tender white, lean flesh. Very delicate and should therefore be prepared simply.

Tench *(lyn):* very bony fish with slimy skin and very flavorful skin.

Catfish *(som):* one of the largest freshwater fish, few bones. Young fish have tender, white, fatty, and aromatic meat.

Trout *(forel'):* one of the most common freshwater fish, today supplied mostly from fish farms. Very tender and flavorful meat.

Perch *(okun'):* firm, easily digestible, and flavorful meat. The fillets with the skin on are suited to roasting.

The port city of Odessa

Odessa is unlike any other place in Ukraine: a bustling port city full of a mixture of languages and peoples. Ukrainians live here next to Russians, Bulgarians, Greeks, and Albanians, there are also Germans as well as Jews. Odessa is considered to be the city of humor, of the dry, oblique, and high-spirited joke. "Do you come from Odessa?" is the start to a typical joke, to which the answer is "No, I am a respectable person." Around 1.2 million people live here, cheerful and cosmopolitan, and surprisingly enough even a little melancholic which many associate with the proximity to the steppe and the sea.

You can try the diverse international and Ukrainian specialties in the cafes and restaurants on the often rundown boulevards and in the bars at the port: juicy Greek olives, Korean-style preserved vegetables, Bulgarian paprika dishes or Turkish-oriental hors d'oeuvres. And everything is washed down with beer, wine, or sparkling wine from the local cellars.

For centuries the port of Odessa was the most important in the Russian empire and therefore in Ukraine and is still one of the most important ports in Eastern Europe today. The cargo ships with industrial and construction goods, with foodstuffs such as oranges, bananas, Indian rice, or tea from Ceylon all dock here. Even under the Soviet Union the *Privoz*, the large bazaar on the outskirts of the city, reveled in the aromas of the big wide world—this is where desires were and still are satisfied. Clothing from a wide variety of countries could and can be found here, as can cosmetics and seductive spice mixtures. The market is also a source of fascination with all of the fragrances of local and exotic fruit.

The acrid aroma of salted, smoked, roasted, preserved, or baked fish combines with the all-pervasive smell of salt water. Mackerel in particular are caught in the Black Sea, as well as herrings sprats, mullet, bullheads, or Baltic herring. The fish dishes served at home or in the city's restaurants are freshly caught and delicious. However,

Above left: A market vendor in Odessa sells dishes made from southern vegetables.

Center left: The *Krasnaya* Hotel is one of Odessa's magnificent buildings from the 19th century.

Left: The open air cafes along Odessa's pedestrian streets lend the city a Mediterranean flair in the summer.

Right: Fresh or dried fish from the Black Sea are part of the staple diet in Odessa.

the magnificent city of Odessa on the Black Sea has also known bad times, being afflicted by regular famines and wars.

Overcoming the ecological problems of recent times such as water and soil pollution requires enormous effort. Of the 26 kinds of fish which were caught in marketable quantities in the 1960s there are now just six for which it is still worth casting the nets. The anchovy catch, which measured 320,000 tonnes in 1984, has shrunk to 15,000 tonnes in just a few years. Some fish species have died out completely.

However, rethinking has been taking place even in Ukraine. Environmental consciousness has been gaining in significance since the start of the 1990s and there is now an environmental protection act and a corresponding ministry with far-reaching authority. In the event of ecological infringements companies can have a financial penalty imposed upon them or can even be shut down. The Green Party founded at the end of 1989 is gaining in support and the positive side of the economic downturn is that this helps the environmental protection since many of the rundown factories from the Soviet era are out of commission and can therefore no longer pollute the natural environment.

People strolling on the famous Potemkin Steps with the monument to the governor of Odessa, Emmanuel Richelieu (1766–1822).

Ukrainian fish dishes

Fashyrovany korop
Stuffed carp

½ cup/15 g dried mushrooms
1 scant cup/150 g buckwheat
1 medium-sized onion, finely chopped
Oil for frying
4 eggs
Salt
Pepper
1–2 garlic cloves, crushed
1 carp weighing about 2¼ lb/1 kg, gutted through the spine at the fish store
Flour and breadcrumbs for crumbing
7 tbsp/100 g melted butter

Wash the dried mushrooms and soak in 1 cup/250 ml cold water for about 30 minutes. Then boil until soft, drain (reserve the liquid), and chop into small pieces. Cook the buckwheat in the reserved liquid for about 25 minutes, adding more water if necessary. Sauté the chopped onion in oil and then combine with the cooked mushrooms, buckwheat, 2 raw eggs, salt, pepper, and the garlic.

Wash the carp thoroughly. Stuff with the filling through the spine. Stitch up the fish with kitchen twine and then coat with flour, the remaining beaten egg, and the breadcrumbs. Fry in oil on all sides until crispy then bake in a preheated oven at 440 ° F/225 °C for about 45 minutes or until cooked.

Before serving remove the twine, cut the fish into portions, and drizzle with the hot melted butter. Serve with steamed carrots and boiled potatoes.

If the carp is not yet prepared for cooking the fins should be cut off first of all.

Then scale the fish with the back of a knife, or with a fish scaler, under running water.

For stuffing the carp is gutted via the spine or have them do it at the fish store.

The carp is stuffed with the filling made from buckwheat, mushrooms, onions, and eggs.

The carp is carefully stitched together with kitchen twine so that the stuffing does not spill out.

The carp is crumbed and then fried before being baked in the oven until cooked.

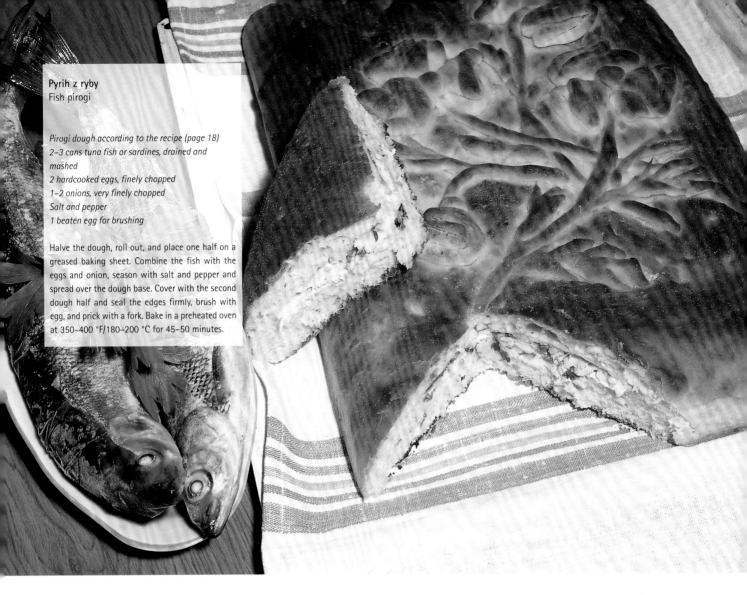

Pyrih z ryby
Fish pirogi

Pirogi dough according to the recipe (page 18)
2–3 cans tuna fish or sardines, drained and
mashed
2 hardcooked eggs, finely chopped
1–2 onions, very finely chopped
Salt and pepper
1 beaten egg for brushing

Halve the dough, roll out, and place one half on a
greased baking sheet. Combine the fish with the
eggs and onion, season with salt and pepper and
spread over the dough base. Cover with the second
dough half and seal the edges firmly, brush with
egg, and prick with a fork. Bake in a preheated oven
at 350–400 °F/180–200 °C for 45–50 minutes.

Zavyvantsi z ryby
Fish rolls
(Not illustrated)

1³/₄ lb/800 g small pike or perch fillets
About 4 slices/100 g white bread, crusts removed
¹/₂ cup/125 ml milk
2 eggs
1 medium-sized onion, finely chopped
Salt and pepper
2 tbsp all-purpose flour
3¹/₂ tbsp/50 g butter

Wash the fillets, pat dry, and put half of them through
a grinder. Soak the white bread in the milk, squeeze
out, mix together with one egg, the onion, salt, pepper, and the ground fish. Spread the filling over the
other fillets, roll them up, and secure with kitchen
twine. Dip the fish rolls in the flour and beaten egg
and fry in the butter. Serve the fish rolls with roast or
mashed potatoes.

Shchuka z khronom
Pike with horseradish

4 pike fillets each weighing 5 oz/150 g, without skin
Salt
1 horseradish root, grated
7 tbsp/100 g butter
³/₄ cup/200 g sour cream
1 tbsp white wine vinegar
1 tbsp sugar
Pepper
¹/₂ bunch each dill and parsley, finely chopped

Wash the pike fillets, pat dry, and season with salt.
Lightly fry the grated horseradish in 2 tablespoons
butter. Carefully place the fish pieces next to one
another in a buttered casserole dish, cover with the
horseradish, pour over the sour cream, cover and cook
for about 40 minutes. Remove the fish pieces with a
slotted spoon and keep them warm. Combine the
cooking stock with the remaining butter, the white

wine vinegar, and the sugar, then season the sauce
with salt and pepper. Serve the fish covered with the
sauce and garnished with the herbs. Serve accompanied by boiled potatoes.

Jewish ghetto

"We used to bake bread from the cheapest, darkest coarse meal, but to us it tasted good without butter," wrote the Jewish stage and film actor Alexander Granach (1893–1945) in *Da geht ein Mensch* (There Goes an Actor). "Oh yes, onions and garlic were hidden because even more bread was devoured with onion and garlic." The Granach family was destitute but they were no exception because their neighbors and their neighbors' neighbors in the east Galician Jewish Ghetto did not fare any better. What they had in common were a lot of children, their proverbial humor which also helped them to get through the hard times, and their cultural traditions.

East Galicia had belonged to Poland from the middle of the 14th century, between 1772 and 1919 it was part of the Habsburg monarchy and today forms the western Ukraine where about 300,000 Jews live. Jews had already been fleeing to east Galicia at the time of the Crusades between the 11th and 13th centuries, but this increased in the 14th century when many Jews who had been subjected to contempt, persecution, and expulsion in western Europe fled to the East. With them they brought their Yiddish language, derived from the Middle High German dialects. A further large wave of immigration followed in the 15th and 16th centuries especially in the wake of the Spanish Inquisition. The Jews were benevolently taken in by the Polish–Catholic nobility because they contributed to trade development. They were also deployed as bailiffs, a position that was to prove fatal for them when Ukrainian farmers and Cossacks joined forces against their Polish masters in the Cossack rebellion of 1648. Thousands of Jews were subjected to cruel deaths or were expelled. In the years that followed the Jewish communities again suffered under the wars and campaigns between Poles, Russians, and Swedes, such that they became noticeably poorer. A wave of migration got underway from the rundown city areas into smaller town and village settlements. That is how the world of the Jewish ghettos came to be and which existed up until the persecution and execution of European Jews in World War II. In most cases these settlements were inhabited solely by Jews who, despite their Christian surroundings, kept to themselves and maintained their own culture. Here they enjoyed religious freedom and extensive communal self-determination. Since Jews were not permitted to own land they mostly lived from petty trade and handcrafts—and primarily from hand to mouth.

It was in reaction to this destitute life that Chassidism developed in east Galicia in the 18th century as a movement toward mysticism and a joyful internal acceptance of life. In the opinion of the founder of this religious current, Rabbi Israel ben Eliser, known as Baal Schem Tov ("Master of the Good Name"), one was closer to the faith when the strict formalism of the Jewish laws was replaced by active humility, benevolence, and self-communion.

Drafty backyards, leaning, closely packed wooden houses and crooked alleyways were crowded around the marketplace in a Jewish ghetto. In the bustling throng between the traders stood clay pots and tin ware with goods, beans for the *cholent*, the Sabbath stew, for example. The aroma of roast onions, unleavened bread or gefilte fish wafted between the yards and the huts.

Jewish recipes and their preparation are closely linked with the laws of the *kashrut*, the Jewish dietary laws. The food has to be kosher, that is "immaculate." Only those mammals that are both ruminants and cloven-hoofed are permitted, such as beef, sheep, and goats. The slaughtering takes place in accordance with specific rules (Kashrut) whereby, above all, the animal must be bled after stunning. Meat and milk dishes are eaten completely separate from one another. Very devout families therefore have two sets of cutlery and crockery, sometimes even two basins for washing up. According to the *Kashrut* fruit, vegetables, eggs, and fish are neutral and can be eaten with both meat and milk dishes. However, only fish with scales and fins are allowed, species such as eel, catfish, or sturgeon are forbidden—and therefore so is caviar. Shellfish are also taboo.

East European Jewish cuisine is multifaceted, tasty, and imaginative if it is a case of making the most out of a little. Even today the Sabbath stew cholent is still prepared the day before as no work is done on the Sabbath. The *kneidl*, or knaidlach, an oblong dumpling made from flour, baking powder, and fat such as suet, is a favorite side dish cooked on top of the cholent. The gefilte fish now known around the world is a classic fish stuffing cooked in the fish skin, made from carp or perch for example. However, it is also often used to refer to small fish dumplings served with carrots and a horseradish and beet sauce.

Kugel, a sweet or savory dish baked in the oven and made from noodles, rice, potatoes, sweet potatoes, parsnips or other vegetables, always set with egg, is also delicious, as are stuffed *blintzes*, pancakes, and pâtés made from minced chicken or goose liver. Fermented cucumbers or cabbage are still a tradition today as are herrings preserved in brine. Compotes and baked dishes based on dried fruit are often served for dessert and Jewish cuisine is renowned for wonderful baked goods with fruit, nuts, almonds, and raisins.

In the Jewish ghetto the daily bread and other foodstuffs were traded on the street.

Lokshen kugel
Noodle bake

Generous 1 lb/500 g ribbon noodle (made with egg)
Salt
4 eggs
7 tbsp/100 g sugar
½ tsp cinnamon
1 pinch nutmeg
2 tbsp honey
7 tbsp/100 g butter, softened
1¼ cups/150 g raisins, washed and scalded
1 cup/100 g walnuts or almonds, roughly chopped
Butter for greasing

Boil the noodles in slightly salted, boiling water, drain, and rinse. Beat the eggs with the sugar. Add the cinnamon, nutmeg, a pinch of salt, honey, and the softened butter. Mix well and fold the mixture into the noodles together with the raisins and nuts. Place in a greased, ovenproof dish and bake in a preheated oven at 350 °F/180 °C for 45–60 minutes. The bake can be served either warm or cold according to preference.
Variation: The dish tastes even better when 2 finely chopped cooking apples are added to the mixture.

Cholent
Sabbath stew
(Serves 6)

¾ cup/150 g each of white and brown beans
1¾ lb/750 g brisket of beef, boned
4 tbsp oil or goose fat
2–3 onions, sliced
2 garlic cloves, sliced
6 medium-sized potatoes, peeled and quartered
¾ cup/150 g pearl barley
1 bay leaf
1 tsp dried thyme
½ tsp paprika
1 tbsp sugar
Salt and pepper

For the kneidl:
1 generous cup/150 g all-purpose flour
½ tsp baking powder
Salt and pepper
⅔ cup/150 g goose fat, or soft margarine
About 6 tbsp cold water
½ bunch parsley, finely chopped

Soak the beans in cold water for at least 8 hours, then drain. Cut the meat into bite-sized pieces and brown in the oil, on all sides, in a large flameproof pan. Remove the meat and fry the onions until soft and then the garlic. Return the meat to the pan, add the soaked beans and the remaining ingredients, sprinkling each layer with salt and pepper. Finally, cover with water, bring to a boil and leave to simmer for 20–30 minutes. In the meantime prepare a dough out of the *kneidl* ingredients, shape into an oblong dumpling and carefully place on top of the meat and beans.

Cover the pan tightly (place a piece of aluminum foil between the pan and the lid if necessary) and slow cook in the oven at 210–250 °F/110 °C for 8–10 hours or overnight. Do not stir! Before serving slice the *kneidl* and serve with the stew.

Carpathian cookery

"Following the superbly appetizing soup, to which—of course—dozens of herbs have contributed the intoxicating fragrance of the Carpathian forests, I am basking in the bliss of a dish which from outside appearances is reminiscent of a simple farmers' breakfast. Of course the potatoes and the eggs play a role in this symphony but, next to more completely different herbs, first fiddle is played by the new find in the Carpathian forests: the unsuspected, unseen, not to mention never eaten mushrooms!" These lines from a travel guide essentially sum up the cuisine of the Ukrainian Carpathian region in the west of the country: it captivates with the straightforward simplicity of the ingredients from the forests, meadows, fields, and gardens. The low range of mountains in the center of Europe, also known as the Forest Carpathians, extends for 175 miles/ 280 km in western Ukraine and the Hoverlya peak rises to 6,652 feet/2,000 m. The sounds of civilization are far removed, the mountains have a tremendous stillness and an intensive aroma—

gentler in the summer when the meadows and the fruit trees are in blossom, stronger in autumn when the earth is moist, the mushrooms are sprouting in the forests, and the smoke from the potato fires is in the air. Descendants of the Huzul, Lemk, and Boyk peoples still live in the Carpathians. They each speak their own dialect, have their own architectural style in part and, in contrast to the predominantly farming population settled on the lowlands of Ukraine, they are primarily engaged in forestry, fishing, and horse and sheep breeding. Anyone who travels to or goes hiking in the Carpathians continually encounters shepherds with large herds, the men themselves often clad in sheepskin. The lamb here is particularly flavorsome as the herbs and grasses of this highland region (melissa, mint, yarrow, nettles, lemon balm, oregano, and wood sorrel,) not only fortify the animals but also flavor the roasts or the lamb soup exquisitely. *Brendzya* also tastes just as delicious and natural, simply with bread and tomatoes or else in salads. The meadows and the extensive mountain forests are a hunter's paradise and deer, venison, wild boar, rabbits, and poultry are popular. Delicious eels are bred in the lakes. Due to the moist, warm climate the cherry, apple, pear, walnut, and hazelnut trees usually produce rich harvests. The cultiva-

tion of oats and corn has been a tradition for centuries whereas wheat and millet do not fare as well. Corn porridge therefore remains part of the staple diet in the Carpathians today. The numerous mineral water springs provide healthy refreshment and the water from these sources is often subjected to further processing. The *Truskavetska* mineral water from Truskavetsk in the lower Carpathians is popular throughout the country. Meat and bacon are frequently smoked in the Carpathians. Green beans with bacon or with a sauce made from sour cream and potatoes, which are baked in the oven with bacon, are a substantial every day meal. *Labsha* are homemade egg noodles, as yellow as sunlight and served with fried cabbage or with hazelnuts and sugar. Who would not agree with the comments of a visitor in this regard: "Heaven only knows how such enchanting harmonies and dissonances were composed in two courses."

The Huzul used to live in the Carpathians as shepherds, farmers, and horse breeders. Their pagoda-like wooden houses are still typical of this forested region today where life still proceeds at its gentle country pace. The locals live from the sheep and the produce that grows in this fertile region.

Baranyna z yablokamy
leg of lamb with apples

3¼ lb/1.5 kg leg of lamb
Salt and pepper
4 garlic cloves, sliced lengthwise into slivers
3½ oz/100 g fatty bacon (salo), diced)
10 medium-sized potatoes, peeled and quartered,
or diced if preferred
3 medium-sized cooking apples, peeled and quartered, or diced
Preserved lingonberries

Wash the leg of lamb and pat dry, rub with salt and
pepper, make little slits and stud with garlic. Put in
a roasting pan. Fry the diced bacon in its own fat
and add to the meat with a little water. Roast in
the oven at 430 °F/220 °C for about 1 hour, regularly basting with the cooking fat. Add the potatoes
and apples and roast for a further 30 minutes.
Serve with gravy and lingonberries.

Kalysha z kvasoleyu
Corn porridge with beans

For the corn porridge:
2 cups/500 ml milk
1 tsp salt
1½ cups/250 g corn meal (polenta)
1 tbsp/15 g butter

Bring the milk, together with 2 cups/500 ml water or
else just 4 cups/1 liter of salted water, to a boil. Add
the corn meal and bring back up to a boil over low
heat. Leave to swell over very low heat, stirring regularly, so that the mixture does not stick.

For the beans:
1¾ lb/750 g green beans
Salt
Summer savory
5½ oz/150 g fatty bacon, finely diced
2 onions, chopped
1 cup/250 g soft sheep's milk cheese
Crushed garlic according to taste

Wash the beans and break into bite-sized pieces. Cook
in a little boiling water with the summer savory for
about 20 minutes, drain. Fry the bacon in a skillet in
its own fat and then sauté the onions in the fat until
soft. Add the beans and briefly sauté together. Serve
the corn porridge with the beans together with the
sheep's milk cheese and garlic.

Meat and poultry

Dusheni nyrky
"Drowned" kidneys

2 veal kidneys, weighing about 12 oz/300 g
Salt and pepper
1 onion, finely chopped
2 tbsp/30 g butter
1 small glass brandy
$\frac{1}{2}$ cup/125 ml meat stock
4 black peppercorns
1 bay leaf
1–2 tbsp all-purpose flour
2 tbsp chopped parsley

Slice the veal kidneys open lengthwise and clean well. Leave them to draw in lightly salted water for 1–2 hours, pat dry thoroughly, and slice thinly. Sauté the onions in the butter until transparent. Add the kidneys and fry briefly. Slake with the brandy, add the stock, peppercorns, and bay leaf. Cover and leave to simmer over a low heat for 5 minutes. Combine the flour with a little cold water, bind the sauce with it and bring back up to a boil, season with salt and pepper. Sprinkle with chopped parsley. Serve with mashed potato or with rice.

Pechena telyatyna z kropom
Roast veal with dill cream sauce

1 veal roast weighing about 3 lb/1.2 kg
Salt and pepper
Oil for frying
2 cups/500 g sour cream
2 bunches dill, finely chopped

Wash the meat and pat dry, season with salt and pepper. Brown on all sides in the oil in a roasting pan. Add a little water and bake in the oven at 430 °F/220 °C for about 1½ hours, adding a little more water if necessary. Remove the meat from the pan, add the sour cream and the chopped dill to the roasting juices, briefly bring to a boil, season with salt and pepper. Slice the meat and serve with the sauce and boiled potatoes.

Nachynena huska
Stuffed goose

7 oz/200 g liver (beef or poultry)
6 garlic cloves, crushed
Salt and pepper
5 eggs, separated
7 tbsp/100 g butter
1 young goose weighing about 5–6 lb/2.5 kg, oven-ready
1 bunch parsley

Dice the liver very finely and then combine with half of the garlic, the salt, pepper, egg yolks, and butter. Beat the egg whites until stiff and carefully fold into the liver stuffing.
Wash out cavity of the goose and pat dry, rub well with salt and pepper. Stuff the goose with the liver stuffing and stitch the cavity shut with kitchen twine. Roast in a preheated oven at 400–430 °F/200–220 °C for about 3 hours, basting the bird with the roasting juices regularly.
Before serving sprinkle the goose with the remaining garlic and garnish with parsley.

Vyprova pechenia z pidlyvoyu z slyvok
Roast pork with plum sauce
(Illustration left)

1³/₄ lb/750 g pork fillet
Salt and pepper
2 tbsp all-purpose flour
3 tbsp pork fat, or oil
1 tbsp vinegar
1 bay leaf
2 cloves
1½ cups/250 g prunes, pitted
1 stale bread roll, crumbed
2 tbs/30 g butter
1 tsp sugar
½ tsp cinnamon

Wash the meat and pat dry thoroughly, then season with salt and pepper, coat in flour and brown well on all sides in the hot fat. Pour in about 1 cup/250 ml hot water, add the vinegar, bay leaf, and cloves and roast at 350 °F/180 °C for 30–40 minutes. In the meantime place the prunes in a saucepan and just cover with hot water. Bring to a boil and simmer over low heat until soft, then push through a sieve with a wooden spoon. Lightly brown the breadcrumbs in the butter and add the prune purée together with a little of the meat juices. Remove the meat and keep warm on a platter. Strain the roasting juices through a sieve, combine with the prune purée and bring to a boil, adding a little water or stock depending on the desired consistency. Season to taste with sugar and cinnamon.
Slice the meat before serving, pour over the sauce and serve with potatoes.

The breasts and thigh bones are removed from the chicken for especially decorative chicken rolls.

Cold butter is then shaped around the bones by hand and left to cool again for a short time.

The chicken breasts are then pressed or beaten flat so that they are easy to roll up.

Each of the buttered bones is now wrapped with a chicken breast.

The chicken rolls are coated in flour, egg, and bread-crumbs and then fried in oil until golden yellow in color.

Kurka po kyivske
Chicken Kiev

¾ cup/175 g cold butter
4 fresh chicken breasts
Salt and pepper
3 tbsp all-purpose flour
2 eggs
Sunflower oil for frying

For the side dish (potato sticks):
Generous 1 lb/500 g potatoes
Oil for frying

Shape the butter into 4 rolls and put these back into the refrigerator. Remove the skin from the chicken breasts and halve them; remove the fillets from the breastbones with a sharp knife, cover the meat with plastic wrap and carefully beat flat. Take care that the edges are particularly thin. Season the meat with salt and pepper, place a roll of butter on each larger breast piece, cover with a fillet piece and roll up together. Coat the rolls one after the other in flour, beaten egg with salt and pepper, and breadcrumbs and then leave to chill for about 2 hours. Heat a generous quantity of oil until very hot and fry the chicken rolls in the fat until golden yellow (about 5 minutes). Leave to drain on paper towels and serve with potato sticks. For the potato sticks peel the potatoes, slice into matchsticks 2–2½ inch/5–6 cm long, fry in a deep-fryer until they are golden brown. Remove, drain, and sprinkle lightly with salt.

Salo

The Myrhorod pig is one of the most important Ukrainian breeds, yielding very high quality bacon, (salo).

It is said that *salo*, pork bacon, is as essential a part of life for Ukrainians as vodka is for the Russians. Since the Middle Ages pork products have been more popular in Ukraine than in most other European cuisines. For example, bustling livestock markets were held in the town of Myrhorod in the Poltava region in the 17th century, where, in addition to other livestock, pigs in particular were traded. Today domestic pigs in the countryside still live a largely natural lifestyle, in the barn in winter and in the pigsty in summer. One of the most important breeds is the Myrhorod pig. They are well built and strong, light in color and have a lot of fat relative to lean meat. The Duroc pig, which was bred in the US from several red breeds, is also popular. Ukrainian farmers, who are experts in their field, feed their animals on corn, barley, beets, sugar beet, and fodder beet. However, *salo* from pigs that have been fattened on bread as used to be the case, is also delicious. Many farmers slaughter the animals themselves for their own use and for sale at the markets. After burning off the bristles the butcher cuts the bacon into slices. *Salo* is usually salted, rolled, tied up, and hung from the roof of a cool cellar or in a barrel made of oak or cherry wood. In the past the barrel was often made airtight and buried underground for two years. Thereafter the *salo* melted like butter in your mouth. It is snow white in color and really does taste like a mixture of fresh

Left: The Ukrainian bacon *salo* goes well with hearty rye bread, garlic, and a glass of *horilka*.

A large selection—*salo* is available in a range of varieties at the Bessarabka Market in Kiev.

butter and lard. It turns slightly yellow with increasing maturity but this does not affect the quality. Since very few families, especially in the towns, have their own cellar nowadays the raw bacon is often salted and frozen in portions. Connoisseurs are able to tell the quality of a *salo* from its color and smell and the purchasing of *salo* always involves tasting and bargaining. Huge pieces of shiny pork bacon are traded over the counters and the prices increase with the proportion of meat. Ukrainians also love pure green bacon, i.e. fresh, without the addition of further ingredients—and of course only from well-fed animals. *Salo* warms you up in the winter cold, it is a source of calories and energy and is ideal for taking out into the fields or as a snack when out and about. Also popular is the pork bacon *soloyna* that contains more meat in proportion to fat. People like to eat it diced and fried *(shkvarky)* with *varenyky* (see page 166), rolled cabbage leaves *(holubtsi)*, or with pork crackling *(smalets)*. *Smalets* is ideal for roasting potatoes, meat, and *dyruny* (potato puffs) or else is simply enjoyed with rye bread and finely chopped garlic. For lunch it is normally finely chopped and fried in a skillet with potatoes or eggs, or else in soup. In the evening it makes a hearty meal with dark bread, salt, onions, and mustard.

There are a number of amusing anecdotes as testimony to the Ukrainians love of bacon: a well-laden Ukrainian is asked by the customs officer whether he is carrying weapons or drugs. Turning bright red he admits that he was not able to do without the latter and unpacks mountains of strong smelling bacon. In answer to the question, what does *salo* have to do with drugs, the Ukrainian answers that he is simply addicted to it.

Sausage from the Ukraine

Snardel'ky do snidanku, for breakfast, the smooth filling, is made from pork and often also beef.

For the specialty *polyadvytsia* pork fillet is first cooked and then gently smoked.

Myslyvs'ka, hunter's sausage, contains spices such as cardamom and pepper in addition to the pork or beef.

Pashtet, the smooth filling is usually made from veal liver and refined with bacon.

The window of this vodka store pays homage to the most common Cossack clichés: hard drinking, bravado, and a penchant for singing.

Cossack culture

One still encounters the Cossack customs in Ukraine today, a people who are considered to be the fighters for Ukrainian independence. The Cossack movement developed in the 15th century when, following the collapse of the Kiev Rus state and the takeover of the country by the Poles and Lithuanians, thousands of Ukrainians fled from the new rulers into the fertile steppe regions north of the Black Sea and the Caucasus. The Cossacks (from the Turk-Tatar *kasak* meaning free man, warrior), settled here in self-governed communities and lived off hunting, fishing, and raids against the Turks and Tatars, later engaging in agriculture along the large rivers such as the Don and the *Dnieper*. In the Cossack uprising of 1648 they rebelled against Poland under the leadership of Bohdan Chmelnitzky. After protracted fighting, Ukraine was split between the Russian Empire and Poland in 1667. In the 18th century the Cossacks came under the command of the Russian army, paralyzing their commitment to Ukrainian independence. They continue to maintain their old traditions even today, however. In independent Ukraine Cossack associations have been formed that keep the old customs alive with national games, folk dancing, elaborate uniforms, and the music of the famous Cossack choirs. In the kitchen the Cossacks are known for their simple, nourishing cuisine, such as meat or fish stews as well as quickly roasted meat. The word shashlik is said to derive from the Cossack *Saporishya* (Russian *Saporoshe*). It is a modification of the Turk-Tatar word *shish* for skewer and means "fish grilled on a skewer."

Background: *Ukrayins'ka* is a homemade sausage made from pork with garlic, which is cooked first and then smoked.

Kyshka, the typically Ukrainian buckwheat blood sausage has a spicy flavor due to the bacon.

Saltseson, brawn, made from head meat is available at the markets in a wide range of varieties.

Ukrainians love *smalets*, pork lard, simply on its own or with crackling and/or onions.

Moskovska, Muscovians, are very fatty sausages made from pork and beef according to Russian tradition.

Homemade high-proof: *samohon*

A kind of mash *(braha)* made from sugar, yeast, and water to make *samohon*. This is fermented and then distilled.

Many Ukrainians distill their *samohon* in simple stills at home. These are often put together very inventively using pots, buckets, and tubes.

The acid test: the proof of the *samohon* is tested with a match because the liquor only burns once it has an alcohol content of more than 50 percent.

"If you have no money, then borrow some, but drink." When times are bad this saying is to be heard everywhere in Ukraine. And since money is often scarce and one also does not really know what is in the cheap rotgut sold on the street corner, people rather distill their liquor themselves. *Samohon*, the homebrew, is a real family phenomenon which is as much at home in the Ukraine as in Russia where it is called *samogon*. It is better value than cheap rotgut, it is purer and also a little less high-proof. Only if the alcohol starts to wake the friendly little devils inside you, your tongue and mouth become numb, and your insides start to glow, is it a really good liquor.

In central Ukraine sugar, water, and yeast are used to make *samohon*, in the south it is made from fruit such grapes, apricots, apples, cherries, or plums; in the north from potatoes. Just over 2 lb/1 kg of sugar takes 3½ oz/100 grams of yeast and 3 quarts/3 liters of warm water. However, since the *vuivarka*, the Soviet washing pot made from enameled sheet metal or iron and still omnipresent today, has a capacity of at least 2¼ US gallons/10 liters and the homebrew ought to last for a long time, one does not usually start distilling with anything less than 6½ lb/3 kg of sugar. The ingredients are mixed and then placed in the *vuivarka* and left in a warm place for a couple of weeks.

The fermented *braha* has been produced after at least 14 days and some people already drink that, as it is not only supposed to be good for the skin, but also especially good for impatience. The pot is then placed on the stove where it is connected to a simple spiral distilling apparatus and the lid is placed on the pot, usually with a flour and water dough to make it airtight. The liquid is then brought to a boil. The steam passes through a pipe or a snake-like tube where it cools down so that the high-proof alcohol can flow off.

The small home stills are usually ancient and primitive. They were often produced for supplementary income or made by friendly engineers in the Soviet establishments. The first liquor to be siphoned off is called *pervak* (the "first") and has an alcohol content of over 70 percent. A flame is then held to the liquor which follows. If it no longer burns, i.e. it is under 50 percent, siphoning is stopped.

A good *samohon* should not be cloudy but, rather, pure and clear as tear drops. Even Nikolai Gogol, the wry aficionado of the depths of the national soul, writing in *The Wij*, a tale from 1835 about a Ukrainian spirit of the same name, knew how closely related the two liquids are: "Since the Ukrainians, once they start quaffing, have to begin kissing each other in tears, the whole taproom was soon resonating with the sounds of their noisy affection: 'Ah Spiridon! Let me kiss you!'—'Come here, Dorosh, come over here! I have to give you a hug!'"

Background: Patience is required for distilling because the *samohon* flows out of the still through a pipe drop by drop.

Horilka with hot chile peppers. The popular brands are *Shustov*, *Nemiroff*, and *Ukrayins'ka*.

Double fire

It really burns—and is high proof. *Horilka* ("the burning one") is the equivalent of Russian vodka and can be distilled from grain, potatoes, or sugar. In popular medicine it is said that one should drink a small glass of this high-proof liquor with a little salt to cure digestive complaints, and a glass with pepper against coughs and colds. There are also flavor variations—chile pepper *horilka* (*Ukrayins'ka z perzem*) with or without honey. *Budmo*—cheers!

Flavorful fruit

Sallow thorn: the *shchets* (sallow thorn, see illustration left) is a slender bush or a shrub belonging to the *Elaeagnaceae* family whose shiny, juicy yellow-pink, fruit ripen between September and October. Sallow thorn is considered to strengthen the immune system and is rich in vitamin C, provitamin A and the B vitamins. The bitter-sweet berries are made into jam or added to yogurt, although they are considered to be most effective as a tonic in tea. For this they are mixed with sugar and left to stand in the sun.

Snowball bush: the *kalyna* (snowball bush, see background illustration), displayed on many Ukrainian textiles, in pictures, and on ceramics is a bush or tree growing up to 16 feet/5 m belonging to the *Caprifoliaceae* family and growing particularly well in moist lime and humus soils. The red berries are poisonous and can even be fatal. The dried bark and the flowers are primarily used in alternative medicine. The snowball bush, which also contains n-valeric acid, has a calming effect and is used primarily against colic, cramps, and coughing, while also being a diuretic.

Fruit varieties

In the late spring when the soil becomes warmer and the air gentler the cherry trees are in full blossom in the gardens. Next to apples, *chereshnya*, sweet cherries and *vyshnya*, black cherries, are among the most important fruit varieties in Ukraine. They are the first of the tree fruit to ripen and they are enjoyed freshly picked or as a filling for *varenyky* and *pyrohy*, pirogi. The round or heart-shaped sweet cherries, refined by crossbreeding, are much larger than the wild variety and range in color from yellow to almost black. The *Krymski vyshni*, Crimean cherries, are very sweet, juicy, large, and dark red while the *Lubska* which are sour, dark-red to black and which grow primarily in northern Ukraine, are also popular, as are varieties such as Napoleona and Rusiava. A typical summer "cherry feast" comprises a cold cherry soup *(veshnevyi sup)*, followed by *varenyky* with cherry filling (see page 167) and finally a red fruit jelly with cherries or a cherry compote. As a cultivated variety the apple tree is Europe's most important fruit plant; there are alleged to have been some 1,500 varieties in the former Russian empire. In Ukraine today apple trees *(yabloka)* make up 70 percent of all fruit trees. They are differentiated according to summer, autumn, and winter varieties and there are more than 60 varieties available at the markets. The white-green *Papirovka*, the dessert apple originating from the Baltic states, ripens early. It is tender and juicy with a sweet-sour taste. The Melba is sweeter, on the other hand, a red-cheeked, summer variety originally of Canadian origin with white, very juicy flesh. The Ukrainian *Slava Pobidyteliam* ("Fame of the Victors") ripens in the autumn, also developing red cheeks on the sunny side and its sweet-sour flesh is particularly flavorful. The red, slightly acid Jonathan and the red striped, sweet and juicy Star crimson are late varieties that remain fresh for a long time when stored in a cool place. The very old Russian varieties include the large yellow late apple *Antonovka* with its sour taste. It does not have a particularly distinctive fragrance but the tree is especially frost-resistant. The large, oblong-shaped, green-red *Kantil Sinap*, originally from the Crimea, is juicy, tender, and is harvested late. Plums, pears, apricots, peaches, gooseberries, grapes, and, in the south, melons are grown on both smallholdings and also on larger plantations.

Wild fruit are just as popular in Ukraine as they are in Russia (see page 125) and wood strawberries, raspberries, blackberries, blueberries, lingonberries, cranberries in the north, as well as sallow thorn and sloes find their way into many a preserving jar. Anyone who takes a walk along the streets of even a high-rise area can see the large, colorful jam and compote jars piled up against the walls of the often glassed-in balconies. Many fruit varieties are dried, plums are even smoked by putting them on a perforated metal sheet which is then placed over beech wood in a special smokehouse. The plums become bitter sweet with a distinctive taste not unlike that of ham or bacon and they lend a special touch to meat dishes such as roast pig. However, they are also served for dessert with whipped cream. Ukrainians gather *hrushi*, wild pears, in the forests. When these almost spherical fruit are very ripe they are slowly dried in the oven and can later be used in compotes or *usvar* (see page 175).

Fruit bowls at the Bessarabka Market in Kiev.

Chernobyl and the consequences

When Reactor No. 4 went up in a blaze at 01.24 hrs at night on April 26, 1986 the residents of the small town of Prypyat 2 miles/3 km away ran out onto a bridge to watch the fiery spectacle. According to official state sources, 20 years later about 4.7 million people still suffer from the direct consequences of the catastrophe, including more than a million children, excluding the huge estimate of unreported cases. An area of a good 58,000 square miles/150,000 sq km is radioactively contaminated, about one third being each in Ukraine, Byelorussia, and in Russia. Fear, often suppressed, but also a lack of information about the current radioactivity levels, has numbed many Ukrainians. Wild fruit, berries, and mushrooms are as in demand as before and are gathered enthusiastically. The majority of people would willingly resort to imported fruit and vegetables but they are unaffordable. So rather than have the table empty due to a lack of money, the worries are pushed aside. People buying at the market however, tend to stick to the traders they know—trust has become a point of honor. The question about the exact origin of a product has been at the top of the list since the reactor disaster because there are also uncontaminated areas.

Spas—the harvest festival

Spas, the Transfiguration of Christ, is the Christian acknowledgement of God as provider of the fruits of the fields. However, the origins of this harvest festival in the Eastern Church go back to the ancient Slavic era and it is still celebrated today in other countries such as Bulgaria, Rumania, and Greece. It is a colorful scene when, on August 19, people in the towns and villages throng to the churches with baskets full of fruit, mostly apples or pears, which are best suited as winter provisions. In fact many people still observe the rule that this year's apples and pears should not be eaten until they have been blessed. In addition to fresh fruit, a range of other delicacies are also served on this day both at home and with friends and family. Poultry stuffed with fruit such as duck with apples appear on the table or carp with honey, *halushky* with fruit, juicy cakes, compote or even apple pancakes—and an incomparable aroma wafts through the villages, streets, houses and apartments.

Background: Giving thanks for food and drink—at a *spas* festival in a west Ukrainian village the priest blesses the fruit and baked goods brought by the faithful during a harvest festival procession.

For the harvest festival fresh fruit are prettily decorated in jars and baskets. Some people in the Ukraine eat the first apples and pears only once they have been blessed.

Fruit delights

Vyshnevy kompot
Cherry compote

Generous 1 lb/500 cherries, pitted
⅔ cup/150 g sugar
Whipping cream as desired

Bring the cherries to a boil with the sugar in 1 cup/ 250 ml water and leave to simmer for 10 minutes. Then remove the fruit and put aside. Reduce the syrup as required; pour over the cherries and leave to cool. Serve as they are or with whipped cream.
Tip: The compote also tastes good with strawberries or raspberries, which should be cooked very briefly.

Yablochna babka
Apple bake

1¾ lb/750 g apples, peeled and cored
Juice of 1 lemon
9 tbsp/125 g sugar
4 eggs, separated
½ cup/125 g sour cream
Generous 1 cup/150 g all-purpose flour
1 tsp cinnamon
1 pinch salt
Butter for greasing
Confectioners' sugar

Cut the apples into small pieces and drizzle with lemon juice immediately to prevent them from becoming brown. Beat the sugar, egg yolks, and sour cream until frothy; add the flour, cinnamon, salt, and apples, stirring all the time. Beat the egg whites to stiff peaks and carefully fold into the mixture. Transfer to a well-greased baking dish, and bake in a preheated oven at 340 °F/175 °C for about 30 minutes.
Serve sprinkled with confectioners' sugar and garnished with apple slices if desired.

Heavily laden with a sweet booty the industrious worker bees fly into the beehive.

The honeycomb sealed by the bees first has to have the wax removed.

The beekeeper then hangs the honeycomb frame from the beehive in the honey extractor.

The extractor is set in motion by hand and the honey flows into the container.

No fear of busy bees—a Ukrainian beekeeper proudly shows off his worker bees.

Beekeeping

Alexander Petrovych is a beekeeper from Cherkassy on the lower stretches of the Dnieper—a beekeeper like his father, his grandfather, his great-grandfather, and their predecessors before them. "The bees," he says, "have always been there and are still there." He nods his head as if confirming his own statement, smiles and says that, without bees, life would come to an end. In the background one can hear a cheerful, busy buzzing in the garden. There are some two million beekeepers in Ukraine, either as primary occupation or as a sideline. Alexander Petrovych owns 25 beehives which is the limit of the capacity for a single beekeeper. He produces about half a metric tonne of honey annually from which he and his family are able to make a living. The ancient Slavs used to trade in *med*, honey, and it remains a valued foodstuff in Ukraine today. Jars filled with 6½ lb/3 kg of honey are a matter of course on many a kitchen shelf. It is eaten as it is, it is used for baking, for desserts, in *kashas* and teas, but also for savory dishes such as carp with honey. Pickled gherkins are eaten as a snack with a dab of honey and the sweet substance is also ideal for glazing poultry. In the past, before sugar made its way into Eastern European cookery, honey was almost the only ingredient used for sweetening.

The popular buckwheat honey is dark, almost cognac-colored, has a spicy taste, and is particularly rich in antibacterial agents. May honey is fragrant, less viscous, very light in color, more expensive and is produced when the bees swarm out to acacias, clover, or raspberries. Sunflower honey shines like pale amber; forest honey from ecologically sound cranberry bushes, linden, or oak trees in remote forests has a high quality and a distinctive flavor.

Every weekend Petrovych packs up his jars, pollen, honeycombs, and wax, boards the train and heads for Kiev, to the market in the old area of Podil. His stand is in the middle of the market hall where other beekeepers have their wares on sale. Slices of open honeycomb are available for testing, wrapped in cellophane paper like candy. When you open them the sticky, sweet substance oozes out over your hands and you have no choice but to lick your fingers clean. Cleverly displayed on top of and next to each other are jars filled with pollen, bee glue (propolis), and of course with a variety of types of honeys such as buckwheat, oak tree, or linden honey, both with and without the honeycomb. His weekend earnings keep Alexander Petrovych in pocket for a good few days. When he comes home in the evenings he treats himself to a swig, maybe more, of *pytnyi med*, mead first of all. He drinks a toast to the bees and to his wife, and then he drinks another glass simply because life can be hard at times. The vitamins in *met* ensure his good health and his good mood claims the beekeeper. If these are as good as the mead, then life has indeed become a little easier.

Honey as a healing agent

In Ukraine honey is used as one of the most important natural remedies in almost every household. Minerals such as potassium, calcium, magnesium, silicic acid, and phosphor, the vitamins C, B1, B2, B6, and biotin, as well as enzymes and amino acids stimulate the body's protective mechanisms and therefore also the metabolic processes. Pieces of honeycomb are not only a popular snack they also help against throat and respiratory infections. Pollen stimulates the production of hemoglobin and encourages the normalization of the blood count in cases of anemia. Particularly valuable is bee glue or propolis due to its antibacterial properties. An alcoholic extract made from propolis is an aid against stomach complaints and strengthens the immune system. Honey and other bee products also work wonders with cosmetics. Honeycomb melted down into wax, combined with pollen and honey, is used as a relaxing face mask while steaming with honey water is used to open and cleanse the pores.

Little mouths in particular are fond of a honeycomb snack and enthusiastically suck out the sweet substance.

Met

Ukrainians enjoy a glass of mead on many occasions. Today mead is available in elegant, labeled bottles but the beekeepers at the market sell homemade mead as well. To make it at home you need to boil water and honey in a ratio of 2:1 for about 3 hours, you then add fresh hop flowers and let everything boil for a further hour. The hops are then removed, the pot is filled with water again up to its original level and brought back up to a boil again briefly. The liquid is clarified through fine cheesecloth, left to cool at room temperature and yeast is then added to make it ferment. The liquid is poured into bottles, sealed with cheesecloth and left to stand at room temperature for about 4 months, after which the mead is then ready to be enjoyed. Sometimes the honey elixir is mixed with strong black tea before being poured into the bottles. Mead is popularly enjoyed after a meal or warmed on a cold winter's evening

Medivnyk
Honey cake

8½ tbsp/125 g butter
5 eggs, separated
1 generous cup/400 g honey
7 tbsp/100 ml strong coffee
3½ cups/500 g all-purpose flour
2 tsp baking powder
Juice and grated rind of 1 organic orange
½ tsp ground nutmeg
½ tsp ground cloves
1 tsp cinnamon
½ tsp salt

Beat the butter with the egg yolks until light and frothy, then fold in the honey, orange juice and rind, and the coffee. Sift the flour with the baking powder and spices, then gradually stir into the butter and egg mixture. Beat the egg whites until stiff and carefully fold into the batter. Place in a greased, square baking pan and bake in a preheated oven at 340 °F/170 °C for 50–60 minutes. Test with a wooden skewer to see if it is cooked: if the skewer comes out clean the cake is ready.

Variation: You can add rum-soaked raisins and/or chopped walnuts to the batter depending on taste.

The famous sparkle: Crimean sparkling wine

Lev Golitzin, the prince with the Crimean estate *Novy Svet* (New World) must have been an ambitious man with excellent taste as well as being a man of vision. In the closing years of the 19th century he developed a fascination for French champagne: he wanted to get to the secret of its famous sparkle. He had begun with his first attempts at producing champagne in 1882 but despite 10 years of strenuous effort there he saw no prospects of success. That had to change. Returning to the Black Sea Golitzin got down to work again—this time very successfully as was soon to become apparent. In 1900 he left for France again, full of optimism, this time heading for the Great Exhibition in Paris with the fruits of his labors in his luggage. Initially he did not give away where his noble beverage was from. Yet when he won the *Grand Prix* for it and disclosed his secret the *Grande Nation of Gourmets* was in uproar. Nevertheless, the rise of the Crimean sparkling wine was not to be stopped.

The very first steps in the production of the wine famous today throughout the world were taken in Sudak in 1799, and shortly thereafter in Alushta (see the map on page 204.) The quantities were insignificant and only intended for the Tsar's court. It was Lev Golitzin who brought about the breakthrough for "Russian champagne" with his large scale and—for the era—modern production methods. The prince had a tunnel 10,500 feet/3,200 m built into a rock face as a "champagne cellar," a further 10,000 feet/2,800 m were added between 1968 and 1985 by subway workers from Charkiv.

Today Crimean sparkling wine matures in the underground labyrinth making up the wine cellars of *Novy Svet* according to the classic bottle fermentation method (see insert) for 3 years at a temperature of 46 to 57 °F/8–14 °C. The wine basis is pressed from red grapes such as Cabernet Sauvignon, Saperavi, Matrassa, and Chindogny as well as from white varieties such as Pinot Gris, Chardonnay, Aligoté, and Rheinriesling.

However, *Novy Svet* is not the only source of excellent sparkling wines in the Crimean; they are also produced in the cellars of the Inkerman wine producers near Sebastopol, for example. Then there are also the sparkling wines from producers in other parts of the countries such as Kiev, Odessa, Artemovsk, and Kharkiv, for instance.

Yet only about 1 percent is produced using the classic bottle fermentation method. This first class Crimean sparkling wine is characterized by its crystal-clear appearance, fine bouquet, harmony, and subtle taste. Today it is exported to more than 20 countries. In Germany Crimean sparkling wine is marketed primarily under the name *Krimskoye*. It is also exported to the US, the UK, and the Netherlands and the producers are constantly seeking new markets.

Methods of sparkling wine production

Classic bottle fermentation method: a *cuvée*, a mixture of wines as a basis is combined with yeast and sugar in the bottle. Depending on the desired quality, this second fermentation takes between nine months and several years. By shaking the bottles and gradually turning them upside down the yeast collects in the neck of the bottles close to the opening, is frozen and removed. After adding the dosage (sugar and wine) the bottle is then fitted, i.e. corked, fitted with a wire holder and labeled. This is how the highest quality sparkling wine is made.

Transvasier method: the difference between this and the classic bottle fermentation method is that, after the fermentation process, the bottles are emptied into a pressure tank. The sparkling wine is then filtered (removal of the yeast), the dosage is added, and then poured into sparkling wine bottles again and fitted.

Tank fermentation method: slightly lower quality sparkling wine can be produced in large quantities by fermenting the wine in pressure tanks. Thereafter the yeast is removed by filtering, the dosage is added, and the bottles are filled and fitted.

Continuous method: the processing of the wine takes place in several small fermentation tanks at a specific pressure. It begins with the continuous dosing of yeast and ends with the addition of the dosage. The most important phases of this very technical production are the filtering, pasteurization, and stabilizing. In order to accelerate the fermentation the individual components such as the *cuvée* (wine mixture) and the yeast are specially treated beforehand and catalysts are added. In this way the entire production process takes less than 100 days and continuously produces sparkling wine ready for bottling with little effort.

Above left: Red, mild sparkling wine contains a large proportion of Cabernet Sauvignon grapes and is refined with other grape varieties such as Saperavi and Matrassa.

Above center: The rosé sparkling wine from the *Novy Svet* cellars has a very fruity bouquet but is only seldom available internationally.

Above right: At *Novy Svet* both dry and semi-sweet white Crimean sparkling wines are made from grape varieties such as Pinto Gris, Chardonnay, Aligoté, and Riesling.

Right: The *Novy Svet* sparkling wine cellars produce a variety of sparkling wines, such as (from left) *Yubileynoye* (rosé), *Shampanskoye* (white) and *Krasnoye* (red). Today the bottles are often still labeled in Russian as they were during the Soviet era because that neighboring country continues to be an important outlet.

Sparkling wine varieties

In the European Union Crimean sparkling wines are categorized according to west European standards and five quality levels are available, whereby the often very good Brut and Dry varieties are unfortunately seldom seen on the market:

Brut: up to 15 grams of sugar per liter

Extra dry: 12 to 20 grams of sugar per liter

Dry: 17 to 35 grams of sugar per liter

Demi-sec = semisweet: 33 to 50 grams sugar per liter

Doux (also "mild" for export): more than 50 (sometimes more than 80!) grams of sugar per liter.

A dry white Crimean sparkling wine goes just as well as a white wine with poultry or fish dishes, while a demi-sec is suited to dessert and cheese. The red demi-sec Crimean sparkling wine, so they say in its homeland, rounds off a successful evening with subtle harmony. In Ukraine itself and in other Eastern European countries it is mostly the demi-sec sparkling wines that are served and together with a clear vodka they give any celebration a cheerful swing and a touch of elegance.

Massandra—the Tsar's winery

The cellar master assesses a Madeira wine.

Ideally you would like to be able to run your finger carefully over the strangely shaped, belly-like bottles—but you do not dare. A sense of reverence prevents you from doing so and when you look a little more closely you notice the double eagle on the royal crest and the Cyrillic letters which are proudly translated for visitors: "Livadia, by Royal Appointment." It is hard to believe that a noble liquid dating back to the days of the last Tsar is lurking under the dusty patina. The sweet grapes of the Crimea are the ideal basis for heavy, sweet wines. Wine varieties such as Tokajer, Madeira, Sherry, Port, and Cahors have been top class wines since the tsarist era. In terms of quality they are definitely comparable to their west European role models but are produced without their specialist technology. The strength of the southern sun produces the sweetness in the grapes whose sugar content reaches up to 35 percent, the midday heat ensures a mild and rounded bouquet. Many people even maintain that the idiosyncratic melancholy of the surroundings makes the wines heavy and full-bodied.

In the first half of the 19th century the Russian Governor General Michail Voronzov had tried to cultivate French grape varieties in the Crimean but the vines he introduced produced only minimal yields. The founding of the Central Institute for Viniculture and Wine Production in Yalta and the relentless work finally led to the first great success in 1891: an outstanding port wine from cabernet grapes.

It was during this era that the last Russian Tsar, Nicholas II, came up with the idea of establishing the "best winery in the world" at Yalta. The ruler's family spent their summers nearby in the Livadia Palace and was therefore partial to a good wine for all their socializing. And so the Massandra winery with its thick walls, towers, and cornices came into being between 1894 and 1897. Servants and soldiers dug tunnels up to 500 feet/150 m long into the earth to form the cellar—an unbelievable achievement with just shovels and picks. The vineyards which today cover almost 43 miles/70 km along the southeast coast of the Black Sea almost extend into the water in some places.

The former tsarist estate is still in state hands today: 92 million US gallons/350 million liters of wine and 800,000 bottles can be stored in the huge cellars at Massandra. The conditions are ideal for allowing wines to mature and rest for decades. A wellspring on site provides the required humidity and the temperature remains constant at 55 to 57 °F/13–14 °C all year round. Connoisseurs throughout the world are particularly fond of the dessert wines from Massandra. The cellars therefore still specialize primarily in sweet, fortified wines, such as a white, a rosé-colored, and a dark to black muscatel, as well as white and red Port, Madeira, and Sherry specialties and varietal fortified dessert wines made from Pinot Gris, Bastardo, and Kokur. Yet red wines also show a great deal of potential, such as the *Alushta* produced primarily from Cabernet Sauvignon. The *Kagor* (Cahors variety) from the Saperavi grape serves not only gourmet purposes: as an altar wine in the Eastern Church it embodies the blood of Christ.

When taking your first steps inside the dignified winery you have the feeling that you are back in the 19th century. Yet what appears as romantic nostalgia to Westerners used to progressive technology is harsh reality for Massandra. Since there is hardly any public money available even for this showpiece project much of the equipment, which has often been in use for half a century or longer, still has to keep going today.

In April 1990 the London auction house Sothebys auctioned more than 13,000 bottles of the noble wines which were up to one hundred years old and which carried Massandra's reputation and the aroma of days gone by with them throughout the world. It is also something very special, even sensual, to remove the seal and uncork one of these bottles with its full-bodied yet subtle contents. You begin to smell, to feel, to hear things. Suddenly you feel the shimmering air of the hot Crimean nights laden with the intoxicating fragrance of grasses and flowers and the faint lapping of the waves. One seems to hear the faint roar of the sea, strains of music drift past, the cheerful smile of enchanting women wearing grandiose turn-of-the-century dresses …

Портвейн
красный
Массанд
1897

Портвейн
красный
Ай-Даниль
1893

Портвейн
красный
Массандра
1900

The Massandra Winery near Yalta was built at the end of the 19th century at the behest of Tsar Nicholas II. The underground vaults of the national estate house up to 92 million US gallons/350 million liters of wine.

Background: The Massandra cellars are a real treasure chest. Some of the wines stored here, such as red port wines, are more than one hundred years old and reach top prices all over the world.

Winegrowing

Switzerland, Germany, Russia, Sweden, Israel, and Canada are among approximately 20 countries that today import Ukrainian wine. Despite the minimal state support a high degree of scientific and technical expertise is used thanks to the untiring commitment of all of those involved in winegrowing activities so that the wine production is able to compete on an international level. A series of winegrowing institutions ensure the optimization of the results. Efforts are underway to further privatize and de-monopolize the market. The "National Program for the Development of Agricultural Production" provides concrete support. Winegrowing and wine products are also seen as an important precursor to greater economic independence. In 1996 Ukraine exported 5.5 million US gallons/21 million liters of wine, sparkling wine, dessert wines, and brandy while three years previously exports had not even amounted to one third of this. The trend is increasing as well.

The Crimean Peninsula with its humid, subtropical climate still produces most of Ukraine's wines. Even in ancient times, when the peninsula was still called Taurien, named after its original inhabitants, a wide range of grape varieties were planted by the Greeks and the Romans. The Greek doctor Hippocrates (c. 460–375 B.C.) held wine in high esteem because it was wonderfully good for the human body—in the case of both the healthy and the sick. One of the oldest grape varieties in the world is the muscatel grape that was very probably brought to the Crimea by the ancient Greeks. It has been proven that it was being cultivated there up to 2,500 years ago. It has remained at home in the Crimea over the centuries—up until recent times. At the start of the 19th century grape varieties from Italy, Greece, Bulgaria, and Germany began a peaceful European coexistence in Ukraine and since the turn of the century the Crimean wines have been making an international name for themselves.

Set against the backdrop of the impressive Crimean mountains are the famous Inkerman cellars. This area near Sebastapol has excellent growing conditions to which the branded wines *Riesling Alkadar*, *Aligoté Zolota Balka* ("Golden Gully") and *Rkatsiteli Inkermanskoye* are testimony. The red wines *Cabernet Sauvignon Kachinskoye* and *Alushta* originate from the western valleys of the Crimea and the Alushta region. Aligoté grapes grow well in the black soil areas of the Ukrainian steppe between Odessa and Kherson. According to the country's wine experts that is where the best branded wine *Perlyna Stepu* ("Pearl of the Steppe") is produced. In the area southwest of Odessa on the Black Sea coast up to the Danube flats the grapes are indulged by the sun and the warmth which give them a natural sweetness. Full-bodied, dry or semisweet table wines such as *Shab*, *Silvaner Dnistrovski*, white *Shabske* or *Zoloti Vorota* ("Golden Gate") are to be enjoyed there. The locals are also proud of their famous brandies such as *Odessa*, *Chornomorski* ("From the Black Sea") or *Zoloti Kniash* ("Golden Prince").

The Cherson area on the lower Dnipro is characterized by fertile sandy soils. The area has a tradition of growing primarily west European grape varieties such as Rheinriesling which came to the country at the start of the 19th century, or Cabernet Sauvignon from which the smooth-tasting red *Oksamyt Ukrainy* ("Ukrainian Velvet") is produced. This wine is the color of ripe, dark cherries; due to its high tannin content it is supposed to be good for stomach complaints. The nearby area of Mykolajiv has also been known as a winegrowing area for centuries, as is the Trans-Carpathian region in western Ukraine. Grapes such as Furmit and Lindenblaetter ripen on the warmer south and southwest facing hillsides while wines such as *Promenyste* ("Shining") made from the pink Tramina grape, *Berehovs'ke* ("From the Riverbank") made from the Welch Riesling grape or *Zakarpats'ke* ("Transcarpathian") made from Rheinriesling grapes are found in the cooler mountain regions.

Horilka z vyna
Wine liqueur

2 cups/500 ml smooth red wine
⅔ cup/150 g sugar
3–4 cloves
1 organic lemon, sliced
1 cup/250 ml samohon, or else schnapps

Bring the wine to a boil with the sugar, cloves, and lemon and leave to simmer for about 10 minutes, then filter through a fine sieve or piece of cloth. Add the *samohon* and pour into a bottle. The liqueur can be drunk straight away.

Tip: If you want to use a very dry wine then add more sugar accordingly.

Map: The winegrowing regions of Ukraine are in the south, on the Crimean Peninsula and in the Transcarpathian area.

WINE REGIONS:
- black soil-steppe areas
- Crimea
- Transcarpathian

0   100 km

Where people still press their own wines the grape juice is often produced with the most simple of presses.

Background: Vines have been grown near Berehove in the Transcarpathian region for centuries.

Solodke: the sweet life

Shulyky
Dough pieces with poppy seed sauce

Generous 2 cups/300 g flour
7 tbsp/100 g butter, chilled
4–5 tbsp sour cream
2 tbsp sugar
2 eggs
Butter for greasing

For the sauce:
1¹⁄₂ cups/200 g poppy seeds
7 tbsp/100 g sugar
3¹⁄₂ tbsp/100 g honey

Cut the butter into small pieces and rub the flour. Add the sour cream, sugar, and eggs and mix to form a dough, then roll out. Place the dough on a greased baking sheet, prick all over with a fork and bake in an oven preheated to 350–400 °F/180–200 °C for about 15 minutes. In the meantime prepare the sauce: soak the poppy seeds in warm water, pat dry and grind, then mix with 1 cup/250 ml water, the sugar, and the honey. Divide the sauce between 4 deep plates. Tear the baked pastry into bite-sized pieces using 2 forks and then place the still warm pastry pieces in the sauce. This dish is best eaten with spoons!

Ukraine and the Habsburgs

Chrin and *smalets* (related to *Kren*, the Austrian word for horseradish, and lard), poppy seed plait and damson dumplings: in some of the old restaurants and coffee shops in Lviv (Lemberg) in western Ukraine you can go back in time and forget about national boundaries. One almost expects to hear a "Yes madam, what will it be?" but then you go ahead and order in Ukrainian anyway. The suitor seeking a girl's hand is known by the same word in both German and western Ukrainian usage. He has probably already eaten his *knedli*, the west Ukrainian dumpling, and will certainly have done so by the time the *schlagbaum*, boom, goes down for the last time.

As a result of the 1772 partition of Poland, Galicia and Lodomeria belonged to Austria. From then on the region came under the influence of the Habsburg monarchy for about 150 years. This influence remains clearly recognizable in both the language and in the cuisine, for example with the coffee house culture and the pastries which originate from Böhmen and Mähren. Thus damson dumplings are today just as much part of the sweet culinary pleasures of Ukraine as the coffee houses are of the restaurant culture.

West Ukrainians are proud of the fact that Georg Franz Kolshitzky, the founder of the first coffee house in Vienna, came from the Lviv area. During the Turkish siege of Vienna in 1683 he had managed to get through the enemy lines on several occasions in order to maintain contact with the Imperial Polish army. Following the victory over the Ottomans as a reward he received three ox wagons laden with sacks of coffee which the Ottomans had left behind during their retreat—the basis for the first "coffee shops" in Vienna.

Today the best coffee in Ukraine is to be found in the old part of Lviv, for example in the dignified coffee house of the George Hotel where one revels in the neo-classical and imperial style of the old rooms, or in *U Kulchyts'koho* ("At Kulchyzki") where you can browse through the latest books and newspapers for hours on end with piano music in the background. In the relaxed atmosphere here you can enjoy a *kavusya*, the "little coffee," for which the beans are ground by hand and enriched with ground coriander, for example. This coffee is always served with the coffee grounds.

Knedli z slyvkoyu
Damson dumplings

1³/₄ lb/750 g mealy potatoes (russets) unpeeled
1¹/₃ cups/200 g all-purpose flour
¹/₃ cup/75 g lard
2 eggs
Salt
Generous 1 lb/500 g damsons, pitted
15 sugar cubes or 15 walnuts
1 cup/50 g breadcrumbs
7 tbsp/100 g sugar
Cinnamon
Generous ³/₄ cup/200 g sour cream

Boil the potatoes in their skins, rinse under cold water, leave until they have finished steaming then remove the skins while they are still hot. Mash the potatoes and combine with the flour, lard, eggs, and ¹/₂ table-spoon salt and knead together well. The dough should not be sticky (knead in a little more flour if necessary). Divide the dough into 12–15 pieces and roll each piece out into a thick circle. Place a sugar cube or a walnut in each damson. Then form the dough into a dumpling around each damson. Bring a saucepan full of lightly salted water to a boil, place the dumplings in the water and cook gently until they rise to the top. Combine the breadcrumbs, sugar, and cinnamon to taste. Coat the dumplings with this mixture and serve warm with sour cream and, if desired, with damson compote.

Would you like a little more? The confectionary factory *Svitoch* sells its sweet temptations in its own store.

Sugar beet

The 19th century was the hey day for the trade in the white gold. As the "Soviet sugar bowl" Ukraine later produced about two thirds of the USSR's sugar. Today the production surpluses from western Europe are sold to the former bulk buyer Russia at dumping prices and there is as good as no export from Ukraine any more. Nevertheless, sugar beet is still in second place after wheat in Ukraine's agricultural production with her fertile black soils. The main growing area is situated around Khmelnitski, Vinnytsya, Cherkassy, Kharkiv, and Poltava as well as around Kiev. For *tsukor*, sugar, production the harvested sugar beet is washed, chopped by machine, and covered with hot water in iron cylinders (diffusors). The resulting rari-fied sugar sap is clarified using lime water, which binds foreign agents, before being thickened and boiled until crystallized. About two thirds of Ukrainian sugar beet is used to produce white crystal sugar, one third is used industrially, especially in chocolate factories, bakeries, for beverage production as well as in the processing of fruit and vegeta-bles. Jams and syrups made from the sweet beets are also popular.

From the bakery

Pechyvo z porichkamy
Blackberry cake

Generous 2 cups/300 g all-purpose flour
7 tbsp/100 g sugar
1 cup + 2 tbsp/250 g butter
½ tsp baking powder
½ cup/125 g sour cream
1 egg
Generous 1 lb/500 g blackberries or other berries e.g. blueberries
Scant 1 cup/100 g confectioners' sugar

Combine the flour, sugar, butter, and baking powder. Add 1 tablespoon water, the sour cream and egg and knead everything together well. Roll the dough out into a circle ¼ inch/½ cm thick and place in a greased pie plate. Shape the sides into an edging. Fill with the berries and sprinkle with confectioners' sugar. Bake in a preheated oven at 440 °F/225 °C for about 40 minutes. Allow to cool before serving.

Verhuny
Deep-fried pastry with sugar

3 egg yolks
1 tbsp sugar
2 tbsp/30 g butter or 100 g sour cream
2 tbsp rum
Generous 2⅓ cups/350 g all-purpose flour
½ tbsp vinegar
½ tsp salt
2¼ lb/1 kg lard
Sugar for sprinkling

Beat the egg yolks with the sugar until white and gradually incorporate the butter or sour cream, rum, flour, vinegar, salt and a maximum of ½ cup/125 ml boiled water, one after the other. The dough must be able to be rolled out and shaped. Roll and cut into strips measuring about 1 x 4 inch/2.5 x 10 cm. Shape these either as pretzels, knotted in the middle, or as twists. Melt the lard in a deep pan and fry the *verhuny* in the hot fat for about 1–2 minutes until golden brown. Sprinkle with sugar immediately and serve.

For an attractive *verhuny* variation a slit is cut in a wider piece of pastry.

Then the ends of the pastry are very carefully pulled through the middle.

This is now the typical *verhuny* shape and just needs to be fried in the fat.

Zavyvanets
Walnut roll

1½ oz/40 g fresh yeast [see method]
2 tbsp lukewarm milk
4½ tbsp/65 g superfine sugar
2 eggs
6 egg yolks
1 cup/250 g heavy cream
½ tsp salt
Vanilla extract
Grated rind of 1 lemon
2 tbsp rum (optional)
3½ cups/500 g all-purpose flour
7 tbsp/100 g butter, melted
1 tbsp breadcrumbs
Egg for brushing

Crumble the yeast into the lukewarm milk, add a pinch of sugar and leave the mixture to rise for about 10 minutes. (If using dried yeast, follow maker's instructions). Beat the eggs and the egg yolks with the sugar until light and frothy, then add the cream, salt, vanilla extract to taste, grated lemon rind and rum if using. Sift the flour into the mixture, add the yeast and work into a smooth dough; knead for 15 minutes. Add the melted butter and knead well again for at least another 15 minutes. Cover with a cloth and leave to rise for 2–3 hours. Knead the dough again and then roll out onto a floured work surface into the shape of a square. Spread either the Walnut filling or the Poppy seed filling (given below) thinly over the dough and then roll up the dough from one side. Carefully place on a greased baking sheet, brush with the beaten egg and leave to rise again for 30 minutes. Bake in a pre-heated oven at 350 °F/180 °C for about 45 minutes.

Walnut filling

4 tbsp heavy cream
1 tbsp sugar
Vanilla extract
2½ cups/300 g walnuts, ground
2–3 tbsp confectioners' sugar
Whites of 2 eggs

Bring the cream to a boil with vanilla extract, to taste. Remove from the heat and combine with the nuts. Fold in the confectioner's sugar and leave to cool. Then fold in the eggs whites.

Poppy seed filling

1¼ cups/300 ml milk
3½ tbsp/50 g sugar
2 cups/250 g poppy seeds, ground
2 tbsp/30 g butter
1 tbsp honey
2 egg whites
Grated rind of ½ lemon
Grated rind of ½ orange

Bring the milk to a boil with the sugar. Add the poppy seeds and leave to swell until the mixture thickens. Add the butter and honey and allow to dry out over a low heat for about 1 minute. Then allow to cool before stirring in the egg whites and the lemon and orange peel.
Tip: If preferred you can also enrich the filling with a dash of rum.

Slyvovyi tort "Hirka"
"Hirka" plum cake

For the dough:
Generous 1 cup + 2 tbsp/250g sugar
7 tbsp/100 g butter
1 egg
1 cup/250 ml heavy cream
2½ tsp baking powder
4 cups/560 g all-purpose flour

For the filling:
Generous 1 lb/500 g prunes, pitted
4 cups/1 liter heavy cream
2 cups/220 g confectioner's sugar
Vanilla extract, to taste
Grated chocolate and/or chocolate couverture

Rinse the prunes, cook until soft and set aside. For the dough: beat the sugar, butter, egg, and cream until light and frothy. Gradually fold in the flour combined with the baking powder and knead into a dough: it should not be too stiff. Roll out the dough into one large oblong measuring about 12 x 6 inch/30 x 15 cm and 15 small rectangles measuring about 12 x 3 inch/ 30 x 8 cm (the lengths should match). Place the large oblong on a greased and floured baking sheet and bake at 340–400 °F/175–200 °C for about 10 minutes and then leave to cool. The base should remain soft and not become too crispy. Place the prepared prunes on the smaller rectangles, roll each of them up lengthways into a thin roll, place on a greased and floured baking sheet and bake at 340–400 °F/175–200 °C for

Ukrainians are fond of sweet cookies with their tea or coffee. Delicious sponge fingers *(bishkopty)* taste even better when covered with chocolate just to make them even more extravagant.

10–15 minutes; leave to cool. For the filling: beat the cream with the sugar until stiff. Spread the cream over the large oblong and place 5 filled rolls on it, spread these with cream, place 4 rolls on top, spread with cream and continue in the same way placing 3, then 2, then 1 roll on top so that you form a pyramid. Spread with the rest of the cream and, optionally, sprinkle with grated chocolate and/or drizzle with chocolate couverture. Keep in a cool place and serve as soon as possible.
Tip: You can also use cherries instead of prunes.

Those who cannot afford branded cigarettes buy loose tobacco and roll their cigarettes themselves.

Tobacco

The original inhabitants of America were the first to take the leaves of the tobacco plant and roll them up, light them, and inhale the smoke for ritual purposes. In around 1520 Christopher Columbus brought leaves and seeds back to Spain, but it was only around 1560 that the enjoyment of tobacco became widespread in Europe—for example through the French diplomat Jean Nicot from whom nicotine takes its name. Sharp businessmen in England and especially in Holland very quickly recognized the blue smoke as a source of quick money.

Tobacco has also been grown in Ukraine since the 17th century, having arrived in the country via Turkey. Due to a tobacco ban it was not allowed to be traded as far as Moscow, until Peter the Great made it acceptable at court at the beginning of the 18th century. The first tobacco factory in the greater Russian empire, to which parts of Ukraine had belonged since 1667, was built in 1718 in Ochtykra in the northeast of present day Ukraine.

The Poltava and Chernihiv areas soon developed into the most important tobacco growing regions in the Russian empire. In the second half of the 19th century about 60 percent of all Russian tobacco outside of the Caucasus was grown there. It was processed locally and also exported to countries like Holland, for example. With the abolishment of serfdom in 1861 a number of small tobacco factories soon appeared while joint stock and trading companies developed at the beginning of the 20th century and which became state-controlled after the assimilation of Ukraine into the Soviet Union (1922).

Today Ukrainian tobacco production is largely in foreign hands. Following Ukraine's independence the company R. J. Reynolds Tobacco International, for example, purchased 70 percent of two large tobacco factories in Krementchuk and in Lviv in the 1990s. Reynolds' production of around 20 billion cigarettes annually equates to almost a quarter of all cigarettes smoked in Ukraine. There is no purely Ukrainian cigarette production to speak of.

Today Ukrainian tobacco *(tyutyun)* is still used primarily for cigarette manufacture, especially in the Chernihiv and Poltava regions as well as in the Crimean and Transcarpathian areas. The two types of the solanaceous herb grown are *Nicotiana tabacum* ("Real Tobacco," or Virginia Tobacco) and *Nicotiana rustica* ("Farmers' Tobacco"). In the former Soviet Union areas the latter is grown on a subsistence basis and is known as *machorka*.

Right: The tobacco leaves ferment while drying in special barns and thus obtain their golden brown color.

The tobacco plant belongs to the family of solanaceous herbs. In summer it forms pink-red flowers.

Davidoff—a man and his cigar

The internationally known Zino Davidoff came from Kiev. He was born in the Ukrainian capital on March 11, 1906. His father, Henri Davidoff, produced tobacco blends for pipes and cigarettes and seems to have infected him with the tobacco virus: Zino was introduced to the art of fine blends as a teenager. In 1911 the Jewish family fled from the pogroms in tsarist Russia and settled in Geneva.

In 1924 Zino Davidoff traveled through the tobacco-producing countries of Latin America in order to learn everything worth knowing about the noble leaf and the art of its production. He joined his father's business upon his return in 1929. The fact that the best quality Cuban cigars were stored in his—for that era new—humidor under favorable conditions soon became known throughout Europe as did the reputation of the young tobacco specialist and his fine nose. He had cigars produced in Cuba in particular; in 1946 he created his famous *Chateaux* range for the Cuban brand *Hoyo de Monterrey* and in 1969 his own brand *Davidoff* which remains a legend today. The cigars are now produced in the Dominican Republic following the dispute between Davidoff and the Cuban government in 1991. Zino Davidoff was able to enthrall people; when he started to talk with all the ardor of a lover, non-smokers became smokers, cheap cigar smoking philistines lowered their heads in reverence before the cigar manufacturer's skill.

Zino Davidoff had very wealthy clients, among their number the Aga Khan, who willing bought a thousand cigars a month, albeit not all simply to smoke, but also to savor and be given away as gifts. The great cigar man once wrote of his clients: "They assess their supplies carefully, mentally they stroll among the shelves, like the owner of a vineyard does in his fields, the art lover among his paintings, the

Zino Davidoff (1906–1994), the most famous cigar manufacturer in the world, came from Ukraine.

collector among his statues." Zino Davidoff died in Geneva in 1994.

RUSSIAN FEDERATION

Republic of
Abkhasia

Gagra

Sokhumi

Ochamchire

BLACK

SEA

Tqvarchili

Svanetia

Mostia

Kazbegi
5033 m

Greater Caucasus

Lentekhi

Ratcha

Rioni

Pasanauri

Aragvi

Alaverdi

Kakhetia

Lagodekhi

South Ossetia

Tskhinvali

Ambrolauri

Imeretia

Kutaisi

Akhmeta Telavi
Dusheti

Zinandali

Gurjaani

Ingur

Mingrelia

Zugdidi

Senaki

Shrosha

Gori

Kura

Mtskheta

Alazani

Dedoplistsqaro

Rioni

Samtredia

Kartli

TBILISI

Iori

Poti

Guria

Abastumani

Borjomi

Rustavi

Ozurgeti

Lesser Caucasus

Bakuriani

Marneuli

GEORGIA

Kobuleti

Khulo

Akhaltsikhe

Akhalkalaki

Kazreti

AZERBAIJAN

Batumi

Autonomous
Republic of Ajaria

0   30 miles/50 km

N

TURKEY

ARMENIA

საქართველო
Georgia

Isabel and Marek Kielian

In no other activity do the Georgians spend so much time together as celebrating. This almost cost them their place in the world, as legend would have it: after God divided the world among the people on it, the Georgians came along to receive their piece of land. God raged: "You are too late." The Georgian envoys apologized: "We were at the table but we didn't forget you. We ate, we raised out glasses to you and thanked you for creating such a beautiful world." These words and the happiness of the people touched the Creator: "The world is indeed already divided up, but there is still one little place that I had reserved for myself. I would like to give this to you." This is how, the Georgians say, they came to live in the most beautiful corner of the world. The country offers a breathtaking interplay of different landscapes and types of climate: lavish vegetation in warm and humid west Georgia, the evergreen subtropical Black Sea coast, forests up to alpine heights with perpetual snow in the Lesser and Greater Caucasus, as well as continental climate in east Georgia with its hot steppe on the border with neighboring Azerbaijan.

There is also a colorful range of people: over its area of close on 27,000 square miles/70,000 sq km, the Georgian nation covers a dozen population groups (see page 222 f). The peaceful juxtaposition of different cultures can be seen at the common table—the pivot and central point in the life of every Caucasian. Even in difficult times, the table will bend under the weight of many different dishes. The mild climate of west Georgia by the Black Sea provides fragrant vegetables for the table such as peppers and eggplants, as well as citrus fruit, fish, cheese, and corn dishes: many dishes made of beef and lamb come from east Georgia, along with wheat bread baked in a clay oven. Across the whole country, herbs such as coriander, basil, and mint, as well as saffron and fenugreek, join to form the secret fragrance of so many vegetable dishes, soups, and meat dishes. Soups and sauces are often prepared using fruit and are served cold in summer; some are served cold throughout the year. Fruits such as cornelian cherries, diverse types of plum, and walnuts not only enrich sweet dishes but also give more solid dishes a characteristic note. Last but not least, the east of the country is considered the cradle of wine, and still produces a few fine drops today, which also give guests from around the world the feeling that they have landed in one of the most beautiful spots on earth.

Previous page: The Greater Caucasus with peaks of over 16,500 feet/5,000 m is omnipresent in the north of Georgia. The pilgrimage church Tsminda Sameba is seated on a ledge in the shadows of the Kazbek mountain.

Homemade specialties made from fruit and nuts are eaten by everyone on Georgia. Sweet coated walnuts (left) and fruit purée pancake rolls (center) are popular treats.

Markets placed between Orient and Occident

"There is a hurly-burly in the market the whole day long; you can see all the Caucasian and west Asiatic types here, … there is earsplitting shouting, noise, screeching. Apart from the locals, there are also many people who have traveled here from different corners, either from villages or from remote locations in the Caucasus." As in the times of the German writer Arthur Leist, who visited the old town market in Tbilisi in the 1880s, it continues in markets in the Georgian capital city to this day.

"Kartopliani gemrieli, lovely potato turnovers" croaks a sprightly old woman, balancing her goods at eye height as she passes through the crowd of people. A walrus-mustachioed butcher tries to push his wheelbarrow laden with freshly slaughtered geese past the clusters of people on his way to the meat department, grumbling loudly. A gallant Azerbaijani smilingly presents the gleaming red center of a cut pomegranate as well as his sparkling gold teeth, while a group of stallholders, looking at the cheeses shining in brine, contest the quality of their *sulguni* (see page 236).

Oriental "busyness" has ruled here since the 12th century, since the Georgian market was named after the Persian word *basari*. Due to its geographical position, Georgia has always been a revolving door between orient and occident. Different types of fruits and vegetables were brought into the country in the baggage trains of numer-

ous conquerors and traders from all points of the compass, and onto its tables: mulberries, peaches, and persimmons, spices such as cinnamon and pepper, eggplants from the East Indies and spinach from Persia. In the 17th and 18th centuries, the Turks brought beans, peppers, corn and tomatoes from the west; the Russian Tsars allowed tea, potatoes, and citrus fruit to be cultivated in Georgia for the first time in the 19th century.

In those days, the traders met in markets outside the city gate and in the caravanserai. Today a growing number of middlemen compete for the limited space in the two large market halls and on their access routes in the capital of Tbilisi. Sidewalks and gateways in the roads of the inner city offer alternatives, and here each day you can find everything from early in the morning to late at night that is needed for the cooking pot. However, the favorite shopping opportunity is the turbulent *Desertiris Basari* at the main station. Everything that grows and is processed in this "Garden of Eden," as the Soviet rulers once called their southerly republic, finds its way to these two floors. Indeed, the current structural crisis in Georgian agriculture has long worked in favor of competition from neighboring countries: pomegranates and melons from Azerbaijan, vegetables from Turkey, and stone fruit from Armenia have become standard offerings.

Only the meat department is firmly in the hands of Georgian men. Loud and verbose negotiations take place here about the juiciest pieces of domestic meat production. Not until they reach here are beef, pork, and lamb carved up as required into portions suitable for large families. The selection of meat is traditionally men's business. Whoever can stand behind his laden stall and understand the art of negotiation and persuasion and also maintain personal relationships with the customers will rule the market. On the other hand, the lonely farmer from Kakhetia looks a little lost, waiting in patient silence to sell his single suckling pig.

Right: The much-loved sulguni cheeses are offered for sale in their fresh and smoked versions.

Left: Dried herbs and spices exude a bewitching fragrance at every Georgian market.

Freshly slaughtered sucking pigs sell like hot cakes. Stuffed, grilled on a spit or roasted, sucking pig is the favorite meal of Georgians and is mainly served at their numerous celebrations.

Pickled delicacies

Pickled vegetables are in season all year round in Georgia; they form part of traditional larder stocks. Any type of fresh vegetable is suitable for pickling, such as chiles, green tomatoes, cucumbers, onions, and young garlic. These freshly harvested delicacies are blanched briefly and pickled without any additions in a 5 or 10 percent brine. Only green tomatoes are first carefully studded with cloves of garlic, dill, and bay leaves.

The king of these salty treats is *jonjoli*, a Georgian specialty made from the flower buds of the bladdernut *(Staphylea pinnata)*. The bladdernut bush, which can go up to 16 feet/5 m tall, grows wild in Georgia up to about 4,000 ft/ 1,200 m above sea level. The spherical buds of the hanging racemes, which are about 5 inch/ 12 cm long, are picked by hand in April and May and pickled entire, along with their stems. The flowers are blanched in boiling water and sprinkled immediately with salt until liquid is drawn out. Then slightly salted water is poured over. Alternatively, the flowers can be placed in layers in salt in preserving jars; when liquid is drawn from the flowers, the mixture is pressed down using a wooden spoon or stone, and as many new flowers and salt as possible are added until the jar is full.

In this way, *jonjoli* keeps for up to one year and is available loose at markets. High-quality *jonjoli* may only be made from fully developed buds and young flowers and taste similar to pickled capers. The Georgians enjoy this specialty as a cold appetizer, as a fine addition to meat dishes or eaten simply with bread.

Jonjoli promotes the digestion and is indispensable as a side dish at any lavish meal.

Many colorful types of vegetables, fresh from the farmers' market, are the be-all and end-all of Georgian cuisine.

Vegetables

Sun-soaked on the Black Sea as far as eastern Kakhetia, plentiful rain in humid, subtropical west Georgia, and a secure water supply in the hot, dry climate of eastern Georgia, it is no wonder that Georgia, with its optimum climatic conditions, was the main supplier of agricultural produce and food for the whole giant empire in the Soviet era. The collapse of the Soviet Union brought domestic agriculture almost to a standstill. The restructuring of the former collective farms is slowly taking place, years after independence, so Georgia's farmers only grow food for the domestic market. Last but not least, restricted electricity supplies and completely obsolete agricultural equipment is forcing unprofitable and uncommercial vegetable cultivation. Limited surpluses go to relatives in town, and seldom to the market. Times of crisis also have their advantages, the lack of pesticides makes domestic vegetables a healthy treat. However, production is currently meeting less than 60 percent of domestic demand, and every season vegetables from Turkish greenhouses, for example, are arriving more frequently on the table in Tbilisi.

Apart from the mountainous regions, all of the vegetable types used in the Georgian kitchen are grown all over the country. Only potatoes flourish better in the higher regions. Even in the spring, the first onions and green salad vegetables are ready to harvest in mild west Georgia. From early summer to sunny autumn, vegetable gardens across the land provide tomatoes, eggplants, cucumbers, and peppers. In autumn these are supplemented by pumpkins, cabbage and beets, and spinach in winter. Vegetable types such as beets and cabbage have been adopted by the Georgians from the Russians, but in their preparation they are given a specifically Georgian twist by adding walnuts and herbs and spices such as coriander and fenugreek. Within the scope of their refortified Christian Orthodox faith, cooked vegetables are considered a particularly pure food for fast days, over one hundred of which are distributed across the year, such as before Easter and before Christmas.

There are only a few traditional forms of vegetable preparation; fresh ingredients are boiled, baked, fried, stewed, salted or preserved in oil. Typically Georgian are *mkhali*, appetizers with vegetables or chicken, in which the ingredients are cooked, then chopped and mixed with walnuts. The much-loved Georgian spice mixture *khmeli suneli* ("mixed herbs," see page 228) provides a distinctive aroma. For *borani*, cooked vegetables such as eggplants, spinach or cabbage are chopped small, mixed with yogurt and served as a cold appetizer. Cucumbers and tomatoes are served—whole or cut up—with fresh herbs such as basil, cilantro and parsley; green salad is mainly served with just herbs, onion, and salt. Salad dressings, as known in Western kitchens, are only slowly being accepted in modern households. They are generally prepared using lemon juice and oil, and sometimes a little sugar is added. Carrot salad is made Russian-style using mayonnaise.

Tsiteli charkhlis potlis mkhali
Beet leaf salad (Not illustrated)

500 g beet leaves, or spinach
1 garlic clove, crushed
½ bunch each of cilantro, dill, parsley, finely chopped
1¼ cups/150 g finely chopped walnuts
2–3 tbsp fresh pomegranate juice, or 1 tbsp wine vinegar
3 tbsp khmeli suneli (1 tsp each of saffron, fenugreek seeds and coriander seeds, ground)
Salt and red peppercorns, ground
Pomegranate seeds, or 1–2 onions, chopped

Blanch the beet leaves, leave to cool, then squeeze out by hand. Chop very finely and mix with the garlic, herbs and nuts. Season to taste with pomegranate juice, spices and salt, and sprinkle with the pomegranate seeds. Serve cold.

Mtsvane lobio kvertskhit
Green beans with egg (1)

Generous 1 lb/500 g green beans, trimmed
Salt
2 medium-sized onions, finely chopped
4 tbsp/60 g butter
½ bunch each of cilantro, dill, celery leaves, parsley and basil, finely chopped
6 eggs

Cut the beans into 3 or 4 pieces and simmer until almost tender in very little water (the water should evaporate completely), then salt lightly. Fry the onions in 2 tablespoons butter until transparent, add the beans and herbs, then the remaining butter and braise for a few minutes, covered. Whisk the eggs together with a little salt. Remove the vegetables from the heat, pour the egg mixture evenly over the top and leave to cook, covered, over the lowest possible heat until the eggs are set.

Nigvziani badrijani
Eggplant with walnuts (2)

Generous 1 lb/1 kg eggplant
Salt
Oil for frying
1½ cups/200 g finely chopped walnuts
2–3 garlic cloves, crushed
Red peppercorns, ground
3 tbsp khmeli suneli (1 tsp each of saffron, fenugreek and coriander seeds, ground)
2–3 tbsp wine vinegar
2 tbsp finely chopped fresh cilantro
Pomegranate seeds to garnish

Wash the eggplants, cut lengthwise into thin slices,
salt and leave to draw, covered, for about 1 hour.
Then drain and press the remaining liquid carefully
from the eggplant slices using paper towels. Fry the
eggplant in hot oil on both sides, remove from the
pan and leave to cool. Crush the walnuts with the
garlic and peppercorns using a pestle and mortar,
add the spice mixture (khmeli suneli) and vinegar,
season with salt, add the cilantro leaves and stir
the mixture to form a paste. Spread the eggplant
slices with it and roll up or fold the ends in. Leave
at room temperature for 2 hours for the flavors to
develop and garnish with pomegranate seeds
before serving.
Tip: Halve small eggplants, fry them, and then
place the filled halves on top of each other (see
photo).

Soko khakhvita da kindzit
Mushrooms with onions and cilantro (3)

3 medium-sized onions, finely chopped
3 tbsp/45 g butter
Generous 1 lb/1 kg mushrooms, cleaned and
halved or quartered
½ cup/125 ml mushroom stock (or diluted mushroom essence)
1¼ cups/150 g finely chopped walnuts
1 bunch of fresh cilantro, finely chopped
Salt
Black pepper

Fry the onions in the butter. Add the mushrooms
and stock and simmer until the mushrooms are just
cooked. Stir in the walnuts and cilantro and season to taste with salt and pepper.

Soups and stews

Soups and stews, called *tsvniani* ("juicy food") in Georgian, took their place on the Caucasian menu about 5,000 years ago with the development of the pottery trade. The cultivation of grain and the raising of livestock, in particular, gained great significance at that time and suggested the preparation of soups based on meat and sour milk. A particular feature of Georgian soups is their generally sour flavor, achieved through the addition of different fruit components. *Kharcho* combines beef with rice, plum sauce, and many different spices. *Chikhirtma* is a tart sharp-flavored soup of lamb or poultry, thickened with egg yolk or whole eggs. So that the egg does not run when heated, it is first mixed with a sour liquid such as fruit juice, *matsoni* (yogurt) or vinegar. The stew called *bosartma* can also be prepared

from lamb or poultry, and additionally contains tomatoes as well a generally acidic component such as pomegranate juice. *Tkemali*, sour plum sauce, (see page 260) is used as a souring agent in substantial soups and not only makes the meat more aromatic but also makes it easier to digest. The hearty soup *khash*, made from innards, is served in Georgia as a hangover cure after celebrating all night, just as in the neighboring countries of Armenia (see page 276) and Azerbaijan. Vegetables used in soups are generally restricted to onions and tomatoes, and only infrequently—such as in summer soup *sapkhulis tsveni* —are other vegetables such as beans, eggplants, and peppers put into the pot with mutton or lamb. During periods of fasting and on hot summer days, tart, meatless soups *(shechamandi)* with

fresh herbs are a Georgian specialty. The two at the top of the list of favorites are cornelian cherry soup *(shindis shechamandi)*, which can be eaten hot or cold, and yogurt soup with egg and herbs *(matsvnis shechamandi)*, which is generally served hot. These soups are frequently thickened with flour.

In Georgia, soups are almost exclusively eaten at home as an everyday meal, or with friends as a first course or as a main meal with bread and salad. However invigorating and tasty the soups may be, they are almost never found on the table at celebrations.

Shindis shechamandi
Cornelian cherry soup

1 ¼ lb/600 g fresh cornelian cherries, pitted
2 level tbsp whole wheat flour
4 cloves of garlic, crushed
Salt
½ bunch of fresh mint, finely chopped

Cook the cornelian cherries in 2 cups/500 ml water for about 10 minutes until soft; leave to cool then strain, reserving a little of the cooking liquid, and push through a sieve.
Stir the whole wheat flour into the slightly cooled cooking liquid, add to the cherry purée and simmer over the lowest possible heat for about 15 minutes, stirring occasionally. Add the crushed garlic cloves and season with salt. Sprinkle over the chopped mint before serving. Serve hot or cold, as desired.

Matsvnis shechamandi
Yogurt soup

1 onion, finely chopped
2 tbsp butter
2 cups/500 g matsoni yogurt (or Turkish yogurt, failing that full fat yogurt)
1 tbsp whole wheat flour
2 eggs
Salt
One handful each of fresh cilantro, tarragon and dill, finely chopped

Fry the onions in the butter. Stir the *matsoni* yogurt, flour, and 1¼ cups/300 ml cold water together thoroughly, pour onto the onions, stir again, bring to a boil then simmer for about 10 minutes. Whisk the eggs, add to the soup, stirring all the time and remove the soup immediately from the heat. Season with salt and sprinkle with the chopped herbs before serving.

Katmis chikhirtma
Chicken soup with egg
(Not illustrated)

1 oven-ready chicken
2 tbsp/30 g chicken fat, or butter
4 medium-sized onions, chopped very fine
1 small head of celery, quartered
1 medium-sized parsley root, halved lengthwise
Salt and pepper
½ tsp cinnamon
½ tbsp ground coriander
3–4 egg yolks
2 tbsp whole wheat or corn flour
Juice of 1–2 lemons
1 tsp saffron powder
½ bunch of each of basil, dill, mint, and parsley, finely chopped

Divide the chicken into portion-sized pieces. Heat the chicken fat removed from the chicken (or the butter) in a deep pan and fry the onions. Add the chicken portions and fry together for about 10 minutes. Pour on sufficient hot water to cover the chicken pieces well. Add the celery, parsley root, salt and pepper and cook over medium heat until the chicken is tender.
Remove the chicken and vegetables from the cooking liquid, keep the chicken warm and season the stock with the cinnamon and coriander. Remove from the heat, whisk the egg yolks with the flour and lemon juice and add to the stock, stirring continually. Add the saffron and herbs and reheat the soup, stirring continually, but do not allow it to boil. Replace the chicken portions in the soup and heat through for a few minutes.
Variation: Breast or leg of lamb can also be used, soured in this case using wine vinegar.

Sapkhulis tsveni
Summer soup

Generous 1 lb/500 g cuts of lamb for soup
Salt
3 bay leaves
3 medium-sized onions, finely chopped
¾ lb/300 g green beans, halved
2 tart apples, sliced
4 medium-sized tomatoes, diced
1 eggplant, diced
1 small dried red chile pepper
1 bunch of parsley

Cut the meat into pieces, put in a pan with 4 cups/1 liter lightly salted water and the bay leaves, bring to a boil, then simmer, covered, for 1 hour over medium heat. Remove the meat and set aside. Leave the stock to cool until the surface fat has hardened, lift this off and use to fry the onions. Bring the stock to a boil, add the meat, apples, and vegetables and simmer for about 30 minutes. Season with salt and sprinkle with parsley.

Kharcho
Hearty beef soup (for 6)
(Not illustrated)

1¾ lb/750 g beef brisket
Salt
¾ cup/150 g rice
6 small onions, finely chopped
3–4 tbsp/60 g butter
2 tbsp corn or whole wheat flour
3 bay leaves
1 medium-sized parsley root, chopped
Black pepper, freshly milled
¾ cup/75 g finely chopped walnut
½ cup/125 ml tkemali sauce (see page 229) or freshly squeezed pomegranate juice
4 tbsp khmeli suneli (1 tsp each of saffron, fenugreek seeds and coriander seeds, ground)
½ tsp paprika
1 pinch of cinnamon
3 garlic cloves, crushed
1 handful of fresh herbs (basil, celery leaves, parsley), finely chopped
2 tbsp finely chopped cilantro leaves

Cut the meat into bite-sized pieces, put in a pan with about 3 quarts/3 liters lightly salted cold water, bring to a boil then simmer on low heat for about 2 hours. Add the rice. Fry the onions in the butter, sprinkle over the flour, add some of the hot stock, stir to thicken and add to the soup with the bay leaves, parsley root and pepper. After about 15 minutes, add the walnuts. When the rice is cooked, add all the other ingredients except the cilantro leaves, and season with salt and pepper. Serve sprinkled with the cilantro.

Variety of people and cuisine

Extensive vineyards in Khaketia, sunny fields of corn in west Georgia, wooded hillsides and clear, fish-filled rivers in the Greater Caucasus—the nature, flora and fauna of Georgia is so diverse, just like the rich variety in its people and population groups. As in other areas of the Caucasus, members of different ethnic and language communities live in Georgia. In the last Soviet population census in 1989, Georgians made up about 72 percent of the population. Outside the Caucasian language family, there was additionally an Armenian minority in Tbilisi and in the Armenian border areas. Russians and Azerbaijanis lived in the larger towns and in the Azerbaijan border areas. After their breakaway from the Soviet Union and the violent conflicts with Abkhazia and Ossetia, there was emigration and flight. A clear figure still cannot be placed on the extent of emigration, as the census of 2002 could not include Abkhazia. The Georgians have lived in the Caucasus for about 4,000 years. In the Middle Ages they made up about 90 percent of the population but in later centuries, particularly after the incorporation of Georgia in the Russian Empire in 1801, there was immigration, primarily by eastern Europeans, but also by Greeks and Russified Germans.

The Republic of Georgia contains three autonomous territories: Adzharia, Abkhazia and South Ossetia. The Adzharians are essentially Muslim Georgians who constitute the bulk of the

Only about three-quarters of the inhabitants of Georgia belong to the Georgian ethnic group. Today, different ethnic groups maintain their language and culture, primarily in the mountain regions, but also in the west.

population in the Autonomous Republic of Adzharia. The Abkhazians, who speak a northwest Caucasian language and are predominantly Muslim, were a minority group in their autonomous Republic which was established in 1930. Their independence movement, which followed the collapse of the Soviet Union, led to the expulsion of around 200,000 Georgians and affiliation with Russia. The Ossetians, who speak an East Iranian language, were granted the autonomous territory of South Ossetia in northern Georgia in 1921. Their demands for unification with the Russian Republic of North Ossetia led to violent clashes in the 1990s and precipitated a large exodus by a large part of the Ossetian population to North Ossetia. Since the Russian-Georgian war of August 2008, South Ossetia has, for all intents and purposes, been cut off from Georgia and has enjoyed—like Abkhazia—questionable independence under Russian protection.

Language is considered the most important distinguishing feature of ethnic differentiation in the population of Georgia. In the opinion of philologists, Georgian (Kartvelian) is one of four southern Caucasian languages, which progressed as the dominant language of literature and the written word, and incorporated related dialects. A second language, Lazish, is spoken in the south of Adzharia in the border area with Turkey and on the Turkish side by the Lazes, a predominantly Muslim group. In large parts of west Georgia (Imeretia, Mingrelia and Guria), Mingrelish is the mother tongue. Finally, the Svans in the high valley of the Inguri have so far been able to retain

Georgian New Year

New Year is the greatest festival for the Georgians. According to the Orthodox church calendar, the festival falls on January 14. However, since the Soviet era, people have been following the Gregorian calendar and celebrate on January 1. On New Year's Eve, a fir tree is set up, decorated with cotton wool, candles, baubles, and toys. The custom in west Georgia is to attach crosses to the points of walnut tree branches and to fasten apples, pomegranates, and candy to them.

The Georgians like to celebrate the New Year with a festive meal, where everything to be found in the kitchen is served up (see page 232). At the New Year, there has to be turkey with walnut sauce (*satsivi*, see page 231) and sucking pig. At midnight, the men reach for fireworks and firearms, the women make wishes while they distribute the tasty nut confection *gozinaki* with the words *ase tkbilad daberdi* ("grow up as sweet as this").

The tradition of *mekvle* is of pagan origin: this New Year messenger formerly sprinkled wheat in the house of the host, but today he brings candy and blesses the house with wine. In principle, anyone can take on the role of the "man who is the first in the New Year to leave a track in the snow." However, only well-disposed New Year messengers are wanted, because it is said: "The year will be like the visit of the *mekvle*." Those who do not play the *mekvle* always keep candy to hand for friends.

their cultural and linguistic independence. In addition, there is also a number of population groups who do not speak their own language but Georgian dialects. Small groups of these mountain people live in the adjacent valleys of the Aragvi with the Mokheven, Khevsuren, Mtiulen, Pshaven and Tushen. Although each of these groups amounts to just a few thousand people, they have retained a number of peculiarities with reference to housing, clothing, cuisine, trade, customs, and oral traditions.

In spite of their ethnic variety, from early on the Georgians felt themselves to be one people, which was strengthened by the adoption of Christianity. The Georgian Orthodox church represents the state religion of Georgia, which has been characterized through history by a remarkable tolerance towards other denominations. The second-oldest Christian state religion after that of Armenia—its roots go back to 337—has been completely independent of the Russian patriarchy since 1992, to which is was subordinate from the Russification of Georgia at the start of the 19th century. In the old town area of Tbilisi, the residential areas of Muslim Azerbaijanis, Armenian Christians, Jewish and Christian Georgians are adjacent to one another. Russian residents of the Orthodox creed, and Roman Catholic and protestant settlers originating from Germany complete the variety of religions. The cultural differences between the ethnic groups are characterized not only by their language and religion but also by their culinary traditions, caused by their geographical conditions. In Kakhetia, extensive vineyards shape the landscape. In the mountainous landscape of west Georgia, on the other hand, only small quantities of individual grape varieties are grown, and tea is cultivated on the lower hills. In Inner Kartli, large fruit and vegetable plantations are characteristic. Whilst there is extensive corn cultivation in west Georgian areas for personal use (see page 235), there are primarily wheat fields in the east. The mountain people, the Svans, Ossetians, Mokhevs, Chevsurs and Tushetians, eat fish from the numerous rivers and lakes in the mountains and for millennia have cultivated forms of preservation of lamb and beef (see page 246). In addition, favorite flavors also vary; the farther west you travel, the more piquant the meals.

Corn cultivation determines the appearance of the landscape in wide areas of Mingrelia (west Georgia), as corn-flour bread is the staple food here. In eastern and central Georgia, on the other hand, wheat is grown for the daily bread.

The Mokhev area of settlement is in the central Caucasus. They belong to the Georgian mountain people who have still retained a considerable amount of regional independence in spite of their low numbers.

Adzharian khachapuri are enriched, after baking, with a raw egg.

Khachapuri—the national dish

The Georgians fall into raptures about *khachapuri*. Like no other meal from the Georgian kitchen, this type of cheese bread stands for national identity and family tradition. It should never be missing from either the everyday or the celebratory table. This national dish tastes light when the dough is prepared with *matson*, similar to yogurt. However, housewives also frequently make a smooth yeast dough which, like the matsoni dough, forms the basis for many khachapuri variants.

Imeruli khachapuri, Imeretic-style cheese or quark bread, is the classic khachapuri. Almost every housewife fries several of these round, cheese-filled flat loaves in an iron pan every day. They are eaten like bread at breakfast, as a snack, and also in the evening. At celebrations, the guests are spoiled with this classic variant and also with *penovani*, lozenge-shaped puff pastry pockets filled with cheese and baked in the oven. Both khachapuri variants are also available at numerous snack kiosks and from street traders at markets or subway stations. In times of crisis, they may also be sold from a hand extended from the window of a ground floor apartment.

The khachapuri variants *achma* and *acharuli* come from Adzharia. The first consists of many layers of dough, cheese, and butter and is prepared like lasagna; in the second variant the dough is filled with cheese and shaped like an oval boat. After baking, a raw egg is placed directly in the hollow. In addition, the khachapuri family also includes *lobiani* made with puréed kidney beans from Racha, *kartopliani* with mashed potato and cream cheese, *pkhlovani* with boiled cabbage fried in butter and cream cheese from Khevsuria and South Ossetia, and *kubdari* with heavily spiced ground meat from Svaneti.

Khachapuri
Georgian cheese bread

For the dough:
¼ liter matsoni yogurt (or Bulgarian or Turkish yogurt, failing that, full fat yogurt)
1 egg
¼ tsp baking powder
Salt
3–3½ cups/450–500 g whole wheat flour

For the filling:
Generous 1 lb/500 g sulguni cheese, (or 8–9 oz/250 g each of buffalo mozzarella and cream cheese)
1 egg
1½ tbsp/50 g butter
Salt
Butter for frying

Make a smooth dough out of the ingredients. Use as much flour as needed to keep the dough light without it sticking to your hands. Leave the dough to rest for about 30 minutes. Meanwhile, prepare the filling. Grate the sulguni cheese and process into a smooth, glutinous mixture with the egg and butter, using either a mixer or a wooden spoon. Season with salt if required (depending on the salt content of the cheese), and divide into 4 balls. Shape the dough also into 4 balls and roll these out to form 8 inch/20 cm circles. Put the cheese fillings in the center of each circle, bring the edges of the dough up and over the filling to enclose, and press firmly together to seal. Carefully press the dough pockets flat until each will fill a large skillet, and then fry individually in the hot butter, covered, before turning them and frying them, uncovered, to finish. Cut each flat loaf into 4 portions and serve hot.

Left: Each Georgian guards her khachapuri recipe like a valuable treasure. It is said that there are as many recipes for these dough pockets as there are female Georgians.

The basic ingredients for khachapuri should be at room temperature so the dough rises well.

Matsoni yogurt makes the dough mild and smooth. If it sticks during kneading, use more flour.

Before the dough pockets filled with cheese are fried, the edges must first be carefully sealed.

225

Eating khinkali is an art—essentially they are eaten in your hand. The small, practical knob made from pasta dough is used as a handle. Thus you can bite easily into the filled dough pocket, but take care to prevent the delicious meat juices running out over your fingers.

Khinkali

The Swabians love their Maultaschen (stuffed pasta), the Italians their ravioli, and the Uzbeks their *manty*. Filled pasta pockets have conquered kitchens from China to Europe. The Mongols, in their attacks westward in the 13th century, brought their ground-meat-filled variant from central Asia to Georgia. Here, this meal of the conquerors has been adopted into their range of national dishes under the name of *khinkali*. Housewifely virtues are measured by the skill in forming the bag of dough: the more folds of pasta

dough that can be pressed together over the filling to form a knob, the greater the devotion of the woman to her family. To eat them, khinkali are held in the fingers by the knob, and pieces are bitten off carefully, so that the meat stock generated in cooking and enclosed in the dough does not run over the hands and clothes.

The steaming pasta pockets on the table only need black pepper and cold beer—their fans enjoy them this way by the dozen. They are loved both as a small, satisfying snack from a street stall and in the form of a main dish or as part of the classic Georgian table (see page 232 f).

The eternal dispute: who invented pasta?

Gourmets and scholars continue to argue: Where does pasta come from and who was the first with the idea of filling pockets of dough with meat? The most widespread theory, which was disproved many years ago, however, was that the Venetian explorer Marco Polo brought the first pasta to Europe from China in about 1295. The Sicilians believe that pasta was brought to their island in ancient times by the Greeks. In Liguria, they think that Genoese traders learned the technique of dough preparation from flour, water and salt on the Mongol steppes, where the nomadic lifestyle did not allow the laborious preparation of yeast dough, and the wind and sun was even better at drying the simple dough used for pasta—which was speeded up when shaped into long strings. What has been verified is that people in China were mixing ground wheat with water and then drying it about 4,000 years ago. Both the Etruscans and the ancient Greeks and Romans were familiar with pasta-type dishes, and the Arabs rolled simple dough into thin sticks and dried them in the sun long before Marco Polo was around.

One can therefore assume that people in different places in the world and independently of each other came to the simple idea of mixing flour from wheat or other cereal types with water and salt, later also with oil, milk or egg, and cooking it in boiling water. Pasta pockets filled with meat could well have come to Europe from the Far East along the Silk Road. They are a practical food for traveling, and they are found everywhere along the legendary route (see also page 328 f): as *manty* in Uzbekistan, as *khinkali* in Georgia, and further north as *varenyky* in the Ukraine and *pelmeni* in Russia.

For khinkali, the dough is rolled out into circles and then one or two spoonfuls of coriander-scented ground meat is placed in the center of each.

When gathering the dough over the meat filling, it is the aim of each Georgian housewife to give the dough as many folds as possible.

Khinkali
Pasta pockets

For the filling:
1¾ lb/750 g ground lamb or mixed ground pork and beef
Salt
Black pepper
3 large onions, chopped very fine
1 bunch of cilantro, chopped fine

For the dough:
4½ cups/650 g all-purpose flour
About ⅔ cup/150 ml lukewarm salt water

Knead together the ground meat with the salt, pepper, onion, cilantro and about 7 tablespoons/100 ml lukewarm water. Prepare a smooth dough from the flour and salt water, roll it out thinly and cut out 6 inch/15 cm circles (using a saucer). Put 1–2 tablespoons of the meat filling into the center of each circle. Gather up the edges of the dough to the center over the filling and pinch neatly together. Put the khinkali in a large pan with boiling, lightly salted water and simmer very gently gently agitating them with a wooden spoon now and again. When the khinkali float to the surface, continue to simmer for about another 6 minutes. Then remove from the water using a skimmer, sprinkle with black pepper and serve hot.

Now the khinkali just need to be cooked.

Khmeli suneli—the flavor of Georgia

The key to the secret of the unmistakable Georgian fragrance of soups, stews, meat, and vegetable dishes is in the ingredients of khmeli suneli ("mixed herbs"). The three indispensable ingredients of this spice mixture give vegetables and meat dishes a hint of the Orient: the enduring bitter yet fresh fragrance is provided by ground fenugreek seeds and flower heads, called "foreign herb" in Georgian *(utskho suneli)* as this plant which occurs from the Mediterranean to China probably found its way to the Caucasus via China and the Silk Road. Finely ground coriander seeds in the spice mixture give an aniseed-type flavor. Saffron, or much more frequently saffron alternatives (see page 231) is the third spice in the trio. The addition of dried and ground parsley, dill, mint or cilantro leaves varies, depending on the house recipe.

The quintessence of Georgian cuisine: sauces

However rich Georgian cuisine appears, it is given its finishing touch through numerous delicious sauces. The former Soviet State and Party leader Nikita Khrushchev assured people on a visit to Tbilisi that the sauce made from *tkemali* plums was so pleasant that even nails would taste excellent in it. This is open to question, but the sauce that originated in Georgia stimulates the senses with very subtle flavors. The refined mixture of tart plums, garlic, and herbs with salt and pepper makes it at once sour, bitter, sharp, peppery and

salty. It tastes outstanding as an accompaniment to all types of meat dishes.

The significance of sauces is undisputed. Neither fish nor meat comes to the table without its own liquid accompaniment. Unlike many other countries in Europe and Asia, Georgian sauces are not based on meat but are founded on fruit, vegetables, walnuts, or poultry stock.

Satsebeli ("for dunking") is the name of sauces made from puréed tart fruit or fruit juices, while *tkemali* plums, cornelian cherries and pomegranates take

pride of place. Tomato sauce (*pamidvris satsebeli*) with garlic and dried herbs is also popular.

These sauces are always prepared independently of the dish with which they are served—often prepared as a batch to last the whole winter. They are always eaten cold. This suits Georgian meals that often last for hours and to which most meat dishes are brought cold; one of the exceptions is shashlik.

Also much loved are dishes with nut sauces, for which ground or crushed walnuts are mixed with

Fresh herbs are a component of all sauces; garlic and paprika, on the other hand, are used frequently but in small quantities. Only *ajika* sauce, which comes from Abkhasia, consists primarily of peppers and obtains its fiery heat from aromatic spices, chiles and garlic. It can be eaten with meat or with bread, vegetables or egg dishes. There are no fixed rules for the use of sauces. Different dishes come about through varying the sauces with a main meal (e.g. fried poultry with *tkemali* or pomegranate sauce) or vice versa: one sauce can be served with different side dishes, such as *Tkemali* sauce with suckling pig, pork or vegetables, and *bazhe* sauce with fish or poultry. For everyday meals, sauces are eaten with roast potatoes, corn porridge or bread.

meat stock or water, but always with a shot of wine vinegar or sour fruit juice. The most important nut sauces are *satsivi* and *bazhe*. *Satsivi* sauce is always based on a poultry stock made from a turkey. Unlike *bazhe* sauce, it contains onions that are fried in the poultry fat, and it is generally thicker. The classic Georgian spice mixture *khmeli suneli* (see box) along with cinnamon and cloves gives it a distinctive note.
For *bazhe* sauce, walnuts, garlic, vinegar and *khmeli suneli* are mixed together with boiling water or poultry stock. It can be rounded off with a splash of home-pressed walnut oil. Here too, fried poultry or even fish is added to the sauce to marinate well before being served cold.

Tkemlis sazebeli
Tkemali plum sauce (1)

2¼ lb/1 kg tkemali plums, or unripe mirabelles or very sour plums
8–10 cloves of garlic, crushed
1 bunch each of dill, cilantro and mint, chopped finely
Salt and pepper

Cut into the fruit lengthwise, pour over about 1⅔ cups/ 400 ml water and simmer over low heat until the stones loosen. Pour off the juice into a pan, remove the pits, purée the fruit, and add as much juice as needed to produce a creamy sauce. Add the garlic and herbs and season with salt and pepper.
The sauce is served cold with meat. It tastes very good with suckling pig, ham, and chicken.

Ajika
Pepper sauce (2)

20 pointed red peppers or capsicums, finely chopped
1 mild red chile pepper, seeded and finely chopped
1 hot chile pepper, seeded and finely chopped
3 tomatoes, skinned and finely chopped
4 whole heads of garlic, skinned and crushed
1 tsp each of fenugreek and coriander seed, ground
1 bunch of cilantro, finely chopped
Salt

Purée all of the ingredients except the cilantro. Season to taste and add the cilantro. The sauce goes well with broiled fish and corn bread.

Mtsvane ajika
Green ajika (3)

7 oz/200 g hot green chile peppers
Large head of garlic, cloves separated and peeled
2 bunches each of cilantro and parsley
1 bunch of white basil
Handful of celery leaves
1½ tbsp/100 g salt

Chop the vegetables and herbs finely and mix, or for a fine sauce push through a grinder, then stir in the salt. Goes well with fried meat dishes.
Tip: To keep the sauce in the store-cupboard for the winter, add another 3½ tablespoons of salt and seal in a screw-topped jar. Leave to stand for at least 2 weeks.

Brotseulis satsebeli nigvzit
Pomegranate sauce with walnuts (4)

1 tsp saffron threads or powder
1 cup/250 ml strong chicken stock
1¼ cups/150 g chopped walnuts
2 tsp paprika
8–10 garlic cloves, crushed
1 bunch of cilantro, finely chopped
1 cup/250 ml freshly pressed pomegranate juice, or blackberry juice
Salt

Dissolve the saffron in the hot chicken stock. Process the walnuts with the paprika, garlic and cilantro into a paste using a pestle and mortar and mix into the cooled saffron-chicken stock, stirring continually. Add the fruit juice and season with salt. It should be very fluid.
Serve the pomegranate sauce cold with fried or poached poultry or fish.
Tip: Obtain fresh pomegranate juice by sieving as many fresh pomegranate seeds as needed to provide the desired quantity of juice.

Shindis satsebeli
Cornelian cherry sauce
(Not illustrated)

Generous 1 lb/500 g ripe cornelian cherries
3 cloves of garlic
1 tsp khmeli suneli (saffron, fenugreek and coriander seeds in equal quantities ground)
Salt and red pepper corns, crushed
1 tsp each of a handful of dill and celery leaves

Pit the fruit and purée. Mix the garlic, spices and herbs with about 7 tablespoons/100 ml of boiling water, stir into the purée and season with salt. Serve the sauce cold with fried or broiled chicken.

Walnuts

The walnut tree probably originates from Asia Minor and spread along the Silk Road as far as China. The Greeks brought it to Europe in the 7th to 5th centuries B.C. Even then the tree enjoyed great respect with its imposing appearance. In Greece, the nuts were called "divine spheres"; the Romans dedicated the majestic timber to Jupiter, which provides the current Latin generic term *Juglans regia* ("Jupiter acorn"). In ancient times, the tree symbolized long life, and even today its fruits are a symbol of fertility and abundance.

Whether the Georgians obtained their love for this nut from their Persian and Arabic conquerors, or whether they had fallen in love with it earlier remains unclear. In any case, even today many customs are witness to the special position and symbolic force of this old cultivated tree. On his travels in Georgia in the mid-18th century, the German traveler Friedrich Guldenstadt observed the rituals of a funeral in the countryside: "The bark of a beautiful walnut tree next to the house of mourning was cut into all the way

around so that it could die at the same time as the owner of the house."

The walnut tree is a deciduous cultivated tree type. It is at home in eastern Turkey, across Armenia, Georgia and Iran to China, Korea, and Japan. It also grows at altitude, loves a sunny, open position and can live for over 150 years. The nuts can be harvested from September to October, about five months after flowering. One tree can produce 45–65 lb/20–30 kg of nuts.

In Georgia, walnut trees can grow up to about 5,000 ft/1,500 m above sea level. The aromatic nuts come from Kakhetia and, like vines, they develop more flavor-forming substances in the bracing continental climate of east Georgia, with its longer period of ripening, than the rapid-growing fruit from warm and humid areas. At harvest time, the farmers spread large cloths under the spherical crowns of the trees and knock down the nuts using long hoes and sticks.

The nut is an absolute must in Georgian cuisine and its possible uses are almost limitless. Walnuts are an indispensable ingredient in many vegetable dishes and sauces, as well as in soups, bean stews, meat and fish dishes, and in baking. They are dunked into thickened grape juice for the typically Georgian confectionary *churchkhela* and

Walnuts are a main component of Georgian cuisine. They are generally shelled by hand. In folk culture they symbolize both miserliness and honesty.

covered in honey and sugar for *gozinaki* candy. Even home-produced walnut oil can be found in some households. For this, the nuts are pounded in a mortar until the amber-colored oil emerges. Walnuts are also frequently used even during periods of fasting. On over 100 days of abstention, these calorific, nutritious nuts are a welcome supplement to the menu. They provide up to 65 percent fat per 100 grams fresh weight, a high proportion of which is in the form of vital unsaturated fatty acids and linoleic acid. In addition to protein, vitamins B1 and C, these nuts provide the body with numerous minerals and trace elements. A form of bottled fruit extremely rich in vitamin C is provided by green nuts *(kaklis muraba)*, harvested when unripe and preserved with plenty of sugar. The Georgians love this as a sweet delicacy.

Dried calendula and marigolds are used in Georgia instead of saffron.

Saffron alternatives

From ancient times to today, saffron has divided humanity into the rich and the poor. The cultivation and processing of this noble plant has always been so labor-intensive and arduous that real saffron (see page 322 f.) has remained the most expensive spice in the world and is seldom used today in Georgia.

Even when the Persian King Darius allowed this valuable delicacy to be grown in the Caucasus in the 5th century B.C., his contemporaries were aware of alternatives to this aromatic plant that provides strong yellow coloring: pot marigolds *(calendula)* were used as the "poor man's saffron" from Persia, across the Caucasus to Greece, and then later in the whole of the Mediterranean area. The dried petals were a popular addition to soups and syrups. In some areas of Georgia, the orange-colored petals are still used to color and flavor sauces. Not as healthy as calendula with its antispasmodic and blood-cleansing effects, but more intense in flavor are the bright yellow to orange colored petals of marigolds *(tagetes)*, also called "Imeretic saffron" in Georgia. Their crushed, dried petals, smelling strongly resinous, are also frequently used in the spice mixture *khmeli suneli* (see page 228) as a saffron alternative. The quantities required are best left up to the experts, as too much of the plant can be poisonous.

Indauris satsivi
Turkey with walnut sauce
(Serves 6 to 8)

1 young turkey weighing about 2–3 kg, oven-ready
3 bay leaves
5 medium onions (11)
1 tbsp finely chopped fresh tarragon
Salt (4)
2½ cups/250 finely ground walnuts (7)
3 garlic cloves, crushed (8)
3 tsp khmeli suneli (1 tsp each of saffron or marigold
(5), fenugreek (1) and coriander seeds (6), ground)
½ tsp ground cinnamon (10)
½ tsp ground cloves (2)
Wine vinegar to taste (3)
2 tbsp fat from the poultry stock
1 tsp paprika (9)

Completely cover the turkey with cold water, add the bay leaves, 1 onion (halved) and tarragon, bring briefly to a boil and then simmer for about 1 hour over the lowest possible heat. Remove the bird from the stock, rub inside and out with salt and roast on a rack in a preheated oven at 350 °F/180 °C until golden brown, basting continually with small quantities of stock. Leave the turkey to cool slightly and then divide carefully into portions. Leave the remaining stock to cool, then skim off the fat. Mix the walnuts, garlic, and spices thoroughly into the vinegar and about 1½ quarts/1½ liters of hot stock (the sauce should not be too thin!). Finely chop the remaining onions and fry in the poultry fat, then add to the sauce and season with salt and paprika. Pour the sauce over the turkey pieces and leave to cool. Satsivi is served cold and is popular with corn porridge (*ghomi*, see page 237).

An evening with Tamada

Sunday afternoon in Tbilisi. The table in the living room is bending under the weight of innumerable plates of cheese, spinach with nuts, trout, cold chicken, suckling pig, and dishes of various delicious cold sauces. As is standard in Georgia, all of the dishes are brought out at once. "A small snack with my family," was how it was described in the invitation from our friend Giorgi. Fifteen family members sit down together with us at the table and start loading the zakuski onto small plates. Giorgi's sister is still looking for places to put the plates of hot corn flatbread, cheese, and pasta dough pockets.

Vaktang, the head of the family, took the chair at the head of the table: "We Georgians say: the guest comes from God. Therefore I would like to thank God for sending these fine people to our table. May their feet bring happiness to our house. *Gaumarjos!*" After this Georgian toast, we lift out glasses, filled with Kakhetian wine. What could we say in response? A look from the master of ceremonies stops me. Giorgi jokes: "Order is the rule at the Georgian table. You must be aware that the *tamada* has supreme power at the table. He determines not only the order of toasts, he also names the people who may speak apart from him." With the expression *alaverdi shentana var*, the tamada gives a guest selected by him the honor of verbosely and poetically developing his toast.

The Georgians could not imagine a celebratory table without a tamada. The high art of celebration is developed not only though cheery dinner parties *(keipi)*, which take place at joyful events such as weddings, Christenings, birthdays, and religious holidays. The progress of simpler meals, invitations, and funeral wakes are also structured by eloquent masters of ceremony and often raised to an art form. The host or the guests generally select an elderly man, rich in life's experiences, for this honorary office. As an expert in the customs and traditions, he celebrates societal standards and religious philosophies of life in a strongly ritualized sequence of toasts. So right at the start, people drink to the celebrant, at a birthday, for example, and then to the host and his family.

Khatuna, Giorgi's wife, serves roast kid and beef cooked in wine. Because of the lack of space, she sets the plates so they overlap slightly and replaces the crockery in front of us. Toasts to relatives, the parents, and those who have died bring tears to the eyes of one woman. With a sonorous voice, the tamada tries to alleviate her pain: "Wine is an agent against grief, but it is not an agent to reduce melancholy. That is why I am now drinking to life. There is much in the world that is beautiful: the strength of the oxen, the dew in the morning, the richness of the earth, the pressing of wine, the smile of a pretty woman, the heart of a knight. But the most beautiful thing is the growth of a new generation. To life and to children: *Gaumarjos!*"

The men empty their glasses; the women sip carefully. Soon, all have flushed cheeks and jackets are hanging over the backs of seats. The great grandfather, who is already rather frail, is brought in, and almost before he is seated he has snaffled some suckling pig and cheese. "*Sakartvelos gaumarjos:* To the homeland of the Georgians! And to that of the guest!" At this point, the old man explains that in his home village there is a custom of drinking the glass empty and then shaking out the last drops, because these indicate the number of enemies. Therefore it is important not to leave too much in the glass. Then he slaps us on the shoulders and says: "But what would a real man be without enemies?"

Where plates have slowly become emptied, the women fill the gaps with cheese here, meat and fish dishes there, and do not enjoy a break until the resonant *kartvel dedas gaumarjos!* sounds: "To the mothers of Georgia!" Drinking horns are brought in and emptied in one movement in a toast to the Georgian folk heroes. These include Queen Tamara (1184–1213), who ruled her land with kindness, tolerance and diplomatic skill, and

The master of ceremonies at the table is a popular motif in Georgian art and literature, as in the painting *Tamada* by the famous naïve painter Niko Pirosmani (1862–1918). The men raise typical ibex horns containing wine for the toast, proposed by the bearded head of the table.

the national poet Shota Rustaveli, whose name has been passed down through the national epic *Vepkhis Tkaosani* ("The Warrior in Tiger Skin") produced at the turn of the 12th century. The heroes of the homeland of the guests are also remembered. In the heat of the living room, the fragrances of spices, roast meat and wine are building up. Tarts and pieces of walnut confectionery, accompanied by a little glass of black tea compete with high-piled bowls of fruit as the finale to the meal. Here and there is a push or a movement, because the hearty dishes remain on the table until the end so that late-arriving guests, who are always welcome, can share in the eating of the whole celebratory meal.

The toasts now stress the positive characteristics of those present. Khatuna smilingly declares: "The table is just like psychotherapy for us. In my home country of Kakhetia, we often say before a feast: come to the table, and let us praise each other." On the way home, we can feel what she meant by this. We feel fortified in every possible way.

So far, only Alexandre Dumas has proved to be more resilient to drink than his hosts at the Georgian table. When the merry French writer of adventure novels such as *The Three Musketeers* and *The Count of Monte Cristo* received a "drinker's certificate" on his travels through Georgia in 1858, like many other foreign guests in the Caucasus, he did not know what had hit him.

Corn is the most important staple foodstuff in west Georgia. The farmers bring large woven carrying baskets of harvest from the fields and empty them in a heap in front of the barn.

Right: Before processing, the women remove the covering leaves and threads from the corncobs.

Corn: the staple

Some west Georgians insist on believing that the cradle of the corn plant lay in Georgia and not in the ancient empires of the Aztecs, Incas, and Maya. For *simindi*, as they call their corn, has over many years become the main basic foodstuff in the western provinces of Imeretia, Mingrelia, and Guria. The golden grain came with Columbus to Spain in 1493, from where it began its triumphal march across the old world. The Turks were particularly helpful in this, as they spread this ancient cultivated plant across their area of authority at that time, from North Africa to Budapest.

In Guria in west Georgia, the Turkish conquerors allowed corn to be cultivated for the first time in the mid-17th century. It felt very much at home in the warm, humid climate that predominated there and spread from Guria to Mingrelia as a competitor to local grains such as millet and wheat.

Although corn is now cultivated across the whole of the country, people in the east of Georgia still make their daily bread from wheat flour. On the other hand, corn flour is used exclusively for the daily bread in west Georgia: *mchadi* is a relatively heavy flatbread. Corn flour is not suitable for airy loaves or thin flatbreads because it lacks the gluten specific to other grain types that is required to hold the dough together.

Corn, honored by the American Indians, is particularly healthy because each grain contains a full load of carbohydrate, high-quality protein, unsaturated fatty acids, and numerous minerals and trace elements such as potassium, magnesium, and fluorine. Fresh corn grains additionally contain pro-vitamin A, B vitamins and vitamin C. The protein building blocks of niacin and lysine can only form correctly when combined with pulses or milk products. Therefore corn porridge *ghomi*, enriched with slices of *sulguni* cheese or beans, or the corn and cheese porridge *elarji* are particularly valuable meals, often the only meal of the day for the west Georgians, who live in comparatively poor conditions. On more lavish tables and at celebrations, corn porridge is popular served with cheese as a starter. White flour corn is preferred for the preparation of porridge and flatbread. Yellow sweetcorn *(tkbili)* is boiled or grilled fresh from the harvest and chewed directly from the cob.

Mchadi
Corn bread

2 cups/200 g corn flour
1 pinch salt

Make a dough from the corn flour, 1 cup/250 ml water, and salt. With cold, wet hands, form the dough into a ball and then spread out about ½ inch/1 cm thick on a baking sheet (ideally one with a non-stick coating) and bake in a preheated oven at 350 °F/180 °C for about 20 minutes. When done, cut the corn flatbread into portions and serve warm, with an appetizer or salads. Will not keep longer than 24 hours.

Variation: Bake a ½-inch/1-cm thick layer of dough for about 10 minutes in a lidded earthenware pan or a pie plate on the hob, then turn and finish cooking, uncovered.

Tip: The quantities required for the dough can also be measured out simply using a measuring beaker or a cup at the ratio of 2:1 (corn flour to water).

Sulguni

Gvantsa Tetrishvili did not want to go without *sulguni* even at times when salaries were low. Therefore the engineer learned how to prepare this Georgian delicacy herself in her one-roomed apartment on the outskirts of Tbilisi. The recipe for this most popular Georgian cheese came from her mother from Mingrelia, and the milk from farmers whose herds of cows and sheep grazed on the edge of her estate. Today, all milk types and mixtures, but mainly cows' milk, are used to make sulguni, a type of fermented cheese originally made just from buffalo milk. The milk is processed fresh or pasteurized.

Gvantsa pours fresh milk from a 5 quart/5-liter container through a cloth into a tall, enamel pan. On her gas stove in the kitchen, she heats the milk to 86 to 95 °F/30–35 °C. A couple of drops of pepsin, an enzyme from the abomasum, available from the pharmacy, initiates the fermentation process. With her finger, Gvantsa regularly checks the temperature in the pan. After about one hour, the milk has turned into a thick, smooth mass. "Now you stir hard," explained the engineer, swinging her wooden spoon. "The temperature must remain even across the whole of the pan." After another 10 minutes on the stove, a little yellowish whey finally starts to form above the jelly-like milk mass.

"Now comes the real work," warns Gvantsa, and turns down the heat as low as possible. Her prac-

ticed fingers carefully crumble the curds of milk into hazelnut-sized pieces, so that the whey can emerge. The curds that are produced are again heated briefly to 86–95 °F/30–35 °C until they are dry and sticky and can be formed into a ball. Gvantsa's hands work very carefully because about 20 percent of the whey must remain in the cheese mass during pressing. The acidic liquid causes the ripening process in the cheese.

Now Gvantsa rubs the cheese with salt and leaves it to rest until next morning in a wooden sieve. These sieves are only used once. A melt test is used to determine whether the mass is sufficiently ripe for processing: After about 3 minutes in water at 176 °F/80 °C, the cheese sample is elastic and stretchy. Gvantsa is pleased. With a sharp knife, she cuts the young cheese into thin slices and melts them in milk heated to 158 °F/70 °C, stirring continuously, to form a smooth, sticky mass. "Like chewing gum," she remarks, and places the cheese mass on the table. Her petite hands, strenuously pulling, folding and rolling, produce a smooth cheese. To keep its form, it is immersed briefly in cold water. Placed in 16–18 percent brine, sulguni will keep in the refrigerator for 14 days, or for just a few days at room temperature.

To make sulguni cheese, buffalo milk is traditionally used. This is heated and then mixed with an enzyme from the abomasum (pepsin).

As a result of the curdling process initiated in this way, the whey gradually collects through stirring and gently pressing the curds.

The curds are formed into a ball by hand, then shaped into a loaf and salted.

Sulguni cheese is placed in salt water so that it will keep. It can be enjoyed fresh or smoked.

Corn porridge *(ghomi)* with sulguni cheese is also served as an appetizer in celebratory meals in west Georgia.

Left, background: Some cheeses show the pattern of the drainage sieve; others are smooth.

Elarji
Corn and cheese porridge

¾ cup/100 g corn semolina
Salt
⅔ cup/100 g very fine corn flour
3 cups/350 g sulguni cheese, or buffalo mozzarella, cut into small pieces

Bring the corn semolina to the boil in 3⅓ cups/800 ml lightly salted water, stirring continually, and then leave to swell for about 10 minutes over the lowest possible heat, stirring occasionally. Gradually sprinkle on the corn flour, stirring continually, and simmer for a further 15 minutes at the lowest possible heat to form a porridge, stirring occasionally to prevent sticking. Remove from the heat, add the cheese and stir over a very low heat until it is completely incorporated. Serve hot.

Corn semolina and corn flour in about equal proportions are the basic ingredients for Georgian corn porridge. For *elarji*, sulguni cheese, popular everywhere, is included.

When the corn porridge has swelled, the sulguni cheese is vigorously stirred in. This should produce a smooth mass with no lumps of cheese.

To serve, Georgian housewives pull the corn and cheese porridge into long strands and arrange it decoratively on a plate.

As an alternative, simple corn porridge *(ghomi)* is also popular with slices of smoked sulguni.

From the rivers and sea

Freshly-caught fish is served not only in the Georgian harbors of the Black Sea such as Poti and Batumi. Meals in the capital city to which people are invited also include fresh fish to give tone, and in the Tbilisi market hall *Desertiris Basari*, the supply ranges from fresh cod from the Baltic, sturgeon from Azerbaijan, through fresh herring from the Black Sea to domestic freshwater fish.

There is a rich variety of the latter in Georgia's rivers and lakes. Four different subspecies of river trout *(kalmachi)* swim about in the cool, oxygen-rich rivers of the Caucasian mountain regions. The Georgians prefer cooking them in salt water and serving them with a rich walnut or cornelian cherry sauce. The preparation of *khramuli*, a fish species that only occurs in the Caucasus is very simple: for the dish *tsotskhali*, the small, shiny, silvery fish are just cooked in boiling water without any salt.

Freshwater barbells like the *chanari*, which can weigh up to 13 lb/6 kg, or the spindle-shaped, pike-like *murtsa* are loved but rare fishing trophies. More frequently, carp *(kobri)* bite, and these are also farmed in ponds and artificial lakes. Their relatively oily flesh is tasty boiled, stewed or fried, and is particularly aromatic stuffed with walnuts and pomegranates seeds. The giant of the freshwater fish is the catfish *(loko)*. This predator can grow up to 16 feet/5 m long and weigh up to 6½ cwt (US)/300 kg. Its very lean flesh is boiled and served with vinegar and cilantro as an incomparable treat.

However, the existence of this commuter between rivers, lakes, and coastal waters is threatened just like the few remaining fish species in the Black Sea. Known in ancient times as a sea very rich in fish, there were still 23 species of fish sheltering here 30 years ago, of which only five now remain. The reason for this is first and foremost over-fishing, as well as sewage and industrial waste, fed into the sea by rivers from the 17 states neighboring the Black Sea basin. In the mid-1980s, the suffering ecosystem was knocked further out of balance. A type of jellyfish, brought into the Black Sea by ships from the Atlantic, robbed the fish of their food base, as they fed on fish larvae and small fish. Since the end of the 1990s, an attempt has been made through a ban on fishing to prevent the eradication of the sturgeon, the flounder, and the Black Sea salmon, which is a popular catch not only for its flesh but also for its roe. The reduction in the stock of herring and sterlett (sturgeon family) should also be arrested in the future through stricter monitoring of the size of catches.

The families of Georgian fishermen like to sell their small, fresh catches by the roadside.

Loqo kindzit
Boiled catfish with cilantro and vinegar

1 oven-ready catfish weighing 1³/₄ lb/800 g
Salt
2 bay leaves
1 bunch of cilantro, finely chopped
¹/₂ cup/125 ml white wine vinegar

Place the oven-ready catfish in a pan or fish kettle. Pour boiling water in to cover the whole fish. Add salt and the bay leaves and poach until tender, covered, for 30–40 minutes, or until tender, over the lowest possible heat, skimming the liquid with a flat skimmer from time to time. Remove the fish from the pan, cut into portions and keep warm in a covered dish. Strain the cooking liquid, stir the finely chopped cilantro into the white wine vinegar and add 1–2 cups of cooking liquid. Pour this sauce over the cooked catfish before serving.

Kalmakhi nigvzit da brotseulit
Stuffed trout with walnuts and pomegranate

4 oven-ready trout, weighing about ¾ lb/300 g each
Salt
1 cup/75 g walnuts, crushed with a pestle and
mortar
2 small onions, chopped finely
Seeds of 1 large pomegranate
2–3 tsp paprika
1 tsp each of ground cinnamon and ground cloves
2 tbsp flour
4 tbsp oil

Wash the trout, rub with salt and leave to rest for
30 minutes. Mix the walnuts, onions, pomegranate
seeds, and spices together. Stuff the fish cavity and
close using wooden toothpicks. Carefully coat in
flour. Heat the oil in a skillet and fry the trout on
both sides until golden brown and crispy.

Shemtsvari zutkhi pamidvrit
Fried sturgeon with tomato sauce

5 medium tomatoes, skinned and sieved
Oil
3 cloves of garlic, chopped
1 small dried chile pepper, seeded and chopped
2 tsp paprika
1 bunch each of cilantro and parsley, chopped
Salt
4 slices of sturgeon, each weighing 5–7 oz/
150–200 g
2 large onions, sliced into rings

Cook the sieved tomatoes in 1–2 tablespoons oil to
achieve a thick sauce. Process the garlic, chile,
paprika, and herbs into a paste using a pestle and
mortar, season with salt, add to the tomato sauce
and simmer for a few minutes. Salt the sturgeon
slices and fry on both sides in oil until crispy.
Arrange the fish on a plate, cover with the fried
onion rings and pour over the tomato sauce.
Variation: The sturgeon can also be served with a
pomegranate sauce (see also page 229).

The tricks of Medea

Without Medea, Jason could not have succeeded in his quest. According to the saga of the Argonauts, the son of the king of Greece set off with his ship to the legendary Colchis in what is now Georgia. His uncle Pelias, King of Iolcos, gave him the task of bringing the Golden Fleece (a sheepskin of pure gold) back to Greece. Only then would he hand over the rule of his kingdom to Jason. This was no simple task, for the Golden Fleece was guarded by a dragon. Luckily, Medea, a herbalist sorceress and the daughter of the king of Colchis, fell in love with Jason. Thanks to her magic and tinctures, the courageous Greek was able to regain the treasure.

Pelias and Jason's father, Æson, had in the interim become old men. However, Medea gave Æson new vitality and youth by taking old blood from him through a cut in his throat and filling him up with fresh blood. With Pelias, as he had not kept his promise to Jason, she settled the score by having him cut into pieces by his daughters under the pretext of receiving a similar rejuvenating cure.

Even today, Medea and her skill in bestowing health and eternal youth are remembered with pride in the former Colchis, now west Georgia and Abkhasia. Some see this herbalist as the first beautician and pharmacist.

The food of the centenarians

The scene is Rezo Gelashvili's garden on the outskirts of Martvili (Mingrelia): in front of the wooden house, a pig is rolling about in the afternoon sunshine. Rezo ends his long working day in the vegetable garden, puts his broom to one side and, from a heavy pottery jug, pours wine into small glasses. The 92-year-old farmer winks at us. His eyes twinkle with vitality and determination. He points toward his garden: "Look over there, my friends! This here and the eternal blue sky above us, that's Georgia and my Garden of Paradise. This little bit of land has fed my family for generations, and everything that my heart desires grows here; here grow the herbs that keep me young and handsome."

Rezo smiles mischievously, exposing perfect, white, sparkling teeth. Rezo has never been ill, he only knows of dentists through hearsay and he tends his field and garden alone with his third wife, the 50-year-old Natela. This sprightly man is no exception. In Georgia in the 1980s, 51 people per 100,000 inhabitants reached the age of 100 or more. Joie de vivre and health into biblical old age are proverbial for all the Caucasian peoples. However, gerontologists have been unable to completely reveal the secret of these Methuselahs, located between the Black Sea and the Caspian Sea. What has been proven is that the traditional food and lifestyles of the Caucasians support long life. Like his forefathers, Rezo eats strength-giving proteins mainly in the form of grain products: "We eat corn or millet porridge at any time of the day. We have *sulguni* cheese or nut oil with it. When working in the fields, a bit of corn flatbread is enough for me. I like to eat that with onion or cucumber."

The main meal in the evening for Rezo and Natela is generally bean or vegetable casseroles, eaten with a little lamb or chicken. Suckling pig, Rezo's favorite meal, is only eaten on special occasions such as family celebrations. The king of all the fitness foods is homemade yogurt (*matsoni*, see box). The immune system is also boosted by eating onions and garlic. Both of these bulbs, containing antibacterial agents, protect against infections. Eaten regularly, they prevent arteriosclerosis and high blood pressure. Polyunsaturated fatty acids, as contained in walnuts, provide unrestricted flow through blood vessels and thus an

Left: Healthy roots—the frequent consumption of onions and garlic could be one reason why many people in the Caucasus reach a very old age in good health.

To make matsoni yogurt, buffalo, cows' or sheep's milk is brought briefly to a boil in order to kill unwanted bacteria.

Then the milk is allowed to cool to about 98 °F/37 °C, and one cup or a small glass of matsoni with its yogurt bacteria is added for each 4 cups/1 liter milk.

Now the whole mixture must rest in an evenly warm place, covered, for at least half a day to allow the bacteria to work.

When ready, the matsoni is poured into jars and then eaten directly as it is, or used as an ingredient. Well cooled, this healthy yogurt will keep for a few days.

Matsoni

For the Georgians and their neighbors, *matsoni* is an ideal thirst-quencher and a healthy source of protein. The thin, liquid yogurt is drunk all day long like water. The health-promoting effect of the lactic-acid bacteria contained in it is medically proven: *L.B. elbrueckii lactis* provides healthy intestinal flora and can thus help to prevent many illnesses, whose cause can be traced back to a weak immune system.

Matsoni is generally made by farmers or in private households. Buffalo or cows' milk, and sometimes also sheep's milk is brought to a boil to kill any putrefactive bacteria. Then the milk is allowed to cool to about 98 °F/37 °C, one cup of matsoni is added for each 1 liter of milk and the whole mixture is left in a warm place for 12 to 24 hours. The lactic acid bacteria change the milk protein, which makes the yogurt acidic, which at the same time means that it will keep longer than fresh milk. Homemade matsoni is sold in jars or bottles at markets. Many dairies have also brought industrially-produced matsoni onto the market, but this does not come close to the flavor of homemade yogurt.

Matsoni is a popular drink and is thinned with water, depending on its consistency. In addition, it is used in yogurt soup (see page 220), and particularly modern Georgians enjoy it with fresh fruit for breakfast. As an alternative to genuine Georgian matsoni, Turkish or Bulgarian yogurt is suitable. It must be a little more liquid and acid than the standard yogurt in many west European countries.

adequate consumption helps to reduce the risk of heart attacks and inflammations.

The many spices and wild herbs that are picked fresh each day and eaten raw, such as basil, cilantro, purslane, parsley, mint, and tarragon, as well as stinging nettles and sorrel, stimulate the metabolism and are rich in vitamins. The varied, vitamin-rich food becomes the purest elixir of life when living conditions are also agreeable: "It is

quite simple," says Rezo contentedly, "I love my daily work in the fresh air, my wonderful wife and my many grandchildren, who always treat me with respect and honor."

Poultry and game birds

Katmis mkhali
Cold chicken appetizer
(Illustration top centre)

1 cooked chicken weighing about 2¼ lb/1 kg
2 cups/200 g walnut kernels, finely chopped
2 cloves garlic, crushed
1½ tsp khmeli suneli (½ tsp each of saffron, fenugreek
and coriander seeds, ground)
1 bunch cilantro, finely chopped
4 scallions, finely chopped
1 tbsp wine vinegar
3–5 tbsp chicken stock
Salt and pepper
Seeds from one pomegranate
1 green bell pepper, finely chopped

Remove the cooked chicken meat from the bones, cut into small pieces and arrange in a deep dish.
Pound the chopped walnuts with the crushed garlic in a pestle and mortar and add the *khmeli suneli*, cilantro, scallions, wine vinegar, and some chicken stock. Season with salt and pepper. Pour this sauce evenly over the chicken.
Set aside for a short time to develop the flavors. Serve garnished with pomegranate seeds and the chopped pepper.

Chakhokhbili
Poultry casserole with tomatoes
(Illustration centre)

1 oven-ready pheasant or 1 large chicken
4 medium-sized onions, cut into half-moon slices
About ⅓ cup/75 g butter
5–6 large tomatoes, skinned and diced
1 bay leaf
1 bunch of mixed herbs (e.g. mint, tarragon, basil, cilantro, parsley, celery leaves), finely chopped
Salt and freshly-ground black pepper
Paprika

Cut the bird into portions and cook in a warmed, heat-proof casserole over low heat, covered, for 5–10 minutes without the addition of any fat or water. Pour off the juices produced and set aside. Fry the meat for 10–15 minutes, uncovered, until lightly golden, turning now and again and adding some of the juices to prevent sticking.
Fry the onions in the butter for a few minutes until they are golden yellow. Then pour on the rest of the liquid or a little water and add to the meat along with the tomatoes and bay leaf.
Cook the whole dish for about 30 minutes over medium heat, covered, stirring now and again. Remove from the heat, add the herbs, season with salt, pepper and paprika and then leave over the lowest possible heat for another 5 minutes.
Fresh bread or potatoes go well with chakhokhbili.

The birth of the city of Tbilisi

Once upon a time, so the story goes, the marshes of the River Mtkvari were covered in forests. This is where King Vakhtang Gorgasali went hunting. In the thickets of the forest, his hunting dogs startled a pheasant; the king's sparrowhawk began hunting the pheasant and soon both birds disappeared from view. The king and his retinue started on a long search and made an amazing discovery: the sparrowhawk and the pheasant were lying in a hot spring, beautifully cooked, as if in a cooking pot. In the fight, both birds had fallen into the steaming water. Fascinated by this natural spectacle, the king reconnoitered the area and came across other hot springs. When the sovereign heard that the water from the springs had healing powers, he decided to found a town on this site. At the end of the 5th century, he named the town *Tbilisi*, from the Georgian word *tbili*, meaning "warm," and its inhabitants still bathe in hot spring water in the public baths.

View of Tbilisi old town—the foreground shows the domes of the public baths, the rooms of which are located underground. The sulfurous waters bubble into the pools at about 104 °F/40 °C.

Shemtsvari tsitsila–tabaka
Pan roast chicken

4 oven-ready young chickens (poussins or squat chickens), each weighing about 14oz/400 g
Paprika
Salt and pepper
4–6 garlic cloves, crushed
About 7 tbsp/100 g butter

Cut open the chickens along the breast bone, starting at the neck, turn over, beat flat and push the ends of the legs and wings through the slit in the breast. Then rub with the spices and garlic. Melt the butter in a large heavy-bottomed skillet or pan, but do not allow to brown. Put the chicken in the skillet, inner side downward and place a flat plate on top, weighted (with a heavy stone). When frying, the chicken must lie very flat on the pan base. Fry over medium heat, turning frequently, for about 30 minutes until golden brown. Serve with *tkemali* sauce (see page 229).

Background: Flatbread and a robust Georgian wine go particularly well with chicken tabaka.

A Georgian national dish is produced from simple ingredients such as a young chicken, garlic, and spices, using a clever method of preparation.

When the legs and wings have been pulled carefully through the slit in the chicken breast, the chicken is rubbed with the spices and garlic.

The chicken is pressed as flat as possible in the buttered pan and weighted down during frying so that it stays flat.

Basturmis mtsvadi
Marinated kebabs

2¼ lb/1 kg pork, beef or lamb
4 large onions
3 bay leaves
½–1 tsp black peppercorns, coarsely crushed
Salt
About 7 tbsp/100 ml wine vinegar
Pomegranate seeds to garnish

Cut the meat into large cubes and dice two of the onions. Marinate the meat for several hours with the onions, bay leaves, peppercorns and some salt in the vinegar, diluted with an equal amount of water. Thread the meat on skewers and grill over a glowing wood fire or charcoal barbeque. Salt to taste. Arrange the kebab skewers on a plate and garnish with rings from the remaining two onions (1) and the pomegranate seeds (2). Pickled green tomatoes (3), pickled bladdernuts (*jonjoli*, 4), tomatoes and scallions (5), wild *alucha* cherry plums (6, see page 260), *tkemali* sauce (7) or purslane (8) are also suitable accompaniments.
Variation: Fry the kebabs and finish them off in the oven.

Meaty meals

Chaqapuli
Lamb with sour plums
(Not illustrated)

7 oz/200 g fresh tkemali *plums*, or alternatively unripe
mirabelles or very sour plums
1¼ lb/600 g lamb suitable for pot-roasting
1 bunch scallions, finely chopped
Salt and pepper
7 tbsp/100 ml wine
½ bunch each of tarragon, cilantro, parsley and dill,
finely chopped

Scald the plums and remove the pits, leave to cool, and
then purée. Cut the lamb into bite-sized pieces and
cook, covered, over low heat without adding any fat.
When liquid starts to form, add the scallions, salt and
pepper, pour on the wine and continue to cook, covered, until the meat is almost tender, adding some hot
water now and again if required. Add the herbs and
puréed plums and enough hot water to cover, and simmer for another 20 minutes over the lowest possible
heat. Season and serve hot.

Kakhuri Katleti
Kakhetian-style meatballs
(Not illustrated)

7 oz/200 g dried cornelian cherries, pitted
2 large onions
Generous 1 lb/500 g ground beef
1 egg
Salt and pepper
Butter for frying

Soften one half of the cornelian cherries in lukewarm
water for at least 30 minutes. Purée or finely grate one
of the two onions. Purée the softened fruit and mix
with the grated onion, the ground beef, egg, salt and
pepper so that it combines a firm mixture. Shape small
oval meatballs from the mixture, press to flatten
slightly and fry on both sides in hot butter. Keep warm.
Finely chop the second onion, fry the remaining cornelian cherries in hot butter, add the second onion and
sweat over low heat. Arrange the meatballs on a serving plate and pour over the cherry mixture.

At *Alaverdoba*, the Georgian harvest festival (see page
249), freshly slaughtered sheep are skinned. Their meat
is cut into small pieces and added directly to the soup
pot on an open fire.

Tskhvris khortsi komshit
Mutton with quinces

1¼ lb/600 g mutton suitable for pot-roasting
3 medium-sized onions, finely chopped
Butter or goose fat for frying
1 cup/250 ml white wine
Salt
4–5 quinces
1 handful of fresh cilantro or parsley, finely chopped

Cut the meat into bite-sized cubes, fry with the onion
in the fat in a deep pan and then braise, covered, for
about 5 minutes. Add the white wine and enough
water to cover the cubes of meat; season with salt
and braise, covered, for about one hour over the lowest possible heat.
Meanwhile, peel the quinces, remove the core area
and cut the fruit into bite-sized cubes. Add the
quinces to the meat and braise, covered, until the
quinces are soft. Season with salt and sprinkle with
freshly chopped cilantro or chopped parsley before
serving.

Meat preservation

Over 3,000 years before the invention of the refrigerator, the people of the Near East and Transcaucasia had mastered the art of preserving meat. As the inhabitants of the rough mountain regions of Georgia still rarely have access to modern technology, the methods of preservation handed down over time are still current, be they ham manufacturing in Svaneti, Racha and parts of Kakhetia, or preserving beef, mutton or lamb by the Tushetians and other mountain people along the Aragvi River.

When placed in cooking salt (salting), moisture, and thus the feeding ground for bacteria, is drawn from the meat. Wood ash has the same effect (potash), and this has been used by the Svans for centuries as an alternative to salt. Dry salting is popular with the Khevsurs and Tushetians—beef or mutton is rubbed with salt and placed in a sealed wooden barrel for several weeks. When juices emerge from the meat, the salt gradually penetrates the muscle fibers and prevents the meat from spoiling. The more recent, air-dried meat specialty is called *kaghi* and can be kept for several months.

Wet salting is frequently the first stage in ham production: For aghmosavluri, and air-dried pork ham from Kakhetia, meat spiced with pepper and garlic is placed in brine for up to 40 days and then finally dried for one week in fresh air in a drying shed.

Smoked ham is a delicacy from the province of Racha. After salting and drying in the cold, pork ham is hung for several hours at a time over several days in the smoke of oak or elm wood. The Khevsurs carve deep cuts in the surface of fatty mutton, so that the spicy aroma also reaches the layers within during smoking.

For *mokheuri kaurma*, a preserved meat specialty of the Mokhevs, made only in the mountains for domestic consumption, different ingredients are used from the fat-tail sheep, the most important breed of sheep in Georgia (see also page 291): the innards and chopped meat of the sheep are sewn into a tube of animal skin, along with the chopped up fat-tail, and boiled in water until tears form on the surface. When buried deep in the earth, this meat can keep for up to one year. *Mokheuri kaurma* is eaten with bread, in stews or with vegetables, and is a practical food eaten by shepherds.

For *shignita*, a sausage made from lamb, the Tushetians fill fat and spiced chopped meat into intestines, whose ends are tied. Dried in a breezy and sunny spot, this sausage specialty can be kept for several years.

Sheep in sheepskin

Before the invention of the cooking pot, people used every possible type of vessel for cooking: bivalve shells, tortoise shells or ostrich eggs. Some of the early practices included cooking in pits in the ground, using heated stones, in vessels made from tree bark or wood and, last but not least, in animal skins. The latter are still used by the Mokhevs, the inhabitants of the high mountains in Georgia, who live as herdsmen and hunters near the Ingushetian border. For *gudis kaurma* ("meat in skin"), a freshly slaughtered sheep is skinned and the cleaned meat cut into large pieces, salted and sewn into the skin with halved onions, garlic cloves, and herbs. The contents of the filled animal skin are then cooked slowly between layers of glowing charcoal and hot ash in a pit in the ground. Comparable in effect to a roasting bag, the natural nutrients and flavors are maintained using this method of cooking, because the meat cooks in its own juice and fat. It is served in deep clay dishes.

Right: In Racha, pork ham is dried and then smoked over oak or elm wood.

Below: Salting is also one of the oldest methods of preservation in Georgia.

Georgian beer

Caucasian mountain inhabitants have been drinking beer since the 4th century B.C. —primarily at ritual events. Many mountain people in northern Georgia held fast to their cults associated with the consumption of beer in spite of their early conversion to Christianity, even after the conquering of Georgia by the Russians and the later period of the Tsars, as described by Konstantin Gamsachurdia (1893–1975) in his history *Mindia*: "On a religious holiday, the Khevsurs gathered at the shrine of Khakhmati … Ibex horns, filled with beer, were passed around the circles … In the great hall of the shrine, the priests and their acolytes sat at a table in a slightly intoxicated state, the ibex horns were passed in sequence from the oldest to the youngest."

Still a traditional drink today for the mountain people of the Khevsurs, Pshavs and Tushetians, in which grain is used in the simplest of ways, this grain juice is being increasingly well received today in the lowlands. The growth of demand was met in 1998 by the Georgian–French brewery "Castel-Sakartvelo," with their modern technology and good beers. In September 2005, the Georgian President Mikhail Saakashvili opened the "Natakhtari" brewery in the place of the same name, to the north of Tbilisi. The computer-controlled plant and the brewers come from the Czech Republic, and the raw materials from Germany.

Georgia is well known for its good beer (from left to right: two varieties of *Kazbegi*, *Topadze* and *Argo*. However, offering toasts using beer is frowned upon.

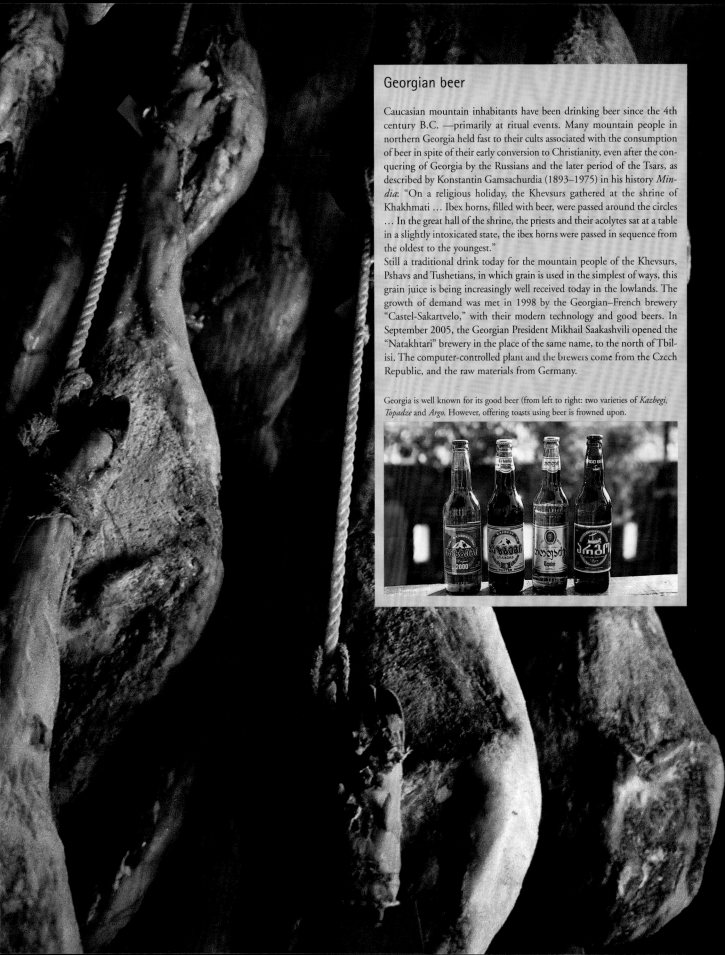

Top left: Traditionally, faithful Christians have their food blessed at the Alaverdoba festival in the cathedral. Bread and salt take pride of place, but people also like to bring their new harvest to the church.

Top right: The 11th-century Alaverdi cathedral in Telavi in east Georgian Kakhetia. It is the scene each year of the Alaverdoba festival, celebrated by both Christians and Muslims.

Left: Just like in pagan times, at the Alaverdoba festival the Georgians sacrifice animals, which are led three times around the cathedral before being slaughtered. Beverages such as wine must are also brought to the church for blessing.

Bottom left: Chickens and other poultry are also blessed in the Alaverdi cathedral and carried three times around the church. They then lose their lives as sacrificial animals or for the celebratory meal that takes place later.

Bottom right: Tents become temporary banqueting halls for the duration of the Alaverdoba, and people dine as opulently as at home. Even the wine flows—but naturally only for the Christians.

Alaverdoba

In early autumn, when the sun starts to bring color to the vine leaves in the east Georgian Alazani valley, and the scent of freshly pressed grapes starts to form in the houses, it is time for *Alaverdoba*. At the place of this archaic harvest festival to the northwest of Telavi, a small church was founded by Josef Alaverdeli in the mid 6th century. It was replaced by a cathedral at the start of the 11th century by the Kakhetian King Kvirike, and has borne the name Alaverdi ever since. How the festival got its name is still disputed to this day. The name of the cathedral may be responsible, but some researchers, on the other hand, think that the god of the sun and fire in pre-Christian times, Aladi, could possibly be the force behind the name's origin. Even at the start of the 20th century, sacrificial festivals are supposed to have taken place around the Alaverdi church in honor of the pagan god.

The festival is older than Christianity, as can be seen in the traditions and practices that can be traced back to pagan fertility cults and were then absorbed into the Christian Alaverdoba. These include the calculation of the date: in past and present times, the moon phases determine the Sunday in September on which the festival starts. For its part, the harvest must be brought in by the last full moon in September, and celebrations take place afterward.

Thanks to these ancient roots, Alaverdoba was and is the festival of all Kakhetians. Neither its Christian consecration in the 6th century, nor the conversion of one fifth of the east Georgian mountain people to Islam in the 17th century under the Persians have changed anything.

The inhabitants of Kakhetia and adjacent provinces make their way to the Alaverdi cathedral at the end of September to take part in the harvest festival within the protection of its walls. It is a bustling festival, which peacefully unites the Christians and the Muslims that live in the Alazani valley.

In the distance, you can hear the rhythmic clapping that accompanies the traditional songs of a Kakhetian trio. As though electrified by the beat of the drum and the lively bagpipe-sounding tone of the zurna, the dancers spin in a circle, stamping their feet, continually spurred on by the applause of the crowds around them. A singer presents old melodies to the sounds of a traditional stringed instrument, he sings of love, the hunt, and wine. Russian pop music from a car radio mixes in with the archaic tunes.

The first freshly slaughtered sacrificial animals (lambs and sheep) are hung up in the trees in large pieces. Knives are sharpened, meat is cut into kebab-sized portions and roasted over the open fire. Large families celebrate their reward for their work over the past year at tables set in their "tabernacles." Alongside grilled meat, they eat baked vegetables, fresh herbs, tomatoes, and cucumbers by the bushel, freshly baked bread from the traditional clay ovens *(tone)* and homemade *sulguni* cheese. Fresh fruit is heaped on the table, and for a sumptuous meal, wine naturally flows like a river.

In cars parked in the dust, children in their best clothes wait for the candies of the season: the grape and nut confectionery *churchkhela* hangs, surrounded by wasps, from wooden sticks like air-dried salami; a wiry old woman stirs a kettle of *pelamushi*, a type of pudding made from grape juice, and thickened with flour (see page 263). Between the fairground stalls and the high-wire dancers, people are pushing towards a ring in which young men are proving their strength. *"Mobrdsandit,* come here to the riding games," calls a man in traditional cavalryman costume, and the clusters of people now gather around him. Alaverdoba is today a material festival, but the pilgrims have still not forgotten the meaning of their festivities even in these modern times—in spite of the fairground hurly-burly and opulent feasts.

Alaverdoba is inseparably linked with the cult of wine. For Christian visitors, wine symbolizes the blood of Christ, and the grapes His tears. The work in the vineyard is, so to speak, service to the Lord. Before the festival, the grapes are picked and pressed, and then traditionally the young juice of the vine is drunk at the Alaverdoba. Before it flows by the liter down people's throats, the farmers have it blessed together with bread in the church. The Christian brothers in faith remain here. However, the Muslims share a ritual with some of them, which neither Islam nor the Christian Orthodox faith actually tolerates: they sacrifice animals—generally sheep—and drive these three times around the house of God before they are slaughtered.

Twilight is now falling, and the grill fires and the glow of bread ovens have long gone out. The sounds of guitars and laughter still come from a "tabernacle," which is decorated with colored rugs made from unspun wool. By nighttime the last religious constraints of the pilgrims fade away. A Muslim family happily accepts an invitation to the "tabernacle" of Christians from a neighboring village. Together they continue to feast, and the bread takes on a ritual significance: it is holy to all Caucasian people when broken, because it is said that bread ends family feuds.

Cooking under an open sky: during the festival, women prepare food on the meadows around the Alaverdi cathedral over open fires.

Transcaucasus, the cradle of wine

For seven millennia, wine has played a part in human culture. Long before Christ said of Himself, "I am the true vine," people in early times paid homage to this old cultivated plant. The Egyptians and the Sumerians, the Greeks and the Romans, consecrated this intoxicating drink to their gods and used the juice of the vine in their religious ceremonies and festivals. On the search for the origins of wine, old historiography, myths and legends point to the region between eastern Anatolia and the Transcaucasus. The first vines grown by humans were planted and the grapes pressed, according to the story of the Creation, on the slopes of Mount Ararat (see page 296). According to legend, the Greek god of wine, Dionysus, brought wine from eastern Asia Minor to Greece. Herodotus, the "father of historiography," was sure that Armenia had to be the land of origin of wine: in his times, ships laden with wine amphorae brought the noble liquid from the Transcaucasus down the Euphrates to Babylon. In early Armenian times,

Background: As in ancient times, clay jugs are still used for storing wine.

Below: Traditional treading of grapes in stone troughs is still customary in many villages.

there were already more than 40 types of vines on the slopes of Ararat. They came about through selection from the wild vine (*Vitis vinifera*), whose home since the last ice age extends through the temperate zones from the shores of Persia on the Caspian Sea to western Europe. Of those which are included with their 40 relatives in the family of ligniferous climbing plants (*vitis*) and which are widespread across the whole of the northern hemisphere, only this Eurasian subspecies is given the name *vinifera*: "wine bearing." Unlike its relatives, it has grapes that naturally tend toward fermentation with their high sugar content and their plentiful juice, yet at the same time are able to build up fresh tasting acids. Traces of their earliest cultivation also lead us to Georgia. Analysis of grape seeds from old sites proves that in the 5th century B.C. cultivated vines were being raised for the purpose of wine production. Five-thousand-year-old grave goods made from finger-sized, silvered pieces of vine wood and wine containers with capacities of up to 5,300 US gallons/20,000 liters are witness to the early place of honor of this old cultivated plant. Its cultivated form was in service in the second half of the 4th century B.C. in the production of this much loved drink over a range extending from Anatolia, through the Transcaucasus to the Zagros Mountains in today's western Iran. With its further expansion to the Near East, three main groups of vines developed, depending on the location, from which over 1,000 cultivated vine types have been produced around the world through further culture and selection. The vine *Vitis vinifera pontica* that originated in Anatolia and the Caucasus is the forerunner of many types that are today cultivated in southeastern Europe and Asia Minor. *Vitis vinifera orientalis* comes from the Jordan valley, and its European descendants include the Chasselas vine, grown in southwestern Germany and Switzerland. Many cold-resistant European red wine types such as Pinot Noir can be traced back to *Vitis vinifera occidentalis*. After the Phoenicians and Romans had laid the foundations for vine cultivation in Europe, the vine captured a place of honor across the whole of the Christian world. For the old Christian countries of the Transcaucasus, however, this drink, equated with the blood of Christ, has more than a religious symbolic power: it is also used to distinguish their identity from that of their Islamic neighbors.

Wine cultivation in Georgia

For many centuries, wine was the elixir of life, which nourished the economy of Georgia, the everyday life of its people, their Christian world view and, through this, their character and their difference from other peoples. Invaders continually tried to subjugate the Georgians by destroying their vines, as in the 16th to 18th centuries, when the Muslim Osmanlis and Persians fought for supremacy in the country. Even in more recent times, there was an action in which the winegrowers had to clear their vines themselves: in 1986, the former Soviet State and Party Leader Mikhail Gorbachev started a campaign to fight alcoholism. A drastic reduction in the production of wine and spirits was wanted, which equated to a deathblow for Georgian winegrowing. However, this campaign only lasted a short time, and Georgia is currently making efforts to rebuild its wine infrastructure.

Although Georgia is known internationally as the "cradle of wine," individual products are almost unknown in the West, as they were sold almost exclusively in the Soviet Union before its political upheavals. After the collapse of the Soviet Union in 1991 and its large market for wine, Georgian wine producers had the bitter experience of realizing that their products were uncompetitive on the world market. In the times of Soviet mass production, the development of individual qualities was impossible due to inadequate investment in modern cellarage techniques.

About 247,100 acres/100,000 hectares of vines were cultivated in the Soviet era, and the harvested grapes were processed in 42 state wine factories. With a transfer to a market economy and economic independence from Russia after the end of the Soviet Union, however, there was a shortage of grain, and an attempt was made to convert vineyards into arable land.

Currently, Georgia has about 148,000 acres/ 60,000 hectares of stocked vineyards, which have already been privatized in part. The Georgians are proud of their large number of vine types, which has been formed through their markedly different types of landscape and associated climatic features, as well as the different soil types of the Greater and Lesser Caucasus. The Institute of Viniculture in Tbilisi has counted about 500 types of vine growing on Georgian soil, out of at least 1,000 known types in the world. Some of these are only regionally significant. About 264,000 US gallons/1 million liters of wine is produced each year—one tenth of the quantity of former years. Numerous cellars have been converted into joint-stock companies, which have gradually been modernizing and introducing Western technologies with the support of foreign investors. At the Pro-Wein 2006 trade fair in Düsseldorf , visitors to the Georgian stand were able to sample several high-quality wines grown under modern conditions.

Harvest time in Kakhetia: the winegrowers proudly carry the fruits of their labor from the vineyard. Grapes grow particularly well on the black soil.

Kantsi, the drinking horn

Drinking horns have been known in many cultures since prehistoric times. In the Caucasus, hunters have for millennia used buffalo, bull or ibex horns as drinking vessels, and this custom has been maintained in Georgian culture to this day. Indeed, drinking horns are still only produced infrequently—unless as souvenirs for tourists—but almost every family has one old piece, passed down from generation to generation and used at festivities. The time for this is traditionally determined by the master of ceremonies at the table (*tamada*, see page 232 f), and the drinking horn is passed from man to man.

Because of its shape, a *kantsi* cannot be placed on the table and one is thus forced to empty it in one draught —a matter of honor for hard-drinking Georgians. A popular anecdote has grown up around these legendary horns. Once upon a time, Tsar Alexander II (1818–1881) invited Prince Gulbaat Chavchavadse to be the *tamada*. At the table, Gulbaat asked for a four-liter drinking horn, raised it to the Tsar and emptied it in one go. When he was about to pass the drinking horn to his neighbor at the table, he noticed that almost all the men had left—the only way out, because the court ceremony did not allow anyone to decline a toast to the sovereign. None of those present felt capable of emptying that giant horn of wine.

Drinking from the traditional *kantsi* is still a male privilege in Georgia.

At the wine harvest festivals here in Kakhetia, the men sing melodious folk part-songs.

Wine regions

Kakhetia

To the east of the capital city of Tbilisi lies the heartland of Georgian wine growing, an extremely fertile region with its brown and black soils and acres of alluvial land. The sunny climate is warm and temperate, almost subtropical. Wind and excessive rainfall from the north are held back by the Greater Caucasus, a range of mountains extending to over 16,500 feet/5,000 m above sea level. About 70 percent of the Georgian wine-growing area is located in Kakhetia with its giant vineyards. The province is characterized by the Alasani and Iori river valleys, which run almost parallel from northwest to southeast. The vines grow on riverside slopes and on fluvial plains at heights between 985 and 2,300 feet/300–700 m above sea level. Due to ideal growing conditions, all types of wine can be obtained from the most important vine types of Rkaziteli, Saparavi, Mtsvane, Khikhvi and Cabernet Sauvignon: dry European-type quality wines, small amounts obtained through the traditional Kakhetian process (see page 254), semisweet and dessert wines, types fortified with alcohol in western European style similar to sherry or port, as well as high quality brandies. The grape harvest *(rtveli)* is celebrated each year by the Kakhetians in colorful festivals.

Kartli

This densely settled area extends over the high plateau run through by the Mtkvari River between the Greater Caucasus in the north and the Lesser Caucasus on the border with Armenia. The climate is hot and dry with harsh winters. Kartli too is one of the original countries of vine cultivation, although its share is only about 15 percent. The most important vine types are Rkaziteli, Chinuri, Mtsvane, Aligoté, and Saperavi, from which dry and fortified table wines and sparking wines are produced.

Imeretia and Racha-Lechkhumi

About 10 percent of Georgian vineyards can be found on the slopes of the foothills of the Greater Caucasus and in the valleys of the Rioni and its tributaries. The climate in both of these provinces is exceedingly warm and humid, with hot summers and mild winters. Mainly Tsolikouri, Tsitska, Krakhuna, and Chkhaveri grapes are cultivated.

The coastal zone

Abkhasia, Mingrelia, Guria and Adsharia lie along the coast of the Black Sea. The climate of this hilly landscape, broken by plains, is subtropical, with frequent rainfall and plenty of warmth. The most important vine types here are Saperavi, Tsolikouri, Chkhaveri, Tetra, Isabella, and Aligoté.

Right: The Georgian vineyards are protected from the cold north wind at the foot of the Greater Caucasus.

Of all the winegrowing areas in Georgia, Kakhetia in the east provides the most grapes. Wine is even grown in the hilly land in the west.

Saperavi: the predominant black grape type has very dark-skinned fruit with slightly colored flesh. The dark, garnet-red wine is produced as a single type or blended with paler types. Due to ripening late, the grapes store high levels of sugar and extracts, but also a great deal of acid, which makes the wines good for keeping.

Rkaziteli: this white grape variety spread so widely from Georgia into all winegrowing areas of the former USSR that today it is one of the 10 most frequently grown vine types in the world. It provides good quality wine: piquant acid, with a flowery to spicy fragrance. In addition, the grapes develop high levels of sweetness and are processed into dessert as well as dry wines.

Isabella: the black grapes are a natural cross between American and European vines. This is one of the most cultivated hybrids in Georgia, Azerbaijan, and other winegrowing areas. Although it is one of the oldest of its type, its global spread is gradually receding. The rosé-colored wines have a hint of strawberry in their fragrance.

The wine harvest continues to be the high point of the year for hard-working winegrowers.

Wines

Winegrowing in Georgia is one of the leading branches of industry. However, winemaking in small operations is generally carried out according to inherited Kakhetian tradition: after the harvest, the grapes end up in a stone or wooden tub and are trodden with bare feet. Then the must is filled into large clay vessels *(kvevri)*. The wine—including the whites when the grapes are well ripened—remains here on the marc for some time even after the end of the fermentation process, which gives the wine more tannins and makes it better at keeping. To keep these earthenware vessels with their capacity of 26 US gallons/100 liters or more cool, they are buried deep in the earth; only their narrow necks are visible and they are sealed airtight with a stone and clay against fungal attack. In many families, wine is pressed in this way after the birth of a son, and it is stored until his wedding. In traditional cellars, wooden casks are hardly ever used.

But times are changing even in Georgia, and today people are turning to West European production methods in large, modernized cellars. The stems are removed, the grapes are crushed mechanically, the must is pressed and fermented for between two and four weeks in stainless steel tanks, then the wine is stabilized and strengthened under the exclusion of air.

The largest wine producer was once called "No. 1." Today, it is called "Georgian Wines and Spirits Comp." (GWS) and is a Georgian–French company, whose wines and spirits are sold by a Dutch subsidiary in Europe, the US, and also in Russia.

The West European idea of wines of certified origin and quality has not yet taken hold, and instead the term "brand wine" is used on the label, which indicates certain grape types and areas of origin. The simpler wines are called "table wine."

The best-known wines carry the names of their original locations, and a journey along the Kakhetian wine route is quite an experience for wine tourists. In addition to the lovely landscape at its most beautiful time of year, during harvesting you can experience the traditional forms of wine preparation and joyous wine festivals at harvest time.

Gurdzhaani is a dry white wine from Rkaziteli and Mtsvane grapes, which ripens for three years in oak casks and has a fine, bitter note. The provincial capital of Telavi was once the seat of the Kakhetian kings; the white wine of the same name pressed from Rkaziteli grapes obtains its bright amber color through its long traditional fermentation process on the marc. Other well-known Kakhetian wines (all with a European-style dry finish) are *Napareuli*, available as white wine from Rkaziteli and Mtsvane, or red wine from the Saperavi grape type, both varieties of which mature for three years in oak casks. *Manavi* is a pure type of white wine from the Mtsvane grape; storage for three years in oak casks produces a very subtle wine. *Tibaani*, produced in accordance with Kakhetian tradition, is much loved in Georgia due to its reported healing effects; its color is that of strong tea and it smells of raisins. Although produced from the white grapes of Rkaziteli and Mtsvane, it has a velvety texture with a light Madeira note.

One of the most exquisite red wines in Georgia is *Teliani*, pressed from Cabernet Sauvignon and enriched with a little Saperavi; it is stored for three years in oak casks, smells of violets and is velvety on the tongue. *Mukuzani*, another of the top red wines stored for three years, is made only of Saperavi grapes and has a robust acidity. In Georgia there are also a few semisweet wines worthy of mention: *Akhmeta* (from Mtsvane), *Akhasheni* and *Kindzmarauli* (both from Saperavi) from Kakhetia, *Khvanchkara* (from local vines) and *Tvishi* (from Tsolikouri) from the Rioni valley and Pirosmani (from Saperavi)—named after the famous Georgian artist of naïve painting, Niko Pirosmani.

Background: The largest wine producer in the country, "Georgian Wines & Spirits Comp.," clearly lays out its extensive range of wines and spirits.

Right: Many old wines are also stored in the cellars of the Chavchavadse family in Tsinandali.

Tsinandali

Tsinandali in the Alazani valley is one of the best-known wine locations in Kakhetia. At the time of the tsars, the very influential ruling Chavchavadse family built a picturesque park here in the English style, along with a residence. Today, the castle houses a lovingly maintained museum that presents the history of the family and gives an insight into the history of winegrowing in Georgia, which is rich in tradition. In the castle garden, there are also a number of witnesses to Georgian viniculture. The large cellar that belongs to it is not only a production site; the old vaults hold some museum pieces, quite apart from the most significant collection of old wine in the country—starting with the year 1814.

Tsinandali is also the name of one of the most well known Georgian white wines. Pressing is not carried out traditionally but as always in accordance with western European methods. This also includes a three-year period of maturation in oak casks. The wine, one of Georgia's best brand wines, is a cuvée of about 85 percent Rkaziteli and 15 percent Mtsvane. The soil and an ideal microclimate mean that wine of almost consistent good quality has been able to be produced each year since 1889. These wines are straw-yellow, dry, and have a pronounced fruit fragrance with just a hint of vanilla. *Tsinandali* received a gold medal at the World Exhibition in Chicago back in 1896.

From the vine to the pot

Kaurma
Liver in wine sauce

Generous 1 lb/500 g liver
4 cups/1 liter milk
2 tbsp/30 g butter or lard
2 medium-sized onions, finely chopped
1¼ cups/300 ml white wine
4 medium-sized tomatoes, skinned and diced
1 bunch each of parsley, cilantro, and dill, finely chopped
1 green bell pepper, diced
1 tsp paprika
Salt and pepper

Rinse the liver, soak in milk for about one hour, then rinse again, blot dry, and cut into finger-sized slices. Soften the onions in a little butter. Cook the strips of liver quickly without additional fat in a covered pan over low heat, pour off any liquid, then fry lightly in butter or lard. Add the onions, pour over the wine, add the tomatoes, and simmer gently until the liver is tender. Add the fresh herbs, bell pepper, and paprika, season with salt and pepper and serve immediately.

Cooking in an earthenware pot

The heart of Georgian pot making beats in the Imeretian village of Shrosha. Since the dawn of time, red earthenware clay has been dug and processed here. This natural material is turned on the wheel or used for free-form shapes. Due to its high proportion of minerals such as mica and quartz, the pot-making material from Shrosha is considered one of the lean clays. With its resilience, it is very suitable for the hand-made crockery made here or for larger vessels. The malleability of this natural material is restricted due to the grainy components, but this has been overcome by the Georgian potters through their dexterity, patience, and experience. After shaping, drying, and firing over several days in a wood-fired kiln, the ceramic remains porous. Therefore wine vessels must be impregnated from the outside using beeswax against moisture and humidity, as they will be buried in the earth, where they remain in good condition for a long time thanks to the cool and damp atmosphere. The inner walls remain untreated, as is the crockery. This has many advantages when used in the kitchen: as the pores can store moisture and release this slowly during cooking, a type of haze is produced in the sealed pot, which protects the food from drying out or sticking. In this way, food can be cooked in its own juice at a relatively low heat without the addition of fat or water. This gentle cooking method retains nutrients and flavors. As the latter also penetrate the pores of the earthenware walls and can have an effect on the flavor of dishes, the Georgians select their vessels according to their function: jugs of different sizes and shapes protect butter and yogurt from spoiling prematurely; a vase-shaped vessel *(dergi)* is used for storing cheese in brine. A wide pan with handles *(sasatsive)* is used for keeping turkey in walnut sauce *(satsivi)*; tall, covered pots such as *kvabi* or *sadoghari* are best for cooking *lobi*, a bean stew, or *chanakhi*, a meat stew. Corn bread or *Khachapuri* are baked without fat in an earthenware frying pan *(ketsi)*. Wine is traditionally stored in giant earthenware vessels: *kvevri* or *chasavali* —which translates as "for going down into," as a person has to climb into the vessel using a ladder for cleaning—can hold up to 660 US gallons/2,500 liters of wine and be 5 feet/1.5 m in diameter and 8 feet/2.5 m high.

Lobio nigvzit
Beans with walnuts

Generous 1 lb/500 g
dried red beans
(e.g. kidney beans)
2 cups/150 g finely chopped walnuts
2–3 garlic cloves, crushed
4–5 tbsp wine vinegar
1 bunch of mixed herbs (e.g. parsley, cilantro, celery leaves, dill), finely chopped
Salt
Parsley and cilantro to garnish

Soak the beans in cold water for at least 6 hours, drain, cover well in fresh cold water and bring to a boil and simmer until soft over low heat, topping up with more hot water if required. Pound the walnuts with the garlic in a mortar, add the wine vinegar and herbs, and mix this paste into the beans. Season with salt. Distribute between about 4 individual ovenproof earthenware bowls and bake in a preheated oven at 340 °F/170 °C for about 15 minutes. Sprinkle with freshly chopped parsley and cilantro before serving.

Gvriti kurdznita da makvlit
Wild pigeon with green grapes and blackberries

4 wild pigeons, oven-ready
Salt
4 tbsp melted butter
Breadcrumbs

For the sauce:
Generous 1 lb/500 g unripe green grapes
Generous 1 lb/500 g blackberries
3 cloves of garlic, crushed
1 bunch each of dill and cilantro, finely chopped
Salt

Salt the pigeons inside and out, brush with melted butter and coat in breadcrumbs. Place in a roasting pan and roast in a preheated oven at 440 °F/225 °C for 30–40 minutes, depending on size, occasionally pouring on some hot stock or water. For the sauce: set a few grapes and berries to one side as a garnish, and extract the juice from the remaining fruit using a juicer. Crush the garlic and herbs in a mortar, add salt, and stir this paste into the fruit juice, mixing well. Arrange the pigeon on a plate, pour over the sauce and serve garnished with grapes and blackberries.

Tolma
Stuffed grape leaves

8–9 oz/250 g each of beef and pork (or about 1 lb/ 500 g of lamb or beef if preferred)
2 large onions
5 cloves of garlic
1 bunch of parsley
$\frac{1}{2}$ tsp khmeli suneli (see page 228)
$\frac{1}{4}$ tsp hot paprika
Salt and pepper
1 cup/175 g cooked rice
4 tbsp tomato paste
About 25 grape leaves

For the yogurt sauce:
2 cups/500 ml matsoni yogurt, (alternatively Turkish or Bulgarian yogurt; failing that, whole milk yogurt)
5 cloves of garlic, crushed
1–2 bunches of mixed herbs (cilantro, parsley, basil), chopped

Grind the beef or pork with the onion, garlic, parsley and spices in a grinder, then mix in the rice and 2 tablespoons of tomato paste, stirring well until evenly mixed.

Remove the stems from the grape leaves, blanch by steaming briefly or pouring boiling water over, then rinse in cold water and leave to drain well and cool.

Shape the meat mixture into 20 small balls or rolls and put one ball on each leaf and roll up from the edges.

Line a pan with two or three grape leaves. Place the stuffed leaves in the pan so they fit closely together and cover with the remaining leaves.

Mix one pinch of paprika and two tablespoons of tomato paste into $\frac{1}{2}$ cup/125 ml water and pour over the grape leaves. Cover with a plate and simmer for 45 minutes over low heat. If necessary, top up with spoonfuls of hot water.

For the sauce: mix the yogurt with the crushed garlic and chopped herbs. Serve the stuffed grape leaves with the yogurt sauce. Eat hot or cold, as desired.

The grape leaves, stems removed, are blanched briefly in boiling water. Then each ball of meat mixture is wrapped in a leaf.

The stuffed grape leaves are placed in a pan lined with grape leaves, then covered with leaves, and cooked in a tomato stock.

When cooked, the stuffed vine leaves (*tolma*) are arranged on a plate and served with a sauce made from *matsoni* yogurt, garlic and herbs.

Citrus fruit

Georgia could have been called the "Citrus Republic" in the Soviet era. The narrow strip of Georgia along the Black Sea coast provided almost 100 percent of the USSR's consumption of these sunny fruit. At the end of the 19th century, the Russian tsars made preparations for enormous sales of citrus fruit by cultivating exotic plants and fruit in the subtropical climate of Abkhasia, Mingrelia, and Adzharia, making their dream come true of having their own colonial goods. The lemon, already successfully cultivated on the western coast, was an encouragement to the colonial masters to lay out gardens for limes, oranges, mandarins, grapefruit, and shaddock (pomelo), unknown in the area at that time.

Under the collective economy in the Soviet Union, these luxury fruit that originated in the Far East became mass goods, ripening over an area of cultivation of 66,700 acres/27,000 hectares. Today, the majority of plantations are in the Autonomous Republic of Abkhasia. However, even in the west of Georgia, 50,000 metric tonnes of these subtropical fruit are picked each year.

Depending on the citrus variety and kind, these providers of vitamin C are harvested between October and the end of March. **Mandarins** are the most widespread. The most popular variant is the thin-skinned satsuma with fruit that is easy to segment. The number of **orange varieties** that have occurred over the course of the centuries through planned and spontaneous hybridization and the introduction of new varieties cannot be overlooked. The best known of these is the early-ripening navel, which is included in the blond oranges group because of its yellowish flesh. Its juicy content has no seeds thanks to a particular cultivation method, and is surrounded by a thick skin that is easy to peel.

The most popular Georgian blood orange type is Karalioki, with its characteristic reddish skin and a strong, occasionally sharp fragrance. The unassuming Meyer lemon, a hybrid between an orange and a lemon, is found as frequently as the classic lemon (see facing page). The fine-pored, light orange colored peel hides an extremely aromatic, acidic to slightly sweet flesh yielding lots of juice.

The **lime** is a tropical fruit, extremely sensitive to the cold, and only grows in particularly well-protected areas in Georgia. Even when fully ripe, the edible skin with its fine fragrance retains its green color, which only turns yellow at low temperatures. The **grapefruit** originally occurred as a cross between an orange and a shaddock. This hybrid, with its yellow or pink colored flesh, has been unable to oust the thick-skinned, large **shaddock** from the Georgian market, in spite of having a higher juice content.

Mandarin: this sweet fruit from China has been cultivated in Georgia for over 100 years.

Orange: there are many different varieties in Georgia of this "Apple from China" (Dutch *appelsina*, late Latin *sina* = China).

Lime: this tropical fruit has aromatic flesh; the juice and peel are used as seasoning.

Shaddock: this giant among citrus fruit can reach a diameter of up to 10 inch/25 cm.

Lemon: very rich in vitamin C. The juice is used to season soups in Georgia.

Grapefruit: this fruit, suspected as being a chance hybrid between a shaddock and an orange, is very juicy.

The lemon

The lemon, originating between the Himalayas and southern China, was a popular cultivated plant in the direct neighborhood of the Transcaucasus in ancient times. However, it was apparently the Turks or the Russians who closed one of the last gaps in the so-called citrus belt by planting lemons on Georgia's Black Sea coast. In this warm zone located between 40° north and 35° south, with its subtropical and temperate climate, the lemon tree produces its best fruit.

As splendidly as renowned types such as the Lisbon and the Villafranca grow in this sunny land, they are hardly considered in traditional Georgian cuisine—with one exception: the juice is a popular seasoning in tart soups such as *chikhirtma*, made from lamb or poultry. The lemon—and above all its juice—is primarily treasured as a remedy as it is believed to strengthen the immune system, thin the blood, and has antibacterial properties. The pectin contained in the peel and flesh helps to dispel poisons and waste products thanks to its superior binding ability. The etheric oils in the peel contain the flavorings that give cakes and desserts their fresh note. Grated lemon peel will keep for several months mixed with honey or sugar, and is a healthy form of sweetmeat.

In the Soviet era, the Caucasian "Citrus Republic" exchanged lemons for diesel. Even today, the fragrant citrus fruits from Georgia are still highly regarded in Moscow's fruit and vegetable markets.

1

3

6

4

5

6

Georgia's heavenly fruit

Cornelian cherry (1): the shrub or small tree with the yellow and red, cherry-like fruit is also known as the cornel cherry or cornus *(Cornus mas)* and is found across almost all of Europe. In central Europe, the cornelian cherry is mainly highly regarded as a hedge plant; in Georgia and in the Caucasus, on the other hand, the sweet-sour fruit *(shindi)* is well received in the kitchen: harvested in September and October, the dried fruit is turned into sauces, jams, liqueurs, fruit loaves, and used in the meatless soup eaten during periods of fasting, *shindis shechamandi* (see page 220).

Plums: sour plum types are preferred in Georgian cuisine. *Tkemali* (2) is a wild, sour plum *(Prunus divaricata Ladeb.)*, which when fully ripe has yellow and red fruit from ¾–1 inch/2–2.5 centimeters in diameter, like the closely related cherry plum *(Prunus cerasifera)*. Both of these, and a variety of the wild cherry plum, originally cultivated by the Persians, *alucha*, with its dark red to violet color, are used to prepare sauces and *tqlap*, a thin cake made from dried fruit purée. To make it, the pitted fruit are cooked until tender in a small amount of water and pressed through a sieve. The purée is then spread on a dampened wooden board and left in the sun to dry.
The mirabelle, also derived from the cherry plum; at least four different types of domestic plum *(Prunus domestica)*; (3) and the small black plum

ghoghnosho (Subspecies prunus insititia L.), all widespread in west Georgia, are well regarded in the kitchen as dessert and preserving fruit.

Jujube (4): the jujube *(unabi, Zizyphus jujube Mill.)* was cultivated in southern Europe in Roman times. It is native from the eastern Mediterranean, through the Near East, to China. In Georgia, the red reddish-brown, oval fruits grow wild on dry slopes. They ripen in August and September and are eaten raw in their skins as a dessert fruit. The flesh is similar in texture to a floury apple and the flavor is a mixture of baked apples and dates. Because of its high sugar content, jujubes are also often made into candied fruits.

Feijoa (5): the feijoa, originally from southern Brazil *(peikhoa, Acca sellowiana)* is a close relative of the guava, and appears similar from the outside. The fruit, with its green, leathery skin, grows in subtropical climatic zones and was brought by the Soviets to the Georgian Black Sea coast as an exotic product to augment this small, subtropical paradise. Due to the pineapple-like flavor of its white to salmon-colored flesh, this fruit, rich in vitamin C, is also called the pineapple guava. The fruits, with their small, edible seeds, ripen from October to December and due to their great gelling ability are suitable for making jams and jellies. They are also popular eaten raw because of their strong fragrance.

Medlar (6): the Latin name *Mespilus germanica L.* is misleading, as the medlar *(zgmartli)* comes from western Asia and today primarily occurs in the Black Sea area (not to be confused with the

loquat *Eriobotrya japonica*, whose fruits are rather smaller and generally yellow). The shrubs of this wild fruit are widespread across the whole of Georgia. The chestnut brown, pear shaped or round fruit ripen in October and November. Only after the effects of frost or over-ripening are the high levels of tannic acid reduced so that the soft flesh becomes acceptable. The fruits contain a lot of malic acid, which encourages digestion, vitamin B2, calcium, and phosphorus, and are eaten fresh or stewed.

Barberries (not shown): this unassuming shrub of the European barberry *(Berberis vulgaris)* that likes growing in dry locations, and whose natural area extends from western Europe across the Caucasus to the north of Iran, must be approached with caution, because apart from the orange to purple-red, elongated berries *(kotsakhuri)*, the plant is highly poisonous! The sour, almost transparent fruit are collected in autumn when fully ripe. The flesh of the fruit provides a real charge of vitamin C, and its high content of malic acid and fruit acids stimulates the digestion. As in Persian cuisine, these dried fruit are also used in Georgia to season meat dishes.

Mulberries

A disease that attacked the leaves of the mulberry tree around 1970 put an end to the fabric from the Tales of the Arabian Nights and a branch of industry for the Georgians for over 1,500 years: silk production. The mulberry tree epidemic stole the food from the silkworms. The tradition of raising silkworms, which started in China about 5,000 years ago, passed along the Silk Road to the Caucasus (see also page 328 f.) In Georgia, silk not only became an important export item and popular fabric for women's clothing, the traditional men's frock coat *(chokha)* was also made from coarsely spun silk yarn.

In 1887, the Caucasian Sericultural Center was founded in Tbilisi. This new university faculty looked into the breeding of healthy silkworms, as did the Ministry of Agriculture. To support this promising branch of industry, credits were issued, and 40 years ago the breeders in the main culti-

vation area of Kakhetia produced about 4,400 metric tonnes of silk pupae.

Today, only the tasty fruit of the mulberry tree is in demand, and these are generally eaten as fresh or stewed fruit or processed into schnapps. But take care—the dark red to black fruit of the black mulberry *(Morus nigra)* is only tasty and edible when fully ripe, shortly before it drops. The white and pink fruit of the white mulberry *(Morus alba)*, on the other hand, has a less distinct fragrance. Its leaves, however, are enjoyed by silkworms and are their main food plant.

Top left: To harvest the ripe mulberries, a man climbs into the tree and shakes the branches by hand with all his might.

Bottom left: The mulberries are caught in a net or plastic sheet. The children often help; harvesting is great fun for them.

Above: Ripe mulberries taste best directly under the tree from which they are harvested— or stewed or turned into jam.

Sweetmeats

Although the Georgians discovered their passion for sweet things in the last few decades, there are very few sweet foods in the Georgian kitchen that could be compared to desserts in European cuisine. Fresh or, in winter, dried or stewed fruit provide a simple finish to traditional meals. Occasionally, outsized cakes may crown the end of a generous spread at a celebratory meal.

Real Georgian sweet dishes are in season in autumn and winter. The juice of fresh grapes is boiled and thickened with flour. The east Georgians use whole wheat flour for this and call this tasty mush *tatara*, and the west Georgian variant using corn flour is called *pelamushi*. This delicacy is served hot or cold at harvest festivals, at New Year, and Christmas in particular. Pela-

mushi is further processed into a classic grape and nut candy for the winter months: in east Georgia, to make *churchkhela*, whole shelled walnuts are threaded onto a cotton thread and dipped several times into the juice and hung up on sticks to dry. For *janjukha* in west Georgia, hazelnuts are similarly used. Before eating, the confectionery is cut into slices. The New Year starts with *gozinaki*. To make these candies, roasted walnuts are caramelized in boiling honey. At New Year there is also *tklapi*, a purée of berries or *tkemali* plums spread into round cakes and dried, also known as *paster* in Armenia (see page 302).

For churchkhela, freshly pressed grape juice is brought to a boil and thickened with flour.

The thick grape mush produced in this way should have the consistency of blancmange.

Threaded walnuts or hazelnuts are dipped in the grape mush and dried several times.

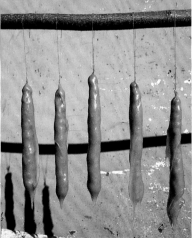

Churchkhela or janjukha can be seen all over the country hanging from trees and balconies to dry.

Tea from Georgia

About 95 percent of the teas produced in the USSR came from Georgia. It was mainly cultivated in subtropical west Georgia on the southern slopes of the Caucasus and was drunk by everyone under the name of "Grusinic tea" (gruzinsky chai). However, the quality could not keep up with the levels on the world market due to radical mass production. Since Georgia's independence, cultivation has fallen rapidly, and today Russia buys its tea primarily from northern India. Since 1995, however, the German tea producer Martin Bauer has invested millions so that Georgia can again produce high-quality tea.

Large-leaved Chinese tea varieties grow particularly well in the west Georgian climate. A few of these are cultivated here, namely the cold-resistant *Colkhis* with its fine rose fragrance. Georgian plantations are currently producing about 60,000 metric tonnes per year, most of which goes to Russia. Eighty percent of the harvest is processed into black tea, and the rest into green tea. Incidentally, the Georgians do not like to hear the name "Grusinic tea," because "Grusinia" comes from the Russian word for Georgia. It has colonial associations and is frowned upon.

Pelamushi
Grape juice dessert
(Not illustrated)

4 cups/1 liter freshly pressed grape juice
About ⅔ cup/100 g whole wheat or corn flour
1 scant cup/100 g finely chopped walnuts

Set aside about ⅔ cup/150 ml of the juice. Bring the rest to a boil in a large pan, stirring continually, then remove from the heat. Whisk the flour well into the reserved cold juice. Then, using a whisk, gradually stir it into the hot juice. Bring to a boil, stirring continually, and simmer over the lowest possible heat for about 30 minutes, stirring occasionally. Pour into a large bowl or individual dishes and leave to cool. Garnish with chopped walnuts before serving.

Left: Not candles or salami—these sweet "sausages" only reveal their secret when eaten. The Georgians particularly enjoy this grape and nut confection, churchkhela, at Christmas, New Year, and at the *Alaverdoba* harvest festival.

The Caucasians were bathing in the Borzhomi waters 2,000 years ago. The spa gardens have invited people to take healthy walks since the end of the19th century.

Where White and Red Tsars took the waters

The composer Peter Ilich Tchaikovsky was deeply moved by his visit to Borzhomi in 1887: "I can only say to you that this is one of the most beautiful places on earth that I have ever seen … Sometimes the beauty that I come across everywhere I go makes me weep. Apart from this, Borzhomi has an additional attraction: there is also excellent mineral water available here in pleasant parks."

The Russian Tsar's family, the Romanovs, provided a boost for Borzhomi in the mid-19th century. After the daughter of the Governor Eugen Golovin, who ruled over the Caucasus at that time, was cured of a serious illness in 1841, the St. Petersburg rubles started to roll into this little Caucasian village. Scientific analysis of the waters was initiated and large spa gardens were laid out.

Select architects were involved in the construction of the summer residences of the nobility. In 1864, Vladimir Shvener designed a Moorish-style castle for Mikhail Romanov, brother of Tsar Alexander II. Master builders traveled from Greece to create a Renaissance-style palace in Likani for Mikhail's son, Nikolay.

However, in a decree in 1919, the new ruler Lenin put an end to the first-class spa, and the aristocratic castles were converted into convalescent homes for the working classes. With the building of about ten additional purpose-built sanatoria, the Borzhomi valley soon developed into one of the largest spas in the Soviet Union. Nevertheless, the top red functionaries preferred the Renaissance palace of the class enemy. The castle in Likani was lovingly done up for Joseph Dzhugashvili, alias Stalin. The Piruza sanatorium, the last one, dating from 1892, survived the decline of the spa caused by recent political reversals. Today, the Tsar's former villa is used as a guest house.

Mineral water from Borzhomi

Mother Nature was not frugal in providing mineral water springs in Georgia. More than a thousand natural springs bubble up from the ground in this small, mountainous country. The leader of what are currently fewer than a dozen economically exploited waters is *Borzhomi*, which comes from the Lesser Caucasus. Both of the alkaline springs were probably known in ancient times. In 1892, seven baths from the 1st century B.C. were discovered during building work by the Yekaterina spring. In those ancient times, the Caucasians only benefited externally from the 100 °F/ 38 °C warm thermal springs.

A taste was acquired for the acidic mineral water in the mid-19th century, after doctors also recommended taking the water internally. Drink cures with *Borzhomi* water quickly became fashionable with the well-to-do across the whole of the empire; Tchaikovsky even compared the salty water with French *Eau de Vichy* during his stay at the spa in the little Caucasian location. When one of the first industrial bottling plants in the whole of the Russian empire was set up in 1896, the healing water was then accessible to the wider masses. At 3,000 milligrams per liter, *Borzhomi* is an extremely mineralized water, which explains its salty, mineral flavor. It is particularly rich in magnesium, calcium, potassium, and sulfates, and in addition it contains about 635 milligrams of salt per liter. To compensate for this, there is also hydrogen carbonate in large quantities which, in conjunction with sodium, reduces blood pressure. This ingredient, absorbed by the water when it passes through different limestone layers on its way to the surface, as at Borzhomi, can also do other things: it exerts a healing effect in the body, regulates the acid-base balance and has a positive effect on gastrointestinal functions. Drunk regularly, this healthy water is successful in treating metabolic disorders, chronic inflammations of the liver and gall bladder, urinary tract disorders and coronary, vascular and neuropathic disorders. *Borzhomi* water is available in *Classic, Light* and *Spring* qualities, and is not only sold in glass bottles but is also available in the ubiquitous plastic bottle. In the Soviet era, *Borzhomi* was exported to more than 20 countries; today, its seriously restricted production mainly enters the domestic market and those of neighboring countries.

Background and below: The highly mineralized healing water from the springs at Borzhomi has been bottled directly on site since 1896. It is the most popular mineral water in Georgia and is available all over the country.

Marcus Würmli

ՀԱՅԱՍՏԱՆ

Armenia

GEORGIA

Lesser Caucasus

Tashir Alaverdi

Stepanavan Idzhevan Berd

Vanadzor Dilijan AZERBAIJAN

Spitak Amvashen

ARMENIA *Shakhdag Range*

Gyumri Hrazdan Sevan

Hrazdan Lake

Aragats Aparan Sevan

Artik 4090 m Charent- Vardenis

Arpa savan Kamo

Ashtarak Aboyvan

Garni *Geghama Range*

Martuni

Ejmiadzin Geghard Djermuk

YEREVAN *Zangezur Range*

Armavir Yeghegnadsor

TURKEY Araks Sisian Goris

Artashat Ararat Areni Arpa

Noravank Vorotan Tatev

Ararat

5137 m Kapan

Azerbaijan Rep.

of Nakhchivan

(Azerbaijan)

0   30 miles/50 km

IRAN Meghri Araks

W e are flying to a hardworking, legendary country. We are in Armenia. In the distance, to the south, the snow-covered peak of Mount Ararat dominates Armenian history. According to the Bible, this is where Noah's ark came to rest, in order to repopulate the earth. A hard task, because Armenia is rocky and volcanic." This is the Chilean poet Pablo Neruda's concise summary of his first impressions of the country in his 1974 autobiography. The Armenians do indeed have another name for their homeland: *Karastan* —the Land of Stones. Ninety percent of the area covered by the present-day state, which is about the size of Belgium, is over 3,250 feet/1,000 meters above sea level. The cliffs are precipitous; rivers and streams carve their way into the mountains, creating space for narrow valleys. On the slopes, anywhere there is sufficient moisture, you find an almost Mediterranean profusion of plants and animals, such as pomegranate, fig, and peach trees, and insects like cicadas and praying mantises. The mountainous regions are covered with high alpine meadows full of herbs and, especially in the northeast, luxuriant deciduous forests make a refreshing contrast to the steppes and semideserts along the river Araks. Sheep and cattle frolic in vast meadows, though only about 17 percent of the land is suitable for agriculture. The winters are cold, and last from around December to March. After a short spring, the hot dry summer extends from May to the end of October. There is very little rainfall, except in spring, so Armenia is only green from March to June.

The Armenian people used to occupy a much greater area that also included present-day eastern Turkey and Cilicia (now southern Turkey). During its thousands of years of history, the country has been under Byzantine, Ottoman, and Persian rule. In the 19th century Armenian territory gradually fell to Russia and in 1920 Armenia came under Soviet rule. With the collapse of the USSR, the country finally gained its independence in 1991. The military conflict with Azerbaijan over the enclave of Nagorno-Karabakh plunged the country into grave economic difficulties.

The Armenians' generosity and community tradition helped them to come through. After all, the extended family is the center of every individual's life. The Armenian for "often" is *hachakh*, and something you often do, *hachakhel*, means "to visit." The Armenians love eating and drinking in the evening with friends, relatives, and neighbors. At family celebrations, the tables groan under the weight of countless appetizers, main courses, salads, soups, and desserts. To produce them, the women often spend long hours standing in the kitchen, and cooking together is seen as a social event. The host does not shy away from getting into debt, because even the best is only just good enough for guests.

Previous page: The 9th century Sevan monastery stands on a peninsula in Lake Sevan.

A trader sells wafer thin *lavash bread* in the market in Yerevan.

Armenian cooking at home and abroad

Wheat grains at different stages of preparation, barley, bread, pomegranates, plums, quinces, dried fruit, raisins, jugs of cheese, sesame oil, very thin fillets of beef, stone tubs containing malt, eight vineyards: an Armenian housewife could start cooking straight away, if these ingredients were fresh. Actually they are the remains of the Urartian city of Teishebaini, excavated by archaeologists on a hill in the modern capital, Yerevan. In fact, Armenian cuisine can be traced back directly to Urartian cooking—so you can still eat here in the same way as 2,500 years ago. From the 9th to the 7th century B.C., the Urartian Empire ruled over the enormous triangle between Lake Van (now in Turkey), Lake Urmia (now in Iran) and Lake Sevan. For centuries, many Armenians lived in "West Armenia," the eastern part of modern Turkey. The genocide of 1.5 million Christian Armenians perpetrated by the Ottomans in 1915 put an abrupt end to the coexistence of the two peoples. However, even though Armenians and Turks are still not exactly friends, common culinary features persist, such as the liking for a slightly sour taste to many foods, often achieved by the addition of yogurt or lemon juice—and in Armenia mainly by adding dried fruits. Meat dishes hold a prime position in both Armenia and Turkey, including the spicy fillet of beef *bastoorma* (Turkish: *pasturma*) and beef sausage *soojookh* (Turkish: *sucuk*). The types of bread known as *lavash* and *matnakash* are eaten in both countries, as is *lahmadjo*, the Middle-Eastern pizza with ground meat that has now become popular in Western Europe and the US. After all, when you eat the countless sweetmeats—the nutty pastries *pakhlava* and *halva* made of wheat flour and honey are just the most famous examples—their common eastern inheritance just melts in your mouth.

The influence of Russian cuisine began in the 19th century, when Russian governors and settlers introduced their national dishes. Appetizers and salads, with ingredients like cabbage and red beet, a few kinds of dark bread, almost all kinds of sausage, pancakes, and above all potatoes, came from Russia. Their penchant for vodka also has Russian origins, though it is rejected as something foreign by many traditionally-minded Armenians.

Mekhitar, the comforter of souls

At the beginning of the 18th century, the Armenian Abbot Mekhitar ("Comforter") fled to Venice with his brothers during the Turkish-Venetian war in order to escape the Islamic Ottomans. He founded a monastery on the little island of San Lazzaro, which remains a stronghold of Armenian learning to this day. The Mekhitarist monks belong to

The monastic liqueur *Mechitarine* from Vienna is a reminder of Abbot Mekhitar, who founded a community of the order in Venice in the 18th century.

the United Armenian Church and through the patriarchy of Cilicia, which has been based in Lebanon since 1930, they have close ties with Rome, whereas in Armenia, the Armenian Apostolic State Church does not recognize the Pope as the supreme authority. A Mekhitarist monastery was founded in Trieste, which was under Habsburg rule at the time but is now part of Italy. After Napoleon's troops conquered the city in 1811, the monastery was moved to the imperial capital, Vienna. Here the monks devoted themselves to producing spirits. Their sweet herbal liqueur named Mechitarine is still produced and sold at the Mekhitarist Monastery in Vienna—a trace of Armenian gastronomy in central Europe.

Everything that the barbecue, kitchen, and cellar can produce is served at Armenian festivities. Specialty sausages, meat dishes, various salads, and *tolma*: fine stuffed vegetables. Wafer-thin lavash bread, wine, and *konjak* are essentials on every Armenian table.

Gifts of food

There are more Armenians living abroad than in the Republic (see Kasten). These Armenian exiles are often very successful, not least because their centuries of experience taught the people of the diaspora how to adapt without abandoning their individuality. This is also true in the field of cooking. The Turks are said to have taken over *tolma* stuffed foods (usually vegetables) from the Armenians as *dolma*. On the other hand, the Armenians in Constantinople took over many elements of seafood cookery, and stuffed mussels, *midye dolma* in Turkish, became an Armenian specialty that was unknown at home, where the sea is far away. Family connections and returning emigrants brought foreign influences into the ancient homeland. These include the parboiled wheat side dish bulgur and the salad *tabule* (see page 273) from the eastern Mediterranean area. Unlike the Georgians, people in Armenia rarely go to luxury restaurants to enjoy food from their own country. On the other hand, Western fast food restaurants are enjoying great popularity. Only one national dish can compete with them, and that is shashlik (kebabs) from a stall in the street. Even at home in modern Armenia, many

The Diaspora

The destiny of the Armenians is characterized by expulsions and forced re-settlements. Their expulsion at the hands of the Turkish Seldjuks in the 11th century marks the beginning of the diaspora. Cilicia, the first independent Armenian kingdom, which was a flourishing cultural center from the 12th to the 14th century, was founded in 1080 outside the mother country—on the northeast coast of the Mediterranean, in the area of the modern Turkish city of Adana. In the 17th century, the Persian Shah Abbas I forcibly resettled Armenian craftsmen, artists, and merchants from Julfa on the banks of the Araks (now in the autonomous Azerbaijani Republic of Nakhchivan) in central Persia, where they were made to help with the building of the city of Isphahan. Their descendents still live there today, in the Armenian district of New Julfa. Many Armenians also left their homeland of their own free will. They founded trading settlements in Constantinople, Venice, Bologna, Lucca, Paris, Marseilles, Amsterdam, Antwerp, and even in Madras and Calcutta. Details about the numbers of Armenians vary considerably. The government estimates the population of the Republic of Armenia at the start of the 21st century at around 3 million. However, as the economic emigration of the 1990s was not fully taken into account, it would be safer to assume a figure of between 2 and 3 million. There are around 5 million Armenians living in other countries—mostly in the US, Russia, Georgia, and France.

traditional dishes are only rarely cooked, probably as a result of the deprivations of the 1990s. By contrast, cookbooks from the 1950s and 1960s provide evidence of a culinary richness that documents the economic upturn and the relative prosperity of Armenia at that time. However, many dishes have also been handed down in the diaspora, and been adapted to suit the conditions there—and in every family.

Armenian beer

In areas where cereals grow, people usually drink beer. This was already the case 6,000 years ago. Reports from that time say that the Sumerians were already brewing beer around 3000 B.C., and the Babylonians had 20 different kinds of beer. The Epic of Gilgamesh (written after 2000 B.C.) tells how a dirty wild ape became a sober, upright human being through beer drinking. As long ago as the 5th century B.C., Herodotus, the Greek "Father of History," expressly praised the quality of Armenian beer.

Today there are two major breweries in Armenia. One produces *Kilikia*, which is named after the old Armenian kingdom now part of modern Turkey, and the other makes *Kotayk*, named after the area that has Hrazdan as its capital. The latter comes in two sorts: a light beer with a blue label and a dark beer with a green label. The taste justifies the Abovian Brewery's claim that they brew their *Kotayk* only from barley and hops, in accordance with the purity regulations. By contrast, with the two kinds of Kilikia, people think they can distinguish an element of rice or corn. Beer is a summertime drink for the Armenians. They meet in one of the many street cafés, order a glass, and chat about anything and everything as they drink.

Two breweries in Armenia produce the popular beers *Kotayk* and *Kilikia*.

Cereal growing

In the beginning plants grew wild—then came the Neolithic revolution. About 10,000 years ago, hunter-gatherers in the Near East began to settle down and turn to agriculture and cattle rearing. The reason for this development probably lay in the fact that people collected wild wheat and in doing so, they sowed the seeds by chance. Suddenly the wheat sprouted around their houses. They took care of the young seedlings, planted the grains deliberately, and eventually bred different varieties.

Armenia still lies in the middle of one of the most important gene centers in the world, comprising the Near East and the Caucasus. For botanists, gene centers are areas in which many wild forms of our cultivated plants are still to be found. In the case of the Near East and Armenia, these are vines, and the four kinds of cereal—wheat, barley, rye, and oats. In order to conserve the original forms of modern cereals, a national park was created in the East of Yerevan, the *Erebuni Argelots*. Plants such as the ancestors of wheat *Aegilops crass*, *Triticum araraticum*, and *Triticum unartu* grow here, along with the early form of rye *Secale vavilovii*.

Armenia is still a land of cereals, especially a land of wheat. The greatest quantities are produced in the northwestern provinces of Shirak, whose capital is Gyumri, and Aragatsotn, which has Ashtarak as its capital. While rye and oats are virtually no longer grown, barley is used for cattle fodder and for brewing beer. Wheat is not only turned into bread, it is also boiled, like rice in other places. It is also used whole or ground in the form of grits, semolina, or as a side dish of par-

An unusual sight—in the country wheat is sometimes still ground by hand using old millstones.

tially-boiled wheat (bulgur). Wheat porridge, wheat added to soups, mixed with salad for *tabule* or as a stuffing for vegetables are just a few of the favorite recipes. Boiled wheat tastes especially good in *khorovu*. A whole lamb is roasted in a hot earth oven *(tonir)* over a metal pot. This contains wheat and twice the quantity of water. The dripping fat and meat juices give the wheat dish its delicious flavor. Handmade whole wheat flour noodles, *arishta*, served with plenty of melted butter are a popular festive dish. Wheat also figures as the grand finale to a festive dinner. After the dessert, the housewife serves a snack of roasted wheat grains.

The Armenians got to know rice dishes through the Russians and their neighbors to the east. They love the many varieties of *plav* (pilaf, Azerbaijani *plov*) (see also pages 312ff). In Armenia they like to add dried fruits, preferably raisins. *Arishtaplav* is a variation of *plav*, in which rice is replaced by noodles. On the other hand, buckwheat is not very widely used, despite the long period of Russian rule. Corn is also rare, though they occasionally eat corn on the cob boiled in water. Special corn dishes, like those made in Georgia, are unknown.

Tabule
Bulgur salad with parsley

7 oz/200 g bulgur wheat
3-4 tomatoes, diced small
3 scallions, chopped
2 bunches parsley, chopped
¹/₂ bunch peppermint, coarsely chopped
Juice of 1 lemon
2-3 tbsp olive oil
Salt and black pepper
Romaine lettuce leaves for garnishing

Put the bulgur in a bowl and pour over just enough boiling water to cover the grain. Stir and leave to swell for about 30 minutes. Strain the bulgur using a fine sieve and squeeze the water out by hand.
Mix all the vegetables and herbs with the bulgur. Make a marinade with the lemon juice, half the olive oil, salt and pepper and use as a dressing for the bulgur salad. Stand in a cold place for at least one hour. Before serving, mix in the remaining olive oil. Serve with flat bread.

Left hand page: The province of Shirak has long been known as the granary of Armenia. Here wheat is grown and harvested in big fields to provide the daily bread.

Our daily bread

Bread *(hats)* is the essential basic food of the Armenian population. This is immediately evident in the everyday language. The expression *hats utel* ("eat bread") is used for "to breakfast," "to lunch," and "to dine." The front-runner among the favorite kinds of bread is *lavash*, a versatile flat bread made of wheat flour and slightly soured. It is bought in wafer-thin oval pieces of a considerable size—about 16 x 36 ins/40 x 90 cm. In the villages, lavash is usually the only kind of bread, and each family makes its own. About once every two months it is baking day, and the traditional *tonir* is heated. This indispensable earth oven is set 3–5 feet/1–1.5 m deep in the ground. It is circular and has a diameter of just over 3 feet/ 1 m. The inner wall is slightly vaulted or barrel-shaped, and is clad with fired bricks. Two hours before baking, the oven is heated by means of a wood fire. Air is fed in through a pipe leading diagonally upward from the bottom of the *tonir* to ground level.

To make 220 lb/100 kg of dough, you need 60 lb/ 27 kg of flour and 6 US gallons/23 liters of water. You knead this with all your might, together with a little sourdough and 2¼ lb/1 kg of salt. After that, the dough has to prove for a good hour and a half until the lactic acid fermentation has got going. Then the women form round loaves, each weighing 10–14 oz/300–400 g. Kneeling on a cushion, they roll it out evenly, using a thin wooden rolling pin. Each loaf is quickly dipped in flour, whirled around in the air, and slapped against the wall of the earth oven using a long, cloth-covered cushion. After only 30 seconds the lavash is baked. Now it can be taken out by hand, but to avoid burning their fingers, they often skillfully yank out the bread with a hook or pull it out with tongs.

In the towns, many women sell lavash from market stalls. However, a simplified baking method has long since been adopted. Though the dough is still rolled out by hand and cunningly shaped by tossing it in the air, the bread is baked between a heated metal plate and a heated metal roller. Fortunately, the result of this semi-industrial lavash production tastes just as good as bread from the *tonir*.

When dried, lavash keeps for up to a year. It is moistened before eating to restore the proper soft consistency. The Armenians use lavash as forks, spoons, and serviettes. They eat with their fingers, especially in the country. Everyone dips lavash into the bowls, collects some of the contents, and wraps it all up in the flat bread. At lunchtime, the

filling usually consists only of a lump of curd cheese with fresh herbs.

Another favorite kind of bread is *matnakas*, bread "pulled with the fingers" made of yeast dough, oval in shape, and marked with long furrows. It tastes best when warm from the oven. This is even more true of "Georgian bread" made with a lot of yeast, which the Armenians simply call *(gruzinsky)* puri, (*gruzinsky*, Russ. "Georgian", *puri*, Georg. "bread").

It usually has a hole in the middle and the taste is reminiscent of the Georgian *khachapuri*, but it is not made with cheese. In the capital Yerevan, the

To make traditional lavash, the women roll out the dough with a wooden rolling pin, and form thin sheets by whirling it through the air.

Before baking, the sheets of dough are placed over a cloth-covered, floured cushion, and slapped against the wall of the hot earth oven.

Lavash is baked in an oven *(tonir)* set into the ground. When it is ready, a woman uses a hook or a pair of tongs to take out the bread.

bakeries and street stalls also sell various Russian types of bread; rye bread *(sev hats)*, the dark, crisp pan loaf *hrasdan* (called after the river and the city of the same name), and a light-colored pan loaf known by the Russian word for loaf *bukhanka*. Bread is always served with an accompaniment, often just a tomato and fresh herbs, but it could also be sausage or cheese.

A particular Armenian specialty in Nagorno-Karabakh and the city of Goris in the east is *zhengyalov hats*, ("bread with greens" in one of the Kharabakh dialects), which is so filling it is almost a meal in itself. It could be compared to a kind of herb pizza, though it is always eaten cold. To make it, they cover a circle of dough with plenty of chopped green herbs. Then they fold half the dough over and knead the edges together. Finally the *zhengyalov hats* is baked in the oven. Unfortunately, this delicious specialty is very hard to get hold of, even in Yerevan.

In modern times it is not just lavash that is to be found in Yerevan street markets but also quite different types of bread. Some kinds, such as the white pan loaf, were adopted from the Russians.

Soups and stews

Khash is a typical men's dish, served with fresh herbs, and accompanied by vodka.

Khash, Armenia's most famous soup, has a legendary reputation throughout the Caucasus. The word comes from *khashel*, "to cook," so it simply means "something cooked." Cow feet and entrails go into the pot, and according to Armenian tradition, the whole process of soaking, cleaning, and cooking should last at least seven days. Men eat khash as early as breakfast time, preferably in company and with plenty of vodka. Women eat khash too, but usually without the entrails. Most importantly, however, women are increasingly dispensing with the tiresome preparation. If you want to eat khash, you go to a restaurant, perhaps in Proshyan Street in Yerevan.

Slow-cooked meat soups are the staples of Armenian cuisine. Shortly before the end of the cooking time comes the crucial turning point when wheat, rice, potatoes or vegetables are added. Prunes, or maybe chestnuts, give this classic mutton broth *bozbash* its characteristic flavor. *Khashlama* is spiced up with tomatoes and paprika. *Kololik* is a meatball soup that also has rice or potatoes added to it, and *putuk* (which, like many Armenian dishes, is named after the earthenware pot in which it is traditionally cooked) combines lamb with chickpeas and vegetables. The chicken soup *chkhrtma* is also widely known.

Of course, when times are hard, the Armenians too make soup with just water, if there is not enough money for meat soup. Rice or wheat-grit soup with vegetables or peas, bean or lentil soup, and of course, milk soups thickened with flour soon fill people up and provide important nutrients. Soups made with dairy products tickle the palate. The yogurt soup *spas* or *tanapoor* (from *tan*, "diluted yogurt" and *apoor*, "soup" or "stew") even contains little pieces of asparagus in addition to cereals and onions. The cold soup *matsnabrdosh* (from *matsun*, "yogurt" and *brdel*, "to crumble," because the soup is eaten with little pieces of lavash) is made from yogurt and water mixed in equal parts, to which cooked eggs, slices of cucumber, dill, and other herbs are added shortly before serving. It is a particularly popular meal to eat during the hot noonday hours.

Khash
"The men's meal"

3¼ lb/1.5 kg cow feet, ready for cooking
Generous 1 lb/500 g cattle entrails (e.g.tripe), ready for cooking, cut in pieces
10 cloves garlic, crushed
Lavash bread, as desired
Salt

Cut the cow feet in half downward and steep in cold water for at least 2 days, changing the water every 3–4 hours if possible.

Cover with plenty of cold water (no salt) and simmer for at least 4 hours, skimming regularly. After 4 hours, add the tripe and simmer for a further 2 hours. The cow feet should fall apart completely (the stock will become as pale as milk during this process). Khash is served in deep plates. At the table, stir in the garlic and crumbled dry lavash a spoonful at a time, and salt to taste. Serve with radish or sour pickled vegetables.

Spas
Yogurt soup with wheat

¾ cup/150 g coarse-ground wheat, bulgur or wheat grits
Salt and pepper
1 egg
3 tbsp/30 g flour
3 cups/800 ml yogurt
1 large onion, finely chopped
2 tbsp/30 g butter
1 bunch each of fresh mint and cilantro, finely chopped

Simmer the cereal in approximately double the quantity of salted water until soft. Beat the egg with flour in a saucepan, mix the yogurt with an equal quantity of water, add to the egg mixture and bring to a boil over a low heat, stirring continuously. Fry the onion in butter and add to the soup with the cereal and herbs. Season with salt and pepper and bring briefly to a boil.

Bozbash
Mutton soup from Yerevan
(Not illustrated)

¾ cup/150 g dried chickpeas
Generous 1 lb/500 g breast of mutton
Salt
1 large onion, sliced
3½ tbsp/50 g butter
6 tbsp tomato paste
2 cups/400 g potatoes, diced
¾ cup/100 g prunes, pitted
2 sour apples, cut in small pieces
Fresh herbs, finely chopped

Soak the chickpeas in water for at least 6 hours. Boil in fresh, unsalted water until tender and drain. Dice the meat and simmer in salted water until almost tender, skimming regularly. Remove the meat from the stock and fry in butter with the onion. Strain the stock, add the meat, chickpeas, and remaining ingredients (except for the herbs), and simmer over medium heat for 15 minutes. Sprinkle with herbs and serve.

Vospapoor
Lentil soup with rice

⅔ cup/150 g red lentils
1–2 large onions, finely chopped
2 tbsp/30 g butter
½ cup/100 g rice
6 tbsp/50 g each of raisins and chopped walnuts
Salt and pepper
1 bunch each of parsley and cilantro

Wash the lentils, and bring to a boil in 1–1½ liter fresh water. Fry the onions in the butter, add to the lentils with the rice, raisins, and walnuts, and season. Simmer for about 30 minutes, until the rice is soft. Serve with the herbs.

Peas and beans

The majority of the Armenian population can only afford to eat meat on special occasions, so it comes as no surprise that people often switch to cheaper sources of protein. Legumes contain 20 to 30 percent protein, which is the same amount as in meat.

Legumes are among the world's oldest cultivated plants. The first beans were cultivated in the Near East. These were broad beans *Vicia faba majo*, also well known as fava beans, *Vicia faba*, which are members of the same family as vetches. These *bakla* are steamed as a vegetable when semi-ripened, or added to soups and stews when fully mature. However, the cultivation of this species is of ever-diminishing importance, as the beans *(lobi)* of the genus Phaseolus, originally from South America, have taken over first place, led by the scarlet runner bean *(Phaseolus coccineus)*. The immature, up to 12-inch-/30-cm-long pods can be found in markets from April until well into the winter. People mostly eat them steamed or boiled and, as with many vegetables, they like to break an egg over them. Combined with chopped walnuts or mixed with yogurt, these beans tickle the palate.

In autumn, the markets are decorated with shiny beans in black and red patterns. Here too the scarlet runner predominates, closely followed by the French or kidney bean, *Phaseolus vulgaris*. A salad of beans and tomatoes is just as popular as an appetizer as puréed beans with walnuts and dried cornelian cherries or *mshosh*, an authentic Armenian lentil purée, flavored with dried apricots. Chickpeas, which originated in Persia and are traditionally much loved in Armenia, are now grown almost entirely in gardens, but they are still indispensable for Lenten meals such as chickpea purée *(topik)* or chickpea soup with plums *(siserapoor)*. Dried peas can be found in Russian-inspired dishes such as meat soups and Russian salad with mayonnaise and small pieces of potato and carrot. Most legumes can make do with very poor soil conditions and adapt perfectly to the country's extremes of climate with its short, cold winters and long, hot, very dry summers. What is more, legumes act as an organic manure because they fertilize the soil through nodule bacteria in their roots. They are able to convert the nitrogen in the air into ammoniac, allowing the plant to produce the essential amino acids it needs. If different plants are grown in this soil the following year, their yield is increased.

Lobov pashet
Red bean purée
(Illustration left)

1¹/₄ cups/250 g dried red beans
1 cup/100 g walnut kernels
1 cup/100 g dried cornelian cherries, soaked and pitted
1 onion, finely chopped
Salt and pepper
1 bunch parsley

Soak the beans in water for at least 6 hours, then bring to a boil and simmer over low heat until tender. Drain and reserve the liquor. Purée the beans. Chop the walnuts and cornelian cherries and mix thoroughly with the bean purée, onion, salt and pepper. Work in enough of the liquor to produce a smooth "dough." Spread the mixture in a serving dish, or form into walnut-sized balls. Put them close together on a plate, and sprinkle with chopped parsley. Serve cold as an appetizer.

Saloradshrov siserapur
Chickpea soup with prunes
(Illustration below left)

1 cup/200 g dried chickpeas
1 cup/100 g prunes
Salt and pepper
1 bunch dill, finely chopped
¹/₂ bunch scallions, finely chopped

Soak the chickpeas for at least 6 hours, then boil until soft in plenty of unsalted water. Drain and reserve the liquor. Soak the prunes in lukewarm water for at least 30 minutes, drain, pit, and cut into small pieces. Rub half the chickpeas through a sieve, mix with the remaining chickpeas and enough liquor to produce a smooth soup. Warm the prunes in this, and season with salt and pepper.
Before serving, sprinkle the chickpea soup with dill and chopped scallions.

Main picture: In the market, beans, cereals, and spices are sold in sacks.

Top insert: Scarlet runners vary from violet to red-brown and often have pale or dark marbling.

Center insert: The best pinto beans in different colors come from Goris in the southeast.

Bottom insert: Pink beans can also be found in farmers' markets in the country.

Beans, cucumbers, scallions, eggplant, and bell peppers are grown in the plain of the river Araks.

Vegetables

In Armenia, where much of the landscape consists of steppes and mountains, vegetables are grown up to a height of about 3900 feet/1200 m above sea level, for example in the area around Yeghegnadzor and Meghri, and in the Alaverdi and Idshevan valleys. In those parts there is sufficient rainfall and nutrient-rich humus soil to provide good conditions for vegetable growing. However, the biggest vegetable-growing area is the Araks Plain, on the edge of which stands the capital Yerevan. Even so, yields here are restricted by the dry nature of the basin, with its poor rainfall distribution and soils that are low in humus. For this reason an extensive irrigation system was set up in Soviet times, but this has not been fully functional since the 1990s.

Every autumn, the land is covered by thick smoke, when the fields and meadows are burnt off in accordance with ancient tradition. This does nothing to improve the soil, as would be possible if it was enriched by working in the residual organic matter. Instead, the wind, which is often very strong, carries off the flakes of ash and the nitrates contained in them. Because the soil is then left completely unprotected, the wind can attack even more fiercely and blow it away.

Since potatoes (kartofil) and cabbage (kaghamb) are not very demanding plants, they top the list of vegetables in the markets. Both are Russian "immigrants" and have therefore not been properly integrated into Armenian cuisine. For instance, there is a favorite Sunday dish of chicken that is simply surrounded by whole potatoes and shoved into the oven. A more successful combination of Russian and Caucasian cuisine can be seen in cabbage salad dressed with lemon juice and mint, which is popular throughout the region, and tolma filled with beans, for which cabbage leaves may be used instead of grape (vine) leaves (see page 282).

In the late summer, eggplant, bell peppers and tomatoes take over the markets. Eggplant (badrijan) is eaten steamed with tomatoes or preferably grilled on a skewer or a baking sheet. As in Russia, "eggplant caviar" (badrijani khaviar) is a specialty they like to serve in winter as an appetizer or accompaniment (see page 26). Pale green bell peppers (paprika, takdegh) are available from May, and dark red ones from August. These are especially popular as kebabs, grilled on steel skewers with pieces of meat. Red peppers pickled with garlic and grape leaves are particularly tasty. They are also the basis of the deliciously hot paste (ajika), which is very popular in Georgia (see page 229). Tomatoes (lolik) are almost always eaten raw and tomato sauces are rare.

Spinach (spanakh), carrots (gasar), pumpkins (dtoom), cucumbers (varoong), romaine lettuce (salat), plenty of onions (sokh), and rather less garlic (sekhtor), all add variety. Because the Armenians love meat above all else, main courses are seldom vegetarian. One exception is the vegetable stew aylasan, containing eggplant, potatoes, peppers, beans, tomatoes, onions, garlic, and herbs.

Many vegetable growers on the Aparan plateau near Mount Ararat still till their fields by hand.

Okra

Okra (bamia) originates from tropical Asia. It is the seedpod of one of the marshmallows, a relative of mallows and hollyhocks. This annual plant loves the heat, grows up to 8 feet/ 2.5 m high and branches out into a bushy shrub. Only a few days elapse between the start of flowering and harvesting. The immature green pods are cut when about 4 inches/ 10 cm long, because later they become woody and fibrous. The hexagonal, approximately finger-thick, beak-shaped okra pods have a sharp bean-like taste that is sour and piquant, yet mild. In Armenia they mostly like to serve them with chicken (see page 294). Okra contain few calories and because of their high mucus content, they help to alleviate stomach complaints.

Aylasan
Vegetable stew (Serves 6)
(Not illustrated)

Generous 1 lb/500 g eggplant
Generous 1 lb/500 g potatoes, peeled and sliced
4 bell peppers (various colors), cut in strips
2 cups/300 g green beans, trimmed and cut in pieces
4 tomatoes, sliced
3–4 onions, sliced
6 cloves garlic, finely chopped
2 bunches kitchen herbs, finely chopped (e.g. parsley, cilantro, basil, thyme)
Salt and pepper
7 tbsp/100 ml oil
7tbsp/100 ml white wine

Peel the eggplant, slice, salt and set aside for 20 minutes. Then press out the juice. Put alternate layers of eggplant and other vegetables in an ovenproof earthenware pot or pudding basin. Sprinkle each layer with herbs, and season sparingly with salt and pepper. Finally drizzle over oil and wine, cover, and stew in a pre-heated oven at 325 °F/160 °C for about 1 hour.

Tip: This dish can also be made with meat. For this, add a generous 1 lb/500 g diced lamb, mutton or beef, and barely cover with water before cooking.

The miracle bulb of the Caucasus

One of the reasons for the proverbial longevity of the people of the Caucasus is said to be the many different ways they use garlic. This bulb, which owes its typical taste and smell to a sulfurous essential oil, contains antibacterial prophylactic substances that are said to be effective against fungal infections and tapeworms, and even against cancer. Garlic is used frequently in Armenian cooking, but not to excess. Its juice was also put to an unusual use here. It was once used as a glue in the production of illuminated manuscripts. Garlic juice was spread over the pages of the manuscript, gold leaf was laid on top, and became firmly attached to the page. This also explains the myth that the Armenians had impregnated their medieval manuscripts—about 15,000 of which are kept in the Manuscript Museum in Yerevan—with garlic to protect them from destructive pests.

Garlic was once used in the production of illuminated manuscripts, as well as in the kitchen.

Tolma: wrapped and filled

At a memorial service for someone who had died, the priest wrapped three stuffed vegetables in a piece of lavash bread and ate it in a single bite. "Father," asked one of the peasants, who noticed this, "how many people in your village are buried in one shroud?" "If the bodies aren't big, it'll be three or four," came the reply.

This anecdote refers to one of the Armenians' culinary passions: stuffed vegetables. What the priest wrapped in the bread had already been wrapped: a *tolm*. The classic *sut tolma*, similar to those we know from other countries such as Georgia, Azerbaijan, Greece, and Turkey, are rice or meatballs wrapped in grape leaves. The Lenten tolma *(pasoots tolma)* contains peas or beans instead of meat and is wrapped in cabbage leaves. In Armenia, they also stuff fruits, such as quinces, apricots, and apples, and vegetables, especially tomatoes, and occasionally onions. Bell peppers stuffed with very finely chopped or grated carrots are delicious. Like all other tolma, these are also placed close together in a pot and stewed in a little stock or water.

Pasoots tolma
Lenten tolma
(Illustration below)

1/2 cup/100 g dried beans
1/2 cup/100 g dried chickpeas
1/2 cup/100 g dried lentils
4 medium onions, finely chopped
2 tbsp oil
1 1/4 cups/250 g wheat grains, boiled until soft
2 bunches parsley, finely chopped
Salt and pepper
24 fresh grape (vine) leaves, could be replaced by
12 cabbage leaves
4 tbsp tomato paste

Soak the beans, peas and lentils separately for at least 6 hours. Boil the beans and chickpeas separately in plenty of fresh, unsalted water until soft. Sauté the onions in oil, mix in the beans, chickpeas, drained lentils, wheat, and herbs, and season with salt and pepper. Blanch the grape or cabbage leaves, drain, and spread out (with grape leaves, lay two together), place 1–2 tablespoons filling in the middle of each, and fold up like an envelope. Place the tolma close together in a pot, stir together the tomato paste and 2–3 cups/145 ml water, pour this over the tolma, and simmer for 20–30 minutes. This dish is usually eaten cold.
Tip: On feast days such as New Year's Eve, the Armenians make Lenten tolma with pickled cabbage leaves.

Khndzorov tolma
Stuffed apples

1 1/4 cups/300 g ground beef, well marbled (i.e. not fat free)
2 onions, finely chopped
1 bunch each of parsley and cilantro, finely chopped
Salt and pepper
Sweet paprika powder
3–4 tbsp/45–60 g butter
2 cups/100 g boiled rice
8 medium apples
Generous 1 lb/500 g ripe tomatoes
About 1/2 cup/125 ml stock

Mix the ground meat with the onions and herbs, season with salt and pepper, and fry gently in butter. Mix with the boiled rice. Cut a lid off each of the apples, remove the core, and carefully take out enough flesh to leave a rim about 5/8 inch/1.5 cm. Chop the fruit flesh finely and mix with the meat stuffing. Fill the apples and put on the lids. Place the stuffed apples in a pot. Blanch the ripe tomatoes briefly in boiling water, skin, and pass through a sieve. Mix the purée with the stock, pour over the apples, cover, and simmer for about 30 minutes, until the apples are tender but not too soft. The dish is served in the cooking juices.

Khapama
Stuffed pumpkin

8–9 oz/250 g dried cornelian cherries
1 small pumpkin, about 3¼ lb/1.5 kg
4 large onions, diced
1 cup/200 g butter
Generous 2 cups/250 g walnuts, chopped
½ tsp cinnamon
Salt and pepper

Soak the cornelian cherries for at least 3 hours in
lukewarm water, then pit. Cut a lid off the stalk end
of the pumpkin, remove the seeds and membranes,
and scoop out the flesh with a spoon, and cut into
dice. Fry the onions in 2 tablespoons butter and
mix with diced pumpkin flesh, cornelian cherries,
walnuts, and seasonings. Stuff the pumpkin with
the filling, put the lid on, and bake in the oven for
about 50 minutes at 350–400 °F/180–200 °C.
Serve stuffed pumpkin with plenty of melted butter.

Ltsonats takdegh
Stuffed bell peppers

8 bell peppers (mixed yellow and red)
Generous 1 lb/500 g carrots
3 tbsp oil
2 onions, finely chopped
1 large ripe tomato
Salt
1 tsp sugar
1 pinch cinnamon
1 bunch parsley, chopped

Cut lids off the peppers, remove the seeds and membrane, and blanch the peppers briefly in boiling water.
Peel the carrots and cut in thin sticks, fry lightly in the
oil, add the onions and fry both together. Blanch the
tomato briefly in boiling water, skin, and dice. Add to
the vegetables and continue cooking for about 5 minutes. Season with salt, sugar, cinnamon, and half the
parsley. Fill the peppers with the mixture, and put on
the lids. Put the peppers in a pot with 1 cup/250 ml
lightly salted water, cover, and simmer until the peppers are tender. Serve with parsley.

St John's wort plays an important part in Armenian natural healing. It lifts the spirits on gray winter days.

Background: In spring, the Armenians like to top up their vitamin reserves with fresh wild herbs, garlic and peppers.

Wild and medicinal herbs

When winter arrives, most kinds of vegetables disappear from the fields, and Armenians live on what they have preserved. For five months they go short of vegetables and vitamins, as there are not enough imports and nothing can be harvested in Armenia until early summer. In March, when the body's vitamin stores are exhausted, the first fresh herbs finally come on to the market. Few countries have more wild herbs in their diet than Armenia.

From March to June, the women of the mountain villages go in search of this green treasure. They sell their harvest by the sackful to the traders in the capital. The range comprises some two dozen herbs. Sorrel *(aveluk)* offers the best additional income. The women plait the juicy leaves into long ropes and allow them to dry. This sorrel has to be soaked before use, and then boiled. The taste is reminiscent of spinach, but it is considerably stronger and spicier.

As early as March, fresh wild onions *(chndshelos)* flood onto the market. They are not unlike the wild leek or ramp that have an assertive onion flavor. Only a month later the markets are over-

Fresh sorrel *(aveluk)*, which sprouts during the first days of spring, is plaited into strings by women and dried. It is soaked in water before use.

The Armenians love mushrooms, and have many different ways of cooking blewits (Lepista saeva personata).

Mushrooms

The Armenians love mushrooms *(sunk)*, but treat them in a completely different way from most central European cooks. Probably through fear of poisoning, they start by boiling almost all mushrooms in water, before preparing them in various different ways. The season begins in spring and ends in late autumn. They collect mainly wild mushrooms, butter fungus, and blewits, and sell them fresh in the market. Many oyster mushrooms come from Dilidjan and Idzhevan. One of the specialties of Armenian cuisine is mushroom soup *(snkapoor)*, which also contains rice, onions, and parsley. There are nutritious versions containing potatoes and noodles, and a typically Armenian variant with plums. Mushrooms also add a special flavor to wheat and rice dishes such as *plav*, and are popular as a filling for *tolma* or cooked for use in salads.

flowing with exotic-looking shoots, especially longleaf sickleweed *(sibekh)* and cow parsley *(mandakh)*. From May on, you can find a special delicacy, the slender, whip-like wild asparagus *(tsnebek)*. A fresh salad of desert candles, known in the West as the cultivated border plant foxtail lily/eremurus (which may not be edible), with eggs and herbs is a traditional Easter dish that has almost vanished into oblivion.

Many basic recipes ensure there is variety in the way herbs are used in the kitchen. For instance, briefly scalded in hot water, then dressed with salt, vinegar, and oil—and the salad is made. Herbs keep their individual flavor best when sautéed in butter. A good strong meat stock, perhaps with mushrooms floating in it, can be turned into a delicious soup with the addition of herbs. Herbs are often eaten in scrambled eggs or omelets as an appetizer or a quick in-between snack. If you really want to take full advantage of the vitamin and nutrient content of wild plants, you should only eat the fresh shoots and the smallest leaves and cook them for as short a time as possible.

Many Armenian dishes are flavored with various potherbs. The most commonly used are red or green-leaved basil, *(rehan)*, cilantro, tarragon, parsley, and dill. Moreover, it is customary to put fresh bunches of these herbs on the appetizer table at a big banquet. In spring a kind of aragula (rocket) *(kotem)* gladdens the hearts of gourmets. There is a long tradition of Armenian herbal medicine going back 3,000 years. The ancient botanist Dioscorides of Cilicia specifically drew attention to the special healing effects of Armenian plants. Nowadays, women everywhere sell small plastic bags of dried medicinal herbs labeled in Armenian, Russian, and sometimes with the Latin botanical name. The bags are filled with mint (for headaches, colds, and digestive problems), wormwood (an appetizer, but to be taken with care, depending on the species), yarrow (for purifying the blood and reducing fever), or St John's wort (for relieving depression), as well as lesser-known plants such as strawflower (*Helichrysum plinthocalyx*, calming, aids the digestion), motherwort (*Leonurus spp.*, for digestive problems, cramps, palpitations) or *Arum orientale*, for chest and stomach complaints.

The tasty trout that can be bought in Yerevan come mainly from fish farms in Garni.

The fishing industry

The most important fish in Armenian cuisine is the pollan or whitefish *(sig)*. The inhabitants of Yerevan even think a memorial should be erected in its honor, because it saved the population from starvation during the crisis in the 1990s. The pollan was brought to Armenia by the Russians in the 1930s from Lake Peipus and Lake Ladoga in western Russia. It bred very well in Lake Sevan, and grows to a weight of up to 1¾ lb/1.5 kg. Fresh pollan can be bought all over Yerevan, and the way it is cooked shows that the Armenians were quick to learn from the Russians. Their smoked pollan is wonderfully juicy. They also serve the finest farmed trout any gourmet could imagine. Of course, these rainbow trout do not owe their characteristic full flavor to industrially produced feedstuffs; they are fattened up on scraps of meat. Originally Armenian waters teemed with a native trout species, the Sevan trout, (scientific name *salmo ischchan*). In Armenian it is called *ischchan*, which actually means "prince"—a very apt name, as there are few more delicious tasting fish. They can compete with the finest salmon, but have pale flesh. The biggest specimens grow to around 3 feet/1 m in length and weigh up to 33 lb/15 kg. However, environmental changes in Lake Sevan and unlimited overfishing have led to the Sevan trout becoming an endangered species.

Brown trout *(karmrachajt)* also live in Armenian rivers, but they do not usually grow very big. The barbel *(beghlu)*, a species native to Lake Sevan and its rivers and that is not found outside this area, is generally considered to be particularly tasty. The southern Araks Plain is the center of the freshwater fish-farming industry. There they mainly rear common carp *(tsatsan)* and silver carp. The scientific name of silver carp is a real tongue-twister: *Hypophthalmichthys molitrix*. Its Russian name is *tolstolobik* ("thick forehead"), and in Armenian it is *pndachakat* (with a "hard forehead") or *hastagluch*, ("thick head"). This member of the carp family, with its conspicuously prominent lower jaw, originates from the Amur region and northern China, and was brought in to stock the fishponds of the countries bordering the Black Sea and the Caspian Sea. There are also wild catfish *(loko)* living in the ponds, some of which can weigh more than 88 lb/40 kg. They make the very best fish kebabs.

Amazingly, Armenia has only a few fish recipes. Around Lake Sevan, the pollan is usually grilled whole. Stuffed Sevan trout *(kutap)* was once considered to be a kind of national dish, but it is now rarely served. Fish is usually boiled or steamed. Crayfish are also simply boiled in water. Western tourists, above all, consider them a special delicacy, because they are not always readily available in other countries—and definitely not at such affordable prices.

Dzkan khorovats
Fish kebabs

4 pollan, each about 300 g, from the fishmonger, with the innards removed through the gills, (not slit along the stomach!), could be replaced by trout, whitefish, etc.
Salt and pepper
⅓ cup/80 g butter
2 lemons, sliced
1 bunch tarragon, finely chopped
Pomegranate seeds

Make several diagonal cuts in the skin of the fish, salt and pepper the fish inside and out, thread lengthwise on skewers and broil, or grill over a barbecue, turning the skewers regularly and brushing the fish from time to time with melted butter.
Serve on a dish with slices of lemon, chopped tarragon, and plenty of pomegranate seeds.

Dzuk giniov
Fish in wine

2¼ lb/1 kg trout, pollan or carp
Salt and pepper
1 bunch tarragon, chopped
Juice of 1 lemon
1 cup/250 ml dry rosé wine
Pomegranate seeds for garnishing (optional)

Cut the fish in pieces, season with salt and pepper, sprinkle with tarragon and drizzle with lemon juice. Leave to marinate for 20–30 minutes. Cover the bottom of a broad, shallow pot with clean thin twigs (or use a steamer), and put the pieces of fish on top. Pour over the wine, close the lid firmly, and steam for 20 minutes over medium heat. If desired, sprinkle with pomegranate seeds before serving.

Cheese from the market

The markets in the towns and villages are brimming over with cheese. Leading the field is brine cheese *(panir)*, every batch of which turns out different. The differences, which are sometimes considerable, are due to the process, the fat content, how long it is matured, or the water content. The Armenians solve the problem of buying the right one by tasting it every time. They do this even with the products of major manufacturers such as *lori* or *hajkakan panir* (Armenian *"pani"*), because even here the quality varies. Many kinds of brine cheese are given a strong individual taste by the addition of green herbs such as parsley, dill, or chives, for instance the almost dry buttermilk cheese *chortan*. Occasionally, you can also find blue cheeses, known unsurprisingly as *rokefor*. Recently, one company has had some success trying to sell people a hard cheese of a type similar to Edam or Emmental. *Tschetschil* or *tel panir* is an Armenian specialty made from sheep's or cow's milk. To make it, the curd is heated to about 185 °F/85 °C, at which temperature it melts, as in a fondue. The strands that form are spun into strings and ropes. The taste of a young tschetschil is reminiscent of mozzarella.

Cheese plays a very small part in Armenian cookery. It is eaten almost exclusively with bread—for breakfast, lunch, or as the prelude to a copious evening meal.

For a quick lunch, they just wrap some curd cheese and fresh herbs in *lavash* bread.

Large illustration, left: The "string" cheeses are known as
Tel Panir (illustrated) or fine-spun Chechil.

Top: Cheese stall in the market in Ejmiadzin.

Above: Homemade yogurt is sold in jars.

Left: Chortan, an almost dry buttermilk cheese.

Alpine pastures

Wherever you look, there are cattle grazing in Armenia. You are as likely to find them on the central reservation of a freeway as in the villages or out on the dry steppes. Around 30 percent of the Armenian land surface is officially designated as grazing land, but in reality it is much more. As a result of massive emigration, countless fields were left fallow and have long been used for grazing. Cattle are also often driven into the forests to search for fodder. From June onward, when there is no more rain and the green plants gradually wither, many farmers move up to higher ground with their cattle. Especially in the volcanic massif of Aragats, the highest mountain in Armenia at 13,300 ft/4,090 m, and along the 30-mile/50-km-long highway from Berd to Chambarakh, the high alpine pastures are strung together like the beads of a rosary. The highest summer pasture on Mount Aragats lies at a height of 9,425 ft/2,900 m.

When it was part of the Soviet Union, Armenia was covered with sovkhosi and kolkhosi (collective farms), but these have not been replaced by cooperatives. Since the rapid privatization of 1991, each farmer has been working for himself any way he can, The poor harvests mean it is not possible to replace old machinery. In the best cases, standardized processes for the manufacture of dairy products have resulted in bigger businesses. In the alpine pastures, the farmers—particularly the Yezidi (see box)—produce their own cheese. It is usually brine cheese *(panir)*, a kind of feta. The basis is cow's or sheep's milk, or both together. During warming, the milk is curdled with rennet. A cloth is used to remove the curd from the whey, and the cheese dough is kept in it for varying lengths of time in different concentrations of salt solution. The former practice of keeping it in sheepskins has gone out of fashion. Butter is still occasionally made in a "butter cradle *(chnotsi)*, a narrow wooden barrel tapering at the ends, that is set swinging like a pendulum. Apart from the buttermilk produced in this way, the farmers in the alpine pastures also make quark, as well as a kind of condensed milk, sour cream with different fat contents, and sweet cream. The dairy farmers' most important product is yogurt *(matsun,* and sheep's milk yogurt is a special favorite. *Matsun* rounds off every meal, and tastes even better with honey drizzled over it. *Tan,* a slightly sour, refreshing drink is made from yogurt and water, perhaps with the addition of a little buttermilk. It is stored in bottles or cartons, to be drunk later by the farmers themselves or sold in the markets.

The Yezidi travel across country with their flocks of sheep.

The Yezidi

The region around the volcano Aragats is the main area of settlement for the ethnic group of the Yezidi. They are true masters of sheep-rearing and the production of sheep milk cheese, which the women sell in the markets. Pens of sheep line the arterial roads around Yerevan. Here anyone who so desires can have a sheep slaughtered by its Yezidi owner and the meat prepared for kebabs.

The Yezidi language is a dialect of Kurdish. The Yezidi are related to the Kurds and have their own monotheistic religion. It includes ancient Babylonian elements, and its teachings are still passed on orally by religious singers. Its roots probably go back to a time even before that of the Persian prophet Zoroaster. The original homeland of the Yezidi was in northern Iraq, where their holy shrine of Lalish lies. The worldwide Yezidi population is estimated at around 300,000. Before the fall of the Soviet Union, there were some 60,000 living in Armenia. During the 1990s, many Yezidi left the country, because they felt threatened after fighting broke out over questions of nationality in the Caucasus. At that time, the women stopped wearing their traditional costume of a pleated gown and headscarf, but now it is increasingly being worn again.

Livestock farming

The Near East is not only considered to be the original home of many of today's commonly cultivated plants. The most important farm animals—sheep, cattle and goats—were also domesticated here. The sheep is reckoned to be the first domestic animal. It was already being farmed around 20,000 years ago. Under the influence of Islam, which the Armenians repeatedly experienced during periods of Persian or Ottoman rule, sheep farming was encouraged, because the eating of pork was forbidden. Nowadays, sheep farming is mainly in the hands of the Kurdish Yezidi. The only breed found in Armenia is the fat-tailed sheep, which gets its name from a heavy pad of fat around the base of the tail that can weigh up to 15 ½ lb/7 kg. The fat is considered to be a delicacy and is indispensable for the preparation of *ravurma*—lamb or mutton preserved in sheep tallow.

The successful breeding of domestic cattle from the aurochs happened about 9,000 years ago. Cattle were probably first used mainly as sacrificial animals. Later people also recognized their material value and used them as currency. This can be seen in the Latin word for money *pecuni*, which has its roots in *pecudes*, "cattle." People were already eating the meat in primitive times, but people soon discovered that cattle could also work and used them as draft animals. Later their milk also became a source of income. Cattle are still the most important domestic animals in Armenia, being kept for both meat and milk. However, there are no clearly distinguishable breeds. All the animals belong to the group of highland breeds, and most of them resemble the Alpine brown cattle with their attractive white muzzles. Armenian beef has a unique, captivating quality. Its steaks can stand comparison with the best cuts from the white Tuscan Chiana or the fine French Charolais. However, dividing it into cuts is not exactly the local butchers' strong suit, as they usually just hack it up with a cleaver. However, this way of dividing the meat has a social element to it. If the slaughtered animal with all its bones is chopped into equal pieces, even the poorest person has a chance of getting hold of a good chunk of meat. Even though western visitors out shopping are delighted by the price of beef, it still remains relatively expensive for the average Armenian.

Pig farming in Armenia is concentrated in wooded areas, especially around the towns of Dilidjan, Idzhevan, Berd and Tatev. There the animals are allowed to run free in the forests and find food for themselves. Many of the piglets have the same clearly visible stripes running along their bodies as young wild boar, so it can be assumed wild boar and domestic pigs still mate now and then. Most domestic pigs are very hairy and hardly ever pink. They more often have dark hair, like some of the Hungarian breeds. Armenian pigs have an active lifestyle that gives their meat a delicious taste that is rarely encountered now in industrialized countries. And the same is said about pigs as about sheep. A pig has to be fat, after all, the flavor is in the fat. This means that they prefer to eat chops with a broad strip of fat round the edge. However, pork is usually served in the form of *khorovats* (kebabs). Chicken also appears on the everyday menu whereas goat is considered unhealthy in Armenia. As a result, very little goat rearing goes on. This has benefits for the soil, which is threatened with erosion, as it does not suffer from the voracious eating habits of these animals that either pull the plants right out of the soil or eat them right down to the root.

Matagh—animal sacrifice

Animal sacrifice *(matagh)* has survived from heathen times right down to the present day—a clear sign that the Armenians will not allow themselves to be robbed of their traditions. Originally, people usually offered the gods large animals like bullocks or lambs. Although the Christian church tried for centuries to forbid such sacrifices, it was never able to maintain the ban for any length of time. In the end, the clergy allowed sacrifices to take place again and gave them a Christian meaning.

Today, the sacrifice is regarded as a votive offering in gratitude for a person being healed or rescued from mortal danger. Famous monasteries or pilgrimage churches, such as Noravank, Gladsor or Gerard, are the setting for matagh. Male animals are sacrificed, because according to the traditional belief, only males can be completely pure. Nowadays the sacrificial victim is usually a rooster. It is brought to the church alive, where it is blessed with salt and ritually slaughtered. The head is left on the church wall as a votive offering. In accordance with a strict tradition, the meat must be divided between seven families. However, this

In the Noravank monastery in the mountains near Yeghegnadsor, animals are still sacrificed today.

rule used to apply to large animals, which are only rarely sacrificed nowadays. Occasionally, the head and feet of an ox that has been slaughtered at home are still brought to the monastery and left in a niche.

A kebab house on Proshyan Street in Yerevan offers shashlik, kebabs, heart and lungs.

Skewered

The host may offer vast quantities of Russian caviar, but no celebration meal is considered a success if just one of the guests sighs, "There weren't even kebabs," because food grilled on skewers is heaven for Armenians. Kebabs *(kyabab)* are an everyday pleasure. They are made with seasoned ground meat, which must always include lamb, formed round a broad skewer and grilled. There are also kebabs in the form of small meatballs on thin skewers. In Yerevan, there are numerous kebab stands that will stay your hunger in between times for the equivalent of about 60 cents. After cooking, the meat is spread on a piece of lavash bread, garnished with salad and sour pickled bell peppers, and wrapped up. Another everyday though less common snack is *shaurma*, which is whole slices of meat grilled on skewers. But the monarch of all dishes on skewers is *khorovats*, or *shashlik* in Russian. In Armenia it is made with pork, or less often lamb. The meat is marinated for a few hours with onions, salt and red paprika powder. The pieces of meat are placed on the skewer alternately with whatever vegetables are in season and grilled, preferably over an open fire.

Fish is also served in the form of kebabs. The favorite fish for kebabs is pollan (see page 286). They are gutted through their gill openings and grilled whole on skewers.

Kebabs are particularly delicious if grapevine twigs are used for fuel. They only take a few minutes to develop an intense heat and they give the meat an exquisite flavor. The preparation and cooking of kebabs is entirely in the hands of the men. The man's duties come to an end only when he has brought the finished kebabs to the table, at which point the women are allowed to use lavash to remove the pieces of meat.

Amarayin khorovats
Summer kebabs

2¼ lb/1 kg pork, e.g. end of neck
Salt
Sweet paprika powder
4 large onions, finely chopped
Juice of 1–2 lemons
2 medium eggplant, roughly diced
3 tomatoes, cut in quarters
2 bell peppers, roughly diced
Fresh herbs, roughly chopped (e.g. parsley, basil, cilantro)
Chives or young scallions, chopped

Cut the meat in bite-sized pieces, sprinkle with salt and paprika powder, mix with the onions, drizzle with lemon juice, and marinate for 2–3 hours. Thread cubes of meat and vegetables on separate skewers and grill over an open fire, turning continuously. Discard the skins from the grilled vegetables and arrange them on a plate with the herbs. Serve the grilled meat with plenty of chives or scallions.

Khorovats tastes best if the meat is grilled over an open charcoal fire.

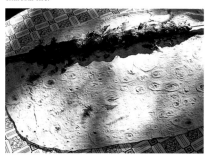

For kebabs, ground meat is shaped round a skewer. The grilled meat and some fresh green herbs are put on a piece of lavash bread.

Then the meat, still on the skewer, is wrapped in the wafer-thin lavash. Only then is the skewer carefully pulled out—and the food is ready to be enjoyed.

Fine beef products

Two appetizers that unfailingly appear on Armenian tables and are usually served to greet visitors on arrival are *bastoorma* and *soojook*.

Bastoorma, known in Turkey as *pasturma*, is a fillet of beef encased in a layer of exquisite herbs and spices. The unique flavor comes from fenugreek, plenty of garlic, hot paprika powder, and black pepper. To make bastoorma, they cut rectangular or fish-shaped fillets and rub them with coarse salt and a little pickling salt, so that they retain their natural blood-red color. After four days, enough water has been drawn out. The pieces of meat are washed and hung to dry for 36 hours in an inner room. During this time, they are pressed every four hours to remove further meat juice. The meat must spend the next two days drying in the open air. Then the spicy-herb paste is spread over them and allowed to soak in for two days. This procedure is repeated three times, with a new coating of paste each time. Then the delicious dried meat is ready to eat, and will keep for months. It is produced both commercially and privately.

Soojookh is a kind of sausage. To make it, beef is cut in small pieces and mixed with salt and pickling salt. Then the meat is stored for a day in a wooden barrel in a special cold store at about 50 °F/10 °C. During this time, the meat juice can run out through holes in the bottom of the barrel. Then the meat is finely chopped, and mixed with salt, pepper, paprika, garlic, and cinnamon. The mixture is put into an intestine and pressed between two boards for three days to give it its typical flattened shape. Then the soojookh is hung up to dry for 10–15 days.

The sausages *yershik* you get in the capital Yerevan are mostly Russian types and of good quality. They include a kind of mortadella and a beer ham. However, if you want to try genuine local meat products, you have to go to the villages. There, for instance, they fill the skin of a piglet with liver, kidney, pieces of meat, and fat, season it well with salt, pepper, and garlic, sew the whole thing up, and boil it slowly in a pot. This delicious specialty is eaten cold.

The beef specialty bastoorma gets its strong taste from a layer of fine herbs and spices.

Meat and poultry dishes

Tezhvezheek
Liver and heart stew

8–9 oz/250 g calf liver
8–9 oz/250 g calf heart
1/3 cup/80 g mutton fat, pork fat, or butter
2 onions, chopped
1–2 large tomatoes
Salt
Pepper
2 bunches fresh herbs, finely chopped, e.g. parsley, dill, tarragon, scallions

Remove the fat and sinew from the liver and heart and clean thoroughly. Dice finely and fry in the hot fat. Add the chopped onions and fry briefly. Blanch the tomatoes briefly in boiling water and peel, then pass through a coarse sieve. Add them to the pan, season with salt and pepper, cover, and simmer for about 15 minutes.
Sprinkle the stew with the fresh chopped herbs before serving.
Tip: If desired, tezhvezheek can also be made with lamb's liver and heart.

Various innards such as the liver, lungs, and heart of calves or lambs form the basis of tezhvezheek.

The Armenians are always generous with onions. For tezhvezheek they only need to be roughly chopped.

Innards have a tendency to become tough quickly when boiled, so they should be cooked for precisely the right length of time.

First the fat and sinew is carefully removed from the innards, then they are finely diced.

The innards are fried first, then the onions are added and finally the tomatoes.

Before serving, tezhvezheek is sprinkled with fresh green herbs. It is best eaten with lavash bread.

Bamiayov kerakoor
Chicken with okra

1 chicken about 3 1/4 lb/1.5 kg, cut in pieces
Salt and pepper
Generous 1 lb/500 g okra
3 tbsp vinegar
2 medium onions, finely chopped
3 tbsp/45 g butter
4 medium tomatoes, cut in four
2 tbsp lemon juice

Poach the chicken pieces in salted water until almost tender, skimming occasionally. Pour off the chicken stock, reserve and keep it warm. Wash the okra, cut off the stalks leaving just enough for the vegetable not to be damaged. Blanch for about 5 minutes in around 1/2 quart/1.5 liters water, to which the vinegar and 1 teaspoon salt have been added, rinse in cold water and leave to drain. Fry the onions in butter, add the chicken, okra and tomatoes and fry briefly. Pour over about 1 cup/250 ml of the chicken stock and the lemon juice, season, cover, and simmer for about 30 minutes over low heat.

Feast days

The Armenians have the longest Christian tradition of any people. In the year 301, the Arsakide ruler Tiridates III made Christianity the state religion and banned heathen cults—twelve years before the Edict of Milan, which simply established the toleration of the Christian Religion in the Roman Empire. Seventeen hundred years later, the Armenian people are strongly characterized by their religion, though the atheistic period of Soviet rule did not leave those who remained in the country unmarked. The great church festivals no longer play a major part in public life, and few of the cultural and culinary traditions connected with them are maintained. However, people still enjoy a celebration, and many families would give the shirts off their backs to be able to treat their guests lavishly. No Armenian banquet is complete without *Kyufta*, a big meat dumpling made from the finest sausage meat, boiled or fried. Fish in the form of *kyufta* or steamed in wine (see page 287) is a traditional dish at Christmas, which is celebrated on January 6th in Armenia. Another feast-day dish is *harissa*, a wheatmeal porridge with chicken, butter and cinnamon that is cooked for a long time. At high Christian festivals it is not customary to eat grilled meat such as *khorovats* (see page 292) that would usually be served to guests on other occasions. Armenian festive meals comprise several courses. As with many eastern styles of cooking, they open with a wealth of appetizers, especially raw and pickled vegetables, herbs, yogurt, the beef specialties *bastoorma* and *soojookh*, cheese, and patés and dips made from lentils, beans and chickpeas. These are followed by hot appetizers of stuffed vegetables, *plav* and soups. The main course is a grill or other meat or fish dish. After that comes a sweet course— *halv*, *pakhlav* or *gata* (see page 304), fresh or dried fruit or puddings such as *anooshapoor*—and finally coffee or tea. The hostess places everything she has prepared on the table, so you might find sour pickled vegetables next to a tempting sweet dessert. Foreign visitors often feel overwhelmed at the sight of the quantity and variety of foods, but should preferably keep this to themselves. The lavishness is all part of the show, and if anything is left over, it reflects all the better on the family honor.

Kyufta
Beef meatballs
(Not illustrated)

2¼ lb/1 kg best beef sausage meat, ordered from the butcher
1 egg
1 small glass brandy
1–2 tbsp salt
1 bunch savory, finely chopped
3 medium onions, very finely chopped
⅔ cup/150 ml milk
2 tbsp all-purpose flour
Paprika powder
About ¾ cup/200 g melted butter

Mix the beef sausage meat with the egg, brandy, salt, savory, onions, milk, paprika powder and 2 tablespoons melted butter to form a smooth paste. Bring water to a boil, and warm a large ladle in it. Use this to form the meat mixture into one large or six smaller meatballs, and place these in the boiling water. When the meatballs rise to the surface, they are done, and should be served immediately with plenty of melted butter.

Garan mis tsiranov
Lamb with apricots

1½ cups/250 g dried apricots, pitted
1¾ lb/800 g shoulder of lamb
Salt
4 medium onions, coarsely chopped
3½ tbsp/50 g butter
About 4 tbsp tomato paste
½ bunch parsley, finely chopped

Soak the apricots in lukewarm water for about 3 hours, drain, reserving the liquor, and leave to drip. Cut the lamb into bite-sized cubes, cover with salted water, and simmer over medium heat for about 20 minutes. Pour off the stock and reserve, and fry the meat cubes in the butter with the onion. Pour over about ¾ cup/200 ml meat stock and 3½ tablespoons of the liquor from the apricots, stir in the tomato paste, add the apricots, cover and simmer for about 30 minutes until the meat is tender, adding more water if needed. To serve, sprinkle with chopped parsley.

Wine

Armenia is considered to be one of the cradles of wine growing. In the 1st century A.D., the Greek geographer Strabo, writing about the fertile land to the south and north of the river Araks, reported, "The people never dig about the vines, although they prune them every fifth year. The new vines begin to fruit in the second year, and when they mature, they yield so much that the people leave a large part of the fruit on the branches."

Fertile lava soils and warm winds make wine-growing possible in four regions of the country, despite the fact that they are relatively high and have cold winters. Most of the grapes are grown in the Araks Plain; the other wine-growing regions are in the northeast of the country around the city of Idzhevan, the area around Yehegnadsor, and three isolated areas around the towns of Goris, Kapan, and Meghri in the southeast.

Industrial wine production in Armenia began in the 1870s. The sector expanded during the period of Soviet rule, though in those 70 years the industry had only one target: quantity. The trouble began with the harvest. The grapes were simply thrown into the back of a truck and not driven to

the factory until the evening, in temperatures of over 95 °F/35 °C. No wonder the white wines, in particular, were oxidized. Also, for decades there was no investment in winemaking technology.

After the break-up of the Soviet Union, wine production suffered a serious collapse and the number of vineyards being worked still continues to fall. However, Armenia is currently trying to free itself from the burden of the past. At the start of the new century, a few distinctly better wines appeared on the market, and since then many new wineries and brands have been established, though many disappear as rapidly as they appeared. Most firms bear the name of the place where the grapes come from, but the grape varieties only rarely figure in the names of the wines. On the whole, however, it can be said that the quality is improving. The area of Armenia devoted to grape growing is currently around 64,250 acres/26,000 hectares, and around 200,000 metric tonnes of grapes are harvested each year, though most of these are for the table. Around 80,000 metric tonnes go to the wineries, which produced some 530,000 US gallons/2 million liters of wine in 2003. From the Araks Plain come the dry white wine *Araks* (produced by Getap) and *Yeraskh* (produced by Eraskh). From the wine region around Yeghegnasdor comes the light, medium sweet red wine *Vernashen* (produced by Getap). *Tushpa* from the firm

Noah is said to have planted a vineyard on Mount Ararat and got drunk tasting his own wine (Genesis 9: 20–24). In the Sistine Chapel in Rome, Michelangelo immortalized the moment when Shem, Ham and Japheth covered their father's nakedness.

of VAN 77, one of the country's most popular wines, comes as a dry red, a sweet red, and also as a white or red muscatel. Finally the Iyevan Wine Plant in the northeast of the country produces a white and a red *Idzhevan*, both of them dry. The sparkling wines *Haikakan Shampain* produced by the firm of Yerevani Shampain Ginineri Gortsaran in the capital are of good quality. The brut and the dry *(chor)* have a distinct note of yeast, which is less evident in the semidry *(kiatchor)*. There are still problems with the strong red wines, which should mature in the wood for several years. Armenia would seem to be perfect for them, especially with the Areni wines, but even expensive bottles are not yet able to fulfill the expectations aroused by the labels. The reasons for this lie mainly in microbiological problems. People are now hoping for an upswing in wine growing and wine technology as a result of increased investment by the major firms and the expertise of western European grape growers and winemakers. The most important prerequisites for this are available, as the natural conditions in Armenia offer great potential.

Grape varieties

A book on Armenian winemaking published in 1996 listed 64 varieties of grapes. However, many farmers have lost all knowledge of the differences between the varieties, and now only a few, mostly local native varieties are used in winemaking.

Areni: the classic grape variety for the once famous dark red wine from Areni and Yeghegnadsor in the south of the country is found almost nowhere outside Armenia and has great potential—thanks to the use of modern winemaking techniques.

Kakhet: this native Armenian variety is used for red dessert wines.

Meghrabujr (the "one that smells of honey"): the Madeleine Angevine and Chasselas (Gutedel) varieties are also included in modern Armenian grape production. Potential for high quality red dessert wine.

Mschali: this aromatic Armenian white-wine grape has at least some share in the best of the current white wines, and also produces fine table grapes that can be stored well into the winter.

Nerkarat: a new Armenian-bred variety currently used for red dessert wine.

Rkaziteli: in Armenia this white grape originating from Georgia (see page 253) is often blended with Mschali.

Voskehat: table wines and various kinds of strong wine are made from this native Armenian white wine grape.

Wine growing within sight of Ararat: extensive grape-growing areas characterize the landscape around the monastery of Chor Virap near Artashat in the plain of the River Araks.

Konyak

The Armenians still like to tell you that Winston Churchill preferred Armenian brandy to French, after tasting it for the first time at the Yalta Conference in 1945. Many Armenians think their *konyak* with its delicate vanilla flavor is well able to stand comparison with French cognac, or at least has the potential to do so. They are probably not too far wrong in that, as when the state companies were privatized, the French Pernod-Ricard group immediately bought the main producer "Yerevanski Konyachny Savod Ararat," founded in 1887. All the same, it will not be possible to buy Armenian konyak in western Europe straight away, as the French would not look too kindly on that kind of competition. The new owners see the "obvious" market for this traditional export product more in the countries of the former Soviet Union, where Armenia meant Konyak, and vice versa. On all bottles sold in Armenia, it still says *Armyanski Konyak* in Russian. In this part of the world, they have never bothered about the fact that the name "cognac," however it is spelt, is reserved for the original French product only.

The Armenians produce their konyak in the same way as the French, through double distillation of white wines, made from Mschali and Rkaziteli grapes, among others. The distillate contains about 70 percent alcohol and is as pale as water. It only gets its darker color after maturing in the wood and with the addition of 7–25 g per liter of sugar coloring. Immediately before bottling, the brandy is diluted with pure water to a strength of 40–50 percent proof. Under the brand name *Ararat* there are many different types that can be divided into groups: ordinary konyak (40–42 percent proof), matured for 3–5 years, brandy matured for up to 10 years (42–57 percent proof) and old konyak. The youngest is the 3-year-old konyak (3-star) that

really deserves high praise for its fine fruity taste. Even experienced palates can scarcely distinguish any further refinement in the 5-year-old (5-star), though many Armenians are convinced that their konyak keeps on getting better with age, as it should. Occasionally even older konyaks turn up in Yerevan fleamarkets, including a 50-year-old from the Soviet era. But the differences between the many different kinds are scarcely perceptible. A second kind of brandy, *Armyanski brandi*, is sold outside the official stores. Even the 3-year-old tastes extremely woody, which cannot only be due to maturing in the wood.

High-proof fruit

The Armenians show true mastery in producing fruit brandies, though this remained a secret for a long time, as Armenian fruit brandies are not sold outside the country. They are mostly distilled at home on a very small scale. Only in Nagorno-Karabakh is there a company producing a very good mulberry brandy. The raw materials for other brandies are various berries, other kinds of grape, apricots, and pears. The results are excellent; the apricot and mulberry brandies, as well as transparent grape brandies can hold their own with the best European products. Brandy made from cornelian cherries *honi oghi* is quite outstanding. It is reminiscent of the rare Alsatian *houx*, distilled from holly berries.

The high art of distillation also finds expression in vodka, which is by far the most frequently drunk liquor in Armenia. It is made only from wheat and tastes incomparably mild—even better than most Russian vodkas, in the opinion of many connoisseurs. Armenia is said to have been the only country in the Soviet Union with no drying-out cells, and in fact, though the Armenians enjoy drinking and drink a lot, they rarely drink too much, and drunks are hardly ever seen. This also has to do with drinking customs, which are much less prescriptive than in Russia. Nobody is forced to empty their glass, so you can drink a dozen toasts with a single small glass. It is enough just to pick up your glass for a moment, even if you do not drink from it.

Background illustration: After double distillation, the konyak matures in wooden barrels for several years.

Facing page, above: The grape must for konyak is still fermented in wooden barrels.

Facing page, below: Fine brandies— *Nairi* and *Dvin*, the two brandies that mature for longer

Left: The Russian labeling of the Yerevan Konyak Factory "Ararat" marks barrel no. 316.

Highland orchard

"The best fruits in the world grow here!" After tasting the fruit that grows here, you can really confirm this patriotic Armenian claim. There are several closely linked reasons for the outstanding quality of the fruit. The strong sunlight ensures sweetness, the winds that blow almost constantly and the temperature variations, especially at heights of above 3,250 feet/1,000 m, promote the formation of acids. As the country does not export any fruit, it is picked when fully ripe and reaches the markets on the same day. Apples and pears, peaches and plums, grapes and berries, plus figs, mulberries, cornelian cherries, and pomegranates head the buyers' favorites.

However, the pride of Armenia is the apricot *(tsiran)*. Even its scientific name is a nod in the direction of this Caucasian country: *Armeniaca vulgaris* or *Prunus armeniaca*, meaning Armenian plum, although the apricot is related to the peach rather than the plum. At any rate, scientists reckon the home of this plant was in Asia Minor, where a number of fruits later cultivated in Europe also originated. The English word apricot is derived from the Latin *praecox* or *praecoquum* ("early"), alluding to *Persicum praecoquum*, the early-ripening peach. The Austrian name "Marille" has its roots in the Italian *armellino*—meaning "Armenian apple." The usually white flowers of this warmth-loving tree appear in April, and the fruit is harvested as early as June. There are no clearly defined apricot varieties in Armenia. Paradoxically, late ripening varieties do not achieve the same melting sweetness as the earlier types, that you cannot help enthusing over—concentrated, juicy, and with the inimitable mildness that sets this fruit apart. Apricots have a permanent place in Armenian cuisine. They are enjoyed in both substantial stews and sweet soups, in meat dishes and desserts, fresh or dried.

Like many other kinds of fruit, the quince is a member of the rose family. Its bittersweet taste only develops during cooking. It can also be dried and used in upmarket dishes.

The rose family

Apricots, quinces, apples, pears, peaches, plus cherries and plums which are also grown in large quantities in Armenia, are all members of the rose family. This family includes a large number of decorative and useful plants. The small country of Armenia can boast 188 species. There are 16 species in the pear genus alone, and 11 species of whitethorn. The names of many species conceal a reference to their Armenian origin, e.g. *Rosa tsangetsura* (Sangesur is an area in the south of the country) or *Sorbus hajastana* (a rowan, and Hajastan means Armenia in the local language). Many have edible fruits, including the Armenian whitethorn *Crataegus armena*, whose floury red berries are threaded on strings and sold.

Quinces *(serkevil)* have also been cultivated in western Asia since very ancient times. They flower in May, and the fruits, which are similar in color and shape to some varieties of pear, can be harvested in October. In the Roman Empire, the quince was sacred to the goddess of love, and it needs devotion if you are going to make use of it, because the raw fruit is not good to eat. However, once cooked, they develop a delicious flavor, and their high pectin content means their juice sets firm to make an aromatic jelly. Quinces are also dried and used in more upmarket cooking, along with other dried fruit, especially apricots.

Left: Apricots betray their origins through their Latin name *Prunus armeniaca* —Armenian plum.

Right: In spring blossoming apricot orchards transform Armenia into a flowering paradise. The sweet varieties can be harvested as early as June.

Dried fruits

When fruit and vegetables are ready for harvesting, Armenian orchards virtually explode. The hardest work is down to the housewives; they have to preserve nature's gifts, so they can have them available in winter too. For instance, apricots are made into sweet compote, jam of the kind the Russians like (*munaba*, Russian *varenye*), or syrup, which is then diluted to taste. In the windy highlands of Armenia, drying is naturally one of the main methods of preserving, and dried fruit adds a pleasant, fruity, slightly sour note to many dishes.

Almost anything is dried, including berries. Dried cherries, apricots, peaches, pears, apples, cornelian cherries, and raisins all taste absolutely delicious. An unusual taste for foreigners is that of dried, not very sweet, slightly floury kaki (Japanese persimmons). These fruits, which have a high water content, can only be dried in an extremely dry climate. For home use they make the least possible effort and dry the fruit with the pits in. On the other hand, fruits that are to be sold later are carefully pitted, cutting them as little as possible. The fruit is laid out in the sun, in which case it must be turned regularly, or threaded on strings and hung in the sun and wind.

The Armenians' passion for stuffing and wrapping extends to dried fruit as well. Figs stuffed with walnuts, or peaches stuffed with chopped walnuts, cinnamon, and sugar are absolutely delicious. Candied fruits are also popular. Specialists candy and dry things like small eggplant, which they stuff with chopped walnuts as well. However, you can only get such delicacies occasionally in the two big markets in Yerevan.

Another dried product is *passer*, thinly rolled sheets of fruit jelly. To make it, they boil up apricots, damsons, plums, peaches, and apples, remove all the thick bits, and purée the remainder. Then they boil the purée until it reaches a glutinous jelly-like consistency, spread the jelly on foil, and dry it in the sun. After a few days these "fruit leaves" can easily be peeled off. They are usually sold as rolls. You just tear off a little piece and eat it, or you can dissolve it in water to make a refreshing drink.

In the grape-growing regions of Armenia, raisins *(chamich)* are still often dried in the sun and wind.

Sweet soups

Sweet soups called *anooshapoor* are an Armenian specialty. They may be made with wheat grains, apricots, mixed dried fruit, or a mixture of everything. They also include sweet porridges like *chavits* made from whole wheat flour, butter, sugar syrup, and sweet cream or *asuda* made with flour and grape syrup. *Anooshapoor* is usually eaten as a hot or cold dessert.

Anooshapoor
Sweet soup with dried fruit

$\frac{1}{2}$ cup/100 g barley grits or wheat bulgur
$\frac{1}{2}$ tsp salt
1 cup/150 g dried apricots, pitted
1$\frac{1}{4}$ cups/150 g raisins
1 cup/150 g prunes, pitted
About $\frac{1}{2}$ cup/ 100 g brown sugar
Chopped almonds or walnuts

Soak the grits or bulgur for about 6 hours, drain, and bring to a boil in about 1$\frac{1}{2}$ quarts/1.5 liter salted water. Add the dried apricots, raisins, prunes, and sugar and simmer for about 90 minutes over the lowest heat.
This sweet dish may be eaten hot or cold. If desired, it may be served with chopped almonds or walnuts.

Dried and candied figs do not merely tickle the palate, they are stuffed with nuts, sugar crystal and cinnamon to make the Armenian specialty *alani*.

Candied and dried apricots, plums, and figs—each stuffed with half a walnut into the bargain—go very well with tea and cakes.

In the country, pears are usually simply dried. However, if they are to be sold, they are dipped in sugar syrup to make them nice and shiny.

To make a dried fruit roulade *(rulet)*, roughly chopped walnuts, fruit jelly and sugar are wrapped in a leaf *(passer)* of apricot jelly.

Sugary fruits: as well as figs and pears, tiny melons are also wonderful for candying. *Soojookh* balls are walnuts in grape jelly.

Of course in the homeland of apricots, everyone eats them dried as well. They taste good as a little snack or in substantial dishes.

One of the most popular of Armenia's pastry specialties is *pakhlava*, which has a lovely nut filling. It comes in the form of tray-baked slices or tiny, individually baked pieces.

Sweet delights

Gata is the most common sweet in Armenia. This general name covers several types of pastry. Some of these are made only of yeast dough, others only of flaky pastry, and there is a third kind that combines the two. The filling *(khoris)* for these cakes consists of a sweet dough with confectioners' sugar and vanilla. The fanciest gata contain nuts and taste rather like the fine Swiss Nusstorte.

Major festivals and celebrations mean a lot of hours spent working together in the kitchen making the classic sweetmeats *pakhlava* (see page 346) and *halva* or the almond cake *nshablit*, among other things. The time-consuming preparation of sweet pastries requiring many different steps is typical. Housewives always make their own flaky pastry, and they have it down to a fine art. Pakhlava comes in different shapes: big squares, little cakes, or even delicious little plaits. Fine spices such as cinnamon, cardamom, cloves, saffron, and vanilla are often used to give these pastries a special flavor.

Nshablit
Almond cookies

6 cups/650 g confectioners' sugar
2 egg whites
5½ cups/500 g ground almonds
1¾ cups/250 g all-purpose flour
Butter for greasing
About 40 whole almonds

Mix the confectioners' sugar with 7 tablespoons hot water. Beat the egg whites stiff, add the sugar while stirring continuously, then stir in the ground almonds. Heat the mixture in a bain-marie (see Glossary), keep the temperature at about 105 °F/40 °C, and stir until the mixture is smooth and even. Cool to room temperature, then work in the flour, stirring continuously. Knead the dough thoroughly, form into small cookies, place on a greased baking sheet, and decorate each one with a whole almond. Bake in a preheated oven at 300 °F/150 °C for about 30 minutes.
Tip: If desired, you can decorate the cookies with frosting.

Halva

3⅓ cups/500 g whole wheat flour
1 scant cup/200 g clarified butter
7 tbsp/200 g runny honey (see Glossary)

Toss the flour in the clarified butter until it is golden yellow in color. Mix with the honey and fry for a further 5 minutes. Spread on a plate or a marble slab, allow to cool, and cut into squares.
Tip: Instead of just whole wheat flour, you can use half flour and half ground sesame.

Gata
Yeast flaky pastries

1½ envelopes/10 g dried yeast
Generous ¾ cup/200 ml lukewarm milk
About 3 generous cups/450 g all-purpose flour
3 eggs
1 pinch salt
7 tbsp/100 g sugar
14 tbsp/200 g soft butter
1 egg yolk

For the filling:
Generous 1⅓ cups/200 g all-purpose flour
⅔ cup/150 g butter, softened
1⅓ cups/150 g confectioners' sugar
1 tsp salt
1 vanilla bean

For the pre-dough, dissolve the yeast in half the milk, take ¾ cup/125 g of the flour and work into a smooth dough. Cover and leave to rest in a warm place for about 30 minutes.
Mix the remaining milk with the eggs, salt, sugar, the remaining flour, and half the butter, add the pre-dough, knead thoroughly, and allow to rest for another 30 minutes, this time in a cool place.
Meantime, prepare the filling. Mix the flour with the melted butter, confectioners' sugar, salt, and the pith scraped out of the vanilla bean, and use your hands to work it to a crumbly consistency. Divide the dough into 4 balls of equal size and the butter into 4 equal portions. Roll out each of the balls to a thickness of about 1⁄16 inch/2 mm, spread with some of the soft butter, and fold over twice. Roll out, butter again, fold up, and roll out again. Go through this procedure 3–5 times. Divide each folded piece of dough in two and roll out each half into an 8 inch/20-cm diameter round about ¼ inch/½ cm thick. Put one quarter of the filling in the center of one round, then cover with a second and press the edges together firmly. Make 4 gata cakes in the same way, prick the tops with a fork, and decorate, brush with egg yolk, and bake in a preheated oven at 350 °F/180 °C for about 30 minutes. Cut in pieces before serving.

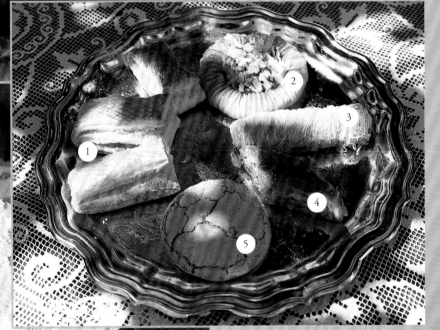

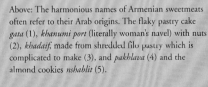

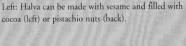

Above: The harmonious names of Armenian sweetmeats often refer to their Arab origins. The flaky pastry cake *gata* (1), *khanumi port* (literally woman's navel) with nuts (2), *khadaif*, made from shredded filo pastry which is complicated to make (3), and *pakhlava* (4) and the almond cookies *nshablit* (5).

Above left: Small pieces of gata are traditionally made from yeast dough. Vanilla adds a delicious extra touch to the filling of flour, butter, and sugar.

Left: Halva can be made with sesame and filled with cocoa (left) or pistachio nuts (back).

The high art of reading coffee grounds

After drinking Armenian coffee, which is not filtered, a thick layer of grounds remains in the cup. If you want to find out about your future, you turn the cup over and leave it to stand for 10 minutes so that the grounds trickle down the sides of the cup in streaks. Then various signs and patterns can be seen in black and white, and imagination rules, when it comes to interpreting them. A dove means a happy marriage, a bed means illness or changes will follow. Scissors indicate quarrelling, a cross means a wedding. Ants mean good fortune, snakes suggest intrigues, and old and new enemies. A crown promises success in all areas of life. The figures 2, 3, 5, and 8 foretell something negative, whereas 1, 4, 7, and 9 allow you to hope for something positive. Letters are interpreted as people's initials. Of course the position of the signs also plays a part. The bottom of the cup is the heart, the sides mean home, and the side opposite where you drank from is "outside." Incidentally, a look into your future does not come cheap. Professional coffee-ground readers in Yerevan charge the equivalent of $13 a sitting for fortune-telling after you have drunk your coffee.

Whether or not you believe the results, reading coffee grounds is considered a serious profession in Yerevan.

Coffee

Black coffee *(sev soorj)* is as commonly drunk and popular in Armenia as espresso in Italy.

In the 15th century, an expedition left Aden in present-day Yemen for southeast Abyssinia, now Ethiopia. They were intending to bring back ivory, but returned with a new discovery from the province of Kaffa—coffee. The Arabs were responsible for distributing it more widely, as they took the beans, which soon became a highly desirable commodity, to the holy city of Mecca and from there to Egypt. In 1517, the Ottomans conquered Egypt and sent sacks of coffee back to Istanbul as booty. There they knew how to handle it and under Suleiman the Magnificent the first coffeehouses were opened so this stimulating beverage could be drunk in public.

At this time, if not before, the Armenians also discovered coffee, though they claim to have known it before the Turks and point with pride to the fact that they have their own word for coffee, *surch*, which means something like "slurped" or "savored." The first café in Vienna, even earlier than the Kolshitzky family's "Kaffeehütte" (see page 206), was supposedly founded by an Armenian merchant in 1688. Coffee had already reached Europe around 1615, arriving first in Venice, where the first cafés opened a few years later. After that it spread rapidly to London, Marseilles, Amsterdam, The Hague, Paris, and Vienna. Everyone was drinking coffee and coffeehouses were all the rage. Roasting houses were set up, especially in the ports. In many places, housewives roasted and ground the beans themselves for centuries, and the Armenians still like to grind their coffee at home. However, you can buy ground coffee in the market, or have your favorite kind ground on the spot in an electric machine. Armenians do not always spend long on making coffee. In offices they mostly make do with any old receptacle and leave the rest to an immersion heater of the kind also commonly found in Russia. Armenian coffee *haikakan soorj* is the equivalent of mocha and is known elsewhere as Greek or Turkish coffee. All the same, it would be a real faux pas to ask for "Turkish Coffee" in an Armenian restaurant. It is easy to prepare. You put a heaped teaspoon of coffee and sugar in a special little brass pot *(serchyeb)* and pour in the amount of boiling water that will fit into a small coffee cup. It is sweetened to taste and relatively weak. They reckon on between a half and one teaspoonful of sugar for each teaspoonful of coffee. Finally they heat the coffee as slowly as possible—the secret of its nice flavor—until it boils. True gourmets slow down the process by placing a tray filled with sand on the hob and placing the brass pot in it.

On special occasions, Armenian coffee is heated very slowly on the hob standing in a layer of sand.

Today many Armenians still buy coffee beans and grind them at home or let the seller grind them to the desired strength.

RUSSIAN FEDERATION

CASPIAN

Quba

Dävädçi

Siyaäzän

Greater Caucasus

Zagatala

GEORGIA

Shaki

Ismayilli

Samaxi

Sumqayit

Abşeron Peninsula

BAKU

Lake Mingäçevir Mingäçevir

Göyçay

Agsu

Agdal

Üçar

Kürdämir

Gobustan

SEA

Üozax

Akstafa

Kür

Tovuz

Sämkir

Gäncä

Yevlax

Xanlar

Naftalan

Bärdä

Sabirabad

Ali-Bayramli

Kür

AZERBAIJAN

Imishli

Salyan

Agdam

Beylagan

Neftçala

Karabakh Range
(belongs to Armenia)

Lesser Caucasus

ARMENIA

Xankändi
(in Armenian, Stepanakert)

Masalli

Araks

IRAN

Länkäran

TURKEY

Autonomous
Republic of
Naxçivan

Naxçivan

Julja

Aras (arm. Araks)

Astara

N

0   30 miles/50 km

Elnara Ismailova

AZƏRBAYCAN

Azerbaijan

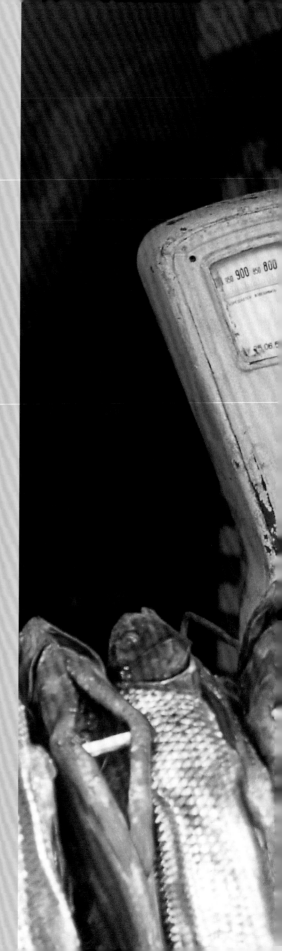

Azerbaijan—the very sound of the name conjures up echoes of the Orient; the air is full of the fragrance of saffron, fresh herbs, and fruity wine; for millions of years little flames of natural gas have lit up the night in the ancient "Land of Fire." The learned men of antiquity were impressed by the variety and fertility of this land on the western shore of the Caspian Sea. In the 1st century B.C., the Greek geographer and historian Strabo wrote of this Garden of Eden at the foot of the Caucasus: "Often two or three crops can be harvested from one seed. It is the first time that, without lying fallow, and reaped in a very primitive way, the earth brings forth fifty-fold."

Protected by the Caucasus, a fertile lowland triangle lies beside the biggest inland sea in the world. Nine climate zones, ranging from Mediterranean to Alpine, can be distinguished within a very small space. Nevertheless, large parts of this country where East and West meet is characterized by a sunny climate with mild winters. The vegetation is equally varied. The country is home to more than 4,500 species of plants, two thirds of all the species in the whole of the Caucasus. Many different kinds of fruit, vegetables, and herbs ripen and develop their full flavor under the southeastern sun. Huge herds of sheep grazing on the green alpine meadows and the steppes provide milk and juicy meat. The rivers teem with trout, pike, and perch. The Caspian Sea also offers unique delicacies, turning every meal into a banquet, and inviting gourmets to indulge themselves. More than 40 different food fish come from Azerbaijan, as well as that irresistible delicacy, caviar. In addition, in the Soviet era, the country was one of the most important providers of salt to the gigantic empire. After the 3rd century, agriculture, animal husbandry, wine growing and cookery were greatly enriched when the caravans of the silk road brought spices, fruits, rice, and natural silk into the country. Thanks to the favorable climate, many of these products soon became naturalized. After the 7th century, the Arabs brought not only Islam but also new ingredients and cooking methods into the country. Nowadays, all these influences are completely integrated into the Azerbaijanis' everyday life, making the food such a colorful kaleido-scope—fragrant saffron rice, countless versions of stuffed vegetables, meat and fine fish from the Caspian Sea grilled over an open fire, fresh herbs, tasty cheeses, desserts and oriental sweetmeats. Wine symbolizes the openness and joie de vivre of this traditionally Islamic country, and tea opens the door to visitors in this house where East and West meet.

Previous page: The apparently timeless region around the ancient cultural center of Shemakha is one of the most delightful areas in Azerbaijan.

Right: The fishseller in Baku proudly presents his gleaming golden smoked fish from the Caspian Sea.

Rice

Rice is the most important source of nourishment for over half of the world's population, and has been for 5,000 years. Rice crops up in ancient legends, and has even been used as a means of payment. Official communications and private notes have found their way onto rice paper. Originating from southern China and the eastern part of India, rice has spread over every continent and continually stimulated innovation and trade.

In Azerbaijan, rice (*chaltik* or *duyu*) is known as the "people's second bread," and archaeological finds in Bejlagan have enabled its use to be traced back to the 9th century. Rice (Latin: *oryza sativa*) was already being cultivated in this area in the Middle Ages and exported to neighboring countries. In the 19th century, there were huge rice fields in the areas of Astara, Lankaran, Shaki-Sagatala, and Guba. At the 1889 Caucasian exhibition in Tbilisi, Azerbaijan was represented by 58 kinds of wheat, 27 of millet and 58 of rice. In 1930, the rice-growing area over Azerbaijan still covered more than 124,000 acres/50,000 hectares. However, as a consequence of the expansion of the more profitable tobacco plantations and the rapid development of vegetable growing in Lankaran, rice-growing land had shrunk to around 4,500 acres/1,800 hectares by the mid 1970s. Since 1992, farmers have been encouraged to start growing rice again, so that demand can increasingly be met from home production. As a result, in 2005 they were able to harvest some 8,300 metric tonnes of rice from 5,718 acres/2,314 hectares of land.

The plant's adaptability makes it possible to use different cultivation methods, with or without artificial watering. No matter whether the rice is sown directly or seedlings are planted out in flooded fields as is customary in Azerbaijan, this is always preceded by intensive soil preparation. After cleaning the rice fields, the flooded soil is manured at the end of November and, in order to avoid nutrient and water loss, the surface of the field is allowed to harden. The ground is not plowed again until the spring. The young plants spend three weeks growing in special nursery beds before being planted out in May. It used to be the custom to celebrate in the fields right next to the last row of seedlings. At the end of August, 18–20 days after flowering, they stop watering the fields. The harvest begins two weeks later. The rice is mown and laid out to dry. After two or three days, it is threshed, husked, and polished by machine.

Rice has a top position in Armenian cuisine. The national dish *plov* comes in countless versions, and rice is also indispensable for soups, desserts and semolina production. Round-grained varieties are used in soups like *toyug shorba* (chicken soup with dried fruit), ground meat stuffings for grape leaves and cabbage rolls, and dumplings for soup.

Plov
Rice with butter and saffron

3 g saffron
5½ cups/1 kg basmati rice
Salt
1 egg yolk
Generous 1⅓ cups/200 g all-purpose flour
About 14 tbsp/200 g clarified butter

Soak the saffron overnight in ¾ cup/200 ml lukewarm water. Wash the rice, and soak for at least 3 hours in 5 quarts/5 liter salted lukewarm water. Make a dough with the egg yolk, flour, 1 pinch salt, and 1 tablespoon clarified butter, and leave to rest for ½ hour. In a large pot, bring 4 quarts/4 liters water to a boil, add salt, and slowly add the drained rice. Boil over high heat for 6–8 minutes until half cooked, stirring occasionally, then strain through a sieve. Roll the dough out to about ⅜ inch/1 cm thick, grease the bottom of the plov pot with a little clarified butter, line it with the dough, and bake on the hob over medium heat for about 15 minutes. Pile the drained rice in a cone-shape on the dough, add layers of clarified butter and saffron, but reserving most of the saffron to pour over the mound of rice right at the end. Place a dishtowel between the pot and lid to make sure it is airtight, and steam the plov over low heat for 1 hour. To serve, put the saffron-yellow peak of the rice mountain on a spare plate, spoon the remaining rice onto a large plate, place the yellow peak on top, and pour over melted butter. Cut the pastry base in pieces and serve with the rice.

A dough is prepared from egg yolk, flour, salt, and clarified butter, and rolled with a wooden rolling pin to make a thin disc the diameter of the rice pot.

While the precooked plov rice is draining, the bottom of the rice pot is greased with clarified butter and lined with the thin disc of dough.

The dough is baked on the hob. Then the drained rice is put into the pot in layers with the butter and saffron liquid. Now the rice is covered and steamed.

When the rice is ready, the yellow peak is put on one side and the lower layers spooned onto a serving dish first. The saffron peak is draped over the top.

Now the layer of baked dough is lifted out of the pot and cut in pieces with a knife. The crisp pieces of dough are arranged on the rice.

The prettily arranged plov rice is served with various meat and vegetable accompaniments. On feast days several accompaniments are served.

Top right: Rice has been cultivated in Azerbaijan since the
Middle Ages. It is the basic food and is mainly grown in
the wetlands of Lankaran.

The freshly harvested rice is husked and polished by
machine. In Azerbaijani cuisine they use almost exclusively white, medium-grain rice.

Festive plov

The Azerbaijani national dish *plov* is the high point of every festive meal and every family celebration. Unlike the pilaf dishes of other eastern countries, where vegetables and meat are often cooked together with the rice, the rice for plov is usually prepared separately from the other ingredients. First it must be washed and soaked. In a special pot that tapers toward the top, the half-cooked, drained rice is shaped into a cone on a bed of dough or rice, an infusion of saffron is poured over it, and the rice is steamed again. After all, the color, consistency and flavor of the rice proves the skill of the cook.

The different versions of plov are determined by the accompaniments—meat or vegetables, sweet or cooked with milk. Plov with lamb is popular as *govurma plovu* or *sabsa govurma plovu*. For *gijmä plovu*, ground lamb is mixed with raisins and chestnuts, while pieces of lamb with eggplant are used in *badimchan plovu*. Among the exceptions are *doshama plovu*, in which fillet of lamb is stewed until juicy and tender underneath the rice, and *pakhla plovu*, for which precooked white beans are put in the pot on layers in between the rice and both are steamed together.

Lovers of poultry enjoy stuffed chicken in the form of *lavangi plovu* or chicken trimmings with onions, eggs, turmeric, lemon juice, and saffron in *chigirtma plovu*. Raisins, almonds, cumin, and saffron flavor the chicken in *toyug plovu*. fish also goes very well with rice, for instance in stuffed Caspian roach (*kutum*, see page 333) or fried salmon with onions in the dish *balig plovu*. With vegetarian plov, they serve dried fruits sautéed in butter, for instance apricots, raisins, and sometimes plums, and also *kuku* or *badimchan chirgitmasi*, omelets with herbs or eggplant. For *süd*, the rice is not cooked in two stages, but boiled in milk until it is soft, and served with raisins as a sugary mountain.

Plov is traditionally eaten with a spoon; a fork is used to break up the accompaniments. Anyone who likes improvising can find countless ways of varying the classic recipes. And if there is any left over, it will taste just as good the next day, when the flavor of the saffron has thoroughly worked its way in. To warm it up, the rice is put in a pot with a few tablespoons of water and heated while stirring gently. All the same, warmed up plov is rarely served to guests, as the rice is no longer "al dente," as it is when freshly steamed.

Lavangi plovu
Plov with stuffed chicken (1)

6 tbsp/50 g raisins
4 medium onions
1¼ cups/150 g shelled walnuts
⅔ cup/150 g plum purée
Salt
Black pepper
1 medium chicken, 2–2¼ lb/900 g–1 kg
Slices of lemon for garnishing

Soak the raisins for at least 30 minutes in lukewarm water. Purée the 4 onions in a blender, wrap in a dish-cloth, squeeze out the juice thoroughly, and put the onion purée in a bowl.

Put the nuts through the blender as well, and add them with the raisins to the onion purée. Stir in the plum purée, (reserving 2–3 tablespoons), and season with salt and pepper.

Wash the chicken, pat dry, salt inside and out, and rub with the remaining plum purée. Fill with the prepared stuffing and roast in a preheated oven at 340–350 °F/170–180 °C for about 45 minutes until crisp and brown. Serve the chicken with the plov rice and garnish with slices of lemon as desired.

Holy rice

The great value still placed on rice and bread today reflects an ancient legend. The Prophet Mohammed praised rice as a sign of culture and source of life. Everyone should therefore treat it with great care.

Khadisha, the prophet's first wife, was an expert at making plov. One winter evening she was preparing this popular dish and had just put the rice on a cloth on a chest in order to check and sort every grain—the smooth white ones for the plov, the worm-eaten ones for the birds. Suddenly a grain of rice fell to the floor.

Mohammed had determined that no food from nature should be spoilt through carelessness or trodden on. So Khadisha looked for the grain, but could not find it, even with her husband's help. Finally, Mohammed suggested letting water into the room, because then the rice grain would float. And indeed, when the family were already standing up to their calves in water, she spotted the grain of rice—a small white bead on the water that was now rescued.

Sabsa govurma plovu
Plov with lamb and herbs (2)

1 g saffron
2¼ lb/1 kg lamb
Salt and pepper
⅔ cup/150 g clarified butter
2 medium onions, finely chopped
1 tbsp lemon juice
5 oz/150 g each of spinach, dill, fresh cilantro and
scallions, finely chopped
Generous ¾ cup/200 g natural yogurt
4–5 cloves garlic, peeled and pressed

Soak the saffron in 7 tablespoons/100 ml lukewarm
water for at least 3 hours. Roughly dice the meat,
season with salt and pepper, and fry in 3½ tablespoons clarified butter. Saute the onions in a little
butter, and add to the meat along with the saffron
and lemon juice. Pour over ¾ cup/200 ml water,
and simmer over medium heat. After about 30 minutes, add the vegetables and herbs, cover well, and
continue cooking over medium heat for a further
20 minutes until the meat is tender, stirring occasionally. Then add the rest of the clarified butter,
stir well, cover, and leave to draw without heat for
another 10 minutes.
Serve with garlic yogurt (yogurt mixed with the
pressed garlic).

Shirin govurma plovu
Sweet plov with dried fruits (3)

Scant 1¼ cups/150 g raisins
1¼ cups/200 g dried apricots
14 tbsp/200 g clarified butter
Sugar to taste

Wash the raisins and dried apricots, cover with
water, soak for about 30 minutes, and drain. Melt
the clarified butter in a pan and fry the fruit over
medium heat until golden brown.
This dried fruit accompaniment is scattered over
the plov rice and sprinkled with sugar.
Variation: Instead of 200 g apricots, you could if
you like use half and half dried apricots and pitted
prunes.

Govurma plovu
Festive plov with meat and chestnuts (4)
(Serves 4–6)

1 cup/100 g cherry plums, pitted
may be replaced by prunes
1¼ lb/600 g lamb or beef
Salt
3 medium onions, halved lengthwise and sliced
7 tbsp/100 g clarified butter
7 oz/200 g chestnuts
Black pepper
1 tbsp turmeric
1 tsp cinnamon

Soak the cherry plums in lukewarm water for 30
minutes. Cut the meat in big cubes of about 1½–
2 oz/40–50 g, simmer in lightly salted water over
medium heat until tender and set aside in the
water they were cooked in. Fry the onions in the
clarified butter until golden. Score the chestnuts,
bring to a boil in salted water, rinse in cold water,
and peel. Add the onions, cherry plums and chestnuts to the meat, add the seasonings and simmer
everything together for 45 minutes over low heat.
Serve separately from the plov.

The Festival of Novruz

Spring—the awakening of nature, love, and life from the winter sleep—is celebrated by Azerbaijanis as *Novruz Bayramy*, the "Festival of the New Day." This important national festival is often thought of as an Islamic New Year festival, though the earliest written evidence from the year 505 B.C. confirms that it has much earlier origins. When the Arabs conquered the Near East in the 7th century A.D. in order to create an Islamic empire, they first encountered bitter opposition from the population of the area of present-day Azerbaijan, who had embraced the religion of the Prophet Zoroaster. The Muslims tried to abolish the old heathen spring festival, but in vain—it was too important. So Novruz was accepted as an Islamic New Year Festival. Even though the religious aspect faded into oblivion during the Soviet era, people still celebrate Novruz on the night of the spring equinox from March 20th to 21st. On this day, the old town center of Baku is transformed into a huge stage. In the streets and squares musicians play, and children and young people dance in national costumes. Women roll herbs in thin sheets of bread and bake pockets of dough filled with herbs, beans, ground lamb or sheep's cheese on iron griddles. The men grill fresh lamb and poultry over open fires, and people sit at long tables and benches and celebrate.

The Novruz symbols probably date back to Zoroastrian times (see page 344). As Zoroaster, the Ancient Iranian founder of the religion, set a high value on the work of the fields, wheat sprouts representing fertility became the most important symbol of the festival. Three weeks before the festival, wheat seedlings are transplanted into flat plates, and later become small "meadows," which adorn every festive table. The women make a special *halva* from wheat germ paste, almonds, walnuts, grape syrup, and spices, rolled into little balls with a walnut in the center as a sign of fruitfulness. These are a traditional gift to friends and family.

Eggs dyed with onion skins and herbs must be on every table at Novruz, because they unite within them the four elements, which are very important symbols of the heathen festival. The shell represents earth, the thin skin air, the egg white water, and the yolk fire. In addition, eggs are also fertility symbols. Before the start of spring they celebrate four holy Tuesdays—rather like the four Sundays in Advent celebrated by Christians. Each is dedicated to one of the elements, and special festival dishes must be served on each one, including mainly various different plovs. On the last Tuesday, they pile up firewood in the courtyards and people dance and sing and play. In the old days, neighbors, friends or relations lowered a sack down the chimney into the house on this day. Now youngsters mostly put a hat outside the door, knock, and hide. The occupants must fill the hat with seven gifts. For the same reason a *khoncha*, a silver tray with seven sweetmeats on it,

stands on the family table during Novruz. It should contain *pakhlava*, a cookie with walnut filling (see page 346), fancy pockets of yeast dough with an almond or hazelnut filling (*shakarbura*), sponge cookies (*shirinchorak*), spicy candies (*nogul*), sugar candy, nuts or dried fruit.

As with any festive meal, the Novruz dinner is long and copious. First there are various cold appetizers, such as salads, bean or eggplant purée, cold omelets with herbs or vegetables, cold stuffed fish, caviar, cheese, cucumbers, and tomatoes. These are eaten with bread *tandir chorak*, a flat yeast bread baked in a clay oven, or *yukha*, a thin unleavened bread. Next come stuffed vegetables (*dolma*), filled dough pockets (*gutab*), or meat or fish kebabs.

The main course is plov, the most important dish in Azerbaijan at festive and Sunday meals (see page 341f.). At Novruz, plov is usually served with several different accompaniments of meat, fish, or vegetables. Regional variations are also expected to appear. In Lankaren they like to serve the rice with stuffed fish; in Gasakh, it comes with lamb, in Baku with lamb and green herbs, and in Shemakha with dried fruit. The refreshing yogurt soup *dovga* (see page 326) is not eaten until after the main course.

A big banquet is rounded off by almonds and nuts, or nowadays also with a gateau as well as nuts and dried fruit. And of course there must be tea, which is served with *murabba* (tea conserve). Traditionally, they drink water or fruit sherbet with their meals, but now they also have lemonade, wine or vodka.

As it was in the days of Zoroaster, fire is the greatest power of the Novruz festival. As soon as night falls over the settlements, noise can be heard from the back yards. In the courtyards and streets people leap seven times over the fire, shouting, "Everything hard, everything sick must burn in the fire!" They want to begin the New Year free from the troubles of the old year. Children and young people, adults and even old people line up in the waiting queues, more and more people leap over the fire in the firm belief that their wishes will come true. Everything will be better in the New Year.

On festive occasions such as the celebration of Novruz, the table is filled to overflowing. The Azerbaijanis say there should not be room for so much as a finger. In the middle is the plov. The accompaniments, assorted appetizers such as stuffed vegetables or dough pockets, fresh herbs, and drinks are arranged around it.

Above left: This young lady was chosen as the Novruz Maiden and on the day of the Novruz festival, she is allowed to carry the flame of spring to the Maidens' Tower in Baku. She is dressed in traditional costume.

Above: During the festival of Novruz, the men grill huge quantities of kebabs at roadside stalls. In the background, a picture of the penniless Novruz clown Kossa, who is fed sweetmeats by the people.

Left: In many town and village squares, children in Azerbaijani national costumes perform traditional dances. They are accompanied by their mothers—and by the sound of countless bands of musicians.

Below left: The courage to leap over the fire at the Novruz festival is passed on from the old to the young. At the start of spring, old troubles are thrown into the fire. That means the New Year can be a happy one, so they say.

Below: Important symbols of the Novruz festival are fresh wheat sprouts representing fertility and the khoncha tray with painted eggs, cookies, dried fruits, nuts, candies, and candles.

Summer vegetable dishes

Yay dolmasi
Stuffed summer vegetables

For the filling:
2¼ lb/1 kg ground lamb
4 medium onions, finely chopped
2 tbsp clarified butter
1 bunch each of basil and cilantro, finely chopped
1 pinch cinnamon
Salt and pepper

4 small eggplant
8 firm tomatoes
8 pale green or yellow bell peppers
4 tbsp clarified butter
About 1⅔ cups/400 ml lamb stock
Yogurt and garlic to taste

For the filling, fry the ground meat and onions together in the clarified butter and mix with the herbs and seasonings. Cut off the stalk end of the eggplant, make a lengthwise slit in each (but do not cut right through), simmer for 2–3 minutes in salted water, allow to cool, then remove the seeds with a spoon. Cut a lid off the tomatoes, and spoon out and reserve the contents. Cut a lid off the stalk end of the bell peppers and remove the seeds. Fill the fruits with the prepared stuffing, put the lids back on the tomatoes and peppers. Melt the clarified butter in a shallow pot, place the vegetables close together in it, and fry. Spread the tomato flesh over them, pour over the stock, cover, and simmer over low heat for about 40 minutes. Serve with garlic yogurt and white bread.

Balgabab gutabi
Baked dough pockets filled with pumpkin

2¼ lb/1 kg pumpkin, peeled and cut in small pieces
4 medium onions, finely chopped
8½ tbsp/120 g clarified butter
1 cup/100 g pomegranate seeds
1 pinch cinnamon
Salt
2⅓ cups/400 g whole wheat flour
1 egg
Butter for brushing

Simmer the pumpkin pieces in a little water for about 20 minutes over low heat until tender. Fry the onions in 2 tablespoons clarified butter until golden, add to the pumpkin and simmer both together for another 10 minutes. Mash the pumpkin mixture with a fork, stir the pomegranate seeds and cinnamon in thoroughly, and season with salt.
With the flour, egg, a pinch of salt and about 1¼ cups/300 ml water make a semisoft, elastic dough. Set aside for 20 minutes. Form into balls the size of a tennis ball. With a wooden rolling pin, roll each ball out into a very thin circle. Place 1–2 tablespoons of filling on half of each circle, fold the other half over and press the edges of the semicircle firmly together. The finished items should not be piled on top of one another! Fry the dough pockets on both sides in the remaining clarified butter, and brush with melted butter before serving.
Variations: these dough pockets are often served with other fillings, for instance with finely chopped green herbs sautéed in clarified butter, beans, or ground lamb flavored with onions and pomegranate seeds, or with sheep's cheese and special mixtures of herbs.

Kuku
Herb omelet

2 scallions, cut in thin rounds
¾ cup/50 g fresh cilantro, finely chopped
1 bunch dill, finely chopped
3 cups/100 g shredded spinach
Salt and pepper
4–5 eggs
1 tbsp whole wheat flour
⅓ cup/80 g clarified butter
Generous ¾ cup/200 g natural yogurt

Mix the scallions, herbs, and spinach in a bowl, and season with salt and pepper. Break the eggs into the herb mixture, sift over the flour, and mix everything together with a large fork. Heat the clarified butter in a pan, pour in the mixture, cover, and cook over low heat for about 20 minutes. When the underside is firm and golden brown, turn the omelet over carefully, and cook the other side. Allow this finished kuku to cool, cut in segments or diamonds, and serve as an appetizer with yogurt and white bread.

Azarbaychan salati
Salad "Azerbaijan"

3 large tomatoes, diced
1 salad cucumber, peeled and diced small
3 sweet bell peppers (the pointed green kind), diced
small
1 romaine lettuce, leaves roughly torn
3 tbsp olive oil
Juice of 1 lemon
1 bunch scallions, finely chopped
Salt and pepper
¾ cup/75 g pomegranate seeds

Mix the diced tomatoes, cucumber, and peppers and
arrange on the lettuce leaves. Make a dressing with
the olive oil, lemon juice, scallions, salt and pepper,
and pour over the salad. To garnish, sprinkle with
pomegranate seeds.

Eggplant

In its homeland of India, eggplant was at first used as a decorative
object on account of its beautiful skin. The early forms had a very
bitter taste, and only a lot of cross-breeding made it into an edible
vegetable. The plant first became known outside the borders of Asia
in the 17th century, and it became widespread in Azerbaijan at the
end of the 18th century, where it was known as *badimchan*. The
conditions in the southern Caucasus are ideal for growing eggplant
outdoors: plenty of sun, summer temperatures over 77 °F/25 °C,
and nutrient-rich soil.

In Azerbaijani cuisine, it is eggplant time from the end of June on.
There are many different recipes for these fruits, which grow to a
length of 3–7 ins/8–28 cm. They range from spicy appetizers and
stews, through substantial meat dishes, to conserves. Stuffed eggplant *(badimchan dolmasi)* are a special favorite, braised with tomatoes and peppers. Simply sliced and fried and brushed with crushed
garlic, eggplant on a piece of flat bread makes a delicious in-between
snack. The Azerbaijanis also love grilling whole eggplant with tomatoes on skewers. The small varieties are best for bite-sized nibbles,
such as pan-fried eggplant stuffed with nuts, or eggplant stuffed
with herbs that has first been blanched, had the seeds removed, and
then been filled with finely-chopped herbs and pickled in vinegar
in big jars.

For winter storage, fresh eggplant purée (as a spread for bread) or
sliced eggplant pickled in vinegar with garlic and peppers, are bottled in large jars. This is because carotene, vitamins B and C, and
potassium can be very useful in cold periods. And anyone suffering
from loss of appetite will certainly be cured by *guratva*. For this specialty, blanched de-seeded eggplant is cut into small pieces, mixed
with chopped apples and quinces, covered with sugar syrup, boiled
and dressed with wine vinegar.

The eggplant, which originated in India, is now one of the country's favorite vegetables.

Sweet chestnuts

When it gets unbearably hot in summer, there is no cooler pleasure than sitting in the shade of a big chestnut tree. The fruits of this tree have been treasured for centuries for medicine and food, while the wood is in demand for making furniture and wine barrels. In Azerbaijan, chestnut trees grow wild in the woods or in plantations at the foot of the Caucasus.

It is said that chestnuts are planted for the future, because they grow very slowly for the first 10 years, and only reach their full height at the age of 60. For this reason, many farmers also plant quicker-growing apple, pear, and peach trees in their chestnut groves. When the chestnuts ripen in October, the prickly, fleshy cases release two or three seeds with firm brown shells covering a thin pale skin that encloses the creamy kernel. At harvest time, any that do not fall onto the cloths spread out on the ground when the trees are shaken are knocked off the trees with poles. Sweet chestnuts *(shabalid)* are divided into several types: *khanlig* (medium sized fruits), *ashlig* and *barguhava* (large), and *farash* (small). To prevent the chestnuts from losing moisture, and consequently their fine flavor, they are kept in trenches lined with leaves or in wooden barrels sunk in rough sand.

In the kitchen, chestnuts are an essential accompaniment to festive *plov*. Their mild flavor gives a delicious finishing touch to other meat dishes such as cabbage rolls. On frosty winter evenings, people eat spit-roasted chestnuts that are then boiled in salted water. They are a favorite snack when simply roasted, and very nutritious, because of their high fat, carbohydrate and mineral content. Chestnut shells have long been used as a hair-dye, or for dyeing fabric and leather.

Right: Overhanging chestnut trees are a feature of the landscape in many parts of Azerbaijan.
Below: Ripe chestnuts released from their case show their gleaming brown shells.

Shabalidli kalam dolmasi
Cabbage rolls stuffed with meat and chestnuts

6 tbsp/80 g round-grain rice
1¼ lb/600 g ground lamb
2 medium onions, finely chopped
2–3 medium tomatoes, peeled and finely chopped
8–9 oz/250 g chestnuts, peeled and finely chopped
¼ cup/60 g fresh cilantro, finely chopped
Salt and pepper
8 oz/200 g lamb bones
About 1¾–2¼ lb/ 800g–1 kg white cabbage leaves, washed and separated
2½ tbsp/40 ml white wine vinegar
1 tbsp sugar
Cinnamon

Soak the rice in cold water for 2 hours. For the filling, mix the ground meat thoroughly with the chopped onions, tomatoes, and chestnuts, and season with salt pepper, and cilantro.

Put the lamb bones in about 4 cups/1 liter cold water, bring to a boil, and simmer gently over medium heat. Blanch the cabbage leaves and allow to cool. Put 1–2 tablespoons of the meat and vegetable filling on each leaf, fold over and roll up the leaves to form oblong roulades.

Place the cabbage rolls close together in layers in a pot, pour over the stock, and simmer for about 45 minutes over low heat. Mix the wine vinegar and sugar, add to the rolls, and leave to draw for about 20 minutes over low heat. To serve, pour a little stock over the rolls, sprinkle with cinnamon to taste. Eat with flat bread.

Olives from Azerbaijan

Olive trees up to 300 years old grow in the center of the capital Baku, bringing a touch of the countryside to many residential areas. Archaeological finds reveal that the evergreen olive tree *(Olea europaea)* flourished on Crete over 5,000 years ago, and later became popular in Egypt, Italy, and Asia Minor. The Greeks called it the "tree of dreams," for the Egyptians it was the symbol of peace, and for the Romans it represented wisdom. In Azerbaijan, olives *(zeytun)* are said to have been known as long ago as the 8th or 9th century in the Shirvat region to the west of Baku, in Karabakh, and on the Abseron peninsula, but the first major grove near the capital was only planted in 1949. Today there are three such plantations. Each tree bears 33–45 lb/15–20kg, maybe even up to 110 lb/50 kg of fruit. In October, they harvest the still not completely ripe green olives, which are particularly good for preserving. The fruits are either picked individually or knocked off the trees with poles. The ripe black olives collected in November are pickled in brine and can be eaten the following day. Because green olives are easy to pit, they are often stuffed with almonds, peppers, garlic, or fresh herbs. They make ideal appetizers and are used as tasty ingredients in countless dishes. Olive oil is produced in Azerbaijan on the Abseron Peninsula, though only in small quantities. It is often used for frying or as a basis for sauces.

Olives are grown in Azerbaijan and pickled in brine after the harvest. They can be found in markets in jars of various sizes—often stuffed with almonds, herbs or garlic.

Saffron

Travelers returning from Azerbaijan in the 9th and 10th centuries told of the precious commodity saffron *(sa'foran)* that could only be weighed and paid for in gold coins—the price was already high in those days. Asia Minor is reckoned to be the home of the sought-after variety of crocus *Crocus sativus*. In the 17th century, French missionaries wrote, "Baku is a beautiful city on the coast of the Caspian Sea. The soil here is very soft and covered with saffron."

In the old days, Azerbaijani women used to blend an infusion of saffron in with the henna when dyeing their hair. This made the color more intense, and the saffron gave the hair a golden sheen and a beguiling scent. Body oils, perfume, and intoxicating drinks containing saffron also aided them in the art of seduction. In addition, a manuscript of 1872 contains details of more than 30 medicines made from saffron. It is still used for dyeing cloth, especially the famous silk shawls from Shakai on the ancient Silk Road (see also page 329).

The climate and soil conditions of the Abseron Peninsula on the coast of the Caspian Sea are perfect for growing saffron, with dry summers and only a little rain and cold weather in autumn and winter. To keep out the wind, which can be very strong, the saffron fields are protected by bands of trees 130–145 feet/40–45 m wide. The bulbs are planted in July and August, as far as possible in straight, parallel rows, to make cultivating and harvesting the fields easier. The bulbs must rest during the autumn and winter, so all that is done in November and December is manuring. In addition, the plants need moisture to develop. If there is plenty of rain, there is no need for additional watering. Almost another year goes by before the plants open their wonderful violet flowers. If the fields are well tended and the plants are carefully harvested, 1,320 lb/600 kg flowers can be collected from 2½ acres/1 hectare of land, yielding the raw material for 13¼ lb/6 kg saffron. The harvest begins at the end of October and must proceed very quickly. It is all over in a maximum of 20 days. The farmers walk through the fields carrying wicker baskets to pick the flowers. Shortly afterwards, nimble fingers separate the violet petals from the orange-brown stigmas. These fine threads were formerly dried in sieves over open fires, but nowadays they use special ovens.

The Azerbaijanis still swear by genuine saffron, and substitutes are frowned on. The reddish dried saffron threads give off an intense spicy scent, but taste slightly bitter if chewed. In the kitchen, an Azerbaijani *plov* (see page 312) without saffron would be unimaginable. Moreover, the infusion is a perfect basis for many soups and meat dishes. This spice gives a wonderful touch of color to sweetmeats. A few grains of saffron turn *pakhlava* (flaky pastries) and cookies the honey color of amber. Saffron is also among the ingredients for tasty sherbet (see page 344), and a few golden threads add a mysterious flavor to tea.

Facing page: Crocus variety *crocus sativus*, which provides the sought-after saffron threads, also grows in poor soil.

Spices

Black pepper *(gara istiot,* Lat. *Piper nigrum),* the oldest spice and the most important in world trade, was sacrificed to the gods in pagan times. Some 700 varieties of pepper flourish in tropical climates. Black pepper grows in Azerbaijan. It gives many dishes the perfect sharpness, acts as a stimulant, prevents flatulence, and cleans out the stomach.

Cumin *(sira,* Lat. *Cuminum cyminum),* a wild and cultivated plant related to dill. It has been prized for 5,000 years for its sharp, spicy flavor. The ground seeds are used in cooking, for instance in bread and marinades. Tea made from cumin seeds is purifying and cleans out the kidneys.

Bay leaves *(dafna yarpagi,* Lat. *Laurus nobilis)* are dried and used to flavor stews, soups, meat dishes like the lamb stew *bazartma,* and marinades. They contain essential oils, vitamin A, iron, and potassium. The blue-black berries of this evergreen tree are also used in medicine.

Cinnamon *(darjin,* Lat. *Cinnamomum zeylanicum)* comes from China and is now imported from Iran or India. Dried cinnamon bark, usually ground, is used for its sweet, aromatic flavor in meat dishes, desserts, and sweetmeats. It is also used in sherbets and added to tea. Cinnamon helps to alleviate digestive problems.

Coriander seeds *(keshnikh tokhumu,* Lat. *Coriandrum sativum)* – dried and ground, is used for its sweetish spicy flavor in baking, but also in marinades and soups, with meat and fish, and in cheese making. Coriander tea can help with kidney, stomach and bowel disorders.

Cloves *(mikhak,* Lat. *Syzygium aromaticum),* the dried buds of this evergreen are mainly imported from Syria. They add flavor to marinades, drinks, soups, compotes, and candies. Cloves are good for sweetening the breath and can be used for toothache and earache.

Cardamom *(khil,* Lat. *Elettaria cardamomum)* is a highly aromatic spice from India, which came to Azerbaijan via the Silk Road. It is very popular for making cookies and as an ingredient in tea and drinks. Chewing the sweet seeds freshens the breath and clears out the kidneys and bowels.

Anis *(Jirä,* Lat. *Pimpinella anisum)* comes originally from Asia Minor and is grown in Azerbaijan on the Abseron Peninsula. The sweet-tasting seeds are used in cookies and for flavoring cheese. The essential oils in anis have a positive effect on the airways. It can be drunk as an infusion or inhaled.

Sumach *(sumach,* Lat. *Rhus Coriaria)* is a wild and cultivated plant in Azerbaijan. It contains acids, sugars and vitamins C and K. When dried and ground, the small sourish fruits of the sumach, also known as the tanner's sumach, are an important ingredient in meat and fish dishes. They neutralize fat and aid the digestion.

Black pepper   Cumin

Bay leaves

Cinnamon

Coriander seeds   Cloves

The stigmas of the saffron flowers must still be picked out by hand. There is as yet no machine that can do it.

The saffron threads are dried in a sieve over an open fire. Nowadays people mostly use gas.

How to treat the delicate threads

Saffron is best bought in the form of threads. They keep their flavor longer than the powder and, what is more, you can be relatively certain that it is genuine saffron and not a cheap substitute. To release the bittersweet taste, saffron—as whole threads or crushed in a mortar—should be soaked in water, wine, vinegar, or lemon juice and then added to the dish to be cooked. It needs warmth in order to develop its characteristic flavor. However, if you drop it straight into hot fat, it loses its delicate taste. The longer saffron is cooked as part of a dish, the more intense the yellow color becomes, but it loses its flavor. If you do not wish to miss out on the bittersweet taste, you should add the saffron toward the end of the cooking time.

Pot herbs

There are very few Azerbaijani recipes that do not contain herbs. Whether it is for appetizers, main courses or snacks, there is always a bunch of cilantro, parsley, mint, tarragon, dill, basil and scallions, which you hold in your fingers and nibble away at. These green plants replace all kinds of vitamin pills. They contain carotene, potassium, calcium, and folic acid, promote good digestion, and make cheese, meat and fish dishes taste even more tempting. Omelet with herbs (*kuku*, see page 318) or dough pockets filled with finely chopped green herbs *(gutab)*, which are baked on an iron griddle over an open fire, are excellent springtime dishes.

To preserve the taste of summer, pot herbs—mixed or individually, whole or finely chopped—are marinated or put in jars with plenty of salt. The salt must be rinsed off before use. Preserved herbs can be used to make green soups, sauces, and herb omelets. Herbs such as mint, marjoram, tarragon, dill, and basil, are also easy to dry—either hung up in a dark, dry place or quickly in the oven or microwave. Used to season soups, salads, and many meat dishes, they bring a wonderful taste of spring to your plate all the year round.

Fragrant herbs can be found in all Azerbaijani markets. They are eaten fresh with every meal, just by nibbling from a bunch.

Cilantro *(keshnikh,* Lat. *Coriandrum sativum)* gives salads and many meat and vegetable dishes a special spicy taste. Wild mountain cilantro is used for yogurt soups and herb dough pockets. The seeds, which are good for the digestion, are used in baking and to flavor fresh cheese.

Parsley *(Jafari,* Lat. *Petroselinum crispum)* can be found in Azerbaijan in the curly or flat-leaf forms. It is used in almost all cooked dishes and in marinades. Celery, which is said to be related to parsley, is also popular. It goes with lamb, herb omelets, and for seasoning preserved vegetables.

Mint *(nana,* Lat. *Mentha)* can be found in several varieties in Azerbaijan. It is cultivated for use in salads, soups, and marinades, and mountain mint is used medicinally to prevent flatulence and stomach cramps.
Water mint *(yarpis,* Lat. *mentha aquatica)* goes well with cheese, in yogurt soup, herb dough pockets, and salads.

Majoram *(marsa,* Lat. *Majorana mortensis monch)* has a strong, spicy scent and is used both fresh and dried. This fragrant herb is a tasty ingredient in salads, many meat, fish, and vegetable dishes, and in marinades. It is used medicinally to treat colic, cramps and migraine.

Tarragon *(tarkhun,* Lat. *Artemisia dracunculus)* in Azerbaijan is smaller and more aromatic than the variety commonly known in Europe. It is used fresh or dried in mixtures of herbs. It is very good in soups and salads, and an indispensable part of the bunches of fresh herbs that come with every meal.

Dill *(shuyud,* Lat. *Anethum graveolum)* is used fresh as a strongly flavored ingredient in salads and bunches of herbs or cooked in soups and meat dishes—especially in lamb *plov* with green herbs (see page 315). The Azerbaijanis make a herbal tea from the seeds that is good for the digestion.

Watercress *(väsäri,* Lat. *Lepidium sativum)* is usually served fresh. It stimulates the appetite and goes very well with cold appetizers, salad, or cheese, and with many other dishes. Because it is high in vitamin C, potassium, calcium, and folic acid, watercress is very healthy.

Thyme *(kakotu,* Lat. *Thymus vulgaris)* contains powerful essential oils and is therefore a popular thirst-quencher when made into a herbal tea that is kind to the stomach. Fresh or dried, it is good for grilled meat or fish, as well as for flavoring vegetables, marinades and sheep's milk cheese *(shor).*

Baby leeks *(kavar,* Lat. *Allium porrum)* have a sharp taste and are used in many dishes in Azerbaijan, especially as an important ingredient in bunches of herbs, but they are also eaten with cheese and cold appetizers. They are almost always served fresh; ordinary onions are used in cooking.

Basil *(reyhan,* Lat. *Ocimum basilicum)* is commonly found in two varieties in Azerbaijan, the red cultivated kind and the wild green variety. This strong-scented herb is used fresh in salads and soups, and when dried it is added to pepper mixtures. Red basil looks very decorative in the ubiquitous herb bunches.

Substantial or light: unusual soups

Hot or cold, with or without meat, with pasta or yogurt—stews and soups are enjoyed all year round. The soups that start off a meal do not usually contain meat, for instance clear broth *(shorba)* with rice or pasta, chickpeas or beans, fresh herbs, saffron, and pomegranate juice.

Yogurt soups are especially popular. *Ovdukh* and *dograma* are not cooked, but are simply mixed together cold, with the addition of cucumbers, herbs, and other fresh ingredients. By contrast, the much-loved *dovga*, made from yogurt diluted with water, and herbs, is cooked on the hob. Even so, this soup too is generally eaten cold, and is often served to round off a festive meal. However, *dovga* can on occasions be served hot, for instance when it is offered as a main course with meat dumplings added to it.

Soups containing pasta require skill and time. *Dushbara* contains mini-tortellini. *Khamrashi* (with small meatballs, beans and noodles), *sulu khingal* (lozenge-shaped pasta, meat and onions in lamb stock), and *arishtali shorba* (with home-made noodles) are so filling that they take the place of a whole meal. The finishing touch is provided by the delicious flavor of fresh herbs such as cilantro, mint, dill, and sometimes cinnamon. With the traditional vinegar and garlic mixture *sirka sarimsa*, everyone can add the seasonings they want at table. On market stalls selling cooked food you see steaming pots of substantial lamb or mutton stews such as *piti* or *bobash*. *Piti* is always prepared in small earthenware pots, glazed on the inside, whereas *bobash* is always cooked in big cauldrons. You can also have *bobash* with chicken, duck, or fish in it, and there must always be chickpeas. Sprinkled with bread, herbs and sumach, these soups are cheap and filling. *Khash* is a soup made of innards and lamb feet, of the kind also known in Georgia, Armenia, the Mediterranean and Central Asia (see page 276). Cilantro, basil, dill, or chopped peppers give a fresh, spicy Azerbaijani taste to the beet soup brought in by the Russians, known here as *borsh*.

Piti
Individual lamb stews

¹/₂ cup/100 g dried chickpeas
1¹/₄ lb/600 g mutton or lamb
1 cup/100 g fresh or ¹/₂ cup/50 g dried cherry plums, or dried sour cherries or if all else fails (!) prunes
1 g saffron
6 medium potatoes, peeled and cut in four
2 medium onions, halved lengthwise and cut in rings
Salt
Pepper
Onions and scallions as accompaniment
Sumach
Dried mint

First soak the dried chickpeas in cold water for 4–5 hours.

Cut the mutton or lamb into 12 portions. Divide the meat and chickpeas between 4 individual stewpots (earthenware pots that are glazed inside are best for this, but you can also use small pudding basins, cover with fresh water and cook slowly in the oven at 250 °F/ 120 °C for 6 hours.

If dried fruit is used, soak for 3–4 hours in lukewarm water. At the same time, soak the saffron for at least 3 hours in ¹/₂ cup/125 ml lukewarm water.

After 6 hours' cooking time, divide the potatoes, onions and cherry plums between the 4 individual pots and cook for a further 45 minutes. Add the saffron infusion, season with salt and pepper, and allow to draw in the hot oven for a further 20 minutes. *Piti* is served in the pot it was cooked in. At table, you first pour the broth into a plate and eat it as soup, then you put the solid ingredients on your plate as a main course. Whole, peeled onions, scallions, sumach, and mint are served separately.

Dushbara
Lamb broth with dough pockets

8–9 oz/250 g lamb bones
1 cup/150 g fine whole wheat flour
1 egg
2 medium onions
Generous 1 lb/500 g ground lamb
Salt and black pepper
¼ cup/60 g fresh cilantro, finely chopped
1 tbsp dried mint
2½ tbsp/40 ml white wine vinegar
4–5 cloves garlic, peeled and crushed

Make a broth with the lamb bones and 5 cups/1¼ liter
water. With the flour, egg, 1 pinch salt, and 7 table-
spoons/100 ml water, make a semifirm elastic dough
and set aside to rest for 20–30 minutes.
Either purée the onions in a blender or chop very fine.
Mix the ground meat with the onions and season with
salt and pepper. Divide the dough into 5–6 portions.
Roll each portion out very thin using a small wooden
rolling pin, cut into squares about ⅝–¾ in/1.5-2 cm,
and put a small amount of filling in the center of each
one. Fold the squares of dough in half either down the
middle or diagonally. They must be small enough to fit
4–5 into a tablespoon. Strain the broth and bring back
to a boil, then simmer the dough pockets in it for
about 5 minutes over medium heat. Before eating, the
soup is sprinkled with cilantro and dried mint. The
wine vinegar is mixed with the garlic and served separately, to be added as desired.

Dograma
Cold yogurt soup with herbs

1⅔ cups/400 ml water, boiled and allowed to cool
3 cups/800 g natural yogurt
10 tbsp/150 g sour cream
1 salad cucumber, peeled and cut in small pieces
1½ cups/150 g leeks, cut in small pieces
1 cup/80 g fresh cilantro, finely chopped
1 bunch dill, finely chopped
½ cup/30 g red basil, finely chopped
1–2 cloves garlic, peeled and crushed
Salt and pepper
About 6 slices/400 g stale white bread, cut in bite-
sized pieces

In a large bowl, stir together the water, yogurt, and
sour cream to the consistency of soup. Pour in the prepared vegetables and herbs, add the garlic, and season the soup with salt and pepper. Chill in the
refrigerator. According to taste, the bread can be
added now or at the table. Dograma is eaten as a cold
appetizer or a refreshing dish between courses.

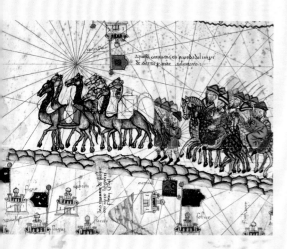

The Silk Road

The "Silk Road" was the world's first transcontinental highway for trade, and came into being at a time when all long-distance transport was entirely undertaken by pack animals. In 183 B.C., the Chinese Emperor Wudi sent the first expedition to the West under Zhang Qian. They soon advanced as far as Persia, and a trade route linking China with the Roman Empire slowly developed. Though at first it was luxury goods such as silk, spices, and rice—depending on the section of the route—that made their way over 4,500 miles/7,000 km through Central Asia to the West, the trade route also acted as a cultural bridge between the Occident and the Far East. The road flourished until the 15th century. Its decline began when Vasco da Gama discovered the sea route from Europe to East Asia in 1498. Incidentally, the term "Silk Road" was coined by the German scholar Ferdinand von Richthofen in the 19th century. The roads, which started from Xian in China, one to the north, the other to the south of the Taklimakan desert, met and divided again in the ancient city of Kashgar. The northern route led over the Pamir mountains to Samarkand and Persia to the south of the Caspian Sea, while the southern route branched off over the Karakorams and ended in India. Its destinations in the West were Damascus and the Black Sea coast. Silk came via the northern branch, and a wide range of spices via the southern route. The sea route, along which the traders of southern India and China mainly transported rice, was known as the "Rice

The various branches of the Silk Road ran for about 4,500 miles/7,000 km from the city of Xian in China westward via Baghdad to Damascus. The road to Constantinople led through the areas of Azerbaijan and Armenia, with a branch off to Georgia.

Left: Around 1270, the merchant Marco Polo traveled along the Silk Road from Venice to China.

Right: In the old caravanserai of Baku, where travelers from the Orient once spent the night, you can now eat like a prince.

Road" before the time of Vasco da Gama. As time went on, all types of goods were transported along all the trade routes.

Of course, the most important commodity on the east-west route was silk. It was made into fabrics of different qualities, and also into paper and sails. The source of the raw material was a state secret in China, and betraying it was punishable by death. But in the 5th century, when a Chinese princess was married to the ruler of an oasis town, she hid silkworm eggs and mulberry leaves in her baggage. This spoilt young lady could not imagine life in a country without silk. A century later, Persian monks commissioned by the Byzantine Emperor Justinian I are said to have smuggled silkworms to Constantinople. That was the start of silk farming outside China. The Byzantine Empire and Persia, which included Azerbaijan at that time, built up their own production. In the high Middle Ages, the trading conditions and variety of goods became ever more diverse.

Fruits such as apricots and melons, nuts, and various herbs were novelties at the time, even rhubarb came to the West by this route. Agriculture and cattle-rearing were also given new

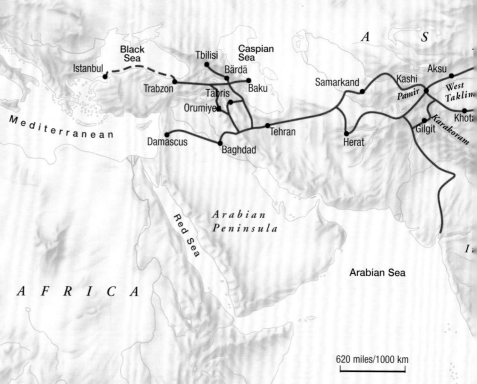

momentum, not to mention the cuisine of the areas along the route. The influence of the nomadic peoples was particularly strong in this respect. During their long journeys across steppes and deserts, the traders—like the nomads—ate camel and horsemeat and drank the milk of these animals. Many dishes that could be cooked over an open fire, such as stews and simple meat dishes that could braise in a cauldron in their own juice and fat, originated in this way.

The caravans that wanted to ship their wares to Constantinople from the Black Sea port of Trebizond, set out from Persia across the area that is now Azerbaijan. The cities of Baku and Barda were important trade centers, especially for silk. Barda in central Azerbaijan also exported dyes made from pomegranates, henna, and chestnuts. Azerbaijani wool and carpets were also in demand. There are even reports of a trade in fish from the Caspian Sea to India.

Fine silk shawls from Shaki in Northern Azerbaijan are still considered a luxury. Silk carpets are the top-quality product of the nation's craftsmen. The Silk Road left strange marks on the culture of the country. The expensive fabrics inspired Azerbaijan's poets, Chinese paints influenced the artists, the techniques of wood and metalworking were an innovation from Persia and Greece. The ornamentation used by the nomads and the oasis-dwellers found its way into textile design, as can now be seen in the famous carpet museum in Baku. Five hundred years after its decline, an international conference in Baku in 1998 decided to reestablish the legendary Silk Road with the help of money from the European Union, and to promote the free exchange of goods between Europe and Asia along the "Europe-Caucasus-Asia Transport Corridor." The initiative has its headquarters in the Old Town in Baku, where the restored buildings of former caravanserais help to create a tangible Silk Road atmosphere. The warehouses are full of antiques and carpets, people drink tea—and nowadays beer and wine as well—in picturesque inn courtyards, and the wonderful fragrance of oriental spices hangs over it all.

The inner courtyard of the restaurant in the old caravanserai in Baku radiates the atmosphere of the Silk Road.

"On the carpet"

In the East, people originally communicated and slept on carpets on the floor. Food was served on white cloths. Now furniture has spread throughout the world, this tradition has almost died out, but it still lives on in many Azerbaijani villages and in a few tearooms and restaurants.

Traditionally there are many schools of carpeting in the country, each one characterized by its own structure, ornamentation, and coloring. A Garabakh is dominated by nature and plant motifs in many colors, while strong red and blue tones and oriental patterns are characteristic of carpets from Guba, and a Gasakh seems very modern and abstract. The custom of having every girl learn carpet-making lives on in the centers of production. The richly-endowed carpet museum in Baku is considered to be one of the finest displays of carpets in the world.

The floors and walls of the houses of the well-to-do were always covered by expensive knotted carpets. The poor could only afford woven kelims. Carpets hang on the walls of many apartments as decoration, fine pieces made of silk or wool on chairs and sofas are a permanent element in interior decoration, and on festive occasions, the food is still often "carpeted" on beautiful runners.

Carpet-sellers offer their wares for sale in the Old Town in Baku, in buildings dating from the time of the Silk Road.

Anxi

Xian

ulf of
ngal

South China Sea

Azerbaijani caviar

Everyone raves about caviar, but people very often forget that during the time of the Soviet Union, most "Russian" caviar came from Azerbaijan. Today, caviar is still an important factor in the country's economy. The stronghold of the Azerbaijani caviar industry is in Neftçala on the Caspian Sea, between Baku and Lankaran. In March, enormous quantities of fresh caviar are on sale in the markets around the processing plants and in the capital. In the back rooms of market booths, whole jars containing over 1 lb/500 g of this precious commodity may change hands—at huge prices (e.g. $ 300) that people in Western countries can only dream of.

In Azerbaijan, caviar *kuru* is usually eaten on buttered flat bread or white bread. Sometimes thin slices of tomato and cucumber are served with it, and also cilantro, dill, and scallions—a delicacy that always goes down well as an appetizer, a snack, or even for breakfast. Because of overfishing and water pollution, in recent years local caviar production has suffered reductions of 20–25 percent—the same as happened on the Russian side of the Caspian Sea. As the second most valuable export after oil, the sturgeon is now protected in Azerbaijan, in the hope that stocks will recover.

Caviar from the Caspian Sea is one of Azerbaijan's finest delicacies.

Most Azerbaijani fishermen on the Caspian Sea ply their trade with very simple equipment.

Treasures of the Caspian Sea

In the 5th century B.C., the Greek historian Herodotus reported that the people around the Caspian Sea and the River Kura lived mainly on fish. The sturgeon was always their favorite catch, and it was not only used for food; the oil was used in cosmetics, and the swim bladder to make glue. One of its uses was in the finishing of oriental ivory figures, as there was a flourishing trade from very early times via the Silk Road (see page 328 f). Today the fishing industry contributes one third of Azerbaijan's national income. Around the shores of the Abseron Peninsula, the Caspian Sea and the River Kura provide a favorable habitat for more than 80 species of fish, around 30 of which are caught for food. Among the most important are several kinds of sturgeon (beluga, sevruga and—now more rarely—fringebarbel sturgeon), Caspian salmon (Lat. *salmo trutta caspius*), which is known as "gold fish" *(gissi balig)* in the language of the country, *kutum* (Caspian roach, Lat. *rutilus frissi kutum*), *kulma* (also a kind of roach, Lat. *rutilus caspicus natio kurensis*), eels, sardines, herring, Baltic herring, gray mullet, plus freshwater fish, such as pike, carp, zander, and perch, known in Azerbaijan as *khan baligi* "the emperor of fish." Though all these species were once found in large numbers, over the last few decades rising fishing quotas and the pollution caused by the chemical industry have led to a decline in fish stocks. Because Azerbaijan does not want to lose this precious gift of nature completely or bankrupt the fishing industry, more investment is now being put into farming fish, such as sturgeon and salmon. To create conditions that are as close as possible to nature, they try to locate the fish farms close to the natural spawning grounds.

Despite the great selection of fish, sturgeon is still the number one choice, when it comes to cooking. Its flesh is often grilled over an open fire, but it is also popular boiled, baked or pan-fried. Ground sturgeon flesh tastes exceptionally good. It is used to make fishcakes and dumplings, or formed into a long sausage shape around a skewer for barbecuing. Smoked sturgeon is delicious, but this fish is especially valuable and sought-after on account of its roe—black caviar (see Kasten).

Recipes for stuffed fish are generally popular. The best fish for this is *kutum* (roach), because of its delicate, juicy, white flesh and firm skin. Other species are used for cold appetizers. Fish is also extremely popular poached, fried, smoked, or in thick soups. A cheap alternative to sturgeon and salmon, which Azerbaijanis can barely afford, is the *kilka* (Baltic herring), a species of small herring that is mostly used for fishcakes. This fish is exported to Russia and the Ukraine in large quantities. There it is dried, and is a great favorite eaten with beer.

Facing page: Sturgeon, beluga and Caspian salmon are also sold smoked in many fish shops.

Insert: In the "Interbalig" fish shop in Baku you can find the jewels of the Caspian Sea, such as fresh sturgeon.

Fish dishes from the rivers and seas

at least 3 hours. Cook the rice in lightly salted water. Make stock from salted water and the head, tail, and fins of the fish, and strain through a fine sieve. Bring the stock to a boil, add the chickpeas and cook until almost soft, then scoop out with a slotted spoon. Process the fish in a blender together with 2 onions, add the rice, mix in the egg, and season with salt and pepper. Wet your hands, and form the fish mixture into balls, putting 1 or 2 cherry plums in the center of each. Finely chop the remaining onion. Return the stock to a boil, and add the onion, potatoes, chickpeas, saffron infusion, and fish balls, and simmer for a further 30 minutes over medium heat. *Balig kuftasi* may be served as a stew, or the broth can be served first, and then the fish, potatoes, and chickpeas separately.

Nara baligindan kabab
Sturgeon kebabs

Generous 1 lb/1 kg sturgeon or swordfish, ready to cook
Salt and Pepper
2 1/2 tbsp/40 g sour cream
Juice of one lemon
4 medium tomatoes, sliced
2 medium onions, cut in rings
1 bunch scallions, cut in rings
Pomegranate syrup (narsharab)
1 tsp sumach

Cut the fish in chunks of 1–1 1/2 oz/40–50 g, season with salt and pepper, and rub with sour cream. Thread the pieces of fish on steel skewers and grill over an open fire for 7–10 minutes, turning once. Remove from the heat, and drizzle with lemon juice. Serve the sturgeon kebabs with tomatoes, onions, scallions, pomegranate syrup, and sumach.

Balig kuftasi
Soup with fish balls

1/2 cup/100 g chickpeas
1 g saffron
5 tbsp/60 g round-grain rice
Salt and pepper
1 3/4 lb/800 g sturgeon or swordfish
3 medium onions
1 egg
1/2 cup/40 g cherry plums, pitted
Generous 1 lb/500 g potatoes, peeled and diced

Soak the chickpeas in cold water for at least 4 hours. Soak the saffron in about 1/2 cup lukewarm water for

For the fish ball soup Balig koftasi, make stock from the head, tail, and fins. Cook the presoaked chickpeas in this stock.

Mix the ground fish, with rice, onions, egg, and seasoning, and form balls stuffed with cherry plums, which you cook in the fish stock with the other ingredients.

The fish broth and the solid contents may be served separately, or all together as a stew, if preferred.

Kutum lavangi
Stuffed Caspian roach

1¹/₂ cups/200 g raisins
¹/₂ cup/100 g dried cherry plums, pitted
2 medium onions, finely chopped
2¹/₂ tbsp/40 g clarified butter
1¹/₄ cups/200 g finely chopped walnuts
Salt and pepper
1 roach, about 2¹/₄ lb/1 kg or other fish (e.g. sea bream) for stuffing, ready to cook
1–2 lemons

Soak the raisins and cherry plums in lukewarm water for at least 30 minutes. For the filling, fry the onions until golden. Add the walnuts, cherry plums and raisins, mix well, and season with salt and pepper. Preheat the oven to 350 °F/180 °C. Rub the fish with salt inside and out, stuff with the filling, sew it up, and bake for about 35–45 minutes in an upright position with the back on top. To serve, drizzle the fish with lemon juice and garnish with slices of lemon. It is eaten with *plov* rice or bread. Stuffed fish is also often served cold as an appetizer.

Lamb

Archaeological finds of lamb bones at Mingäçevir in the west and rock paintings in Gobustan provide evidence that sheep have been reared in Azerbaijan for at least 10,000 years. Wool was already being exported to Russia in the Middle Ages, and the fine fleece of the Merino sheep is still much in demand for the textile industry. The Bosach, Garabach and Shirvan breeds are farmed for their meat.

Summer is the most important time for the shepherds. From the end of April to October, they move with their flocks across the mountain pastures. In their summer quarters, they shear the sheep, make cheese and butter, and slaughter animals according to their needs. The meat is baked in a lot of salt to preserve it, and then stored in a cool cellar in its own fat. It is served up in winter in stews and other meat dishes, together with vegetables and herbs.

Lamb also has a special religious significance in the Islamic faith. Every year, at the end of the Ramadan fast, a young animal is slaughtered as a celebratory offering and shared between relatives, friends, and neighbors. No part of it may be thrown away. It is as a result of this tradition that Azerbaijani cuisine has so many different dishes made from every part of the lamb.

Sabsa govurma, the intriguing mixture of green herbs and pieces of braised lamb, brings spring to the table (see page 315). The festive accompaniment to *plov* is lamb with chestnuts and plums. The delicate meat also defines the taste of stews such as *piti* or dumplings *kufta*. The dish *bosartma* comes from the shepherds' kitchen. After slaughtering, the meat is cut in big pieces while it is still warm, and stewed with onions in its own juices in a copper cauldron over an open fire. *Chiz biz* is a stew of chopped lamb liver, onions, and potatoes. Other innards, along with the feet, are boiled to make the soup *khash* (see page 276). However, the best bit is reckoned to be the ram lamb's testicles *(khaya)*. Grilled, roasted, or braised, the delicate pale meat is a truly Epicurean experience. Kebabs *shishlik* are also an indispensable part of Azerbaijani cuisine. The meat is either unseasoned or marinated beforehand in vinegar with onions, bay leaves, salt, and pepper. Sometimes the pieces of meat are put on the skewer alternately with tomatoes, eggplant, and peppers, and grilled directly over an open fire until golden brown. They are served with bunches of fresh cilantro, parsley, mint, tarragon, dill, basil, and scallions, and with sour pomegranate syrup *(narsharab)*.

Azerbaijani shepherds have always driven their flocks across country. They search for fragrant herbs that will give the milk and cheese a delicious flavor.

The truth is in the head

In Azerbaijan, there are many children's games played with the bones from lambs' feet that have persisted since heathen times. Sheep horn is used to make combs and buttons. These are still occasionally made by farmers and shepherds, and also by craftsmen.

The origin of foretelling the future when lambs are slaughtered also lies hidden in the dim and distant past. A shepherd told us about something that happened in a village of the kind you can still come across from time to time. In a murky room with a fire blazing in the middle of it, stood an old woman with the head of a freshly-slaughtered lamb in her hand. On the fire was a big pot of water. A young pregnant woman waiting outside the door was visibly excited. "Will the first child be a boy or a girl?" She was still in doubt as to whether the old woman could foretell the future. The lamb's head now lay in the pot of boiling water. The old woman took it out, opened the lower jaw wide, and looked attentively into the throat. It was completely clean. "It will be a boy," said the soothsayer. "If there was still meat hanging in the throat, it would be a girl." Later the young woman did in fact give birth to a boy—so our storyteller assured us.

In summer, farmers and shepherds make cheese. The sour milk cheese *motal* matures in a sheepskin bag, with the hairy side, which has previously been dried out with salt, wrapped firmly round the cheese dough. This is still sold in markets, but on the farms you can also get cream cheese with mint, cilantro, and cloves, homemade yogurt, and freshly churned butter.

At the sheep market in Imishli, the sellers wait for takers. Buying is men's work. The best customers are the families of couples getting married. They buy several animals at a time for their wedding party—and they are so happy, they hardly bargain at all for lower prices.

Lamb and beef specialties

Nargovurmasi
Beef with chestnuts and pomegranate

1 g saffron
2¼ lb/1 kg marbled beef, e.g. shoulder
Salt and pepper
8½ tbsp/125 g clarified butter
Scant 1 lb/400 g chestnuts, boiled and peeled
4 medium onions, cut in two lengthwise and then in rings
1½ cups/150 g pomegranate seeds
50 g fresh cilantro, finely chopped
50 g dill, finely chopped

Soak the saffron in about ½ cup lukewarm water for at least 3 hours. Cut the beef into about 12 pieces, season with salt and pepper, and fry on all sides in half the clarified butter. Quarter the chestnuts. Fry the onions in the remaining clarified butter until golden. Pour the meat, chestnuts, and fried onions into a pot, add 1 cup/200 ml water, cover, and simmer over low heat for about 1 hour. When the meat and chestnuts are tender, add the pomegranate seeds, and simmer for a further 10–12 minutes.

Sprinkle with the herbs, and serve with *plov* rice or bread.

Arshuman kuftasi
Ground meatball with chicken
(serves 8–10)

For the filling:
1 cup/100 g cherry plums, pitted
¾ lb/300 g chestnuts
1 chicken, about 900 g
Salt
½ tsp saffron powder

For the meatball:
2¼ lb/1 kg onions
2 eggs
5½ lb/2.5 kg ground leg of lamb
1 bunch fresh cilantro, finely chopped
1 bunch dill, finely chopped
1 tbsp turmeric
1 tsp cinnamon
Salt and pepper
2 eggs, hardcooked and shelled
Dried mint
Green herbs and sumach for serving

For the filling for the ground meat ball, soak the pitted cherry plums in lukewarm water for at least 30 minutes. Score the chestnuts, boil in water, rinse in cold water, and peel, using your fingers or a small kitchen knife.

Simmer the whole chicken in lightly salted water for 20–30 minutes and remove from the stock. Rub it inside and out with saffron powder and stuff it with the chestnuts and cherry plums.

For the meat ball, purée the onions in a blender and mix them with the egg and the ground lamb. Add the cilantro and dill and mix thoroughly.

Spread the ground lamb evenly on a large piece of cheesecloth. Lay the stuffed chicken in the middle, place the hardcooked eggs at the sides under the wings then, with the aid of the cheesecloth, press the ground meat all around the chicken to form a ball. When the stuffed chicken is thoroughly encased, tie a knot in the top of the cheesecloth.

In a large saucepan, bring 5–6 quarts/5–6 liter lightly salted water or meat stock to a boil, and simmer the meat ball for about 1½–2 hours, keeping it just below boiling point, and skimming occasionally.

Remove the cooked meat ball from the pan, place on a large flat plate, and leave to "set" for a few minutes. Carefully remove the gauze and cut the meat ball into portions. Serve the stock separately, and sprinkle with dried mint. This dish is accompanied by green herbs as desired, sumach, and white bread.

In Azerbaijan, kebabs are a national dish, just as they are in Georgia and Armenia. Fresh pieces of lamb or beef are stuck on steel skewers, salted, and grilled over an open fire.

Make an elastic dough from flour, eggs, salt, and water, and cut into handy portions. Roll out with a thin rolling pin.

Cut the dough in diamonds, holding it with your fingers to prevent it from tearing.

Boil the dough diamonds in salted water, then scoop out with a slotted spoon.

Giyma khingal
Noodles with lamb

For the noodles:

2 eggs
2²/₃ cups/400 g whole wheat flour
Salt

For the accompaniment:

0.5 g saffron
1¹/₄ lb/600 g mutton or lamb
Salt
Pepper
5 medium onions, chopped
²/₃ cup/150 g clarified butter
Generous ³/₄ cup/200 g natural yogurt
4–5 cloves garlic, peeled and crushed

Using the eggs, flour, and salt, plus about ³/₄ cup/ 200 ml water, make a semifirm, elastic dough and set aside to rest for about 30 minutes. Then divide the dough into portions the size of a tennis ball and roll out to a thickness of about ¹/₁₆ inch/2 mm. Cut the dough in diamonds about 2x2 inches/5x5 cm, lay them side by side on a floured surface, sprinkle with flour

Fried mutton or lamb has a strong flavor and saffron onions are used to take the edge off it.

and leave to dry for about 30 minutes. In the mean-time, bring 3 quarts/3 liter water to a boil, add salt, and then boil about a quarter of the dough diamonds in it for 8–12 minutes. Scoop them out with a slotted spoon and lay them side by side on a large flat plate. Do the same with the remaining 3 portions.

For the accompaniment, soak the saffron in 7 table-spoons/100 ml lukewarm water for at least 3 hours. Using a sharp knife, cut the meat up very finely, and season with salt and pepper. Fry well with 1–2 chopped onions in 3 tablespoons clarified butter. Fry the rest of the onions thoroughly in the remaining clarified butter, then add the saffron infusion. Spread the meat and the saffron-onion mixture over the noo-dles, and serve immediately with garlic yogurt.

Variations: khingal noodles are eaten with various accompaniments; as well as fish and poultry, it could be vegetables (e.g. beans) or onion omelet. It is rec-ommended that the accompaniments are prepared in advance, so they just have to be warmed up again before the meal. One or more accompaniments can then be served on fresh noodles, always with garlic yogurt.

Place the khingal noodles on a plate while still warm, and spread with a mixture of yogurt and garlic.

Onions are used for both the meat accompaniment and for mixing into a sauce with clarified butter and saffron.

Game birds and waterfowl

Zaman's grandfather was a passionate hunter. Like his ancestors thousands of years ago, he would pursue game with no weapons, only his decoys to lure his prey. And by all accounts, he seems to have been very successful. As a child, Zaman witnessed the old man, using only the ploy of stalking them and the power of his own hands, regularly killing pheasants, coots, quails, partridges, and hares, and once he even brought home a wolf. In addition, it was customary at that time to train birds of prey to catch small animals and bring them back.

Like many young men of his times, Zaman Novrusov, later a journalist in Baku, inherited a love of hunting from his grandfather and father during his boyhood in the region of Garabakh (Karabakh). During World War II, wildfowl were the most important source of animal food. When his father died during the war, Zaman inherited a triple-barreled gun for hunting, and had to feed the family from then on. Later, when the country's food situation had improved once more, Zaman moved to the capital Baku, and hunting became a hobby. But for the indigenous people in country districts around Lankaran or in Karabakh, it is still a part of everyday life. A very popular place for wildfowling is the district around the city of Lankaran in the southeast of Azerbaijan, and Zaman too is always drawn back to the area. Because of its extensive woodlands and marshes and its mild, subtropical climate on the shores of the Caspian Sea, this region is not only a popular destination for family outings but also the home of many species of waterfowl, which find the countless small islands an ideal habitat.

In order to be able to control and protect the stocks of game, which also include red deer, roe deer, and wild boar, over the last few years the state has imposed close seasons for particular species and set up conservation areas. In Lankaran, these are Gisilagadj and Hirkan. The coot (gashgaldag) is best hunted in winter, because the birds swim in great numbers on the ice-free stretches of frozen lakes. However, there is an old hunting rule that applies here too: only shoot as much as you need.

Spring is the time for wild geese (vahshi gas and little bustard). The most beautiful bird, beloved of hunters and lovers of wildlife, is the quail variety turach. Its plumage might have been the work of an artist: white spots shining on a black breast, a red ring round its neck, and wings that shimmer with every color. The utterly exquisite pale flesh of the turach tastes a bit like that of a very young

goose, whereas the coot has fine, dark flesh with a flavor that reminds you that it feeds on fish from the lake. As they were centuries ago, the birds are plucked, drawn, and spit-roasted over an open fire or baked in an underground clay oven (tandir). Famous specialties from Lankaran are stuffed wildfowl, and the appetizer fissinjan made of wildfowl with pomegranate and walnuts.

Lankaransayagi fissinjan
Wildfowl with walnut, Lankaran style

1 coot about 1¾ lb/750 g, ready to cook, can be replaced by pheasant or chicken
1 whole pomegranate
2¼ lb/1 kg onions
3 cups/400 g walnuts
1 tbsp plum purée
2 tbsp sugar
Pepper and salt

Divide the fowl with its bones into portions. Wash the pomegranate, prick several times, and wrap in cheesecloth or a very thin dish towel (the fruit gives the dish flavor and color. Put the whole onions with the meat and pomegranate in a pot, cover with lightly salted water, and boil for about 1 hour, adding water and skimming as required. When the meat is tender, strain everything through a sieve, and pour the stock back into the pot. Put the boiled onions and the walnuts through the grinder, and stir into the stock. Add the plum purée and sugar, and boil to make a smooth, thick sauce. Season with salt and pepper. To serve, arrange the portions of cooked fowl on a plate and pour over the nut and plum purée. Fissinjan is eaten with bread or the classic plov rice.

Winegrowers and wine

"Anyone who plants a vine is worthy of the greatest respect," runs an Azerbaijani proverb, and in the national epic *Kitabi Dada Gorgud* ("The Book of Grandfather Korkud," preserved in print in the 16th century) it says, "In the gardens on our mountains, the grapes are deep black. The juice of these grapes is fragrant, and whoever drinks it will acquire great strength."

Grapes have grown in Azerbaijan since primeval times. Archaeological excavations in Akstafa brought to light grape seeds from the 5th to 4th centuries B.C. Near Khanlar, they discovered 2000–3000-year-old fruit seeds in a barrel, as well as earthenware pots used in winemaking, the stones of a wine press, and large jugs. In the 1st century A.D., the Greek historian and geographer Strabo enthused about the luxuriant fertility of the vineyards along the river Aras.

When Islam spread through Azerbaijan in the 7th century, the wine making tradition was affected, because the Koran forbids both the making and drinking of wine. In order not to be obliged to give up the "drink born under the sun," the "orthodox believers" countered with a parable. The Holy Prophet was crossing the road and saw two people who had ordered wine with their meal. Politely, he wished them, *"Halal!"* ("Good health!"). But on his way back, he encountered the pitiful sight of the drunken men lying on the ground, and he called out, *"Haram!"* ("Forbidden"). The ban therefore referred not to the drink, but to the condition of the men.

Even if the story has no truth in it, many Eastern scholars have praised wine as a precious gift but censured its misuse. To avoid Mohammed's ban, they described drinking wine as necessary, since it has medicinal properties as long as it is taken in moderation. This allowed wine growing to continue in Azerbaijan. From the time Tsar Peter the Great came to power in Russia, court life had begun to follow the western model and in the 18th century the demand for wine had increased enormously. This meant that wine growing in the foothills of the Caucasus also experienced a big upturn. At the end of the 19th century, peasant farmers from Württemberg in Germany fleeing from high taxes and poverty came via Russia to Azerbaijan, and settled in the northwest around the city of Gandsha. In the towns they founded—Helenendorf (Khanlar), Annenfeld (Shamkhor), and Traubenfeld (Tovus)—there are still many buildings in the original German Baroque style. Fertile soils and good quality grapes, combined with their own wine growing tradition, provided

the best conditions for the Germans to get into wine production. The vines of the Shamaki area in particular produced grapes of the best quality for making fine fruity wines. These attracted great admiration, not just in Azerbaijan, but also on the international wine market.

New agricultural cooperatives and smaller wineries gave new impetus to wine growing at the start of the 20th century. After Azerbaijan was incorporated into the USSR in 1922, the private companies became wine sovkhosi; larger industrial companies also began producing sparkling wine, brandy, and vodka. In the years leading up to 1985, the "No.1" wine factory near Baku alone—whose very name indicates its importance in the Azerbaijani wine industry—employed 1,300 workers and produced around 75 million liters of these alcoholic beverages annually. After Mikhail Gorbachev's anti-alcohol campaigns (see page 251), in 1996 production had fallen to 10 percent of what it had once been, and was now mainly wine. The grape growing area had shrunk from just under 300,000 hectares in the 1980s to around 50,000 hectares at the turn of the century. The slopes of the Great and Small Caucasus have a temperate climate, and in the marshland around the rivers Aras and Kura and along the shores of the Caspian Sea, it is hot and dry. The wild vine, which still grows abundantly, gave rise to more than 100 native varieties of grape for white, red, and rosé wines. The most important are listed here:

Bayan Shira is a late ripening white variety, used for table and dessert wines and the basis for sparkling wine. **Madrasa** (also known internation-

ally as **Matrassa**) has a striking deep black color. Because it has a sugar content of around 20 percent, it is frequently used for dessert wines of the Cahors type *(kagor)*. The red table wine of the same name is a high-quality branded wine. **Khindogny** is the grape of the Garabakh region, with fruits containing at least 18 percent sugar. The deep garnet red table or dessert wines are of good quality and mostly retain a high residual sweetness.

Azerbaijani red wine (l to r): *Karavan-Saray, Maiden Tower,* named after the symbol of the old Town in Baku, and *Seven Beauties*. For export, the bottles are labeled in Russian and English.

Some of Azerbaijan's countless grape varieties are also sold in the markets as table grapes.

Pomegranates

The trail of the pomegranate leads back to the tomb of Ramses IV, and to the Book of Numbers (20,5), where the Children of Israel thirsting in the wilderness longed for pomegranates, as well as grain, vines, figs, and water. But the pomegranate has also been identified as the fruit of the tree of knowledge, with which Eve is supposed to have led Adam astray. On ceremonial occasions, when the high priests of the Old Testament entered the Holy of Holies, they wore a robe, the hem of which was trimmed with bells and representations of pomegranates. This fruit also has an important role in Islam and in arabesque ornamentation. In many Azerbaijani tales and folk poems, the woman is compared to a pomegranate (*nar*)—fruitful, tempting, intoxicating, and refreshing. On long journeys the fruits were carried in the baggage of the caravans for quenching the thirst and as a valuable medicine.

The original home of the pomegranate is thought to have been in ancient Persia and the Azerbaijani districts under its control. Because of the favorable climate with plenty of sun and warmth, the trees flourish from Central Azerbaijan to Karabakh. At the end of May, the cities of Sabirabad, Goytshay, Udshar, and Agdam, and the pomegranate orchards watered by the Mingäçevir reservoir, are enveloped in a fairytale cloud of pink blossom. Some pomegranate varieties were formerly grown only for decoration. Apart from size, the varieties preferred for cooking are distinguished by their taste. *Girmizgabig* ("red skin" is sour, whereas *chahrai guloysha* ("rose

Pomegranate sauces and syrups add a touch of sourness to meat and fish dishes.

face") is sweet. The seeds of the semisweet variety *nasikgabig* (delicate skin") are often used with onions to garnish meat dishes such as *nargovurma* (see page 336), to make them lighter and more digestible. Pomegranate syrup *narsharab* made from the sour varieties, has a similarly positive effect, and is an essential ingredient in dishes containing sturgeon and other fish and meat. A little bowl of seeds mixed with sugar is reckoned to be a "vitamin C bomb". People who do not have good teeth but have plenty of strength in their hands knead the fruit in their hands until it is soft, pierce a hole in the skin, and squeeze out the juice. This refreshing drink is known as the "blood of the sun." In Azerbaijan, they erect special well-ventilated buildings for storing the fruit. The temperature should be around 34–36 °F/ 1–2 °C with 80–85 percent humidity. Covered in wood shavings, pomegranates can be stored for several months in this way. It is mainly the leathery skin and internal "partitions" that keep the fruit fresh. Hippocrates used to prescribe the juice as a remedy for chest pains and stomach problems, and it is also said to reduce fever and help to cure coughs. More recent findings have led to pomegranates being used to treat diabetes, malaria, high blood pressure, and asthma. However, these splendid fruits have one disadvantage: they leave stains that are hard to remove. Carpetweavers make good use of this by using pomegranate skins to dye wool any color from yellow to deepest black.

A salad of pomegranate seeds, onion rings, and herbs makes meat dishes easier to digest.

At the end of May, the delicate red flowers of the pomegranate trees shine out around the Mingäçevir reservoir.

Myth and magic

The number of mysteries and legends concerning the pomegranate is almost as great as the number of seeds it contains. The ancient Phoenicians, Greeks, and Romans all considered it an erotic fertility symbol on account of its many seeds. Azerbaijani mythology also credits the pomegranate with the power to convey fertility. This is expressed in one of their legends. It was the time of sowing. As always, the farmers had made lavish preparations for the spring festival of *Novruz*. The oxen were adorned with bells and colorful cloths on their horns. The banquet was spread and the musicians struck up. The oldest man in the village was given the honor of entering the field first and beginning the sowing. With a linen bag of wheat grains over his shoulder and a pomegranate in his hand, he walked into the field. As he scattered the grain over the earth, he cut up the pomegranate, took out the seeds, and scattered them too, saying "May the earth bring forth as many beautiful grains of wheat as the seeds of this pomegranate." His wish was granted—the yield from this sowing was greater than any before.

Because of its beauty, in Azerbaijan the pomegranate is compared to a woman. In many cultures, this fruit has always had a ritual significance.

Dried figs, along with nuts and chestnuts, are used to flavor sweet and savory dishes.

Figs and kakis

Full of shame, Adam and Eve reached for the fig leaves after they had eaten the fruit of the tree of knowledge. The fig tree also plays an important part in the legend of the founding of Rome. The basket containing the outcast twins Romulus and Remus was thrown into the Tiber and washed up under a fig tree.

The fig *(anjir)*, a member of the mulberry family, comes from southwest Asia. Fig trees were natu-

ralized thousands of years ago on the Abseron Peninsula and the west of Azerbaijan, and at the beginning of the 21st century they were being grown over an area of around 445 acres/180 hectares. Fig trees can live to be over 100 years old, but they are very sensitive to wind and rain. From their seventh year, they bear 110–220 lb/ 50–100 kg of fruit annually. In the strict botanical sense, the fig is not a fruit, but an inflorescence. Apart from one deep purple variety, most of the local figs have a wafer-thin, yellowish skin, and are deliciously sweet and soft. There was a good reason why they were popularly used as a sweetener before sugar was known.

The ripening time from August on is also known in Azerbaijan as "fig time" *(anjir vakhti)*. In the gardens of the summer cottages, the fruit already appears on the table at breakfast time, along with bread and cheese. Syrup and compote keep the housewives busy at harvest time, as does fig jam *anjir murabbasi*. When dried, these quickly perishable fruits make a healthy and nourishing snack. They are said to stimulate the circulation and promote good digestion.

Unlike figs, kaki or Japanese persimmons *(Khurma* or *sharg khurmasi)*, keep longer and can be eaten fresh well into the cold days of winter. They probably originated from China. In the Caucasian region, they were first cultivated in the Black Sea area of Georgia at the beginning of the 19th century. From there they came to Azerbaijan. The planting of orchards began around 1930, and today cultivation is focused in the central and western parts of the country. The most important

varieties are Khiakume, Gasho, and Sidles (from the English word *seedless*). In shape kakis, the fruit of the oriental persimmon *(diaspyros kaki)*, resemble fairly large beef tomatoes, but are not related to them. A single fruit can weigh 3–3½ oz/80–90 g. During ripening, the color of the skin and flesh can change from green to yellow and dark orange. Unripe kakis are inedible, because of their high tannic acid content, whereas the mature fruits have delicate clinging flesh and a very intense sweet taste. The skin of ripe kakis is easy to peel off, and may even burst by itself.

For Azerbaijanis, kakis make a welcome fresh dessert or a delicious snack. They are eaten ice cold, spooned straight from the skin. In the country, the women thread them on strings and dry them in the air. Chestnut-brown dried kakis are not only as sweet as sugar but also nourishing. Fresh kakis have a slight laxative effect, are beneficial for anemia and stomach ailments and, in addition to sugar, they contain plenty of vitamins A and C, plus potassium and copper.

Right: Kakis are carefully picked from the tree (main picture) and after the harvest they are hung on strings in the sun to dry (small insert).

Below: In Azerbaijan, fresh figs are often eaten at breakfast to provide energy, but they also come dried or in the form of jam, syrup or compote.

Anjir murabbasi
Fig jam

2¼ lb/1 kg fresh figs
5½ cups/1 kg sugar
1 tsp citric acid
1 pinch vanilla

Put the figs in a large cooking pot, spread the sugar over evenly, cover, and set aside for 8–10 hours. Then simmer over low heat for 50–60 minutes, stirring carefully from time to time without squashing the fruit. Finally add the citric acid and vanilla, and leave to cool. This jam is eaten with a teaspoon to accompany tea. As a special treat, fig jam is spread on buttered white bread and served for breakfast or a delicious snack.

Land of fire

In the country's original language, Azerbaijan means "highly prized fire," and the inhabitants still call their homeland "Land of Fire." This name holds within it the ancient history of the area and is connected with valuable mineral resources and heathen traditions. In the Azerbaijani faith, fire is a symbol of warmth and eternity.

From time immemorial, fires have blazed where natural gas finds a way to the surface through cracks in the earth and ignites spontaneously. The significance this element has always had in Azerbaijan can be seen if you visit the 12,000-year-old massif of Gobustan "Land of cliffs," where there are rock paintings of people dancing round the fire. From the 6th Century B.C., Zoroastrianism spread across the eastern TransCaucasus. The core of the teachings of Zoroaster, the Persian prophet and founder of this religion, was the worship of fire. An extravagant feast was held once a year under the sign of fire. The temple of fire Atashgyakh (from *atash*: fire) on the Abseron Peninsula is evidence of Zoroastrian fire worship by one of the sources of natural gas that still burn continuously. Many ancient places of worship were destroyed by the followers of Islam in the 7th century. Only Atashgyakh was rebuilt and is now a museum and a popular place of pilgrimage. The basic premises of Zoroaster's teachings, the worship of fire and the belief in its mystical power, found their way into Azerbaijani tradition. That is why the festival of Novruz (see page 316) is still sumptuously celebrated with cultural and culinary attractions—after all, fire is the cook's most important assistant.

At the beginning of the 19th century, gushing sources of wealth were discovered under the Caspian Sea. The oil and natural gas installations are the modern "places of worship," which now interest the whole world.

Since the time of Zoroaster, the Azerbaijanis have revered fire. Near Baku, flares of natural gas burn from cracks in the earth. This inextinguishable power was worshiped in the temple Atashgyakh, before the Arabs brought Islam to the country.

Sherbet

In Azerbaijan and everywhere in the Near East, sherbet *(sharbat)*—from the Arabic *sharbat*, from which the word sorbet is also derived—is a favorite drink. Long before desserts came on the scene, it was the finale of the multiple-course ceremonial banquet. Later it became customary to serve sherbet to guests for refreshment or to a woman after a strenuous childbirth. It was also a popular drink on wedding nights. To accompany *plov*, stuffed vegetables *(dolma)*, many meat dishes, and at weddings and funerals, sherbet is made from roses, and from saffron, mint, basil, lemons, apricots or pomegranates, preferably with a shot of rosewater.

Almost all sherbets have the same basic recipe: hot water is poured over fruits or leaves, sweetened to taste, and left to cool. Made with lemon, saffron, or berries, it also tastes good hot. Sherbet can also be made quickly and easily with *bakmas*, a thick syrup of melons, figs, grapes or mulberries. Boiled milk mixed with sweetened water, basil seeds, attar of roses, vanilla, and a shot of vodka makes the delicious long drink milk sherbet.

Nane sharbati
Mint sherbet

1 handful fresh mint, finely chopped
7 tbsp/100 g sugar

Pour 3½ tablespoons freshly boiled water over the mint, leave to draw for 4 hours, strain, mix with sugar, and serve on ice.

Limon sharbati
Lemon sherbet

1 pinch saffron powder
Peel and juice of 1 untreated lemon
¼ tsp coriander seeds
10½ tbsp/150 g sugar

Dissolve the saffron in about ½ cup water. Chop the lemon peel fine, pour over 2 cups/500 ml hot water, add the coriander seeds, and leave to draw for 4 hours. Strain, and mix in the lemon juice and sugar. Add the saffron infusion and serve the sherbet well chilled.

Rosy meals

The Roman Emperor Nero (37–68 A.D.) commanded that, for a banquet in his palace, the table should be decorated with roses. Fulfilling his desire cost the emperor no less than a barrel of gold coins. In the east, mentions of this most beautiful of all flowers go back as far as around 1400 B.C. It was prized as the "fragrance of the gods" in ancient Egypt, and in India it is the symbol of love. Precious perfumes have been made from attar of roses for thousands of years, especially in Persia, but also in Azerbaijan. In Azerbaijani, the rose is called *gissilgul* "golden flower." About 40 of the 400 or so species that exist in the world flourish here. The varieties *Yusyarpag* ("100 petals"), *Gasanlig*, and *Liana* are particularly suitable for the production of essential oils as ingredients for perfume. It takes no less than a metric tonne of rose flowers to produce 0.8 kg of attar of roses. Jams and rosewater for tea are made from the variety Gasanlig ("for the pot"). A small spoonful of rosebud jam on the tongue gives tea an exotic sweetness. Connoisseurs even scatter rose petals in the cup, giving it a unique fresh taste. However, the high point of a tea ceremony is rose sugar. To make it, you mix fresh rose petals with honey and allow it all to draw in the sun until the sugar crystallizes. The result tastes fabulous, and is supposed to be beneficial for anemia. An unusual delicacy is *gulab*, a distillation of rose petals. A teaspoonful of this rosewater in the tea has proved effective as a cure for insomnia and nervousness. Just the scent of it is calming. Perhaps that is why it became a ritual for the mourners to wash their face and hands in *gulab* after a visit to the cemetery, in order to breathe in the odor of life again.

Tea and sherbet made from fruits, saffron, or rose petals is served with silver and crystal tableware, and according to ancient custom, with oil lamps on the table. It is accompanied by cookies, sweetmeats, and jam.

Nar sharbati
Pomegranate sherbet

9 tbsp/120 g sugar
2 pomegranates (producing about 7 tbsp/100 ml freshly squeezed juice)

Boil 2 cups/500 ml water, dissolve the sugar in it, and leave to cool. Knead the pomegranates until soft, make a cut in one side and press firmly, catching the juice. Mix the juice with the sugar water, leave to draw for 2–3 hours, and serve chilled.

Gisilgul sharbati
Rose sherbet

2 oz/60 g petals from deep red, unsprayed roses
9 tbsp/120 g sugar
1 pinch citric acid

Pour 2 cups/500 ml hot, boiled water over the rose petals, add the sugar, and leave to draw for 9–10 hours. Then strain, add the citric acid and stand in a cold place. If desired, serve the rose sherbet on ice.

The ingredients for the filling are walnuts, sugar, and cardamom. The dough is made with milk, yeast, egg, butter, and flour. It is brushed with saffron and egg.

Before the walnuts for the filling are ground, they are roasted in a pan without fat. That way they keep their spicy flavor.

Pakhlava
Walnut pastry

For the dough:
Approx. 7 tbsp/100 ml lukewarm whole milk
2½ tsp/10 g dried yeast
Salt
1 egg
¼ cup/60 g melted butter
1¾ cups/240 g flour

For the filling:
2 cups/200 g walnut kernels, roasted without fat and ground fine
Scant 1 cup/200 g sugar
¼ tsp each powdered cardamom and vanilla
1 pinch each powdered anis and cloves
3½ tbsp/50 g melted butter
1 beaten egg
¼ tsp saffron powder
2 heaped tsp sugar

The ground walnuts are mixed with sugar, cardamom, vanilla, and powdered anis and cloves.

The first layer of dough is rolled out and pressed into the greased pan. The first layer of filling goes on top of it.

Mix the yeast into the milk and leave in a warm place to prove. Sift the flour with a pinch of salt, make a well in the center, mix in the egg, melted butter, and yeast, and knead to a dough. Leave to rise for about 1 hour.

Stir together the walnuts, sugar, and spices. Divide the finished dough into 8 equal balls. Roll them out into approximately 8 inch/20 cm circles—2 about 1½–2 inch/4–5 cm thick, and the remaining 6 wafer thin. Place the circles of dough and the filling in layers in a buttered round cake pan, beginning with one of the thicker layers of dough and ending with the other.

Beat the saffron with the egg and brush the top of the pakhlava with it. Then cut the whole thing in diamonds. Place ½ walnut in the middle of each diamond, and bake the pakhlava in the preheated oven for about 35 minutes at 350–400 °F/180–200 °C.

While it is baking, prepare the syrup. Boil ¾ cup/200 ml water and dissolve the sugar in it. Pour over the hot pastries and bake for a further 15 minutes. Carefully remove the pakhlava from the pan while still warm, and allow to cool. This sweetmeat is served with tea, and is best prepared a few days in advance.

The next layer is rolled out thinner and folded, to make it easier to place in the pan.

Now the walnut filling is covered with the next layer of dough. The dough is only unfolded when it is in the pan.

The final layer of dough is brushed with saffron and egg and pressed against the sides of the baking pan.

Before baking, the pakhlava is cut in diamonds, and half a walnut is placed on each piece.

Sugar syrup is poured over the baked pakhlava, which then goes back in the oven.

Azerbaijanis most like to eat the sweet walnut pastry with tea—at any time of the day.

Everyone in Azerbaijan eats yeast dough and flaky pastry pockets. They are very popular sweet, but are also sold as fast food with savory fillings such as meat, herbs, and cheese.

Sweetmeats from the Orient

The Azerbaijanis are just as keen on sweet things as their Turkish neighbors. They would give anything for *murabba*, the homemade fig conserve with whole fruits, white cherries filled with hazelnuts, peaches, walnuts, watermelons, strawberries, apricots, or eggplant. Sugar cubes for the tea, bonbons and candy are often flavored with coriander seeds, cinnamon, cardamom, cloves, and anis. For special occasions, small cookies and pastries are equally popular.

The most important ingredients of fine cookies and pastries are spices and nuts, for instance as a filling for sweet dough pockets (*shakarbura*), wedges of dough with walnuts or almonds (*boruchug*) or filled rolls of dough (*Shemakha mutakkasi*). *Nasik* is a flaky pastry with saffron filling. Above all, *pakhlava*, a pastry with a nut filling and soaked with sherbet or sugar syrup, makes life sweeter. The city of Shaki is famous for the most expensive form of this sticky delicacy, which is made here using rice flour. However, this time-consuming and complicated procedure is increasingly being taken over by machinery in factories. It is not only children who love *shakar chorak* ("sugar

bread"), a kind of sponge cake) and *bamiya* (long cookies made from a kind of choux pastry). *Rabat lukum* is similar to what the West knows as Turkish Delight but may also have nuts added, *Sudshug*, walnuts candied in grape syrup, are also known in Georgia and Armenia (see page 362). For celebrations and feast days it is traditional to serve very special sweet pastries. *Halva*, fried pieces of dough with honey, sugar syrup and butter, are meant to comfort the grief-stricken at funerals. After a birth, *guymag*, (flour fried with syrup and

butter until crisp) gives the new mother strength and is supposed to stimulate her milk. In winter, *khashil*, a porridge of flour, with sugar and butter, warms you pleasantly from the inside.

All these sweet things, and the much-loved chocolate, honey, walnut or fruit gateaux, are eaten as desserts, with tea, or as a sweet snack to cheer you up. In addition, these sweet goodies are traditional gifts with symbolic powers. For instance, when a betrothal is celebrated, the bridegroom's family must bring plenty of sweetmeats with them, symbolizing the young couple's future happiness.

Tea culture

"The first glass is a must, the second holds hidden treasures, the third brings bad luck, so the fourth is right. And once you have started on the fifth, you might as well drink fifteen." This saying is dedicated to the Azerbaijani's favorite—tea.

This slightly bitter infusion is made from the dried flower buds and young leaves of the tea bush (Lat. *camellia sinensis*), which probably originated in western China. The theory is that it was already being harvested there 4,500 years ago. In the Middle Ages, the tea plant and the knowledge of how to cultivate it came along the Silk Road to the Caspian Sea, but *chay* probably did not become the Azerbaijani's undisputed national drink until the beginning of the 19th century. Tea drinking is still an everyday ceremony.

Conditions in the Lankaran-Astara area are ideal for growing tea, with plenty of sun, nutrient-rich soils, and a mild climate. The first major plantations were started around 1900, and from the middle of the 20th century the flourishing tea industry supplied the entire Soviet Union. At its height, up to 30,000 metric tonnes a year came on to the market. The tea seeds are sown in greenhouses in November/December, and the seedlings are planted out in January. Three months later the soil needs water and fertilizer, plus a dose of nitrogen (important for combating molds) in October, so the plants are better able to survive the winter. The first meager harvest can take place after five years, but once it reaches the age of 20, the tea bush produces generous yields for 80 years and longer. Connoisseurs confirm that the best quality tea is picked in July and August—just one of the six harvests that are possible each season, at intervals of 15 to 20 days. The leaves, which may be picked by hand or machine, are fermented in the 14 factories currently operating in the country. Oxidation reduces the tannin content and activates the caffeine. During this process the leaves acquire the red-brown color that later gives tea its golden hue. Tearooms near the markets, where the men would gather, were once typical of Azerbaijan, but in their original form, they are becoming rarer and rarer. However, the tradition of immediately serving fresh tea, even to unexpected visitors, is maintained in every family. It does not usually take long to ask—after all, the first glass is a must.

Large quantities of the raw material for Azerbaijani tea come from the plantations in Lankaran, where the precious leaves are often picked by hand.

The tea ceremony

For the Azerbaijanis, tea is a part of life. Its preparation is almost a ritual. Rinse out a ceramic teapot with freshly boiled water, put in a teaspoonful of tealeaves per glass, pour on boiling water, and leave it to stand for three minutes. Pour some of the tea into glasses through a strainer, and add boiling water, if desired. The theory is that after 20 minutes tea is no longer fresh. *Chay* is drunk from special tulip-shaped glasses *(armudu stakan)*, and with good reason, because the tea at the top of the glass has always cooled down a little and is therefore ready to drink, while the narrow "waist" keeps the tea lower down hot for longer.

How to drink freshly made tea in Azerbaijan: place a sugar cube in the mouth, and drink the tea over it a sip at a time, while the sugar slowly dissolves.

Among all the different kinds, black (as distinct from green or herbal) tea is the most important in Azerbaijan—drunk on its own, or with cardamom, cinnamon, mint, saffron, or rosewater. To go with it, they serve slices of lemon, sugar, or cubes of sugar candy. The lemon slices are put straight into the glass, whereas the sugar cubes are melted slowly in the mouth, so the sweetness can be enjoyed sip by sip with the tea. They do the same thing with the fruit conserves *(murabba)*, which are eaten with a spoon from small bowls. Black tea is believed to stimulate the heart and circulation, and for headache, toothache, fever, or tiredness, the Azerbaijani's first recommendation is just a single remedy—*chay!*

After the break-up of the Soviet Union, the Azerbaijani tea processing industry suffered setbacks, in some cases severe. The machinery is out of date, and so the tea is often processed by hand in the factories. In any case, tea is mostly sorted by experts, and in that way quality is maintained—that is the most important of all for the Azerbaijanis.

Russia

History

From the Kievan Rus to the Moscow Tsars

"Rus" is the name of the first East Slavic state, as well as originally being a name for the Varangians—Scandinavian warriors and traders who settled in northern Russia together with the Slavic tribes in the late 8th century. Prince Oleg, a scion of the Scandinavian Rurik dynasty, pushed southward towards Kiev in the 9th century and united it with Novgorod in the north. The Kievan Rus was set up along the trade route from the Baltic to the Black Sea and on to Byzantium, with which the East Slavic kingdom also formed a close political relationship. In 988, Prince Vladimir elevated the Byzantine version of Christianity to the state religion of the Rus, which rang in the birth of the Russian Orthodox Church. Under Yaroslav the Wise, the kingdom blossomed politically and culturally, and magnificent churches, monasteries, and libraries were founded. In the 11th century, there were power struggles between Yaroslav's five sons and encroachments by nomads from the steppes, so new political centers were formed in the northeast of the Rus, and the kingdom broke into several principalities.

The lack of unity between the Russian principalities was partly responsible for a dramatic turning point in Russian history—the rule of the Tatars. After their attack on the southern Russian steppes, they conquered Kiev in 1240 and set up their center of power on the lower Volga. Soon almost all of Russia had to pay tribute to the Golden Horde, as the Tatar-Mongol troops were called, because of the impression given by the gold-decorated tent of their Khan. If they brought death and devastation to the country, and to the south in particular, their leadership also essentially brought political and religious order to Russia—by exploiting the estrangement of the princes for their own interests.

The Prince of Moscow, Ivan I, descended from Muscovite Ruriks, was granted the title of Grand Prince by the Khan in 1328, which allowed him to collect the Tatar's tax. He also ran his own treasury, which gave him the name *Kalita* ("Moneybags"). Using this money, he began the so-called Collection of Russian countries, the annexation of other principalities through the purchase of estates and a skilled matrimonial policy. The northwest and the northeast of Russia were united under the leadership of Moscow. The capital of the leader of the Russian Orthodox Church, the Metropolitan, was moved to this ambitious center of the kingdom. After the seizure of Constantinople by the Turks in 1453, Moscow declared itself "The Third Rome." Ivan III, who married the niece of the last Byzantine emperor in 1472, saw himself as the autocrat of the whole of Russia and the sole legitimate head of Christianity after Rome and Byzantium. In about 1480, he was finally able to shake off Tatar rule. His successor, Ivan IV (1530–1584), called "The Terrible," opened the gate to Siberia, with its legendary wealth of natural treasures, by conquering the Tatar city of Kasan, and suppressed the people of the Volga. In 1547, he had himself crowned the first Russian Tsar by the Moscow Metropolitan. His noble followers (Boyars) were rewarded with estates, which increasingly deprived the resident farmers of their rights. In 1649, serfdom was finally legally established. There was again social unrest. The greatest uprising, which also included the people of the Volga as well as the farmers, took place in 1670/71 under the leadership of the Cossack Stepan Razin.

The leadership of Ivan IV was followed by a "time of turmoil" (*smuta*), during which different contenders for the throne of the Tsar, such as the "false Dmitri," posed as legitimate heirs to the throne and put the country through troubled and on occasion rulerless times. Internal political peace gradually returned to the country from 1613 onward, under Mikhail, the first Tsar from the old noble lineage of the Romanovs.

Russia as a European superpower

He forcefully opened up Russia to Europe: Peter I (1682–1725) was the first Tsar who traveled abroad to the west. He was deeply impressed by the advances he saw there—in sea travel, trade, industry, and agriculture. He was impatient to modernize his people and did not hesitate to impose a "Beard Tax," which was supposed to stop his subjects from wearing the traditional long beard. In 1721, he provided Russia with access to the Baltic through victory over Sweden, and moved the capital city to St. Petersburg, whose marshes surrounding the River Neva took many human lives. This became the baroque residence of the European superpower, Tsarina Catherine II ("the Great"), who strengthened this position in the second half of the 18th century. The Russian empire expanded with the incorporation of Polish areas to the west, gained access to the Black Sea, and pushed forward in its penetration of Siberia.

In the first half of the 19th century, Russia turned from being the "rescuer" of Europe to its "gendarme." In 1812, Napoleon was defeated in his campaign in the "Patriotic War" by the cruel climate and the resistance of the people—which sealed the end of his control of the continent, and Tsar Alexander I was feted as a liberator. His successor, Nicholas I, on the other hand, gained doubtful fame in the management of his authoritarian police state. Intellectuals and young nobles fought against this autocracy with uprisings and assassinations. In 1861, the "liberator Tsar" Alexander II finally ordered the lifting of serfdom. Many of the farmers, now impoverished through rental payments, went to the cities and there formed a rapidly growing proletariat. The first workers' parties were founded, and there were strikes and unrest. These peaked in the St. Petersburg "Bloody Sunday," when the Tsar's guards caused a bloodbath among workers peacefully demonstrating in front of the Winter Palace. This event was the trigger for the first Russian revolution of 1905, which included all classes of society and wrested an advisory civil representation of the people (*Duma*) from the Tsar—the first Russian parliament.

From the Soviet Union to the present day

World War I led to the military and economic collapse of the country, then to the February Revolution in 1917, and the abolition of the monarchy. A civil government was formed, which was dismissed in the same year in the course of the violent October Revolution by a radical communist splinter group of the social democrats under the leadership of Vladimir Ilyich Lenin. These *Bolsheviks* ("majority") were only able to consolidate their leadership after a three-year bloody civil war. In 1922, the Soviet Union was founded: the member countries were Russia, with its capital city now moved back to Moscow, the Ukraine, White Russia, Georgia, Armenia, and Azerbaijan; the Central Asiatic Republics were added a few years later. In the same year, Josef Stalin, from Georgia, was named the Secretary of the Central Committee of the Communist Party. He knew how to expand his power base and pushed himself forward as Lenin's successor. Up until his death in 1953, he exerted a dictatorial form of leadership, in which millions of people were victims of arbitrary political "cleansing" and internment in Siberian punishment camps, *gulags*. The land belonging to the farmers was

Even today, life in the country is still characterized by hardship and poverty in Russia's severe climate.

The Russian Orthodox Church played a substantial part in the power of the state up until the Petrine reforms, and today remains a cornerstone of how Russians see themselves.

forcibly collectivized and farmed in large agricultural operations, the so-called kolkhoz. To carry out gigantic projects in the name of the industrialization of this enormous country, the Soviet state ruthlessly exploited both people and nature.

Despite a pact of nonaggression between Stalin and Hitler, the Soviet Union was attacked in June 1941 by the German army. The "Great Patriotic War," as the Russians called World War II, brought unimaginable harm to the country, with millions slaughtered. Finally, the Red Army was able to free the USSR and Eastern Europe from Hitler—as allies of the US. However, instead of an alliance between these two world powers, a Cold War between the two political systems began soon after 1945. The Soviet empire sealed itself off. Stalin's successor, Nikita Krushchev, introduced a phase of de-Stalinization and reforms, but this was dissolved after 1964 through a 20-year period of restoration and stagnation under Leonid Brezhnev and his aged successors. Not until 1985 was a change rung in with the election of the youngest Politburo member, Mikhail Gorbachev, as head of state. Perestroika and glasnost, reorganization of real, existing communism and transparency through the liberalization of policies on information and culture led to the collapse of the whole system—not only in the Soviet Union but also in the Eastern European "brother states." A failed attempt at a communist putsch in 1991 led to the dissolution of the Soviet Union. It was replaced by a loose "Community of Independent States" (CIS). In spite of openness and electoral freedom in the Russian Federation, black economy corruption and nepotism still continue. Both the domestic market economy and democratization continue to struggle due to the mafia organizations in which politics have become embroiled since the Soviet era and independent company founders, bankers, and

journalists "disappear." Broad classes of the population are becoming poorer, as the state often does not pay out pensions or salaries for months and regions in the provinces and constituent republics are neglected. At the start of the 21st century, Russia is attempting to stabilize its economy under President Vladimir Putin with the assistance of foreign investment, and to redefine its role in the international community of states—great tasks for a giant country with a turbulent history.

Language

Russian is an Indo-Germanic language and, together with Ukrainian and White Russian, belongs to the group of East Slavic languages. Although there was a common East Slavic language during the time of the Kievan Rus, after the empire was split, the languages each developed separately. All three use the Cyrillic alphabet. It is based on Greek capital letters, and is named after the Greek slave missionary Cyril. Together with his brother Methodius, he developed the precursor to the Cyrillic alphabet, the Glagolitic alphabet, in order to spread the Good News to the Slavs in their own language. Their Bible translations from the Greek are the foundation of Old Church Slavonic. The complicated standard language of Church Slavonic and everyday colloquial language existed in parallel for centuries. At the start of the 18th century, the keen reformer Peter the Great also exerted himself in this area. He introduced the "civil script," which has remained standard to this day, which took over from the Old Church Slavonic spelling. Books and new terms streamed into Russia from the west. As in other European countries, French became the language of the nobles. Intellectuals and poets, such as Mikhail Lomonossov (1711–1765), the

writer of the first grammar book for the new Russian, and Nikolai Karamsin (1766–1826) contributed to the modernization and development of Russian. The actual creator of modern Russian literary language was Alexander Pushkin (1799–1837), who united elements of Church Slavonic with the vernacular, finally surmounting the old division.

In the orthographic reform of 1918, the last letters that were no longer enunciated were finally removed from the Church Slavonic alphabet. The language was soon influenced by the socialist structure and was characterized by functionality and abbreviations. Under Stalin, an emotive style spread that glorified the achievements of the Soviet Union and its leader, which set the tone not just for literature but also the language of policy and everyday language. Perestroika brought a flood of new words into the language under the influence of Western culture.

Russian has a continued significance in education, science, politics, trade, and transport in many states that are now independent, such as the Ukraine, Kazakhstan, and Lapland, due to the continuing high proportion of Russian speakers.

Ukraine

History

Ukraine—center of the Kievan Rus state in the 10th century—developed into a cohesive region in terms of language and culture following the Tatar incursion in the 13th century. The Union of Lublin between Poland and Lithuania made the country, which had been split between the two powers since the 14th century, subject to the Polish crown in 1569. The Polish-Ukrainian nobility constituted an upper class that increasingly had disenfranchised Ukrainian farmers working their estates. Under the **Brest Church Union** of 1596 the Ukrainian areas were united even more closely with the Catholic nobility in Poland in terms of the union of the Ukrainian Orthodox Church with Rome. This met with determined opposition from the peasant population, however. In the face of increasing pressure from their landlords in the steppe areas many fled north of the Black Sea to the Cossacks. Originally a warlike Tatar people, due to the immigration of Ukrainian and Russian serfs since the 16th century the Cossacks were primarily East Slavs. The hatred for the landowners and their mostly Jewish bailiffs exploded in the great **Cossack rebellion** in 1648 which made large areas of Ukraine into a Polish wasteland and which was accompanied by terrible massacres within the Jewish communities. Unable to match the superiority of Poland and Lithuania on their own, the Cossacks accepted the **Treaty of Pereyaslav** in 1654 and came under the protection of the Orthodox Christian Russian empire, providing military services for the Tsar in securing the borders against the Ottoman vassal nation of the Crimean Tatars. The treaty brought Russia into open conflict with Poland and the opponents **divided the Ukraine** along the Dnipro in 1667. The eastern part including Kiev came under the Russian empire. Under Peter I. the Cossacks were unable to maintain their independence between the fronts in the Great Northern War (1700–1721) against Sweden. With the defeat of the Ottoman Empire and the final annexation of Krimkhanat, Catherine the Great gained access to the Black Sea and incorporated the Cossack areas into her empire in 1783.

A *nationalist movement* developed in Ukraine in the 19th century. While the Habsburg Empire, to which the southwestern areas of Ukraine had belonged since 1772 due to the division of Poland, supported the national cultural movement among the Ukrainian population, Russia was carrying out an increasing Russianization of the east Ukrainian upper classes. It was only with the popular revolution of 1905 that the Ukrainians were able to publish newspapers in their own language, a development which was soon to be hindered again by Russia, however.

In World War I west and east Ukrainians had to fight against each other on the front between Austria and Russia but in 1917, with the approaching downfall of both empires, a spontaneous **independence movement** took hold in all areas of the country. In January 1918 the Ukrainian and West Ukrainian republics were formed and were unified a year later. The young nation was to meet its downfall after only a few weeks, how-

The Crimea—and its landmark, the lookout point "the swallows' nest"—became a bone of contention between Ukraine and Russia following independence.

ever. As the center of the civil war between the Bolsheviks, antirevolutionary troops, and the Polish army it proved to be too weak on its own without allies. In June 1920 the Bolsheviks took power in Kiev and in 1922 Ukraine became a **member of the Soviet Union**. Lenin's relatively liberal economic and nationalist policies led to a rapid recovery in the country in the years that followed. The Ukrainization of the party cadres was actively encouraged and Ukrainian became the official language for the first time. Under Stalin, however, Moscow rejected the Leninist internationalism and made Soviet patriotism the official ideology. The enforced collectivization, which was carried out with particular severity in Ukraine, led to failed harvests followed by a terrible **famine** to which entire villages fell victim in 1932/33. The Soviet leadership also used political "cleansing" to suppress the national independence movement and replaced the Ukrainian farmers and intellectuals, who "disappeared" due to deportation and execution, with Russians.

Following the Stalinist terror some Ukrainians saw the **German occupation in World War II** as a liberation. It soon became apparent, however, that the new rulers saw the fertile country simply as a "bread basket" for feeding the "Reich." They abducted the Ukrainian civilians and carried out the planned extermination of the Jews. The Red Army found a wasteland when it returned in 1943/44. In 1947 the Russian Ukrainian Nikita Khrushchev undertook the rebuilding of the country. As First Secretary of the Soviet Communist Party he granted Ukraine greater cultural freedom from 1956 and ensured the Ukrainization of the party cadres in Kiev. Yet the subsequent Brezhnev era was again one of radical Russianization policies, characterized by repression and censorship. Resistance movements began to form, and they spread increasingly from 1986 onward, provoked by the attempts of the Soviet authorities to downplay the catastrophe at the nuclear power plant of **Chernobyl** and the ensuing procrastination of counter measures. In 1991, Ukraine declared its **independence**. Its first/second president, Leonid Kuchma/Kravchuk struck a compromise with Moscow. Furthermore, when the Ukraine was accepted into

the Council of Europe and began industrial relations with the NATO, its rapprochement to the West became manifest. After apparent vote-rigging during the presidential elections of 2004, mass protests formed which have gone down in history as the »**Orange Revolution**.« The Supreme Court ruled that a run-off ballot between pro-Russian Viktor Janukovitch and Viktor Jushtchenko, who leant more towards western Europe, was invalid. When the ballot was repeated, Jushtchenko was declared the winner and new president. However, shortly afterwards power struggles developed in the orange party between Jushtchenko and Yulia Tymoshenko. In the meantime, the country fell into stagnation. Eventually, in 2010, the frustrated population elected Janukovitch for president. He expanded his own power and increased relations with Russia again. In late 2013, large parts of the population gathered in Kiev to protest against Janukovitch's government. Eventually, in February 2014 the **Euromaidan** demonstrations led to the downfall of President Janukovitch. The ensuing developments are putting a serious strain on the republic.

Language

The characterization of a Ukrainian identity in the 14th century also led to the development of a linguistically cohesive identity relative to the Russians and Byelorussians. Under Polish rule Ukrainian was subjected to Latin and Polish influences as the official and literary languages. Like Russian Ukrainian uses the Cyrillic alphabet and up until the 18th century also shared the division between two language levels—the Slavic Church language and popular speech. The progressive administrative and social integration of eastern Ukraine into the Russian empire since the division of the country led to the dissemination of the Russian language at the expense of the Ukrainian oriented Slavic Church language and Latin. It was only within the context of the cultural renaissance movement of the 19th century that Ukrainians began to promote their own language and literature. Popular speech formed the basis for the development of modern literary Ukrainian which, in the works of the nationalist writer Taras Shevchenko (1814–1861), led to the reunification with the Slavic Church language. As a result of the ban on Ukrainian language publications in the Russian empire, and the relocation of cultural life to Austrian Galicia, the literary language incorporated numerous west Ukrainian elements during the decades prior to World War I. The decade-long efforts to achieve the authorization of their own language was an essential element in the fight for independence by the eastern Ukrainians. With the declaration of independence in 1918 Ukrainian finally became the official language and the language of literature but had to give way to Russian again during the Soviet era. The declaration of Ukrainian as the national language on January 1, 1990 heralded the rebirth of a nation.

Georgia

History

Sakartvelo is what the Georgians call their country between the Greater and Lesser Caucasus, meaning "Land of the Kartlians," from Kartli, an east Georgian province. Georgia has been settled since the early Stone Age. It entered written history in the 6th century B.C. In west Georgia at this time, the state of Kolkhis arose, which was influenced culturally and economically by the Greeks, but which kept its political sovereignty for centuries. At about the same time, the kingdom of Iberia developed in east Georgia, which was dependent on the Persians.

Both Kolkhis and Iberia became part of the Roman empire in the 1st century B.C. and remained so for 400 years. In 337, Iberia elevated Christianity to the state religion and thus became the second Christian state after Armenia. Kolkhis-Laiska, a principality that emerged from the old Kolkhis, also adopted the Christian religion.

In the 5th century, the power of the east Roman Empire of Byzantium became weaker, but at the same time the Persians strengthened. Both of these competing powers frequently fought their battles on Georgian soil. One outstanding leader at this time was King Vakhtang Gorgassali, who briefly obtained independence for his country of Iberia in 483. The provincial nobles after him, however, ruled under the direction of Persia or Byzantium. From the mid-7th century onward, the governors of the Arabic Kalifs were a new factor in the power struggle in Georgia. For centuries they pushed forward the Islamization of the country against bitter resistance from the majority of the population.

After the end of the Arab occupation, the desire for a centralized kingdom and a united state grew. In 975, King Bagrat III ascended the throne and brought together almost all of the provinces in east and west Georgia to form one kingdom. His successors, however, had to fight the Turkish people that invaded under the leadership of the Seldshuks. These people were finally defeated by King Davit IV, who ascended the throne in 1089 and led Georgia into its "Golden Age." Davit expanded his kingdom through war, but he also built roads and bridges, abolished the privileges of nobles, founded academies of science and art and was characterized by his religious tolerance. By the first half of the 13th century, this time of flowering was past. Georgia's position of power crumbled and the Mongols conquered the country. They placed different leaders on the throne and then removed them—until Giorgi V ascended to the throne in 1314. In 1336, he invited all the provincial princes to a celebratory meal and had those beheaded who were friendly to the Mongols. Thus the power of the Mongols was broken, but their example became accepted: by the end of the 14th century, the Mongol Timur (also Tamerlane) led his devastating campaign of conquest through Georgia.

In 1453, the Ottoman Turks conquered Constantinople, and Iran simultaneously found new power under the Safavids. Georgia, now consisting of three kingdoms (Imeretia, Kartli, and Kakhetia) and numerous principalities became a bone of contention between Turkey and Persia.

In order not to become a Christian enclave crushed between these warring powers, Erkele II, king of Kartli and Kakhetia, signed a protectorate agreement in 1783 with the expanding Christian Orthodox superpower of Russia, which had declared war on Turkey. However, the Russians did not keep to it, but annexed east Georgia in 1801, Imeretia in 1810, and other areas later on. The Georgian leaders were replaced by Russian military governors; the Georgian church was made subject to the Russian church and Russian became the official language. This reckless annexation led to several unsuccessful uprisings. On the other hand, Georgia was again geographically reunited by the Russians.

In the 19th century, many Georgians studied in Russia and Western Europe and brought socialist thinking home with them. Radical intellectual groups were set up, from which also emerged the most infamous Georgian, Josef Dzhugashvili, alias Stalin (1879–1953). After the October Revolution in 1917, Georgia wanted to separate from Russia and declared its independence in 1918. In 1921, however, the Red Army marched in, and the country became part of the Union of Socialist Soviet Republics. Although the Georgians also fell victim by the dozen to Stalinist "cleansings," Stalin is still honored by many as a national hero.

After World War II, during which many Georgians died in the ranks of the Red Army, the country did relatively well under the socialist planned economy, and it developed into the tourist center of the Soviet Union. Like other Soviet Republics, Georgia declared its independence in 1991. The following years were characterized by great political instability, criminality, and economic decline. The first President was Zviad Gamsakhurdia, who was deposed in 1992, but then instigated a revolt to regain power. It was suppressed by Georgian governmental troops with Russian support. The areas of South Ossetia and Abkhasia, which were autonomous in Soviet times, declared their independence from Georgia, and the Abkhasians in particular met with resistance from the Georgians. Military conflict was the result. The Georgian troops were defeated and had to withdraw. Recognized by neither the Georgians nor the international community, Abkhasia is today to a large extent effectually independent.

In 1995, Eduard Shevardnadze, the former Soviet Foreign Minister under Mikhail Gorbachev, became the country's president and increasingly but not undisputedly stabilized the country both politically and economically.

The "Rose Revolution" at the end of 2003 deposed Shevardnadze. His successor, Mikhail Saakashvili, is pursuing a course focused on Europe and the US.

Language

Georgian is the official language of Georgia and, together with Svan, Megrelian, and Laz, which are used as additional colloquial languages in the regions, form the group of south Caucasian languages. In addition, there are numerous dialects. Georgian is, however, the written language common to them all. The origin of Georgian is unknown, and its relationship to other language groups cannot be ascertained. Georgian script probably developed in the 5th century under the influence of the Greek and Aramaic alphabets. First there was *Khutsuri*, the "church script" used for religious texts. This developed into a secular "military script," *Mkhedruli*, in the 11th century, which was modified in the 17th century into its current written form.

In linguistic history, Old Georgian differs from New Georgian, which developed in the 12th century; however, Old Georgian was not completely superseded until the mid-19th century. The New Georgian vocabulary contains many New Persian, Turkish, and Russian elements.

The equestrian statue of the legendary King Vakhtang Gorgassali looks down on the Georgian capital of Tbilisi.

Armenia

History

The origins of the Armenian people, known to themselves as *Haj*, remain a mystery. Probably around the end of the 7th century B.C., an Indo-European people migrated from the west into the area between Lakes Van, Sevan, and Urmia, where they encountered the crumbling Urartian empire. As the Armenians took over many elements of Urartian culture, such as the myths surrounding Mount Ararat, the irrigation system, cattle farming, and wine growing, whereas their language has Indo-European roots, modern Armenians see themselves as the descendants of both nations.

The name *Armina* appears for the first time in the year 521 B.C., on a stele of the Persian king Darius I (522–486 B.C.), testifying to the rule of the Persian Achaemenides over the Armenian highlands, which stretched in a northward curve from Lake Urmia to the Valley of the Euphrates. An independent **Armenian kingdom** grew up during the 2nd century B.C. under Tigranes II (95–55 B.C.), it extended from the Caspian Sea to the Mediterranean Coast—the greatest size any Armenian state would ever reach. However, this edifice soon crumbled and Armenia once again found itself in the role of a dependent buffer state at the edge of the Roman Empire. During the prolonged power struggle between Rome and Persia in the first centuries A.D., Armenia was constantly invaded, and finally crushed and divided between the combatants at the end of the

The Khor Virap monastery at the foot of Mount Ararat, now in Turkey, where Noah's Ark is said to have landed.

4th century. At the same time, the Armenian people were given power and unity under the Arsakide king Tiridates III, who was converted to Christianity by St. Gregory the Illuminator. As a result, Armenia became the first country in the world to adopt the new faith as a state religion in 301 A.D. This step encouraged the spiritual life, and Armenian literature experienced its **Golden Age** in the 5th century. Manuscripts from this period have survived and are housed in the Manuscript Museum in Yerevan.

A significant change of political balance in the Near East came about with the **Arab Conquests** in the name of Islam in the 7th century. Byzantium tottered, the Persian Empire fell apart and, from that time on, the governors in eastern Armenia were appointed by the caliphs. If this constricted position between the great powers of east and west was particularly unfavorable for Armenia's independent development well into the Middle Ages, this was completely halted after the 11th century by new powers arriving from the east. In 1064 the country was raided by the Turkish Seljuks, it was overrun by the Mongols in the 12th century, and devastated in the 14th century by the ravaging expeditions of Tamerlane. Many fled before the **Seljuk Storm**—reckoned to be the start of the *spyurk* (diaspora)—to the remaining Byzantine area of Asia Minor, or founded new communities in Georgia, the Crimea, Moldavia, Poland, and Galicia.

The dispersal allowed the Armenian **Principality of Cilicia** on the southeast coast of modern Turkey to come into being outside the original settlement area. Its rise was aided by the First Crusade in the 11th century. At the end of the 13th century, this state was recognized as a kingdom by the German and Byzantine emperors, and until its conquest by the Mamelukes in the 14th century, it was an important center for trade between east and west.

After the 15th century, most areas of Armenian settlement were under **Ottoman rule**, though the eastern part, roughly equating to the area of the modern state, was conquered by the Shah of Persia in the 17th century. Taking advantage of the increasing weakness of the Ottoman Empire and Persia, Russia advanced into the Caucasus at the beginning of the 19th century, and annexed the Persian provinces of Yerevan, Karabakh, and Nakhichevan.

Inspired by the nationalist movements in Europe, the call for Armenian self-rule within the Ottoman Empire grew loud as the 19th century wore on. In the end, they were officially granted autonomy, but this had no practical consequences. Instead, Sultan Abdul Hamid acted with the utmost brutality against the people in eastern Asia Minor. In the 1890s, up to 150,000 Armenians fell victim to state-organized pogroms. After the outbreak of World War I, these persecutions became systematic. With the evident intention of exterminating every Armenian living on Ottoman land, they began in the spring of 1915 with the execution without trial of thousands of Armenian intellectuals in Constantinople (now Istanbul). Then the Armenian inhabitants of the six eastern provinces of the empire, where they represented the biggest ethnic group, were murdered by state decree or deported to the Syrian desert and left to starve. In all, almost 1.5 million people fell victim to the *egern* ("atrocities"). The persecution meant the end of Armenian life in the western part

of their homeland, and is seen as the first **genocide** of the 20th century. No admission of guilt on the part of the Turkish State has yet been made.

After the implosion of the Russian and Ottoman empires, the **first modern-day independent state** was founded in the former Russian part of Armenia in 1918. However, caught between the great powers to the north and west as they regained their strength, it did not last very long. In 1920, Armenia was forced to recognize the current borders and, under pressure from the Russians, to declare itself a Soviet republic and, together with Georgia and Azerbaijan, it formed the TransCaucasian Soviet Republic in 1922 and became a member of the **Soviet Union**. After World War II, thanks to its pleasing economic development, the Soviet Socialist Republic of Armenia was able to create the framework for a national revival, which also included ritual commemoration of the genocide. Gorbachev's reforming policies reawakened the desire for independence, though the conflict with Azerbaijan over Nagorno-Karabakh also threw national sentiments into turmoil. When the Soviet Union broke up in 1991, Armenia declared its **independence**. The young state put Azerbaijan under military threat, but the price of victory was political isolation and an economic blockade. At the start of the 21st century, Armenia's biggest task is to find a way out of the economic crisis, acquire international allies, and make peace with Azerbaijan.

Language

Armenian is its own branch of the **Indo-European family of languages** and shows only a distant relationship to Greek and Persian. The country's conversion to Christianity was critically important for the development of the language. The faithful had to be able to read the holy scriptures in their own language, so around the year 400, the monk Mesrop Masrots was given the task of creating **an alphabet of its own** for the country and translating the Bible. This script is still in use today, and the language of the Ancient Armenian scriptures is still the language of church services. In recent times, two literary languages have developed: New West Armenian and New East Armenian. The first is based on the Constantinople (Istanbul) dialect and is currently spoken in Turkey, the Near East, Europe, and America. The latter is based on the Yerevan dialect and is now used in Armenia, Georgia, Azerbaijan, Russia, and Iran.

Language and religion have been the pillars of Armenian culture holding the scattered people together for 1600 years. Now that there is an Armenian state, the ever-threatening loss of the language in the diaspora can no longer endanger the continuing existence of Armenian traditions.

Azerbaijan

History

In ancient times, the land on the west coast of the Caspian Sea was mostly ruled from Persia, and populated mainly by Iranians, mingled with nomadic Turkish tribes, Caucasian Albanians and Kurds. At the time of the Persian Achaemenides, overthrown by Alexander the Great around 330 B.C., the natural fires on the Abseron Peninsula are said to have inspired the **Prophet Zoroaster** (c. 630–550 B.C.). His monotheistic cult spread here as in the rest of Iran, and was preached for centuries. Remains of churches in what is now Azerbaijani territory also bear witness to a Christian state that has been known as Albania since the 4th century but has nothing to do with the country in the Balkans. By contrast, the south of the country, Atropatene, was incorporated into the resurgent Persian Empire under the Sassanides (226–651), who wanted to establish a pan-Achaemenidian empire. A crucial turning point came in the 7th century. The Persian State crumbled under the **Arab onslaught** and Azerbaijan also became part of the Muslim world.

The Azerbaijanis value the diverse heritage of their country, but they are mainly descended from the **Oguzes**, who migrated from the east. This nomadic Turkish people originally came from the region around the Aral Sea, then in the 11th century, under the rule of the Seldjuk dynasty, they settled to the west of the Caspian Sea and in Asia Minor, where they mixed with the indigenous inhabitants. The migration of the Turks caused a change in the population of the pan-Seldjuk empire which, in the period around 1090, stretched from the Indus to the Mediterranean. At the same time, Persian was the language spoken at court, and the much-admired Persian culture was able to develop.

The Mongolian Il-Khans (1258–1335) extended the Azerbaijani trading center of Tabriz and made it their capital, and even the revival of Iran in the 16th century under the Safavid Shah Ismael (1487–1524) was achieved from Azerbaijan. After centuries of foreign rule and fragmentation, he succeeded in uniting Iran by military force and bringing in **Shia** teachings. This brought about the opposition between the Azerbaijanis in western Iran and the Sunni Turks under Ottoman rule, though they were still linked by a common language and origin. During the collapse of central authority in Persia in the 18th century, independent khanates were set up in Azerbaijan, which increasingly came within Russia's sphere of interest. At the beginning of the 19th century, the area now occupied by Azerbaijan and Armenia finally became Russian after two Russo-Persian wars, while the greater part around Tabriz south of the Aral Sea remained in Persian hands.

At first the fact that they were now part of the empire of the Tsars made little change to the traditional oriental way of life. But at the end of the 19th century oil, the gold of the machine age, drew businessmen to Baku from all over the Russian Empire. Around 1900, over half the world's oil came from Azerbaijan. Big European companies such as the Nobel Brothers, the Rothschilds, and Siemens opened branches in the booming city. Alongside the Western Europeans, it was mainly

The oriental lifestyle that is typical of modern Azerbaijanis has its roots in their history.

the Russians and Armenians who ran the businesses, determined the policies, and lived in the central districts of the cosmopolitan city, because they had the advantage over the indigenous Muslims in respect of education and wealth. By contrast, Azerbaijanis did not make up even half the population of Baku, and had little say in affairs.

The Russian conquest opened up the country to European culture, science, and ideas. Even the national consciousness, which would normally be foreign to the universalism of the Muslim world, fell on the fertile soil of an underprivileged ethnic group. At the beginning of the 20th century, with the slogan "Turkicize, Islamicize, Europeanize," intellectuals attempted to form a **nation between East and West**. In the turmoil of the civil war, in May 1918, Azerbaijani nationalists seized the opportunity to found an **independent state**, for which they chose the geographical name of Azerbaijan, which had rarely been used before. But as early as 1920, the Red Army marched in and enforced the founding of a Soviet Socialist Republic, which became part of the Soviet Union in 1922 and, along with Georgia and Armenia, belonged to the TransCaucasian Federal Soviet Socialist Republic.

During the 71 years of **Soviet rule**, the country underwent a radical change. As in other parts of the Soviet Union, they pushed ahead with industrialization and urbanization, the economy grew, and the general level of education improved. However, the positive impetus was bought at the cost of the Russification of the country, the suppression of Islam, and the countless people who fell victim to the Stalinist terror, especially among the intellectual and religious elite. A limited liberalization of public life began under Khrushchev, but even so, in the 1960s oil production—the life-blood of the Azerbaijani economy—almost came to a standstill. However, Soviet penetration of society did not succeed in making people forget the idea of an independent Azerbaijan. In 1988, when the Armenians, who rep-

resented the great majority of the population of Nagorno-Karabakh and had run the autonomous region within Azerbaijan during the Soviet era—demanded that the region should become part of the Armenian "motherland," the spark of nationalism was kindled in Azerbaijan as well. The war that followed led to the independence of both countries, but at the same time, it aroused nationalism and hatred and precipitated the new states into a deep crisis. After changing fortunes in the war, the Armenians have been in control of the Republic of Nagorno-Karabakh since the cease-fire of 1994, which has not, however, been internationally recognized. So the **Second Azerbaijani Republic**, founded in 1991, is still plagued by the unresolved conflict over Nagorno-Karabakh, a depressed economy, and the increasingly repressive policies of the former communist Heydar Aliyev and his successor, his son Ilham. The hope of future prosperity remains, if the oil wells begin to spurt again, and also of a peace settlement, which is a prerequisite for the economic use of the country's natural resources.

Language

Like Turkish, Azerbaijani or Azeri belongs to the southwestern or Oguz group of **Turkish languages**. Turkish languages show a high degree of similarity and mutual comprehensibility, and are agglutinative languages.

An Azerbaijani literary language developed in the 14th century and reached a peak with the poet Mehmed Fuzuli in the 16th century. In the 19th century, with a new generation of writers influenced by European literary forms, a modern written language, based on the spoken form, established itself in the Russian part of the country. At the beginning of the 20th century, when the wave of **pan-Turkism**, the idea of uniting all the Turkish peoples, rose high, a trend appeared—as it did in Ottoman Turkey—toward purifying the language of the many Arabic and Persian elements, which was not fully carried through after the country's incorporation into the Soviet Union.

Soviet language policy was conflicting. On the one hand, the status of Azerbaijani was enhanced by a comprehensive literacy program; on the other hand, after World War II, Russian in particular gained in prestige, because it was the only language that offered access to higher education and the social elite. This meant that bilingualism became the norm, and loss of the mother tongue was by no means uncommon in the upper strata of society. In addition, the frequent **changes of alphabet** (1923 Roman alphabet, 1929 ban on Arabic script, 1937 Cyrillic alphabet, 1991 Roman alphabet again) still make written communication difficult. Since 1991, Azerbaijani has been the only official language, but it will be some time yet, before it has completely worked its way through.

The authors

Hartmut Moreike started his career in radio as a qualified journalist (Leipzig) and philosopher (Moscow), and moved from economics editor, through magazine reporter, to travel writer. He has had adventurous trips through Russia from the North Pole to the Gobi desert. In his novellas, stories, and four novels, the author draws realistic images of life in Russia and always shows his profound knowledge of everyday life, the culture and history of this enormous country between Europe and Asia.

Alexey Kozlachov comes from Zhukovsky in the Moscow area, and graduated from the Moscow College of Literature (the Gorki Institute). He has worked for many years in Russia as a journalist on newspapers such as Literaturnaya Rossiya, Rossiyskaya gazeta and Kto-est-Kto. Until 2004, he was the editor and chief editor of an independent newspaper in the Moscow area, and now lives in Cologne as a freelance author and journalist on cultural and socio-political subjects.

Beate Blaha, a journalist with a background in print and radio, as well as a graduate of the German School of Journalism in Munich, has worked for over 20 years as an author and movie maker with Bavarian Television, specializing in Eastern and Southeastern Europe. She has traveled extensively in the Ukraine. In addition to social subjects and humanitarian projects, this enthusiastic amateur cook is primarily devoted to this land and its people—and with a particular love of its culinary aspects.

Isabel Kielian was employed by the city of Freiburg in its department for representation and town twinning for cultural exchanges with Eastern Europe after her studies in culture and many years spent working as a journalist. She spent 1998 to 2000 in the Georgian capital of Tbilisi as a lecturer sent by the Goethe Institute, where she made an intensive study of the country and its people, together with her husband, the Polish lawyer and Eastern European expert Marek Kielian. After a few years with the Goethe Institute in Zagreb, they both now live in Helsinki.

Marcus Würmli studied science and arts in Basel, Catania and Vienna, receiving a doctorate in Vienna in 1971. The scientist is an author, translator and publisher of over 500 nonfiction and reference books—including books on gastronomy and wine. From 1999 to 2003, he researched the nature and culture of Armenia and has lived since 2005 in eastern China.

Elnara Ismailova comes from the Azerbaijani capital of Baku. She inherited her enthusiasm for the cookery of her home country from her grandmother and mother. Since 1995, she has lived in Germany and has made a name for herself in Europe as a solo pianist and lecturer at the Folkwang College in Essen. The fact that she sees herself not just as an ambassador for music but also Azerbaijani cuisine is proven regularly at gourmet evenings in her elective home in Cologne.

Acknowledgements

Hundreds of people contribute to the success of a large project such as this volume, which came into being in countries in which travel is not always easy and many doors only open through the help of good contacts. The publisher and editors would therefore like expressly to thank all those people and institutions for their support and help— including all of those not explicitly named by us or listed here individually. Our particular thanks go to our families and all our friends who encouraged the team during the project. We would like to thank Helga Schmid, in Gilching, for support and advice to the photographer en route and at home. We would like to thank Gerhard Gleinser and Werner Kopainigg from the "Bogenhauser Hof" restaurant in Munich for beautiful food subjects in Germany, as well as Porzellan und Decoration Schmidt, in Gilching.

The publisher would like to thank the following in particular: Sebnem Yavuz for corrections and creation of the index; Svetlana Dadasheva, Larissa Rumyanzeva and Alexander Verzeiser for their help on questions of Russian food culture and language; Elsa Alimova for her commitment in procuring images in Russia and Georgia.

Russia

We would like to thank Daniela Scarpati, Cologne/Moscow, for her indispensable cooperation and translation of the text by Alexey Kozlachkov into German, as well as the culinary expert and author, Vyacheslav Alatorzev, for many invaluable consultation sessions. We would like to thank Lothar and Christa Pindeus, at the Austrian Embassy in Moscow, for their advice, market visits, and successful meals; also Vera Ukhanova, who cooked us Russian meals on occasion, and her husband. We would like to thank Olga von Elsner, Munich, for her informed support in the design and research of recipes, Tian Zaochnaya, Munich, for research on the subject of the "Itelmens" and contacts in Kamchatka. In addition, we would like to thank Ute Bretschneider for her assistance with the English transliterations.

The author Hartmut Moreike would like to thank the following persons and institutions:
Abbess Juliana from the Convent of the Conception, Moscow
Academy of Sciences, Siberian Department, Omsk/Akademgorodok
Tatyana Dozenko, Moscow
G. Frodin, Reiseagentur für Jedermann, Berlin
Journalists' House, Moscow
Vitaliy Klimov, Moscow
Reza Koroyi, Imperial Kaviar GmbH, Berlin
Viktor Koslikin, Press Attaché of the Embassy of the Russian Federation in Germany, Berlin
Olga Martynova and Olga Tokareva, the Krasny Oktyabr chocolate factory, Moscow
Lenin Library, Moscow
Marina Malysheva and Alexander Stepanov, Hotel Metropol, Moscow
Metropolitan Kiryll, Archbishop of Moscow
Moskauer Deutsche Zeitung
Tatyana Neshelskaya, Moscow
Yevgeniy Pashkov, Chamber of Trade and Industry of the Russian Federation in Germany, Berlin
International organization Porodnennye Goroda, Moscow
Sergey Sanne, Rc. Legal Matters Bochkaryov, St. Petersburg
Juriy Sheldakov, OAO Moscow Distillery "Cristall"
Vladimir S. Vassilyev, Moscow
Svetlana Venzislizkaya, OAO Moskovskiy Kombinat "Kolomenskoye"

The photographer would like to thank the following for their support:
Sergey and Natasha Arfanidi, Irkutsk
Claudia Schweikert, Heinrich Möderle, and Roland Holzer, the Balchug Kempinski hotel, Moscow
Restaurant Berenevka, Kostroma
Bogolyubovo monastery, Vladimir
Manfred and Tatyana Brockmann and the members of the St. Paul's community, Vladivostok
Dmitriy Burninov, Aeroflot Moscow
Vyacheslav Medkov, Club snatokov russkoy vodki, Vladimir
Julia Ilinikh and Engelbert Gamsriegler, Grand Hotel Europa, St. Petersburg
Grand Imperial Russian restaurant-salon, Moscow
Renate and Helmut Grünert, Gilching
Dr. Christoph Hahn, Munich
Galina Kobylnikova, Intourist hotel, Irkutsk
Helena Aleksandrovna Klimova, Vladimir Dyal, and Lyudmila Loginova, Elista
Lomonossov state porcelain factory, St. Petersburg
Valentina Yakovlevna Marchenko, Kostroma
The Naurus restaurant, Kasan
Oleg Nikotovich, Kovran
Nostalgie restaurant, Vladivostok
Vladimir Ivanovich Efimov and Tatyana Petrovna Martinova, the OAO hotel, Vladimir
Prof. Viktoria Petrasheva, Kovran
Maria and Hans Pfänder, Biolandhof, Schwabmünchen
Sergey E. Gutsait, the Podvoriye restaurant, Pavlovsk
Galina G. Prokhorova, Tula
Adelheid Rabus, Munich
Aleksandr Petrovich Ribakov, Vladimir
Jörg Schulze, Villingen-Schwenningen
Viktor Shikhorev, Tula
Staryy Wek restaurant, Irkutsk
State Fishing Company, Vladivostok
Peter Steger, Erlangen
Valentine Nikolayevna Sukhanova, Kasan
Traktir restaurant, Susdal
Christina Tschischova, Irkutsk
Vera Nikoliyevna Ukhanova and Alexsandr Sergeyevich Ukhanov, Moscow
Versailles hotel, Vladivostok
The vodka factory and vodka association, Vladimir
The vodka museum, Uglich
U Solotykh Vorot restaurant, Vladimir
Aleksandr Yeshov, Kostroma
Nadine Vacheslavnovna Yevrasova

Ukraine

We would like to particularly thank Prof. Dr. Nicolas Szafoval from the Ukrainian Free University in Munich and his wife Tanya Tarapacky for continual support and advice. We would also like to thank Oleksiy Nesnov for his assistance with the English transliterations.

The author Beate Blaha would like to thank:
Cornelia Greiner, Munich
Ludmilla Klimova, Kiev
Elena Kovalenko, Lugansk
Dr. Lera Maryushenko, Kharkiv
Dr. Igor Mishenko, Gauting
Olexander Petrovych, Cherkassy

The photographer would like to thank the following for their support:
Ivan Bobyn, Munich
Natalia and Peter Diychuk, Sokolivka
Frau Ficak, the Ukrainian boarding school, Munich
Vladimir Gokov, Kiev
Kiev open-air museum
Bogdan Kluchuk, Sokolivka
Luba Kokot, Lviv
Korneluk family, Kosiv
Georgiy Kosykh, Consul General of the Ukraine, Munich
Massandra winegrowing estate
Peter Mozoluk, the Ukrainian Institute, Munich
The Neptune restaurant, Lviv
Novyy Svit sparkling wine cellar, Sudak
The Oselya restaurant, Lviv
Georg B. Udovenko, the Prolisok chalet hotel, Kiev
Vladimir Anatolevich Matvizin, the Shinok Ukrainian restaurant, Moscow
The Viennese Café, Lviv
Valodimir and Anatolii Pavlovski, the Yarivtsi restaurant, Kiev

Georgia

We would like to thank in particular Khatuna Gamesardazhvili and her whole family in Tbilisi and west Georgia, as well as Mzekala Atkhaidse, Tbilisi/Munich, for her untiring support of our work. In addition, we would like to thank Dr. Giuli Kvrivishvili for her help with the transliteration of Georgian terms into English.

The authors would like to thank the following:
Dr. Maia Akhalkatsi, Tibilisi
Manana Akhalkatsi, Tibilisi
The Anzi restaurant, Tibilisi
Chavchavdse family, Tibilisi
Prof. Dr. Dali Bakhtadse, Tibilisi
Ia Beyanizhvili, Ruispiri
Beyanizhvili family, Ruispiri/Telavi
Borzhomi mineral water
CARTU mineral water, Tibilisi
Maia Dcamukakhvili, Tibilisi
Dsveli Sikvaruli café, Tibilisi
Manoni Eradse, Tibilisi
Khatuna Gamesardashvili, Tibilisi
Nathela Gvenetadse, Tibilisi
Dr. Nugsar Ihgenti, Tibilisi

Kabanchik restuarant, Moscow
Rainer Kaufmann, the Kartli hotel, Tibilisi
Lali Khocholava, Tibilisi
Dr. Marina Khvedelidse, Tibilisi
David Khikovani, GWS wincs, Tibilisi
Maia Khvedelidse, Tibilisi
Eteri Mesurnishvili, Tibilisi
Ledy Mossidse, Tibilisi
Prof. Dr. Yuri Mossidse, Tibilisi
Mukhranthubani restaurant, Tibilisi
Sachashniko restaurant, Tibilisi
Eka Sakalashvili, Tibilisi
Ms Sanikidse, the Georgian embassy, Berlin
Ulrike Schmidmeier, Munich

Armenia

Our thanks go to Anna Bowman for her assistance with the transliteration of Armenian terms into English.

SAS Market Anush Urakhutioun, Erivan
Ararat restaurant, Erivan
Dolmama restaurant, Erivan
Granatus Pastry Shop, Erivan
Dr. Tessa Hofmann, Berlin, for her work on the design
Alina Hovsoian, Erivan
Hovsoian family, Erivan
Albert Isahakian family, Erivan
Gulnara Mannkian, Edshmiadsin
Gilbert Moumdyan, Riemerling near Munich
Oyakh restaurant, Erivan
Svir cheese company, Erivan
Karagyozian Gagik Vaginakovikh, Berg Aragaz
Rouben Vassilian, Poing
Yerevan Brandy Company Ararat, Erivan

Azerbaijan

Our particular thanks go to S. E. Husseinaga Ssadigov, former ambassador of the Republic of Azerbaijan in Germany, and his wife Rafiga Ssadigova, as well as Svetlana Ismailova and Telman Ismailov in Baku for providing many contacts, for wonderful culinary experiences, and for their committed support of our project. We would like to thank Jeyhun Hasanov for his assistance with the transliteration of Azerbaijani terms into English.

Dr. Firdosiya Akhmedova
Irshad Aliev, Minister of Agriculture of the Republic of Azerbaijan, Baku
Semfira Babayeva, Baku
Dilshad Bayramova, Guba
Faig Iskändärov, Baku
Käräm Iskändärov, Dämirtshilär
Musa Bagirov, the Köytäpä restaurant, Baku
Karavanserei restaurant, Baku
Elbrus Mamedov, Baku
Mugam restaurant, Baku
Zaman Novrusov, Baku
Samira Patzer-Ismailova and Jürgen Patzer, Cologne
State tea factory, Länkoran
Tomas Wild, Cologne
Eldar Yunussov, Baku

Bibliography

All countries

Cuisine and food

Chamberlain, L. *The Food and Cooking of Russia (At Table)*, 1982.
Foulkes, C. (ed.). *Larousse Wine*, 1995.
Johnson, H. and J. Robinson. *The World Atlas of Wine*, 2001.
Johnson, H. *Hugh Johnson's Pocket Wine Book*, 2007.
Johnson, H. *Hugh Johnson's Wine Companion: The Encyclopedia of Wines, Vineyards & Winemakers*, 2003.
Mack, G.R. and A. Surina. *Food Culture in Russia and Central Asia* (Food Culture around the World), 2005.
Marvel, T. (ed.). *Frank Schoonmaker's Dictionary of Wines*, 1951.
Meyer, A.L. and J.N. Vann. *The Appetizer Atlas: A World of Small Bites*, 2003.
Nelson, K. Shaw. *Cuisines of the Caucasus Mountains: Recipes, Drinks, and Lore from Armenia, Azerbaijan, Georgia, and Russia*, 2002.
Steurer, R. *Weinhandbuch*, 1995.
Uvezian, S. *Cooking from the Caucasus*, 1984.
Ward, S. *Russian Regional Recipes: Classic Dishes from Moscow and St. Petersburg, the Russian Federation and Moldova, the Baltic States, Georgia, Armenia and Azerbaijan, Central Asia and Kazakhstan*, 1993.
Ward, S. *Russian Festive Cooking*, 1995

History, culture and travel

Benet, S. *How to Live to be 100: The lifestyle of the people of the Caucasus*, 1976.
Dumas, A. *Adventures in Caucasia*, trans. A.E. Murch, 1962.
Kaufmann, R. *Caucasus. Georgia, Armenia, Azerbaijan.* Munich/London/New York, 2000.
Leitner, A. and D. Burkhart. *Von Festen und Feirn in der Slavische Literaturen*, 1999.
Mikdash-Shamailov, L. *Mountain Jews: Customs and Daily Life in the Caucasus*, 2003.
Pushkin, A. *Journey to Arzrum*, Trans. edn., 1974.
Tolstoi, L.N. *Fables, Tales and Stories. A Captive in the Caucasus*, 1978.

Russia

Cuisine and food

Bremzen, A. von and J. Welchman. *Please to the Table: The Russian Cookbook*, 1990.
Chamberlain, L. *The Food and Cooking of Eastern Europe (At Table)*, 2006.
Classic Russian Cooking: Elena Molokhovets' "A Gift to Young Housewives", 1998 edition.
Goldstein, D. *A Taste of Russia: A Cookbook of Russian Hospitality*, 1999.
Kropotkin, A. *The Best of Russian Cooking*, 1993.
Papashvily, H. *Russian Cooking*, 1969.
Petrovskaya, K. *Russian Cookbook*, 1992.
Time Life Books. *Russian Cooking*, (Foods of the World series), 1969.
Usov, V. *Russian Cooking*, 1996.
Volokh, A. and M. Manus *The Art of Russian Cuisine*, 1983.
Wisniewski, I. and W. Lingwood. *Vodka: Discovering, Exploring, Enjoying*, 2003.
Rose, J. *The Vodka Cookbook*, 2005.

History, culture and travel

Adler, W. *Trans-Siberian Express*, 2001.
Almedingen, E. M. *The Romanovs. 3 Centuries of an Ill-fated Dynasty*, 1966.
Briggs, A.D.P. *Alexander Pushkin: A Celebration of Russia's Best-Loved Writer*, 1999.
Cracroft, J. *The Revolution of Peter the Great*, 2006.
Davletshin, T. *Cultural Life in the Tatar Autonomous Republic*, 1953.
Figes, O. *Natasha's Dance: A Cultural History of Russia*, 2003.
Fisher-Ruge, L. *Survival in Russia: Chaos and Hope in Everyday Life*, 1993.
Gilbert, M. *The Routledge Atlas of Russian History: From 800 B.C. to the Present Day*, 2002.
Gogol, N. *Dead Souls*. trans. R. Pevear and L. Volokhovsky.
Habsburg, von G. *Fabergé. Fantasies and Treasures*. Munich, 1996.
Habibis, M. *Russia – Culture Smart: A Quick Guide to Customs and Etiquette*, 2006.
Kappeler, A. *The Russian Empire: A Multi-Ethnic History*, 2001.
Kloberdanz, T.J. *Thunder on the Steppe: Volga German Folklife in a Changing Russia*, 1994.
Massie, R.K. *Peter the Great*, 2001.
McNeese, T. *The Volga River*, 2005.
Murrell, K.B. *Discovering the Moscow Countryside: An Illustrated Guide to Russia's Heartland*, 2001.
Pesman, D. *Russia and Soul: An Exploration*, 2000.
Pushkin, A. S. *Eugene Onegin. A Novel in Verse*, trans. J.E. Falen, 1998.
Ralton, W.R. Sheddon. *The Songs of the Russian People as Illustrative of Slavonic Mythology and Russian Social Life*, 2006.
Richmond, S. and M. Horees. *Lonely Planet Trans-Siberian Railway: A Classic Overland Route*, 2002.
Rössing, R. and P. Balocco. *Reise durch Russland*, 1995.
Strayer, R.W. *Why Did the Soviet Union Collapse? – Understanding Historical Change*, 1998.
Thomas, B. *Trans-Siberian Handbook, 6th edition: Includes Rail Route Guide and 25 City Guides*, 2004.
Tikhomirov, V. *Russia after Yeltsin*, 2001.
Toht, P. and B. Moulder. *Daily Life in Ancient and Modern Moscow*, 2001.
Villiers, Marq de. *Down the Volga: A Journey through Mother Russia in a Time of Troubles*, 1992.
Wachtel, M. *The Cambridge Introduction to Russian Poetry*, 2004
Warth, R.D. *Nicholas II: The Life and Reign of Russia's Last Monarch*, 1997.
World Book Publishing. *Christmas in Russia (Christmas Around the World series)*, 2001.

Ukraine

Cuisine and food

Asala, J. *Ukrainian Recipes*, 1996.
Cramon-Taubadel, S, and I. Akimova *Fostering Sustainable Growth in Ukraine*, 2002.
Farley, M.P. *Festive Ukrainian Cooking*, 1990.
Hoffman, L. and F. Möllers. *Ukraine on the Road to Europe*, 2001.
Stechishin, S. *Traditional Ukrainian Cookery*, 1982.
Ukrainian Women's Assoc. of Canada, Yorkton Branch, *A Book of Tested Recipes, [Cooking Ukrainian style, traditional and modern recipes]*, 1977.
Zahny, B. *The Best of Ukrainian Cooking*, 1994.

History, culture, and travel

Ascherson, N. *Black Sea*. 1996.
Gogol, N. *The Collected Tales of Nicolai Gogol*, 1999.
Kubijovye, V. and H.S. Danylo (Eds.). *Encyclopedia of Ukraine*, vols I–V, 1993.
Lüdemann, E. *Ukraine*, 2001.
Reid, A. *Borderland: A Journey through the History of the Ukraine*, 2000.
Schevenko, A. *Ukraine – Cultural Smart: A Quick Guide to Customs and Etiquette*, 2006.
Wilson, A. *The Ukrainians: Unexpected Nation*, 2002.
World Book Publishing. *Christmas in Ukraine (Christmas Around the World series)*, 1997.
Zborowski, M. and E. Herzog. *Life is with the People: The Culture of the Shtetl*, 1992.

Georgia

Cuisine and food

Abashidze, V., L. Loladze and G. Ciaureli *Georgian Wines*, 1984.
Aken, N. von and J. Harrisson, *The Great Exotic Fruit Book*, 1995.
Chamberlain, L. *The Food and Cooking of Eastern Europe*, 2006.
Fussell, B. *The Story of Corn*, 2004.
Goldstein, D. *The Georgian Feast: The Vibrant Culture and Savory Food of the Republic of Georgia*, 1999.
Green, A. *The Bean Bible*. 2000.
Margvelashvili, J. *The Classic Cuisine of Soviet Georgia: History, Traditions, and Recipes*, 1991.
Siegel, H. and K. Gillingham. *The Totally Corn Cookbook*, 1994.

History, culture, and travel

Baddeley, J.F. *The Russian Conquest of the Caucasus*, 2006.
Bodenstedt, F. *A Thousand and One Days in the Orient*, 1992.
Chatwin, M. E. *Sociocultural Transformation and Foodways*, 1997.
Curtis, G.E. *A Country Study*, 2004.
Dzhavakhishvili, G.D. *Georgia: Land of the Golden Fleece< P>*, 1960.
Gamsakhurdia, K. *Mindia, the Son of Hogay and Other Stories By Georgian Writers*, 1984.
Hewitt, G. *A Georgian Reader*, 1996.
Klaproth, J. von (Ed.). *Dr. J. A. Güldenstädts Travels to Georgia and Imereti*, (1815).
Lang, D.M. *A Modern History of Georgia (Caucasus World)*, 2007.
MacGovern, P. E. *Ancient Wine: The Search for the Origins of Viniculture*, 2003.
McGovern, P.E., S. Fleming and S. Katz. *Origins and Ancient History of Wine (Food and Nutrition in History and Anthropology)*, 2000.
Nasmyth, P. *Georgia: In the Mountains of Poetry*, 1998.
Nasmyth, P. *Walking in the Caucasus*, 2006.
Rayfield, D. *The Literature of Georgia: A History*, 2000.
Rosen, R. and J.J. Foxx. *Georgia: Sover-

Tchaikovsky, P. I. *The Diaries. Edited and translated by Hans-Joachim Grimm*, 1992.

Armenia

Cuisine and food

Antreassian, A. *Armenian Cooking Today*, 1977.

Antreassian, A. *Armenian Cooking*, 1989.

Antreassian. A., M. Jebejian and A. Zanazanian. *Classic Armenian Recipes: Cooking without Meat*, 1994.

Baboian, R. *The Art of Armenian Cooking*, 1971.

Batmanglij, N. *Silk Road Cooking: A Vegetarian Journey*, 2002.

Chirinian, L. *Secrets of Cooking: Armenian/Lebanese/Persian*, 1986.

Ghazarian, B. *Simply Armenian: Naturally Healthy Ethnic Cooking Made Easy*, 2004.

Glants, M. and J.S. Toomre. *Food in Russian History and Culture*, 1997.

Uzevian, S. *The Cuisine of Armenia*, 2001.

Vitz, E.B. *A Continual Feast: A Cookbook to Celebrate the Joys of Family and Faith throughout the Christian Year*, 1991.

Wise, V. Jenanyan. *The Armenian Table: More than 165 Treasured Recipes that Bring Together Ancient Flavors and 21st-Century Style*, 2004.

History, culture, and travel

Abrahamian, L., N. Sweezy and S. Sweezy. *Armenian Folk Arts, Culture and Identity*, 2001.

Baliozian, A. *Armenians: Their History and Culture*, 1980.

Bournoutian, G.A. *A Concise History of the Armenian People: From Ancient Times to the Present*, 2002.

Dadrian, V.N. *The History of the Armenian Genocide: Ethnic Conflict from the Balkans to Anatolia to the Caucasus*, 2004.

Holding, N. *Armenia: The Bradt Travel Guide*, 2004.

Hovannisian, R. *The Armenian People from Ancient to Modern Times: The Dynastic Periods: From Antiquity to the Fourteenth Century*, 1997.

Karanian, M. and R. Kurkjian. *The Stone Garden Guide to Armenia and Karabakh*, 2006.

Masters, T. and R. Plunkett. *Lonely Planet Guide: Georgia, Armenia & Azerbaijan*, 2004.

Sakayan, D. *Armenian Proverbs*, 1995.

Samuelian, T.J. *Classical Armenian Culture*, 1982.

Neruda, Pablo. *The Essential Neruda: Selected Poems*, 2004.

Azerbaijan

Cuisine and food

Akhmedov, A. *Azerbaijan Cookery*, 1986.

Basan, G. *Turkish Cooking: Classic traditions, Fresh ingredients, Authentic flavors, Aromatic recipes*, 2006

Basan, G. and J. Basan. *Classic Turkish Cooking*, 1997.

Hazelton, J.W. *Persimmons (Kaki) from Seed to Supper*, 2000.

Humphries, J. *The Essential Saffron Companion*, 1998.

Willard, P. *Secrets of the Saffron: The Vagabond Life of the World's Most Seductive Spice*, 2002.

Zak, V. *20,000 Secrets of Tea: The Most Effective Ways to Benefit from Nature's Healing Herbs*, 1999.

History, culture, and travel

Bonavia, J., C. Baumer, W. Lindsay and Wu Qi. *The Silk Road: Xi'an to Kashgar*, 7th edn., 2004.

Cheneviere, A. *Travels in the Orient in Marco Polo's Footsteps*, 1996.

Cheneviere, A. *Central Asia: The Sons of Tamburlaine*, 2001.

Elliott, M. *Azerbaijan: With Excursions to Georgia*, 2006.

Hopkirk, P. *Foreign Devils on the Silk Road. The Search for the Lost Cities and Treasures of Chinese Central Asia*, 1986

King, D.C. *Azerbaijan* (Cultures of the World), 2006.

Major, J.S., B.J. Belanus and Yo-Yo Ma. *Caravan to America: Living Arts of the Silk Road*, 2002.

Waal, T. de. *Black Garden: Armenia and Azerbaijan through Peace and War*, 2004.

Whitfield, S. *Life Along the Silk Road*, 2001.

Wood, F. *The Silk Road: Two Thousand Years in the Heart of Asia*, 2004

Yo-Yo Ma and E. ten Grotenhuis. *Along the Silk Road* (Asian Art and Culture), 2002.

359

Text credits

Texts in the chapter on Russia, p. 16–85, 88/89, 102/103, 120–123, 125–135: Hartmut Moreike; p. 86/87, 90–101, 104–111, 114–119: Alexey Koslachkov.

"Russian meals and eating habits" in the chapter on Russia, p. 20: Tanja Krombach

Eugen Onegin by Pushkin, verses appearing on p.64/65, translation by Charles H. Johnston

"Alkhalalalay—the ritual festival of the Itelmens" in the chapter on Russia, p. 112: Tjan Zaotschnaja, Munich, and Marion Trutter

"Birch sap" in the chapter on Russia, p. 120: Beate Blaha, Gauting

"Cossack culture" in the chapter on the Ukraine, p. 191: Marion Trutter

"Methods of sparkling wine production" in the chapter on the Ukraine, p. 200: Dr. Wolfgang Thomann, Ingelheim

"Variety of people and cuisine" in the chapter on Georgia, p. 222/223: Prof. Dr. Jörg Stadelbauer, Freiburg, and Tanja Krombach

"The eternal dispute: who invented pasta?", and "Tea from Georgia" in the chapter on Georgia, p. 227 and p. 263 by Marion Trutter

"Wine cultivation in Georgia," "Wine regions," "Wines" and "Tsinandali" in the chapter on Georgia, p. 251-255: Dr. Wolfgang Thomann, Ingelheim

"Russia: history and language", "Ukraine: history and language" in the appendix, p. 350-352: Tanja Krombach

"Georgia: history and language" in the appendix, p. 353: Ronit Jariv

"Armenia: history and language" and "Azerbaijan: history and language" in the appendix, p. 354/355: Maren Tribukait

Picture credits

l. = left; r. = right; c. = center; a. – above; b. = below

All pictures:
© Gregor M. Schmid

With the exception of:
© R.-J. Bouteville
51 r. (red-tinted russula)

© Christoph Büschel
320 b.l.

© Günter Beer/Beer Photography
246, 323 a.l.; 323, c.l.

© Chaumeton/Nature
51 l. (bay bolete)

© www.cybis.se
Photo: Petra Ossovski Larsson: 120 c.b.

© Davidoff & Cie S. A. Geneva
211 a.r., 294 b.l.

© Gettyimages
64 a.r.; 88 b.; 129 b.r.; 151 a.l.; 182

© Grospas/Nature
51 r. (honey agaric), l. (boletus edulis)

© Houdou/Nature
51 l. (meadow mushroom)

© IAN
159 a.r.

© IFA-Bilderteam-Bail & Spiegel
164

© Peter Korniss
111 b.r.

© Brigitte Krauth, Saarbrücken
26 a.

© Y. Lanceau
51 r. (chanterelle), l. (saffron milk cap)

© Ria Novosti
76/77, 77 b.r.; 117 a.

© Okapia KG, Germany
115 b.r., 117 c.l., 117 c., 117 c.r., 117 b.l., 117 c.b., 117 b.r.; photo: René Arnault: 107 c.r.; photo: G. Büttner: 89 c.r. (ocean perch)

© Jürgens Ost and Europa-Photo
110/111, 114/115

© Martin Rutkiewicz
192/193, 192 a.l.; 192 c.l.; 192 b.l.

© Scala, Florence
296

© Sara Shahin
231 a.r.

© Stockfood
Photo: Harry Bischof: 177; photo: Ottmar Diez: 51 r. (red capped Scaber Stalk); photo: Susie M. Eising: 89 a.l. (herring), 89 c.l.; (mackerel), 124, 171 r., 177 b.l. (trout); photo: Losito & Losito snc: 306/307; photo: Karl Newedel: 54/55; photo: Orion Press: 109 a.r.; photo: Rees, Peter: 89 b.r. (turbot); photo: Maximilian Stock LTD: 32 c.l., 33 a.r., 89 b.l. (plaice), 89 b.l. (sprat), 90 a.r., 300 b.l.; photo: Teubner Foodfoto: 89 b. (cod); photo: TH Foto-Werbung: 325 b.r.

© Tandem Verlag GmbH
322 b.r.; photo: Günter Beer: 28/29, 52, 88 a.l.; 170/171, 227 a.l., 273 a.r., 325 a.l. (tarragon), 325 b.c. (scallions); photo: Christoph Büschel: 38/39, 177 a.r. (pike), a.l. (carp), a.r. (common eel), c.r. (tench), b.r. (perch); photo: Johnson: 313; photo: Werner Stapelfeldt: 323; photo: Ruprecht Stempell: 177 c. (catfish), 199 b.l., 258 a.c, a.r., b.l., b.r., 259, 324 a.l. (cilantro), b.l. (mint), 325 a.c. (dill)

© WILDLIFE
121 (background); photo: D. Harms: 121 four small photos

© Manfred Wirtz
138/139, 178 a.l., 178 c.l., 178 b.l., 178/179, 179 b.r.

© Wostok
291 b.r.

Index of dishes (Page numbers for illustrated dishes are shown in bold)

English recipe index

Foreign language recipe index by country

Index

Glossary

Agar-agar is a setting agent made from species of SE Asian seaweed and is popular with vegetarians instead of gelatin (see below). It can be found in natural food stores.

Al dente is a popular culinary term taken from the Italian to mean "to the tooth." This means that the food being cooked, e.g. pasta, rice etc. must not be overcooked, but still retain "a bite" to it, so regular testing during cooking is recommended.

Bain marie (or water bath) is a traditional method of cooking where the food to be cooked is placed in its dish in a larger container (usually a roasting pan) into which hot water is poured. This enables sauces and custard-based dishes to be cooked gently without curdling. It is also a method of melting chocolate.

Clarified butter is prepared by melting unsalted butter over low heat or in a microwave (see maker's instructions). Skim off any foam and let stand until the solids settle. Pour off the clear liquid, discarding the sediment, and allow to set. Clarified butter does not burn while frying and has a pure clean flavor.

Gelatin comes in powdered or, in many European countries, in leaf (thin sheets) form. It is a matter of preference but many cooks consider that the leaf form produces a clearer and more elegant set.

Grinder (called a mincer in the UK) is a piece of manually operated kitchen equipment that was used for decades before the food processor arrived. In fact, it is still preferred by many cooks when preparing certain types of meat or vegetables where a coarse texture is required. When using a food processor it is recommended that it is "pulsed" rather than run continuously to prevent the ingredient being over processed and losing its texture.

Kefir originated from the mountain range of the Caucasus and was traditionally made from camel's milk, but nowadays it is made from cow's milk. It is not dissimilar to a liquid yogurt. It can be found in specialist stores and delicatessens, especially those that stock foodstuffs from Eastern European countries.

Lard is rendered/clarified pork fat. It is richer than most other fats and is an essential ingredient for the piecrust that surrounds raised-crust pork pies. It is a popular fat for deep-frying in many countries and where dieting is not paramount. If a recipe specifies lard it should not be substituted with shortening, which is made from vegetable oils, and does not have the same essential properties.

Millet is rich in protein and is cooked like rice. It makes a pleasant addition to dishes like pilaf or in salads and is a possible alternative to buckwheat on occasions. It can be obtained from natural food stores.

Quark is a soft, unripened cheese with the flavor and texture of sour cream and can be obtained in a low-fat or nonfat version. It has a richer texture than low-fat yogurt. A reasonable substitute can be made using fromage blanc drained through a cheesecloth.

Parsley root (also known as Hamburg parsley). Much European and Eastern European cooking uses this vegetable, which can be found occasionally, in season, at some farmers' markets or upmarket foodstores. Its main culinary purpose is as a basis for soups and stews, but celery can be used as a substitute.

Wheat grains are used in many European and Eastern European dishes when potatoes or other staple foods may be in short supply. They add a very authentic texture and flavor to recipes that call for their addition, and can be found in natural food stores. Bulgur wheat is a good substitute.

British Cookery Terms

US	UK	US	UK
bacon	streaky (other US varieties	grape leaves	vine leaves
such as back, Canadian etc.	as described)	ground meat	minced meat (mince)
baked potato	jacket potato	ham (cured)	gammon
beets	beetroot	heaping	heaped
bell peppers	sweet peppers	heavy (whipping) cream	double cream
broil	grill	innards or variety meats	offal
broiler	oven grill	parsley root	Hamburg parsley
buckwheat grits	buckwheat meal	pit	stone (of fruits)
candy	sweets	porcini	ceps or boletus mushrooms
candied	glacé	rise	prove
chile	chilli pepper	scallions	spring onions
chocolate, dark bittersweet	plain chocolate	seed	pip
cilantro	fresh coriander	shrimp	prawn
cookie	biscuit (sweet)	slivered almonds	flaked almonds
corn	sweetcorn, maize	soft curd cheese	Quark, fromage frais
cornstarch	cornflour	sugar, confectioner's	icing sugar
eggplant	aubergine	sugar, superfine	castor sugar
envelope	sachet (e.g. of gelatine)	tomato paste	tomato purée
flour, all purpose	plain flour	vanilla bean	vanilla pod
flour, whole wheat	wholemeal flour	whole milk	full-cream milk
gelatin	gelatine	zucchini	courgettes